"DEMOCRACY IS IN THE STREETS"

From Port Huron to the Siege of Chicago

by
JAMES MILLER

SIMON AND SCHUSTER
New York

Copyright © 1987 by James Miller
All rights reserved
including the right of reproduction
in whole or in part in any form
Published by Simon and Schuster
A Division of Simon & Schuster, Inc.
Simon & Schuster Building
Rockefeller Center
1230 Avenue of the Americas
New York, New York 10020
SIMON AND SCHUSTER and colophon are registered trademarks of
Simon & Schuster, Inc.
Designed by Irving Perkins Associates
Manufactured in the United States of America

3   5   7   9   10   8   6   4   2

Library of Congress Cataloging-in-Publication Data
Miller, James, date
"Democracy is in the streets."
Bibliography: p. 379-416.
Includes index.
1. Radicals—United States—Biography.
2. College students—United States—Political
activity—Biography.   3. Students for a Democratic
Society (U.S.)—History.   4. United States—Social
conditions—1960–   .   5. Student movements—
United States.   I. Title.
HN90.R3M47 1987   378'.1981   86-26180
ISBN: 0-671-53056-9

Acknowledgment is hereby made for permission to quote interview material
and poetry from the following publishers and copyright holders, to whom all
rights are reserved:

"Tom Hayden: The Rolling Stone Interview." By Tim Findley, from *Rolling Stone*, Oct.
26 and Nov. 9, 1972. By Straight Arrow Publishers, Inc. Copyright © 1972. All Rights
Reserved. Reprinted by permission.

"Movement." By Todd Gitlin. Copyright © 1965 by *The Nation*. All rights reserved. Used
by permission.

"To Those Born Later." By Bertolt Brecht. Copyright © 1976 by Eyre Methuen, Ltd.
Reprinted from *Bertolt Brecht Poems 1913–1956* by permission of the publisher, Methuen, Inc., by arrangement with Suhrkamp Verlag, Frankfurt. All rights reserved. Used
by permission.

For Alexander, Michael, and Their Generation:

"Men fight and lose the battle, and the thing that they fought for comes about in spite of their defeat, and when it comes, turns out not to be what they meant, and other men have to fight for what they meant under another name."

—William Morris, "A Dream of John Ball" (1886)

CONTENTS

INTRODUCTION

THE PHILOSOPHERS HAVE ONLY *INTERPRETED* THE WORLD IN VARIOUS WAYS; THE POINT IS TO *CHANGE* IT.

> —Karl Marx
> "Theses on Feuerbach" (1845)

NOT THE SLIGHTEST INDICATION OF CHANGE ANYWHERE. THE CANCER OF TIME IS EATING US AWAY. OUR HEROES HAVE KILLED THEMSELVES, OR ARE KILLING THEMSELVES. THE HERO, THEN, IS NOT TIME, BUT TIMELESSNESS. WE MUST GET IN STEP, A LOCK STEP, TOWARD THE PRISON OF DEATH. THERE IS NO ESCAPE. THE WEATHER WILL NOT CHANGE.

> —Henry Miller
> *Tropic of Cancer* (1934)

PORT HURON AND THE LOST HISTORY OF THE NEW LEFT

On June 12, 1962, 59 people came to Port Huron, Michigan, to draft a platform for a new kind of politics. They came from New York and Michigan, Ohio and Pennsylvania, Georgia and Texas. Most were young students; many were veterans of civil rights work in the South. A handful of older trade-union activists and Socialist Party leaders also attended. They all had come to hammer out a manifesto for an organization called Students for a Democratic Society—at the time, an obscure offshoot of the equally obscure League for Industrial Democracy. The conference quickly erupted into an angry debate between Michael Harrington, the veteran socialist, and the young activists, led by twenty-two-year-old Tom Hayden. For three days, the delegates wrangled over ideas, wording, emphasis. Finally, on June 16, as dawn broke over Lake Huron, the student group overwhelmingly voted to ratify the manifesto, to be called simply *The Port Huron Statement*.

This statement is one of the pivotal documents in post-war American history. Its publication was crucial in catapulting SDS to national prominence. It also helped to popularize an idea that would exercise a profound influence over the radical politics of the next decade: the idea of "participatory democracy." This idea came to define the New Left of the Sixties, as countless young people put democracy to the test in communes and small collectives.

"We are people of this generation," began *The Port Huron Statement*, "bred in at least modest comfort, housed now in universities, looking uncomfortably to the world we inherit." Again and again, the sixty-three-page document sounds themes that would echo

13

throughout the Sixties. On utopian ideals: "Doubt has replaced hopefulness—and men act out a defeatism that is labelled realistic. . . . The first effort, then, should be to state a vision: what is the perimeter of human possibility in this epoch?" On the human potential: "We regard men as infinitely precious and possessed of unfulfilled capacities for reason, freedom, and love." On the individual: "The goal of man and society should be human independence: . . . finding a meaning of life that is personally authentic." On community: "Human relationships should involve fraternity and honesty." On politics: "We seek the establishment of a democracy of individual participation, governed by two central aims: that the individual share in those social decisions determining the quality and direction of his life; that society be organized to encourage independence in men and provide the media for their common participation." On the source of social change: "In a time of supposed prosperity, moral complacency, and political manipulation, a new left cannot rely on only aching stomachs to be the engine force of social reform. The case for change, for alternatives that will involve uncomfortable personal efforts, must be argued as never before. The university is a relevant place for such activities."

The hopes first expressed in *The Port Huron Statement* animated some of the most prominent activists in the civil rights and anti-war movements, and inspired many of the students involved in the protests that shook America in the late Sixties, briefly raising the specter of civil war. At the same time, *The Port Huron Statement* remains a document of considerable intrinsic interest and intellectual substance. It captures the New Left at its most thoughtful and plainspoken; it shows clear debts to native traditions of progressive reform and pragmatism; and, in a powerful and provocative way, it weaves together a cogent critique of American society with a romantic yearning for new personal values. It is remarkable for the freshness of its vision, the candor of its sentiments, the fervor of its moral tone, the apparently earnest way it holds American liberalism accountable to its loftiest ideals. It is remarkable, too, for the absence of bellicose rhetoric and Marxist jargon. The constructive temper of *The Port Huron Statement* belies stereotypes of the bomb-throwing radical that arose in the late Sixties. Because it appeared in the infancy of the Movement, it is unscarred by the subsequent frustration and rage that distort popular perceptions to this day. In the 1980s, this youthful manifesto retains a surprising timeliness, perhaps because Ronald Reagan's era of cultural retrenchment and expansive jingoism has amounted to an effort to re-create the self-satisfied complacency of Eisenhower's America.

Who were the political pioneers who drafted this document? What brought them to Port Huron? What were the origins of their discontent, and of their ideas? What was the point of their critique, and what use did they subsequently make of it? What became of their ideals and their quest for "participatory democracy" during the upheavals of the Sixties? How did a vision of democratic renewal evolve into a mass movement of violent protest? What, finally, is the legacy of Port Huron and the New Left it inspired?

The search for answers to these questions sent me back to the early Sixties—the focus of much of this book and the period when a distinctively *New* Left first crystallized in America. It is a period relatively lacking in documentation. No minutes exist for the Port Huron conference. Some of the most important early experiments in participatory democracy deliberately scorned fixed record-keeping. More than twenty years later, the veterans of Port Huron themselves often have trouble filling in the gaps, and some are less than eager to dredge up their past. Those who are still active in politics understandably want to keep their energy focused on current affairs. And those who have embarked on new careers sometimes wish to keep a distance from the political ideals that once gave fire to their lives.

Despite these problems, the documents I did find and the Port Huron veterans I met introduced me to an unfamiliar world of intellectual and political ferment, peopled by a small group of fiercely committed activists. Sublimely convinced of their power to make history, this tiny band of students succeeded in creating a striking new rhetoric of American radicalism. Committed to living by the light of their own convictions, they undertook a variety of bold experiments in organizing voiceless citizens and in establishing their own small communities of perfect freedom. Through a deliberately open-minded process of collective decision-making, they formulated a flexible strategy for social change that, for a time, proved surprisingly effective, briefly making the New Left an important factor in American politics.

In mapping this terrain, I felt a little like an explorer who has chanced upon a lost continent, even though there exists a good contemporary guide published in 1966: Jack Newfield's *A Prophetic Minority*. Yet the world that Newfield so vividly described had, in effect, been blown to bits by the events of the late Sixties. Fueled by the hostility of many American students to the war in Vietnam, the New Left after 1965 quickly mushroomed into a mass movement that aggressively challenged the legitimacy of America's political institutions. Ironically, the growing militance of blacks and young students made the achievements of the earlier activists seem, even to themselves, like an irrelevant, insufficiently radical pre-history. Increasingly ashamed of their middle-class origins, many were eager to deny the academic context of their original political interests. The spectacular demonstrations, riots and student strikes of the later Sixties, lavishly covered in the mass media, made memories of the early days seem pale by comparison. The intellectual foundations of the New Left were ignored, repudiated, forgotten. Then, when the Movement collapsed, at the end of the decade, in the face of government repression and its own self-destructive violence, leaving behind a fog of tear gas, drugs and pseudo-Marxist cant, many survivors, shaken by the experience, chose to leave the past buried —lost hopes, perhaps, but no more illusions.

As a result, most Americans have never heard of Port Huron, and many scholarly accounts continue to recycle misleading assertions about the origins of the New Left. It is often said, for example, that the early New Left was "innocent of ideology" and not properly "political"; that it owed its key ideas, including "participatory democracy," to the example of black civil rights activists in the South; that it was marked by a naive faith in liberalism which somehow issued in a vaguely anarchistic and wildly utopian scheme for decentralized self-government and rule-by-consensus.[1]

In fact, as we shall see, the students who met at Port Huron were widely read, relatively savvy and scarcely orthodox in their political outlook. Their democratic idealism at first owed little to Marxism, anarchism or the mainstream liberalism of a John F. Kennedy. They took their central political ideas not from the civil rights movement, but rather from the tradition of civic republicanism that links Aristotle to John Dewey. After 1962, they pursued a challenging yet undoctrinaire program for social change. Perhaps some of them at the outset were too sanguine in their assessment of the Democratic Party. One thing is certain: they helped launch America's last great experiment in democratic idealism.

The nature and results of that experiment remain highly controversial. Reviled by conservatives and sometimes disavowed as an adolescent episode by veteran radicals themselves, the New Left has found few defenders. To the sociologist Daniel Bell, it represented "the guttering last gasps of a romanticism soured by rancor and impotence." To Tom Hayden in 1977, it was a paradoxical failure: "We ended a war, toppled two Presidents, desegregated the South, broke other barriers of discrimination. How could we accomplish so much and have so little in the end?"[2]

Hayden's question has an enduring personal resonance for me. In

the late Sixties, I was a member of SDS. I was, of course, opposed to
the war in Vietnam. But I was also attracted by the vision of participatory democracy, although at the time I scarcely understood its
intellectual provenance. In 1968 I demonstrated in Chicago, and in
1969 I attended the final convention of SDS. Neither a Weatherman
nor a Progressive Labor Maoist, I worked with Murray Bookchin on
an anarchist platform that went undebated after the convention
splintered. In the years since, I have devoted two scholarly books of
intellectual history to reassessing—sympathetically, but critically
—some of the convictions I formed during the Sixties: that human
beings naturally long to be free; that a just society would enable
individuals to develop a satisfying sense of personal worth, creativity and distinctiveness; that a participatory democracy is the best
way to embody such a society. I have also written professionally
about rock and roll, once considered the vanguard art form of the
counterculture. Analyzing Rousseau, Marx and the French existentialists, however, has left me profoundly skeptical of the assumptions about human nature and the good society held by many
radicals; and a decade of covering the music business has left me
cynical about the "revolutionary" potential of youth. The New Left
was obviously in some respects a dead end—indeed, for many years
I did not want to think about the Sixties at all, since I had grown
ashamed of my youthful naïveté. At the same time, as a mood of
smug tranquillity began to settle over the political culture of the
United States in the early Eighties, I found myself increasingly uncomfortable with both the neoconservative scorn and the facile nostalgia that have typified popular attitudes about the Sixties. There
was a lot more complexity and substance to the tumultuous radical
subculture of that decade than a film like *The Big Chill* or a critic
like Daniel Bell would admit. The New Left, after all, grew out of
problems that still plague American society: poverty, racism, the
arms race, the narrow limits of participation and social change feasible through electoral politics. What, then, *was* the significance of
the New Left? After more than a decade spent addressing that question obliquely, I have tried in this book to settle accounts with my
past more directly.

The form that I have chosen is biographical. By focusing narrowly
on the experience of a few of the young radicals who ratified *The
Port Huron Statement* and took its political vision to heart, I have
tried to recapture, from the inside, some of the excitement and sense
of adventure that made the idea of participatory democracy come
alive in the Sixties. There are limits to such an approach: the broader

context of social and historical forces recedes into the background, and there is always a danger that the significance of events will be distorted as a consequence. In addition, a biographical approach, particularly one organized around a central theme, participatory democracy, and focused narrowly on a handful of leaders, can by itself offer only clues, not answers, to questions about the rise and fall of the New Left as a mass movement.

Still, there is no more vivid way to tell a story that, in many respects, is really quite astonishing. *The Port Huron Statement*, after all, was written and ratified by a handful of inexperienced students. Taking themselves seriously as citizens and activists, they were anything but typical. Yet by exemplifying a spirit of friendship, intellectual passion and political daring, they succeeded, against all odds, in catalyzing a Movement that attracted hundreds of thousands of converts throughout the Sixties. The manifesto they created may well have been, as Kirkpatrick Sale says in his standard history of SDS, "the most widely distributed document of the American left in the Sixties."[3] Veterans of the Port Huron conference subsequently played a leading role in refining the document's key ideas and putting them into practice. Testing the limits of liberalism, some of them plunged into organizing the unemployed. Sickened by the growing American involvement in Vietnam, others staged the first major march in Washington against the war. They journeyed to Hanoi, disrupted the Democratic Convention in 1968, and helped shut down major universities. Their story illuminates an era. Yet for years, *The Port Huron Statement* has been out of print and, like the New Left it inspired, all but forgotten. Here is a crucial episode in American history that deserves to be exhumed—and carefully reappraised, in the light of my generation's mature experience.

PART ONE

REDISCOVERING POLITICS

I WILL NOT DISSEMBLE MY HOPE, THAT EACH PERSON
WHOM I ADDRESS HAS FELT HIS OWN CALL TO CAST
ASIDE ALL EVIL CUSTOMS, TIMIDITIES, AND LIMITA-
TIONS, AND TO BE IN HIS PLACE A FREE AND HELPFUL
MAN, A REFORMER, A BENEFACTOR, NOT CONTENT TO
SLIP ALONG THROUGH THE WORLD LIKE A FOOTMAN
OR A SPY, ESCAPING BY HIS NIMBLENESS AND APOL-
OGIES AS MANY KNOCKS AS HE CAN, BUT A BRAVE
AND UPRIGHT MAN, WHO MUST FIND OR CUT A
STRAIGHT ROAD TO EVERYTHING EXCELLENT IN THE
EARTH, AND NOT ONLY GO HONORABLY HIMSELF,
BUT MAKE IT EASIER FOR ALL WHO FOLLOW HIM, TO
GO IN HONOR AND WITH BENEFIT.

—Ralph Waldo Emerson
"Man the Reformer" (1841)

CHAPTER ONE

OUT OF APATHY

F OR YOUNG RADICALS, 1968 was a year of unforgettable chaos
and hope. In Saigon in January, at the height of the Tet Offensive, Communist troops stormed the American embassy and
attacked ostensibly safe cities throughout South Vietnam. In Paris
in May, militants paralyzed France with a general strike, and nearly
toppled the government of Charles de Gaulle. In Prague, a democratic new form of Communism flourished briefly, until Russian
tanks crushed the renegade regime of Alexander Dubček in August.
In the United States, Martin Luther King, Jr., and Robert F. Kennedy
were assassinated. A U.S. officer in Vietnam declared that he had
"bombed a city to save it." "Burn your money," urged a radical
leaflet. "Burn your houses and you will be free." Cities were torched,
students seized universities, President Johnson withdrew his bid for
reelection. Police and protesters clashed in downtown Chicago in
August during the Democratic Convention. Chicago Mayor Richard
Daley, arguing with Connecticut Senator Abraham Ribicoff, defended his Draconian policies toward protesters in these terms:
"Fuck you you Jew son of a bitch you lousy motherfucker go
home."[1]
  Mention the Sixties and the vivid furies of this one remarkable
year naturally spring to mind. Many Americans first heard of the
New Left in 1968. It may be the only year in post-war American
history when many intelligent people sincerely believed that a revolution was about to occur, though few could explain what this
might mean. "The sense that something epic was happening was
pretty hard to miss," said Tom Hayden four years later: "There was

no way to avoid the fact that everything was going to come to a showdown . . . a liturgical showdown that everyone would participate in and be affected by in the whole country, in the whole world."[2]

What Hayden called the "epic" sense of 1968 is still striking. It is also slightly misleading. As Hayden dimly perceived at the time, this "liturgical showdown"—an unholy ritual of theatrical violence —would ill serve his own sense of a higher political purpose. In the immediate aftermath of the events of 1968, facing trial and imprisonment for his role in the demonstrations in Chicago, Hayden spoke of a "whirlwind" and his sense of "plunging." He admitted that repression and violence would "turn attention away from our ideas and our political philosophy, which is basically democratic." Yet this recognition was clouded by Hayden's own belief that the blame for the violence lay solely with the U.S. Government and that "resistance" to the government was therefore legitimate.[3] This kind of logic, which bewitched activists after 1968, reinforced the climate of violence and played a part, just as Hayden had warned, in consigning the New Left's philosophy of democracy to oblivion.

How had Tom Hayden arrived at this pass? How had the New Left? How had America?

The events of 1968 cannot answer these questions. What climaxed in the streets of Chicago had begun, for Hayden and many other young radicals, a decade before in the dormitories and classrooms of college campuses across America. Hayden attended the University of Michigan from 1957 until 1961, becoming editor of the student newspaper and an oracle of the new student activism. It was in Ann Arbor that Hayden met the three fellow students—Alan Haber, Sharon Jeffrey and Bob Ross—who would persuade him to become a full-time activist. All of them played key roles in planning the Port Huron conference; they all subsequently became important leaders of the New Left. The story of how each developed a passion for politics and discovered the others is a small drama with large consequences.

On a Different Track

The notion of the New Left as a movement of college activists dedicated to an ideal of democracy was, to a surprising extent, the creation of one man: Robert Alan Haber. In the late Fifties, Haber was Ann Arbor's resident radical. Those who knew him describe a reticent visionary. Soft-spoken and brooding, he talked very slowly and very, very deliberately. He methodically presented his political views as a set of propositions to be pondered, debated and—if his arguments seemed cogent—acted upon. A perpetual student who was older than his classmates, he was balding, bearded, instantly identifiable as somebody different. He was a model of rationality who maintained an air of mystery.

As the eight-year presidency of Republican Dwight D. Eisenhower drew to a close, Haber began to argue that advocates of radical social change had, for the first time since the Thirties, cause for optimism. The key was not the proletariat, as socialists for more than a century had believed; the key was students. Throughout the world, students were on the move. Glaring injustices such as racism were stirring American students as well, after a decade of political apathy. What these American students needed, Haber argued, was an organization that could illuminate the connections between issues like the arms race, poverty and racism and the discontents of the students themselves. The concept that would illuminate these connections was democracy. The poor and blacks and students—who could not even vote until they were twenty-one—all lacked a voice in the larger society; the fate of all three groups was in the hands of somebody else. An organization that pointed this out could mobilize students as a pressure group able to stimulate debate on a variety of issues. Students for a Democratic Society—SDS—had the potential to become such an organization. Through SDS, students, perhaps, could make history.[4]

Haber, like many other young radicals of his generation, inherited his interest in politics. Born in 1936, he was named for Robert La Follette, the Senator from Wisconsin and prominent Progressive. His father, William, was a first-generation immigrant of Rumanian Jewish ancestry who had studied at the University of Wisconsin in the Twenties, when the university was a hotbed of Progressive opinion. A self-possessed and magnetic man, William Haber was renowned as an economist and labor arbitrator. By sentiment attached to Norman Thomas and the Socialist Party, he energetically supported Franklin Roosevelt and the New Deal, playing an important role in the creation of the Social Security system. In 1936, he accepted a post at the University of Michigan, where he taught until his retirement. But he remained a prominent figure in Washington, D.C. During World War II, he worked for the War Manpower Commission. He chaired the Federal Advisory Council on Employment Security. And in 1948, he moved his family to Frankfurt, Germany, where he served for a year as the adviser on Jewish affairs to the commander-in-chief of U.S. forces in Germany and Austria.

The family's stay in Germany had a profound impact on the twelve-year-old Alan. "It was the first time I heard the expression V.I.P.," he says. "My father was a Very Important Person, called a major general, even though he was a civilian." The family lived in palatial quarters requisitioned by the military. His father advised survivors from the concentration camps, many of whom wanted passports to go to Palestine in order to fight for Israel. "While we talked about these things over the dinner table," says Alan, "there were German servants waiting on us."[5] In the young boy's mind, the many faces of power—the perquisites of rank, the ability to command the obedience of others, the capacity of tyrants to torture and kill—took on a graphic immediacy.

So did the devastation of war. Most Americans of his generation were shielded from the horrors of World War II. But Alan was free to wander among the bombed-out ruins of Frankfurt. He still has an album of photographs showing the destruction: snapshot after snapshot of rubble and debris. "I was a little kid from Ann Arbor coming into *that*," he says, pointing at one of the pictures. "It was very exciting, the smashness of it all. But it was also awful. The *waste* of beautiful things I felt a lot. The first six months of our stay was in Frankfurt. Then the occupation army shifted, and we moved to Heidelberg. Heidelberg was a city that had not been bombed—in exchange, I was told, for the British Museum. So I could see what was left. It made me anti-war, just viscerally."

Alan returned to Ann Arbor "on a different track." "When I came back," he says, "I had seen more than any other kid I knew." An adolescent drawing that he has kept shows him "in some sort of space capsule: this is clearly me hooking on to something, trying to deal with guns and swords and government." By the time Alan Haber entered the University of Michigan in 1954, he viewed himself as a progressive, if not a radical—and certainly as someone with ideas of his own.

Michigan's Multiversity

Michigan in the mid-Fifties was hardly the ideal place for a young nonconformist to find sympathy and support. The school epitomized the post-war "multiversity"—a mammoth institution catering to a mutiplicity of constituents, from freshmen in Ann Arbor to the Joint Chiefs of Staff in Washington. Professors at the university pioneered in the development of missile guidance systems. By the early Sixties, Michigan had more contracts with the National Aeronautics and Space Administration than any other university in the country. In his annual report for 1958–1959, University of Michigan President Harlan Hatcher proudly declared that "various areas of University teaching have recognized the cold-war struggle and have reflected their concern in our teaching programs." He mentioned not only the creation of a new Institute of Science and Technology, but also the establishment of departments of "Near Eastern Studies and Slavic Languages and Literatures for instruction in South Asia" —testimony to the growing American interest in the Third World as European colonialism drew to an end. "The Soviet nation has seen with perfect clarity," warned Hatcher, that "knowledge through research . . . is the secret of our greatness. . . . It is imperative that our progress at this University be rapid, continuous and strong." Otherwise, the Soviets might "overtake, surpass, master the Americans."[6]

Like other institutions of higher education throughout the country, the University of Michigan in the mid-Fifties was in the midst of a rapid expansion. Seventeen thousand students registered in 1952, and in the next decade that number nearly doubled. Much of the growth came in graduate studies: by 1959, 38 percent of the students were in the Graduate School or in graduate professional programs. These burgeoning enrollment figures show the impact of America's post-war baby boom. They also reflect perhaps the most remarkable single feature of the Fifties: America's unprecedented affluence. Throughout the decade, Detroit's automobile industry paced an exuberant economy. From 1950 through 1970, the Gross National Product of the United States grew at an annual average rate of 3.9 percent, the best performance in the nation's history. Michigan prospered, and so did the University. In 1958, salaries at the University of Michigan were ranked third in the nation.[7]

The university in this period developed a national reputation in several fields, including political science. In 1948, members of the Survey Research Center in Ann Arbor had undertaken the first national study of the presidential vote using probability sampling. Over the next decade, the "Michigan school," as those connected with the Center were sometimes called, used statistics on voting to paint a "portrait of an electorate almost wholly without detailed information about decision making in government." Given the apathy and ignorance of ordinary citizens, the "Michigan School" concluded that democracy was a business best left to elites. Happily,

they were able to report that this was how democracy in fact functioned in America: experts in office formulated policy, closely monitored by the active, informed representatives of various special
interest groups.[8]

The University of Michigan reflected national trends in the Fifties
in all of these areas: the marshaling of resources for the Cold War,
the celebration of the status quo, the faith in social engineering, the
spectacular growth of scientific research with military applications,
particularly after Russia beat the United States into space with *Sput-
nik* in 1957. Still, the university was so large that it included a broad
range of scholars. On the faculty were traditional humanists, a handful of social critics, even a few well-known mavericks such as Kenneth Boulding, a systems theorist and practicing Quaker who
studied techniques for attaining a "peaceful equilibrium" among
nation-states.[9]

Creeping Socialism

When Alan Haber entered the university, he almost immediately
plunged into extracurricular political activity. "As soon as I got to
the college," he recalls, "there was an issue on campus: the firing of
H. Chandler Davis."

Davis was a young instructor in the mathematics department. In
May of 1954, a subcommittee of the House Un-American Activities
Committee had questioned Davis about his ties to the Communist
Party. Citing not the Fifth Amendment, as was customary, but the
First, Davis had refused to answer—a gesture of defiance that virtually guaranteed his subsequent indictment for contempt of Congress. The evening after his appearance before the subcommittee,
the university's president announced that he had suspended Davis
"without prejudice" pending an investigation. Four months later,
after Davis had refused to cooperate with the university investigation, he was dismissed. University president Hatcher argued that
"nobody's freedom has been invaded or abridged," since the Communists were not a "political party in our traditional and accepted
sense of American freedom," but rather "a skilled and crafty and
relentless intrigue which, if successful, would deliver us into the
hands of those who would destroy our freedoms."[10]

The Davis case aroused the concern of civil libertarians throughout the country. The Bill of Rights Fund awarded him $2,000 in
recognition of his courageous stand. In Ann Arbor, students and

faculty protested his dismissal. "I got signed up into the cause," says Haber. He recalls that his father, who maintained a prudent reserve in public, in private criticized the university and encouraged his son.

Although Alan had entered college as a chemistry major, he was fascinated by history, philosophy and social criticism. A voracious reader and eclectic autodidact, he remembers being struck by the Marxist economist Maurice Dobb and the Fabian socialists Sidney and Beatrice Webb. Edward Bellamy's turn-of-the-century utopian novel *Looking Backward* was "an eye-opener to me—that society could be a whole different way. And that it was in some way a matter for people to choose how we wanted it. Living in Germany after the war, I had seen the Marshall Plan kick into gear. I saw how changeable the world was." Haber's unusual background and unfettered imagination made him restless with the impersonality and frivolity of campus life. He began to hang out at the Folklore Society with Ann Arbor's small coterie of radicals. After two semesters, he dropped out of school altogether, beginning a protracted odyssey as an on-again, off-again student and free-lance gadfly.

These were hard years for the left in America. The political inquisition staged by the House Un-American Activities Committee and by Senator Joseph McCarthy had created an atmosphere of hysteria and fear. For some Communists, the government harassment fostered a sense of beleaguered righteousness. Others retreated into a cowed silence. Democratic socialists meanwhile struggled to dissociate themselves from the totalitarian legacy of Leninism. In intellectual terms, they were successful: in 1954, Irving Howe founded *Dissent*, a lively journal that defended socialist ideas and critical perspectives on American society, in part by vigorously attacking Communism and the repressive policies of the Soviet state. When Nikita Khrushchev denounced the crimes of Stalin at the Communist Party's Twentieth Party Congress in February of 1956, he only confirmed what critics like Howe already knew. Khrushchev's revelations, followed by the Soviet invasion of Hungary that autumn, nonetheless stunned Communists throughout the world, triggering a number of new defections. In New York City, the high school and college branches of the Labor Youth League, which had been organized by the Communist Party, dissolved themselves. The Communist youth movement never fully recovered.

Most Americans, though, knew nothing of these developments. In the popular mind, socialism and communism were two words for the same evil. "Creeping socialism" was widely feared and often detected—for example, in the sinister spread of fluoridated water supplies. Critics implied that socialism would turn supermarkets into dreary commissaries that offered but one brand of cornflakes: the American Dream betrayed.

In this context, young radicals in Ann Arbor and elsewhere found themselves allied with other nonconformists on the fringes of the mainstream culture. "There was this very avant-garde scene that I was a part of," says Haber. One of his neighbors and friends was Gordon Mumma, who was just beginning the experiments with electronic music that would make his reputation; Marge Piercy, the novelist, was part of the same network. Linked by their love of coffee and serious conversation, Ann Arbor's clique of self-styled bohemians congregated at the Michigan Union Grill, where they could linger for a dime.

This was the constituency that elected Haber to a seat on the Student Government Council in 1958. Mumma helped design his poster, while Haber wrote the platform. "I wasn't running as a major radical or anything," says Haber. "I just got this artwork out, and mobilized this network of people. There weren't more than two hundred people in the avant-garde crowd, but they were willing to cover all the bulletin boards. I went around to all the different fraternities and sororities. I learned how to run a campaign."

Among Haber's friends was an older radical named T. Robert Yamada. A Japanese-American whose family had been interned during World War II, Yamada had gone to the University of Wisconsin, where he was a member of the Wisconsin Liberal Club. By the late Fifties, he had become a fixture on the Ann Arbor scene, working at Marshall's Bookstore, the best in town, and supervising an extracurricular Political Issues Club at the university. A committed democratic socialist, Yamada bore the nickname "Lefty." It was Yamada who persuaded Alan Haber in 1958, shortly after his election to the student government, to become an active socialist.[11]

The organization that Yamada persuaded Haber to join was called the Student League for Industrial Democracy—inelegantly known as SLID. Its most glittering asset was its past. In 1905, the novelist Upton Sinclair had helped to found SLID's precursor, the Intercollegiate Socialist Society. Its mission was to bring the message of socialism to American college students. Among its original sponsors were Clarence Darrow and Jack London, who became the Society's first president. Over the next decade, its small but illustrious membership included Norman Thomas, Walter Lippmann and John Reed. The Red Scare of 1919, the creation of the American Communist Party and the resulting split among American socialists nearly destroyed the Society. In 1925, the survivors, in an effort to deflect popular fears about socialism, elected to change the organization's name to "The League for Industrial Democracy." The new organization hoped to attract "all believers in education for strengthening democratic principles and practices in every aspect of our common life." Such rhetoric was, in fact, a throwback to the early days of American socialism, when Eugene Debs, the movement's spiritual leader, had repeatedly stressed the redemptive potential of the American republican tradition.[12]

The virtues of that tradition, however, seemed patently questionable to a growing number of radicals. During the Depression of the Thirties, the heyday of American Communism, the League for Industrial Democracy plodded along, trying to serve up socialist near-beer (to borrow a quip from John Dos Passos) to young radicals intoxicated by the success of the Russian Revolution. The League nevertheless continued to attract eminent figures, including the philosopher Sidney Hook and Walter Reuther, later head of the United Auto Workers. John Dewey served briefly as president.

Through the rise and fall of American Communism and the American Socialist Party, through World War II and its Cold War aftermath, through the witch-hunts of the McCarthy era, the League for Industrial Democracy somehow survived. So did its campus wing, the Student League for Industrial Democracy, despite a disastrous merger in the late Thirties with the Communist-dominated American Student Union.[13] Experiences like this left the League fearful of Communist Party infiltration and bitterly opposed to any form of cooperation with Party members. Centered in New York City and kept afloat financially by trade-union contributions, particularly from the needle trades, LID by the Fifties had become a tax-exempt sinecure—a kind of dignified retirement home for aging social democrats. They were keepers of the socialist flame, mortified that Communists might steal their fire.

Despite its feebleness as an organization, SLID had several things to offer students like Yamada and Haber. Other left-wing student groups of the period, bedeviled by government hostility and student apathy, had withdrawn into an arid Marxist scholasticism. SLID's main rival in the late Fifties, the Young People's Socialist League (YPSL), the youth wing of the Socialist Party, endlessly rehearsed the debates of the Thirties between Trotsky and Stalin. SLID, by contrast, precisely because of its noncommittal emphasis on education, appeared paradoxically pliable and relevant. Its rhetoric of democracy avoided scaring people with the word "socialism" and

evoked honored American political traditions. Its list of distinguished alumni suggested a rich legacy of pragmatic radicalism. And
to explain its ideas, the League sponsored effective speakers such as
Norman Thomas and Michael Harrington, one of the most articulate
young radicals in America. The League also maintained strong ties
with liberals and the labor movement: Walter Reuther remained a
prominent patron.

Alan's father welcomed his son's new affiliation. William Haber
was himself a supporter of the League for Industrial Democracy and
a friend of its most prominent Ann Arbor member, Neil Staebler, at
the time chairman of the state Democratic Party. Through his SLID
and family connections, Alan got a job working for Staebler. "I filed
his letters to the whole patronage machine," says Alan, "so I saw
how it worked." His political education continued apace on campus.
In addition to his student-government duties, he helped Yamada run
the Political Issues Club. In the spring of 1958, the club featured
programs on the Algerian revolution; "corporate capitalism—drift
to a new tyranny?"; "philosophical nihilism"; the "hidden persuaders in our midst"; "mass society and democracy"; "liberalism—
rhetoric or principle?"; and, to end the semester, "treason of the
intellectual: careerism vs. critical function."[14]

The correspondence between Yamada, Haber and SLID headquarters in New York makes it plain that the Ann Arbor chapter was fast
becoming an anomaly. On other campuses, SLID chapters, where
they existed at all, were sputtering along; the organization's national
convention in 1958 attracted only thirteen students.[15] Yet the Michigan branch, thanks to the success of the Political Issues Club, began
to thrive. The reason was Alan Haber.

In the summer of 1958, Haber wrote an extraordinary letter to the
SLID headquarters in New York City. Yamada had suggested informally that Haber might be a good choice for a position on the SLID
Executive Committee. Though this was his first formal contact with
the national office, Haber was anything but deferential, offering his
outspoken opinions on SLID at some length.

"I am definitely interested in participating in SLID," he wrote.
Even in "as hopeless a place as Michigan," change was possible:
"You have to take it as an article of faith that getting people to think
is worthwhile in itself and that wherever enough people are made
aware of contemporary problems and the values at stake, their force
will somehow be felt and some element of reason and dignity will
find its way into the modern world." Haber nonetheless expressed
alarm that SLID sometimes seemed to be "suffocating under a blan-

ket of slogans, euphemisms and empty jargon." A proposed national conference on "Work and Its Discontents" provoked him to an extended critique that remains one of the best examples of his intellectual style.

"I hope," Haber admonished, "that you can deal with the problems of the worker in a capitalist society with more objectivity than I feel is indicated by the formulation of the question. . . . Before you can ask, 'What kind of frustration does the worker feel?' you have to ask, does he feel frustration? . . . And what do you mean by frustration? is it just a modern and more acceptable synonym for alienation? . . . And further, why do you make at the outset what seems to be an assumption that this frustration, if it exists, is a product of the institutional structure (whatever that is) and that social reform should a priori focus on modifying the allegedly delinquent institutions? . . . Why should you initially exlude the possibility that this frustration is a result of value conflict within the worker? . . . What are the paramount values for the American worker? . . . If they are not the values he should have, why not? and how does he get them? and what role do institutions play in producing them? What institutions? . . . A reappraisal of goals and objectives is always a worthwhile undertaking; but if it is to be fruitful, if it is to contribute to your understanding of the realities of this 'age of Prosperity,' and if it is to suggest ways of implementing your values . . . then it cannot begin by assuming what it wishes to demonstrate."[16]

Act *Now*

With his freewheeling skepticism, growing sophistication about organization and energetic faith that "reason and dignity" could be restored to their proper place in modern life, Haber combined talents that rarely mix in politics. On a campus like Michigan, his style stood out. Unlike the Young Democrats, he was grappling with big issues. Unlike the arcane doctrinaires of the Young People's Socialist League, he insisted on the virtues of plain talk and self-criticism. He began to win converts. One of the first and most important was a freshman named Sharon Jeffrey.

Like Haber, she had grown up in a family that took the notion of citizenship very seriously. Her parents were both active socialists and veteran trade-union organizers who worked for the United Auto Workers in Detroit. After the war, with the Socialist Party in retreat, both of them had become involved in the Democratic party, regarding it as the best available vehicle for social reform. Sharon's mother, Mildred, was an outspoken feminist and one of the most prominent women in the Democratic party, serving in the Sixties and Seventies on the Democratic National Committee and the national board of Americans for Democratic Action, before becoming president of the National Women's Political Caucus.

"I was marching in union picket lines at the age of five," says Sharon. As a student in grade school, she organized her classes to support Adlai Stevenson, and helped get out the vote on election day. Though her parents encouraged her to think for herself, the family's patron saints were never in doubt: "We discussed the ideals of Walter Reuther and the UAW, and of Eleanor Roosevelt." Senators and mayors regularly visited the house. Talking about politics was "like drinking milk."[17]

Her temperament was bubbly, but her convictions were anything but evanescent. Deeply serious and capable of stubborn defiance, Sharon crossed swords with her grade-school principal over the issue of wearing blue jeans: "She took me out of class and had a discussion with me about what little girls are supposed to wear. I was aggressive and competitive and wanted to be in the clothes I was going to be in right after school so I could play." Years later, when she was at a beach with high school classmates, Sharon saw a girlfriend from outside her neighborhood walk by holding hands with a black boyfriend. "My high school friends were horrified," she recalls. "That evening, at a party, they sat all around me in a circle and asked me the classic question: Would *you* marry a black?" For her, the question admitted of only one answer. For months afterward, she was harassed by taunting phone calls.

Sharon entered the University of Michigan in January, 1959. She anticipated intellectual stimulation and the excitement of meeting new friends. She found bored students, large classes, professors droning into microphones. "My expectations were that college would offer intellectual discussion around significant philosophical, political and social issues. And that the professors would definitely be interested in their students, that students would definitely be interested in ideas, that people would have a sense of meaning and purpose to their lives, and value interaction and personal relationships. And *none* of that, none of that at any level was present."

Disillusioned by her classes and put off by the fevered preparations in her dormitory for sorority rush, Sharon cast about for a campus political group to join. She visited the Young Democrats, who were "very dull"—they expended more energy passing out buttons than they did discussing the issues. "There wasn't any substance to them.

There wasn't any heart." She tried the Young People's Socialist League, but "they were way off in some foreign land. They had *very* intellectual discussions about the Russian Revolution and how that would impact on American socialism. It seemed irrelevant."

Jeffrey kept searching—and in the fall of 1959, after one miserable semester, she finally found what she had been looking for. The occasion was a meeting to plan a civil rights conference. Some ten or twenty students attended. The person talking was Alan Haber. His speech was the answer. "It had vision, it had purpose, it had meaning," she says. "He was also smart enough to know that you have to organize around specifics. That's everything that I really responded to." She fell in love.

Haber's plan was to organize a SLID conference on "Human Rights in the North." The specific point of the conference was "to provide students with leadership skills and perspectives for necessary action against discrimination." The agenda was designed to link racial problems in the community with those on campus—the topics included segregated dorms, fraternities and sororities. As Haber's flyer for the conference emphasized, he hoped to heal "the gap between professional and citizen." "The responsibility for putting an end to discrimination should not be placed on the shoulders of the professional," such as the social worker and government official. "THE CITIZEN MUST TAKE THE INITIATIVE, MUST SET THE COURSE FOR THE PROFESSIONAL TO FOLLOW, MUST PROVIDE THE ENERGY REQUIRED FOR THE SOCIAL ACTION PROGRAM TO EFFECT PERMANENT IMPROVEMENT." In inviting students from other colleges to attend, Haber also stressed his vision of the campus as "a laboratory where students test ideas and techniques which are later used in all areas of society."[18]

Together, Haber and Jeffrey set about organizing the conference. Al plied Sharon with Drambuie and three-course home-cooked meals, reading her his poetry and then discussing how to recruit students. On her own she went after women students in her dormitory, treating the communal bathroom as her private union hall. "I looked like them," she says: "Given that I'm a blonde right out of the Midwest, I could communicate with all of the straight Midwesterners there." Haber, meanwhile, was "burning on all fronts," going out on the road to other campuses to drum up interest in the conference, becoming freshly excited by his academic work, maintaining his involvement in campus politics but turning down an opportunity to become president of the student government: "I said no, I'm going to do this conference, I'm going to change the world."[19]

On February 1, 1960, four black college students in Greensboro,

North Carolina, made Haber's immodest ambition seem a little more plausible. Sitting down at the lunch counter reserved for whites only in a local F. W. Woolworth store, they ordered coffee and doughnuts. The waitress refused to serve them. They remained at their seats. Rather than have them arrested, the store's manager instructed employees to ignore them. Elated by the results, the students returned to campus after the store closed and organized a larger sit-in the next morning.

The demonstration in Greensboro had grown out of rambling late-night discussions among the four students, who were freshmen at North Carolina A&T College. Since 1954, when the Supreme Court had ruled in *Brown v. Board of Education of Topeka*, that legally enforced segregation was unconstitutional, demands for change had been gathering force in the South. The students in Greensboro, excited by the promise of progress, had spent weeks talking about racism and the ethics of action, about Gandhi and the Christian virtue of love, about apathy, fear and resignation. They talked about people who talked but never acted. As they talked, a course of action crystallized. Resurrecting a tactic that had been tried several months before by students in Durham, twenty miles away, the four students planned their own sit-in.

Unexpectedly, their protest caught fire. On February 2, the second Greensboro sit-in attracted the notice of local reporters. By that evening, the news was on the national wire services. Within a week, similar protests against Jim Crow had spread throughout the South. By mid-April, according to one estimate, some 50,000 students had participated in sit-ins.[20]

In Ann Arbor, Al Haber was ecstatic. "I heard the word right away," he says. "I was on the student government, so the word came from NSA [the National Student Association], I think. We very quickly got facts about what was going on, besides what was coming in on the news." He called up the Greensboro students and invited them to attend the Ann Arbor human-rights conference. To Haber, the message of the sit-ins was simple: "Act *now*."

As the sit-in movement gathered steam, students in the North started to organize sympathy boycotts of the chain stores targeted in the South, F. W. Woolworth and S. S. Kresge. In Ann Arbor, the picketing began in March and continued into the spring. The pickets were an organizer's dream. "They required a minimal commitment," says Sharon Jeffrey. "People had to talk about it and say that that's what they were doing. But it was only two hours in the afternoon."

On March 11, *The Michigan Daily*, the campus newspaper, endorsed the pickets in a melodramatic editorial: "Thousands in the South and East boycott stores and march in protest . . . In Houston, Felton Turner, a 27-year-old Negro, is taken to a quiet glade where men beat him with chains, then slice 'KKK' into his chest and stomach. In Washington, the Senate hesitates, then continues to filibuster. . . . In Ann Arbor, young liberals plan to spend a Saturday afternoon picketing a dress shop and two dime stores. The public is invited."[21]

For the student who wrote this editorial, an aspiring reporter named Thomas Hayden, the sit-ins and pickets were the stuff of high political drama, a morality play come to life. "It excited me," he says looking back, "but it excited me first as something I was writing about. I could become quite passionate about it as a journalist."[22]

But for other Michigan students, the sympathy pickets were the introduction to a new kind of politics. A host of previously passive students began to show up regularly to picket the Ann Arbor stores. They were joined by organizers from YPSL and SLID. Haber and Jeffrey worked the picket lines looking for recruits and inviting people to come to the human-rights conference, which was set to begin on April 28. Since the Greensboro students had agreed to attend the conference, Haber and Jeffrey had no trouble generating interest.

One of the picketers intrigued by the conference was Bob Ross, a seventeen-year-old freshman at the time. "I had never walked a picket line," says Ross, "I didn't know anything about it, I felt awkward and embarrassed and it was just—it was the Jewish thing. If you're silent, you're complicit." A native New Yorker, he had grown up in a family with long-standing radical convictions and a wariness, in response to McCarthyism, about expressing them. His stepfather, a garment worker, had been involved in the "popular front" politics of the Thirties, when the Communist Party tried to broaden its appeal by sponsoring a variety of satellite groups more or less dominated by the Party. His mother, a teacher, was a pacifist and a social democrat. She had been an active member of the Teachers' Union, which the Communist Party had dominated, but had resigned from the union at the height of the McCarthy era after several Communist members had lost their teaching jobs.

His trip to Ann Arbor in the fall of 1959 was the first time Bob Ross had been west of the Catskills. Like Jeffrey, he was a serious student who was shocked at the beer-drinking frivolity of the dominant fraternity culture he discovered. He also had to contend with the anti-Semitism of the Greek-letter societies. Shortly after he arrived, some students in his dormitory began drawing swastikas on the walls. Furious, Ross fought back, throwing food at the culprits, harassing them in the halls, challenging them to fight. They backed down. By definition a misfit in Ann Arbor's Midwestern and Protestant culture, Ross gravitated toward the coffee klatsch at the Michigan Union Grill. He wore turtleneck sweaters and hosted a jazz program on the campus radio station—he revered the great bop saxophonist Charlie Parker. That fall, at a speech by attorney Leonard Boudin on the H. Chandler Davis case, he discovered that many of the friends he had met through his jazz show were also interested in civil liberties. He joined Ann Arbor's avant-garde scene.

The Southern sit-ins were a revelation to Ross. "I read about the sympathy pickets," he says, "and immediately had a crisis of conscience: oughtn't I to be there? Up to that point, I had always thought that a good person, a progressive person, was a person with the right atjtitudes, the right opinions. If you were a socialist, you were for socialized medicine. And there was a genuine impotence to the conception. Politics was what you were for and against—not what you *did*. My parents were people who, in fact, had been politically intimidated, who for survival and other reasons had withdrawn from activity. But here were people who were *doing* something."[23]

From Protest to Radicalism

In Ann Arbor, Haber's conference on human rights climaxed a spring of radical activity. The conference brought together activists and intellectuals, newcomers and old hands, heroes like the Greensboro four and local freshmen such as Ross. For Haber and Jeffrey, the gathering confirmed their conviction that the left in America was on the move again. And the two featured speakers, James Farmer and Michael Harrington, suggested a vital continuity between the generations—a largely unspoken tradition that would nourish the young radicals, often without their knowledge, and enable Farmer and Harrington to play leading roles in the events of the following years.

At forty-one, Farmer was Program Director of the National Association for the Advancement of Colored People (NAACP). A former organizer for SLID, he would in several months become the national director of CORE, the Congress of Racial Equality—an organization that he had helped found in 1942. A preacher's kid from the Deep South, inspired by Tolstoy and the Harlem Renaissance and trained at the theological school of Howard University, Farmer in 1941 had prepared a plan for a "Gandhi-type movement of nonviolent direct action against segregation" while he was working as a field secretary for the Quaker Fellowship of Reconciliation. The following year, Farmer put his plan to the test with CORE, which organized the first civil-rights sit-ins in American history in May, 1942. The students in Greensboro knew none of this history. But by their own action, they had given fresh impetus to Farmer's ideals. The man himself, says Haber, "was embracing, friendly, a deep resonance." He embodied the Quaker stand in American radicalism, with its emphasis on moral suasion and face-to-face discussion as the way to achieve peace, concord, consensus—the Blessed Community.[24]

At thirty-two, Michael Harrington was a member of LID and the elder statesman of the Young People's Socialist League. An orator of dazzling eloquence and burning moral passion, he was already Norman Thomas' heir apparent. Raised a Roman Catholic in St. Louis and trained by the Jesuits, he had entered radical politics through the Catholic Worker, Dorothy Day's mission to the Bowery. An austere anarchist-pacifist commune, the Catholic Worker was ruled by the admonition "to see Christ in every man"—including, as Harrington recalls, "the pathetic, shambling, shivering creature who would wander in off the streets with his pants caked with urine and his face scabbed with blood." When he left the Worker—and the Catholic faith—in the early Fifties, it was to become a militant in the Young Socialist League, a small, ferociously anti-Stalinist Marxist sect. Schooled in the intricacies of metaphysics, he was a master of scholastic forms of argument, with an intimate knowledge of the entire Marxist canon. Yet at the same time, he was tough-minded and pragmatic, with a ready grasp of statistics and the specifics of social policy. Once an uncompromising apostle of revolution, he had become convinced that America's authentic labor party already existed, dormant, within the Democratic Party. But he did not forget the suffering that he had seen on the Bowery: in 1959, he published an article in *Commentary* magazine on the persistence of poverty in America which would become the basis for the book that would make him famous three years later, *The Other America*.[25]

Farmer and Harrington both offered living proof that radicals could spring from native American soil. They both illustrated the vitality and variety of dissenting religious traditions. For both, the moral appeal of socialism was central. Their participation, together with the presence of the Greensboro students, helped make the Ann Arbor human-rights conference a minor milestone: some 150 students from both the South and the North attended, forging ties that would become the basis of a durable alliance.[26]

The conference also marked a kind of maiden voyage for SDS, or Students for a Democratic Society, as SLID had been rebaptized a few months before. The name change, Haber recalls, had no special significance: "SLID was just a laughable name," he says, "particularly for an organization in decline." The Ann Arbor conference was a fitting fresh start. Impressed by Haber's work on the conference, the elders of LID offered him the job of SDS Field Secretary—in effect, the organization's roving ambassador to the campuses. Haber accepted.

Before leaving for the first official convention of SDS in New York that June, Haber made a special effort to sign up Bob Ross, who had come to his attention at the conference. Haber pursued him doggedly. "It was a classical political recruitment thing," says Ross. "He had an intensity, in fact a vision, about a new student movement. The vision was democratic: the idea that being a democrat was radical, that it went to the roots of our problems and led to radical change. He had endless patience. He didn't have a lot of endurance, but he would stay with you. You could fall asleep in your chair, wake up—and there he would be, ready to go again." Ross signed on. And in June, he joined Sharon and Al in the Michigan delegation at the convention.

The meeting was something of an anticlimax. Jeffrey remembers a handful of students in attendance—perhaps two dozen. The University of Michigan chapter alone brought eleven members—a bloc of votes that ensured Haber's election as SDS president.

The theme of the convention was "Student Radicalism—1960." After opening-night speeches on the history of student radicalism by Norman Thomas, James Farmer and political columnist Murray Kempton of *The New York Post*, the convention settled into debate about the nature of student radicalism, the purpose of SDS and the connection between intellectual commitment and direct action. According to the enthusiastic official account (which claimed an attendance considerably higher—70—than most participants remember), "a major area of concern throughout the discussions was the distinction between liberal activity, which attempts to realize the American Dream, and radical activity, which proposes fundamental changes in that dream and which suggests alternatives." There was lively debate about the value of organizing student protests against civil defense drills—one speaker thought such protests diverted attention from the criticism of American foreign policy, while another argued that the protests set the stage for such criticism. The group voiced general agreement with the concept of "Cartesian radicalism," as one participant called it: the constant asking of "Why—why the poor, why meaningless work?" Haber urged that the organization take an aggressively multi-issue approach: "SDS," he said, "can ask questions in one area, and then try consciously to relate them to problems in other areas; this is radicalism in the broadest sense." The conference closed with a speech by Dwight Macdonald of *The New Yorker*, who spoke on "The Relevance of Anarchy."[27]

As conventions go, it was not much. At the time, SDS claimed some eight chapters and 250 members.[28] A realist might well have been discouraged—but not Alan Haber. That summer, the new SDS president took stock of the situation and summarized his thinking in his most important piece of writing yet, "From Protest to Radicalism: An Appraisal of the Student Movement 1960."

"Pessimism and cynicism have given way to direct action," declared Haber. "We have spoken at last, with vigor, idealism and urgency." He explained the new mood among students in terms that rang true to his own experience. The movement had grown "out of the memories of wars, atomic explosions, and race riots—out of a heritage of absurdity." On many campuses, the avant-garde had taken the lead: "The term 'beat,' " explained Haber, "has come to characterize all those who have deviated from the traditional college patterns. They are variously professional students, bohemians, political types, and non-students who still seem to be around." Their lax "dress standards" sometimes alienated mainstream students and needlessly limited the appeal of the political issues they embraced. Still, "this group in time of dissension and irresolution, acts, and in so doing, takes the first step toward radicalism; the participation crystallizes commitment."

Despite the hopeful tone, the crux of Haber's paper concerned the limits of the current student activism in the North. "The issues for which we have been fighting are so clear and so right, and the commitment we demand so slight, that we should expect much greater success." Motivated by a sense of shame about the injustices visited upon others in another place, the Northern students in the sympathy pickets lacked "a positive interpersonal dynamic, for we are not close enough to the issues." The protesters often remained stuck on a single issue, such as Jim Crow: "Direct action is not seen as a lever in the total process of social change. We call for disarmament, but we say nothing of what to do with the manpower, resources, industrial plant, and capital equipment that are tied up in the military machine. Problems of poverty, health care, wasted agricultural and natural resources, meaningless work—these issues arouse students neither to demonstration nor discussion. Even in respect to civil rights, we do not speak to the essentials of social equality." The Southern students, by contrast, "operate in a community context" defined, in part, by the moral traditions of the black Church. The justice that they demanded was "justice for themselves."

To deepen the student movement in the North, Haber proposed treating "participation as a continuing educational process." Organizers should present issues in a broad analytic context. Instead of being regarded as an end in itself, direct action should become the pretext for "a deeper appraisal of social problems," drawing on the Northern student's special talent for "discussion, research and debate."

"It must be said," Haber concluded, "that America is not fertile ground for radical or particularly deep social protest." A sober appraisal of the number of students involved in the protests warranted "a fairly modest view of the success of the movement." The challenge was to move the "radical fringe" into the mainstream. "The novelty and the great hope is that other students—undergraduates and those not involved with the liberal movement since childhood —are becoming involved and assuming leadership positions."[29]

Haber's election as SDS president required that he move to New York City. But before the summer was over, he had entrusted the flagship SDS chapter at the University of Michigan to Jeffrey and Ross. In keeping with his views on "the great hope" for radicalism, Haber instructed the two of them to work hard on recruiting a promising new prospect he had spotted—a student conspicuously lacking in a liberal political background. Their target was the incoming editor of *The Michigan Daily* and a man destined to become one of the most famous radicals of the Sixties: Tom Hayden.

CHAPTER TWO

ON THE ROAD

"I DIDN'T GET POLITICAL," Tom Hayden has said. "Things got political." One day in the spring of 1960, Al Haber appeared in Hayden's office at *The Michigan Daily*. "He was the campus radical," recalls Hayden. "He had a beard and a lot of books and he just knew a lot, and he was much older than anyone else, and he came over to talk to me about the sit-in movement. He explained to me that sit-ins had been used by the labor movement and how they were being used by the black students, that it was very important that we come to their defense and that we see that this cause was our cause."[1] Hayden listened. Haber was persuasive. Shortly afterward, Hayden wrote *The Michigan Daily* editorial in support of the sympathy pickets in Ann Arbor. Overcoming his own discomfort at the prospect, he briefly joined the picket lines.

Trim, athletic and casual—for years, untucked shirttails and tennis shoes were his trademark—Hayden cut a striking figure. With "heavy lidded eyes in a pocked landscape of a face," he looked, as Gary Wills once described him, like a "punier Richard Boone as Paladin."[2] He was soft-spoken and serious, a student of philosophy. He drove a motorcycle. He admired Albert Camus and James Dean. At the age of twenty, he had panache, passion, a way with words—language, like the open road, was a source of adventure.

It is no wonder that Al Haber coveted his talents for SDS. "Bob Ross and Sharon Jeffrey and Al were this great little cabal," says Hayden. "They came out of the left, the labor left, and politics for them was an active way of life. I was the guy born out of Middle America, with no socialist or labor parents. We all became friends,

41

but the difference was that they were of the previous left, I wasn't, and they had a great yearning to be part of some new, natural party."[3] Hayden seemed to offer hope that such a "new, natural party" might actually come into being. For Haber, Jeffrey and Ross —and soon, also for Hayden himself—his biography assumed a certain prophetic aura. His experience epitomized the possibilities for a new kind of American radicalism, born of a restless desire to see ideas in action. He became the archetype of the new student radical.

Faith

Thomas Emmett Hayden, named by his Catholic parents for Saint Thomas Aquinas, was born on December 11, 1939, in Royal Oak, Michigan. A predominantly Protestant suburb twelve miles from Detroit, dotted with the cheap shingled homes of automobile workers, Royal Oak in the Thirties became a magnet for Catholics and conservative populists, drawn by the widely heard radio broadcasts of the local Catholic priest, Father Charles E. Coughlin, the controversial critic of corporate avarice and Communist atheism. Hayden's father, as he later described him, was "a Republican populist" with "a stubborn Irish will, a sense that things usually go wrong for the honest person, and an uncanny ability to wait in patience for large-mouth bass." An accountant for Chrysler, he joined the Marines in World War II. "He was changed somehow after the war," Hayden recalls. "He started spending more time drinking down at the American Legion hall, and drifted away from my mother."[4] His parents were finally divorced, leaving Tom to be raised primarily by his mother, who took a job as film librarian for the local school district.

An only child, Hayden grew up in an atmosphere of austere frugality. One visitor to the family dinner table recalls Mrs. Hayden dishing out mashed potatoes, teaspoon by teaspoon. "She said, 'Oh, we've got to get every bit of potato to fill up our boys.' She scraped off those potatoes like there wasn't another potato where they came from. It was that kind of household."[5]

Through the eighth grade, Hayden attended the school of his local parish, the Shrine of the Little Flower, where Coughlin remained the priest. Though Coughlin's radio jeremiads, which had grown increasingly anti-Semitic, had been silenced by Church superiors in 1942, the priest continued to sprinkle his Sunday sermons with warnings about the evils of Communism. The parish school reflected Coughlin's harshly conservative temperament. Hayden has recalled that beatings were administered "to teach you a Christian lesson." His mother, a liberal and tolerant person, was embarrassed by Coughlin's opinions, and tried to shelter her son from them. "I dealt with the insecurity of being an outsider," he recalled in 1968, "by becoming a brainy, advanced kid in class, winning spelling contests and reading aloud from Saint Thomas Aquinas to enrapture the nuns in the second grade."[6]

It was his intellectual earnestness that precipitated his apostasy. "The thing about the Church is the threat of hell. I was afraid that if they were right, you could get in a lot of trouble." When Hayden left the parish school and entered Royal Oak High School, he became friends with several Jews who lived in an adjacent neighborhood. As he knew from his parish schooling, such people were condemned to roast in hell. "I was scared—but I could not imagine all my friends going to hell and me going to heaven because I was born a Catholic." His reflections triggered a crisis of conscience, leaving his faith shaken.[7]

Rebellion

Hayden spent his summers as a teenager working on a fishing boat on the Ausable River and Lake Huron. "My hero," he says, "was the guy who ran the fishing boat—Howard Brubaker. He was the complete entrepreneur. He did for a living what he wanted to do all the time, which was fish." Hayden's most passionate interests were athletic: apart from fishing, often with his father, he played baseball, football, basketball and, above all, tennis. His talents as a tennis player—he once placed third in state doubles—took him far from Royal Oak. On the manicured tennis courts of Grosse Pointe, he discovered the upper class: "I knew these people were different. . . . They didn't seem to sweat." He became an editor of the high school newspaper, had an abortive love affair with a girl from a wealthy family (her mother disapproved of the match) and began to thumb his nose at authority. One of his idols was Holden Caulfield, the protagonist of J. D. Salinger's novel *The Catcher in the Rye*. Another was Alfred E. Neuman, the moronic mascot of *Mad*, the monthly cartoon magazine that lampooned the absurdity of advertising and American popular culture. In the same spirit, Hayden produced an underground newspaper that he called *The Daily Smirker*. He nearly did not get his high school diploma after he published a risibly patriotic editorial in the school paper that spelled out, encoded in the first letter of each paragraph, "GO TO HELL."[8]

Hayden entered the University of Michigan in the fall of 1957. "I had to live in a dorm with thirteen hundred guys," Hayden later recalled, "that was worse than a public housing project. There were no written rules, you couldn't even find out what the rules were or how to change them. It was a system of absolutely arbitrary authority. You couldn't have girls in the room, or even in the library. You couldn't do anything." He looked on, bemused, at the petty violence that flared up in the dorms. "One day the guys started a riot in the cafeteria to protest the rule that you had to wear coats and ties. Some guys threw food at the housemother, and they got thrown out of school. . . . I couldn't understand it—no due process, no hearings." Hayden wrote about the incident in *The Michigan Daily*; he formed a group to meet with members of the law-school faculty to discuss the case. But nothing happened. "It was a big thing to me," he recalled in 1968. "I didn't plan it, it just happened. But if something like that happens a few times you start looking for a new view of the world."[9]

Hayden's experience as a freshman fueled his unruliness. In his sophomore year, he chose as a roommate a self-styled heartlands rebel. "What I shared with him was that both of us were totally enamored of James Dean, motorcycles, and t-shirts and Levi's, a lot of beer parties and getting involved in sort of the fringe, bohemian culture of the campus." The two of them bought a motorcycle. "We used to drive up and down the hills of the university arboretum. . . . We would try to see how close we could come to killing ourselves."[10]

Hayden enjoyed flirting with danger—but he also loved books, writing, the world of ideas. Becoming a reporter for *The Michigan Daily*, he covered campus life and dreamed of becoming a foreign correspondent. He attended Walter Kaufmann's course on existentialism and the classes on political philosophy taught by a young professor named Arnold Kaufman. Hayden read Plato and Aristotle, Camus and Sartre, John Dewey and Jacques Maritain, Rainer Maria Rilke, Ignazio Silone, Norman O. Brown. "Part of me," he says, "was with that world, and part of me was planning to be a journalist, covering the great events of our times. The reconciliation of all this was becoming an activist."

Commitment

Hayden did not become an activist overnight. "I became a revolutionary in bits and stages," he stressed in a 1968 interview. "It was a cumulative process in which one commitment led to another. You start with little commitments, then you go through turning points —people you meet, actions you take, events you see—and pretty soon you find yourself as a professional radical."[11]

The first turning point, as we have seen, came in March of 1960, when Hayden covered the sympathy pickets in Ann Arbor for *The Michigan Daily*. The *Daily* was one of the oldest and most distinguished college newspapers in America, with a long tradition of editorial excellence and independence. Hayden was about to become the paper's editor—a job that not only gave him clout on campus but also made him an important figure in organizations like the National Student Association. For all his hell-raising, he was on track for a career in journalism.

The sympathy pickets piqued Hayden's conscience. But it was Jack Kerouac who proved instrumental in changing his life. After reading *On the Road* in the spring of 1960, Hayden resolved to hitchhike across the country to California.[12] His ultimate destination was Los Angeles, where he planned to cover the Democratic Convention for the *Daily*. But his first stop was Berkeley—the once and future Mecca of radical student politics.

"I got to Berkeley," Hayden recalls, "and went up to a woman who was giving out leaflets at Sproul Plaza. I asked if she knew anywhere where I could meet with political people and maybe get an apartment or someplace to stay. I wanted to see where the sit-ins and other things had happened, where students had been arrested. She gave me some names and I wound up in a house with the people who formed SLATE, the student political party."[13]

The roots of SLATE went back to 1957, when a coalition of liberals and radicals first tried, unsuccessfully, to field a slate of candidates for student government. Berkeley, like Michigan, was a sprawling multiversity, and many of the same issues were raised by radicals on both campuses: racial discrimination in fraternities and sororities, infringement of free speech, the madness of the spiraling nuclear arms race.

Hayden's visit to the Bay Area came on the heels of a tumultuous school year marked by the first real stirrings of a broadly based radical student movement at Berkeley. The fall semester had begun with an angry debate over the expulsion of a student who had gone on a hunger strike in protest over the college rule making military training in the Reserve Officer's Training Corps (ROTC) compulsory. In an effort to clamp down on such incidents, the university president, Clark Kerr, issued a set of "directives." A sanctioned campus group, Kerr decreed, "may not be affiliated with any partisan, political or religious group, nor have as one of its purposes the taking of positions with reference to the off-campus political, religious, economic, international or other issues of the time."[14]

The "Kerr directives," as they were called, failed to deter political dissent. Like their counterparts at Michigan, radicals at Berkeley demonstrated their sympathy for the Southern student sit-ins in the spring of 1960. Shortly afterward, they protested the execution of Caryl Chessman, a convicted rapist who had eloquently pleaded his innocence. Perhaps the strangest—and funniest—controversy of all involved a grammar test that the University of California administered to incoming freshmen. One of the essay questions for the May, 1959, version of the test had asked, "What are the dangers to a democracy of a national police organization, like the FBI, which operates secretly and is unresponsive to public criticism?" In February, 1960, *The Daily Californian*, Berkeley's campus newspaper, reported that an American Legion officer, convinced that this essay question was a piece of "vicious Communist propaganda," had written to the governor of California demanding that it be deleted. In a letter to the *Californian* a few weeks later, FBI director J. Edgar Hoover professed himself "deeply shocked" to see his bureau described as "a national police organization." The Board of Regents of the university then withdrew the question, prompting the *Californian* in an editorial to suggest calling Hoover's men "Boy Scout Troop #55 of Washington, D.C."[15]

For Berkeley radicals, the climax of the year came on May 13, 1960, or "Black Friday," as it was later called. The occasion was a demonstration against the House Un-American Activities Committee (HUAC). A symbol of irrational anti-Communism and a leftover from the McCarthy era of witch-hunts against radicals, the Committee was holding two weeks of hearings in San Francisco on disloyalty and subversion in the Bay Area. On "Black Friday," police officers attacked some 200 protesters on the steps of San Francisco's City Hall, where the hearings were being held. After shooting jets of water at the nonviolent but noisy throng, police waded in to beat people, flinging demonstrators one by one down the steps of City Hall. The confrontation gave the student left its first martyrs. Indeed, Hayden's desire to behold the scene of the incident and to understand its meaning had been a powerful factor in his decision to visit the Bay Area.[16]

Hayden was taken in hand by the Berkeley activists. "They looked on me probably as a raw gem to be polished," he says. "Here's a student editor, we'll politicize him and he'll go back and form a

political party in Ann Arbor, just like SLATE." One new local acquaintance, Herb Mills, an apostle of the new student left, arranged
a kind of political grand tour. "He drove me out to Livermore one
day," Hayden has recalled, "and showed me the nuclear reactor,
where all the hydrogen bombs were made, with the fence around it,
and he described the nuclear weapons and the arms race. And then
another day, [he] drove me out into the fields and valleys, and he
told me about the Chicanos and the farm workers, and the conditions under which they labor." [17]

This impromptu political education had its desired effect. By the
time Hayden arrived in Los Angeles for the Democratic Convention,
he was beginning to see himself as an activist as well as a reporter.
He came with Herb Mills, who had helped plan a nonviolent demonstration outside the convention hall, in order to remind the delegates of the need for a strong civil rights plank in the Party platform.
When he was not busy inside the hall, Hayden joined the picket line
outside.

His articles on the convention for *The Michigan Daily* clearly
reflect the excitement of the political awakening that he was experiencing. He filed a piece criticizing Adlai Stevenson, a sentimental
favorite of liberals and the Democratic standard-bearer in the two
previous presidential campaigns, who was facing his last hurrah.
"Most agree," wrote Hayden, "that practical politics involves operation on two broad levels: the level of ideas, and the nonintellectual
level of personality and image." Stevenson had ideas, he thought,
but only a fuzzy image: "partly because of his seemingly ethical
decision not to mix politics with thinking," wrote Hayden, Stevenson was not "destined for the Presidency." John F. Kennedy, the
convention's eventual nominee, by contrast struck Hayden as "an
ambivalent character. . . . There is a serious discrepancy in Kennedy
between what he says and what he does." He was nevertheless fascinated by the candidate's personality: Kennedy was "a politician
dedicated to public greatness but at the same time calculating and
opportunistic." His image might be hollow—Hayden found his ideas
vague—but Kennedy "has inspired this convention with the promise of political victory, with the promise of vigorous and tenacious
party leadership, with the promise of youth." He does not say as
much, but Hayden leaves the impression that an effective politician
would somehow combine the intellectual seriousness of Stevenson,
the glamour and guile of Kennedy—and, of course, the courage of
the young student radicals, the subject of another report that Hayden
filed from the convention. [18]

Ironically, the figure who perhaps most deeply affected Hayden at the convention was neither a student radical nor a candidate for President: it was Martin Luther King, Jr., already the most prominent civil rights leader of his generation. "Meeting King," says Hayden, "transformed me. There I was, with pencil in hand, trying to conduct an objective interview with Martin Luther King, whose whole implicit message was: 'Stop writing, start acting.' That was a compelling moment. It seemed so absurd to be a student writing about students taking action, as opposed to becoming more of a committed writer and thinker, with commitment coming first."[19]

Hayden was ready to take the next step. In August, he delivered his first major piece of political advocacy, a speech to a student conference on political action held near Monterey, California, and sponsored by SLATE. "How," asked Hayden in his speech, "can the active minority" of students "alter the world-image of the inactive majority?" Most students, he asserted, were interested in private rather than public welfare; most were selfish, not idealistic. Their sense of what was politically feasible had been shaped by "an image of society as an all-powerful, impossible to alter, mechanical creature. The conscientious but uncommitted student withdraws from the complexities and dangers of the social scene."

The "fervent minority," by contrast, offered a model of "existential commitment." In his speech, Hayden asserted that a committed student "has not only become aware of the breadth and complexity of persons and ideas, but has also become intensely attached to a specific position. In many cases . . . his personal attitudes have been severely reversed. He has made a decision demanding guts." The sit-ins and demonstrations were "risky, shoot-for-the-moon affairs, based not on personal security desires but on a willingness to deal with the uncertain." To arouse the required courage and conscience of bystanders, declared Hayden, the student movement had to become "evangelical, that is, it must attract converts."[20]

This speech is remarkable for its awkward, almost painfully earnest rhetoric of risk, "guts" and "existential commitment." It is also remarkable for its image of evangelical outreach: long after he had left the institutional Church, as we shall see, Hayden's Catholic upbringing continued to shape his figures of speech, his habits of thought, his moral sensibility.

Hayden ended the summer with a trip to the University of Minnesota, where the National Student Association (NSA) was holding its annual congress. The NSA had been founded in 1947 as a forum for student politicians and editors. By 1960, it had become the most important and prestigious student organization in the country. Years afterward, Hayden complained that the "power politics of NSA" taught participants how "to be an American politician: delegations, bloc voting, hustling people, campaigning, becoming a monster."[21] That may be true. But at the time, Hayden was elated to have the opportunity to meet other student leaders from around the country.

The NSA played a paradoxical role in the history of post-war American radicalism. Though only a few students knew it at the time, the organization was funded and controlled by the CIA. The agency hoped that a liberal, militantly anti-Communist youth organization could advance the national interest, particularly at the international youth festivals where Communist groups often played an active role. At the same time, radicals unaware of the CIA connection regarded the NSA as a convenient forum for airing ideas and winning converts. One such radical was Al Haber, who came to the 1960 congress looking for SDS recruits; he also brought along a position paper on "The Student and the Total Community," which he hoped the organization would adopt.

The 1960 congress, as Hayden later described it, "began in an atmosphere of reaction against 'student movements' and 'student action,' especially among student government representatives who presumably set out for status through artificial 'politics' and instead were finding themselves trapped in real controversy." Activists nevertheless succeeded in dominating the congress. In the end, the NSA passed as a new basic policy declaration Haber's statement on "The Student and the Total Community." In explicit opposition to the views enshrined in the Kerr directives, Haber's text declared that the role of student "involves a commitment to an educational process that extends beyond classroom training. It involves also the attainment of knowledge and the development of skills and habits of mind and action necessary for responsible participation in the affairs of government and society on all levels—campus, community, state, national, international." A student "operating in this role is one both dedicated to truth and to preparing himself for leadership in a democratic society; he must be prepared to face the challenges of modern life and he must be willing to confront the crucial issues of public policy that affect him beyond the classroom and that determine the course of his society."[22]

Some students at the congress came close to exemplifying Haber's lofty vision of civic responsibility. At the time, Hayden, like Haber, was particularly impressed by a handful of Southern civil rights activists. One was Charles McDew of the Student Non-Violent Coordinating Committee (SNCC), a recently formed, loosely structured coalition of militant black and white students dedicated to direct action against racism in the spirit of the Southern sit-ins. Another was Tim Jenkins, a black student and member of SNCC who became an NSA officer that year. Above all, there was Sandra "Casey" Cason, a white SNCC activist from Austin, Texas, who would become Hayden's first wife.

Casey had grown up in the small, deeply religious community of Victoria, Texas, an only child raised by a divorced and uncommonly liberal mother. From early in life she had felt "different." Rejected by the sorority of her choice at the University of Texas, she became active in the YWCA and the Christian Faith and Life Community, two local church groups with a long tradition of conscientious objection to segregation and racial prejudice. Like virtually every other Southern civil rights activist, Casey formed her radical convictions in a religious context. She tried to live in the light of SNCC's moral credo: "Through nonviolence, courage displaces fear; love transforms hate. Acceptance dissipates prejudice; hope ends despair. Peace dominates war; faith reconciles doubt. Mutual regard cancels enmity. Justice for all overcomes injustice. The redemptive community supersedes systems of gross social immorality."[23]

Casey and her Southern colleagues obviously had made an "existential commitment" to the civil rights movement. Courageous, daring, steadfast, they were willing to fight for what they believed and to take responsibility for the consequences. They represented the kind of political activism that Hayden now hoped to propagate in Ann Arbor.[24]

The Art of Political Discussion

Hayden returned to the University of Michigan full of enthusiasm for direct action and excited by "the prospect of young people being able to change things drastically."[25] But his first action was literary. In an astonishing series of editorials and articles that September, he declared the dawning of a new era of protest.

Some of these pieces were largely reportorial. "Why This Erupting Generation?" he asked in one. He answered his question by examining causes that ranged from the Cold War to the "rise of the Paperback Book." "It is a generation," he wrote, "which cannot avoid reading criticism of itself and its fathers; indeed, the media have flooded the market with inexpensive paperbacks such as 'The Lonely Crowd' [by David Riesman], 'The Hidden Persuaders' [Vance

Packard's breathless exposé of manipulative advertising], 'The Organization Man' [by William Whyte]." Even more significant, according to Hayden, was the long shadow cast by the Cold War. "The present student generation was born on the brink of war and has never seen their country at more than wobbling peace," he wrote. "Theirs is a generation whose optimism has been squelched since the pre-Korea days, a generation stultified and frustrated by intense cold war pressures, particularly as those pressures have been illustrated in the unique concept of The Bomb."[26]

Hayden's characterization of "the critical world context" was alarming. "It is a world," he wrote, "apparently without leaders, a world of vast confusion, changing cultures, strained by the nearness of total war, and it has been in such shape throughout the life of almost every student." The moral climate seemed bleak: "In recent times spokesmen as disparate as Riesman and the existentialists have been concerned with the actual breakdown of dogma and tradition and the resultant society which seems directionless, decisionless, amoral."[27]

Hayden portrayed a world spinning out of control. But his aim was to spur commitment. He maintained that the "fundamental issues before the student today are quite clear: is he capable of rationally thinking through his position? Is he responsible? Does he care for others passionately enough to think and act in their interests? Can he actually bring about change in social order, or is he politically impotent?" Like Camus in *The Rebel*, Hayden presented moral resolve as a bulwark against nihilism, rooted in the wish (in Camus's words) "to serve justice so as not to add to the injustice of the human condition, to insist on plain language so as not to increase the universal falsehood, and to wager, in spite of human misery, for happiness."[28]

In Hayden's eyes, the new student activists proved "that individual commitment to action"—precisely in Camus's sense of a moral wager "without the aid of eternal values"—was "in fact possible." The students' sense of idealism, he observed, had been shaped by "Mill and classic liberalism," "Jefferson's attitudes on liberty," "Gandhi's principles of non-violent action," and "Camus's concept of the human struggle and commitment." The student activists were harbingers of "a revolution that would reduce complexity to moral simplicity, that would restore emotion to religion, that would in fact give man back his 'roots.'" By moving "from legal action to direct action, from a bureaucratic to an individualistic process," they had already shown that "it is still possible for the individual to

unashamedly speak simple, unconfused truths about his relation
with other individuals." They had demonstrated a "new willingness
to take up responsibilities of the individual to the democratic
order."[29]

To illustrate his argument, Hayden introduced Sandra Cason: "I
cannot say to a person who suffers injustice, 'Wait,' " he quoted
Cason: "Perhaps you can. I can't. And having decided that I cannot
urge caution I must stand with him. If I had known that not a single
lunch counter would open as a result of my action I could not have
done differently than I did. If I had known violence would result, I
could not have done differently than I did. I am thankful for the sit-
ins if for no other reason than that they provided me with an opportunity for making a slogan into a reality, by turning a decision into
an action. It seems to me that this is what life is all about."[30]

Convinced activists in Ann Arbor like Bob Ross scarcely noticed
Hayden's articles. "As far as I was concerned," says Ross, "he was
just another guy jumping on the bandwagon. Great, fine, the *Daily*'s
on our side." But Richard Flacks, another reader, took note: "I remember thinking: This is really brilliant." At the time, Flacks was
a social-psychology graduate student interested in the changing political climate on campus. "Hayden was definitely reading signs,"
says Flacks, "but he was also stringing them together and making
them into a larger reality than they yet were. It was a kind of myth-
making."[31]

Hayden tacitly admitted what he was doing. "We must not so
readily assume our 'ideals' cannot be realized," he wrote in an editorial excoriating "myopic realism." "Even if some seem to be unrealizable, we must at least recognize them as myths having a
valuable, operative reality, and we must use them as standards." He
quoted Plato: "In everything that exists, there is at work an imaginative force, which is determined by ideals." And he quoted Jacques
Maritain: "What your intellect and reason have to win is something
which is not to be measured or manipulated by scientific tools . . .
this is the universe of intelligent being and of the sacred character of
truth as such. You will then be able to show the world how human
action may be reconciled with and permeated by an ideal which is
more real than reality, and why it is possible and right to die for
liberty."[32]

At the age of twenty, Tom Hayden was anxious to show that he
had "guts." Like Al Haber, he wanted to change the world. He knew
that a small but growing number of students shared his ambition.
He was ready to work to translate his ideas into some form of polit-

ical organization. But his special talent was with words. As the editor of *The Michigan Daily*, he held a position of real influence. His growing political commitment found its most striking expression in language—a place of mythopoeic possibilities, "more real than reality."

The pieces that he wrote for *The Michigan Daily* helped thrust Hayden into the vanguard of student activists. Yet Hayden himself was characteristically impatient to move beyond the printed page. During the school year, he explored a variety of different forms of political action. The most important of these was VOICE, the student political party that he founded that fall. Modeled on SLATE, VOICE ran candidates for student government on a platform that presented national issues in a campus context: among the party's concerns were student rights, discrimination in fraternities and sororities, free speech in the university. But it was Hayden's handling of a scandal involving the Dean of Women that made perhaps the deepest impression on activists like Ross and Jeffrey.

For years, it had been rumored that the Dean of Women kept tabs on white coeds who dated black men, using local cabdrivers as informants and then sending letters to the girls' parents. When Hayden became editor of the *Daily*, he gathered together a number of letters from female graduates of the university documenting the Dean's behavior. At a meeting with the Dean and other administration officials, Hayden then threatened to publish the letters unless she resigned. She resigned.

"That was behind the scenes," says Jeffrey. "But everybody knew. This had been an issue that had been around for a long time. It was a perfect example of how discrimination exists, but nobody's willing to stand up and do something about it. And it was a perfect example of how direct action could make a difference."[33]

With his evident political cunning and flair for drama, Hayden had little trouble enlisting both Jeffrey and Ross in VOICE. With Al Haber away in New York, there was scarcely anything specific for SDS members in Ann Arbor to do. VOICE offered a plan of action. "The whole idea," says Jeffrey, "was to relate radical ideas to students on campus."

That spring, Hayden took his ideas a step further. In an article written for *The Michigan Daily*, he suggested that the university sponsor a conference that would bring together students, administrators and faculty members to discuss the future of the campus community. "The University must work relentlessly at being a face-to-face, rather than a mass society," wrote Hayden. To foster a sense of genuine community required a "democratization of decision-making." "If decisions are the sole work of an isolated few rather than of a participating many," he warned, "alienation from the University complex will emerge, because the University will be just that: a complex, not a community."[34]

Hayden's stress on the "democratization of decision-making" brought him close to Haber's views on democracy as the key to developing a multi-issue organ of radical education. Throughout the school year, Ross and Jeffrey worked at persuading Hayden to join SDS. As they saw it, he was an activist in need of a more sophisticated organizational and ideological framework—the kind of framework SDS claimed to provide. "Tom was definitely an emerging leader and had a very caring heart," says Jeffrey, who freely admits the condescension in her attitude at the time. "But he didn't have any politics. He didn't understand economics." He was not, in short, a traditional leftist. "I remember cold winter evenings," says Jeffrey, "where we broke up anything we could use as wood to feed to the fire, because we were having these long discussions—about organizing, about the meaning of direct action, about strategy and tactics. We wanted to demonstrate to Tom a political foundation for what he was doing."

Hayden was not a willing quarry. "Their view," he says of Jeffrey and Ross, "was that things weren't happening unless you were signing up people to become card-carrying members of this organization-in-the-making, the SDS. My view was that things were happening very well, thank you, without any assistance from these groups out of the morbid traditions of the left centered in New York City. I'm very much, with faults and virtues, the independent American, arising innocently out of the ashes of the East and Europe."[35]

SDS wasn't the only organization eager to recruit Hayden. Michael Harrington recalls an abortive effort to interest him in joining the Young People's Socialist League. "When I would have discussions with Tom about joining YPSL, his attitude was that he agreed with me on almost all practical and political questions—working within the Democratic Party, political realignment, the centrality of the civil rights movement, the centrality of economic demands going beyond breaking down juridical Jim Crow. He'd say, 'I agree with you. But where I disagree with you is that you use the word "socialism," which is a European word, which simply cuts off your American audience.' And what he was essentially telling me was that he wanted to have a different language. He wanted to speak American."[36]

Hayden briefly considered working full time for the National Student Association. He was also intrigued by the idea of starting an entirely new organization, in order "to re-create," as he put it at the time, "the art of political discussion with a democratic and non-sectarian flavor."[37] But he had no background or training for the venture, and few potential allies.

Haber, Jeffrey and Ross finally prevailed upon him. In principle, SDS was an educational organization designed to stimulate political debate. Its rhetoric of democracy was suitably nonsectarian and all-American. "The accommodation," Hayden recalls, "was that SDS would be fundamentally new, but it would retain this tie to LID, for the sake of some sort of tradition I didn't understand, but also for money." Since Hayden had just married Sandra Cason, who wanted to continue working with SNCC in the South, Haber proposed that Hayden after his graduation in June become SDS Field Secretary and establish an office in Atlanta. It was a clever plan: it sent the newlyweds south, resolving a potential tension in their marriage; it gave Hayden autonomy as well as authority; and it secured for SDS one of the most promising young radical publicists in America.

Witness to a Revolution

For all of Hayden's gloomy talk of moral chaos, this was a time of heady optimism for many young Americans. Early in 1961, the newly elected President, John F. Kennedy, had set the tone with his inaugural address. "Let the word go forth from this time and place," said the President, "to friend and foe alike, that the torch has been passed to a new generation of Americans." At forty-three, Kennedy was the youngest of America's elected Presidents. Radiating vigor and vitality, he cultivated an aura of youthful idealism. In a dramatic late-night speech at the University of Michigan during his Presidential campaign, for example, Kennedy had endorsed the idea of a Peace Corps—an idea ardently promoted by students in Ann Arbor, including Tom Hayden. "I was next to him," recalls Hayden, who covered the speech for the *Daily*: "A most dramatic and thrilling moment for students, who previously were ignored as non-voters."[38] Assuming control of a prospering economy, Kennedy promised to institute a new, chivalrous era of civic pride.

Buoyed by such hopes, the Southern civil rights movement had entered a new phase of militant protest. In May, 1961, James Farmer of CORE led a biracial group onto a bus in Washington, D.C., and

headed south on a "Freedom Ride." He had planned the trip to test
a recent Supreme Court decision that had outlawed racial discrimination in interstate-bus terminals. After a violent mob greeted the
Freedom Riders in Alabama, SNCC joined the protesters. Martin
Luther King voiced his sympathy. And President Kennedy, who had
championed civil rights in his campaign, was finally forced to offer
the riders federal protection.[39]

By the fall of 1961, when Tom and Casey Hayden arrived in Atlanta, the mood among civil rights activists was upbeat. Believing
that they had won a tacit pledge of cooperation from the Kennedy
administration to protect activists by enforcing the Civil Rights Acts
of 1957 and 1960, SNCC organizers were planning to launch an
ambitious project to educate and register voters in the deep rural
South. Living in a house near the national headquarters of SNCC,
Hayden became the official SDS liaison to the Southern civil rights
movement; Casey meanwhile worked for a YWCA human-relations
project headed by Ella Baker, a soft-spoken civil rights veteran and
one of the founders of SNCC.[40]

Hayden himself, oddly enough, had never seriously considered
joining SNCC, despite his marriage to Casey and his admiration for
activists like Charles McDew and Tim Jenkins. "Part of me believed
that we should be arousing the nation's students, and SNCC was
regional," he recalls. "Another part of me believed that the issue of
the Bomb was important, also the issue of university reform. You
couldn't arouse a whole generation to consciousness and to life just
around a regional civil rights issue."[41]

Whatever his reservations about SNCC as an organization, Hayden was unequivocal in his enthusiasm for the group's political
style. From the outset, SNCC had sharply distinguished itself from
the Southern Christian Leadership Conference of Martin Luther
King by its emphasis on "group-centered leadership" as well as direct action. Distrusting the charismatic authority of a figure like
King, SNCC in 1960 declared that "it is important to keep the movement democratic and to avoid struggles for personal leadership"—
goals in evident harmony with Hayden's own emerging political
convictions. He viewed the militants in SNCC as "the cutting
edge," the moral vanguard—the young people showing white students cloistered on college campuses the real meaning of courage,
commitment and democratic responsibility. "That was a very creative, revolutionary period," Hayden recalled with some nostalgia in
1968. "There was tremendous unity, meetings in churches with
overflowing crowds, nonviolent demonstrations. There was that

great optimism that only exists at the beginning of a movement. People were in a state of religious fervor. I began to unlearn everything I had been taught at college. Mechanics, maids, unemployed people taking things into their own hands. I kept wondering, where did these people come from? Really, where have I been?"[42]

Hayden's firsthand involvement in the Southern civil rights struggle had begun early in 1961. In February, he had journeyed to rural Fayette County, Tennessee, to report for *The Michigan Daily* on the plight of sharecroppers evicted from their land after they had attempted to register to vote. Though Fayette County was predominantly black, not a single black citizen had been registered to vote in eighty years. With evident sympathy, Hayden had described the county's "Freedom Village"—a tent city, in fact—established by the evicted sharecroppers with the assistance of James Forman, a seasoned black radical from Chicago who would shortly join SNCC and become its executive secretary. In Tennessee, Hayden was moved by the spectacle of poor people coming to grips not just with their need for "food and other physical essentials," but also with their need for "essentials of a different order—the right to vote and participate in the democratic order."[43]

Although his article for the *Daily* did not mention the fact, he had gone to Fayette County as an activist as well as a reporter, helping to deliver food supplies to the sharecroppers in Freedom Village. "That's the first time I ever encountered a mob," he later recalled. "We were walking down the street and we ran into a gang that was just waiting for us with belts and clubs. We walked the other way as quickly as possible and went to the newspaper office and called the cops. But they just joined the toughs. We got in our car and raced out of town. They followed us for fifty miles before we lost them."[44]

Hayden's experience in Fayette County gave a preview of what would happen that fall in McComb, Mississippi, and nearby Amite County—the site of the pilot SNCC voter-registration project. "McComb, Mississippi (pop. 13,000) is not an extraordinary city," Hayden wrote in one of his periodic mimeographed reports to the SDS membership on developments in the South. A passenger traveling through the town "will glimpse a cramped downtown section, mostly low buildings, a small single-corridored City Hall, local cars and small trucks angle-parked, surrounded by a spread of modest, usually white-frame or brick, often tree-embroidered, little homes. If perceptive, the passenger will see that on one side of the railroad tracks there are fewer buildings, more rising dust, and only an occasional moving vehicle. A local citizen will tell the passenger cordially, 'That's Burgland town over there. That's where our niggers live.' "[45]

SNCC activists had entered McComb in July and begun canvassing door to door in August. They were led by Bob Moses, a quiet and introspective twenty-six-year-old black organizer who had recently quit his job as a New York City schoolteacher in order to work full time for SNCC. Born on the edge of a Harlem housing project, Moses had attended a series of elite schools, earning his M.A. in philosophy at Harvard. As an organizer, he had the salient virtues of humility and courage. Moses was a student of Camus; his rhetoric was poetic, his moral stance defiant. He admired, he wrote in 1961, men "who dare to stand in a strong sun and cast a sharp shadow." It is no wonder that Bob Moses quickly became a hero to young white radicals like Hayden—they spoke the same language.[46]

While Moses and his colleagues attempted to register voters, other SNCC militants arrived in McComb and began to use nonviolent direct action in an effort to desegregate public facilities. Their efforts quickly sparked an outbreak of vigilantism and a spate of arrests of SNCC organizers on trumped-up charges. On August 29, Moses had the effrontery to press charges of his own against a cousin of the local sheriff, who had beaten him severely without provocation. Though his assailant was acquitted, Moses and SNCC, more determined than ever, redoubled their efforts. Then, on September 25, a local white politician shot and killed Herbert Lee, fifty-two, a local black leader and veteran member of the NAACP who had been helping Moses in his registration efforts. The politician claimed self-defense; he was absolved by a coroner's jury. Further protests produced still more violence and more arrests. On October 4, three SNCC organizers as well as 110 black high school students were arrested for disturbing the peace after a demonstration in front of City Hall.[47]

The jailing of the SNCC leaders and many of the local activists effectively ended the McComb project, though sporadic demonstrations continued into December. Efforts to persuade the Justice Department to intervene proved unsuccessful. Despite the setbacks and a bitter sense that the Kennedy administration had betrayed its promise of support, McComb came to symbolize the deepening militance and stirring moral dignity of the civil rights struggle—particularly for the many sympathetic radicals who read "Revolution in Mississippi," Hayden's vivid dispatch from the battlefront.

Hayden had arrived in McComb on October 9 with Paul Potter, an Oberlin student sympathetic to the young radicals who was also the

NSA National Affairs Vice President. The two of them planned to use the NSA and SDS to get word out on what was happening in McComb. Hayden has recalled how Bob Moses smuggled them in from the airport: "We had to stay in a motel and arrange, by clandestine means, to meet a car in a darkened section of the black ghetto. . . . We had to be let out of a rented car, and lie on the back floor of a parked car in a parking lot. Somebody then picked it up and drove us—because it would have been too dangerous for whites and blacks to be in the same vehicle, even at night. They drove us to a house where all of the shutters were drawn, the windows were reinforced, and we had a meeting in the cellar with Bob and some other people to talk about the voter registration campaign. In other words, we were having to use, at that point, clandestine means to discuss the most conventional kind of tactic, namely the registration of voters, because what we were up against was a whole organized system that was out to kill us. And that was a very devastating thing to discover."[48]

It was also tremendously exciting. Here was life lived on the edge: a situation of mortal danger was forging a community of shared risk. "On a theoretical level," says Hayden, looking back, "you can say that we believed in wanting to make history and achieve civil rights. But there was something else: the middle-class emptiness of alienation that people talk about, and then suddenly confronting commitment. The whole emotion of defining not only yourself, but also your life by risking your life, and testing whether you're willing to die for your beliefs, was *the* powerful motive, I believe."[49]

Hayden's sense of his own motives shaped the reports that he wrote. He strove for a dry, documentary style, designed, as he wrote at the time, "to make facts real." But he was especially fascinated by scenes of brutal injustice and senseless suffering, and by the spectacle of ordinary people trying to come to terms with powerlessness and personal tragedy. By making these specific "facts real," he hoped, as he admitted at the time, to "evoke not reader interest but productive commitment." "Perhaps this situation cannot be made real," mused Hayden in the first draft of his report from McComb. In a series of rhetorical questions, he expressed his despair at adequately conveying the "real" truth—that is, the moral urgency of the situation: "Does it become more real in noting that a white man connected with the broadcasting system there sees the solution to the problem in 'throwing those little niggers in one bag, cutting their nuts off, and dropping the bag in the river?' . . . Does it become more real in recognizing that those Negroes are down there, digging in, and in more danger than nearly any student in this American generation has faced? What does it take? When do we begin to see it all not as remote but as breathing urgency into our beings and meaning into our ideals? [James] Baldwin said last year that these kids are the only really free people in the country; perhaps he is right. They have decided not to protest but to transform as well, and that is revolution. They have decided it is time right now—not in a minute, not after this one more committee meets, not after we have the legal defense and court costs promised—to give blood and body if necessary for social justice, for freedom, for the common life, and for the creation of dignity for the enslaved, and thereby for us all."[50]

If Hayden's picture of SNCC was highly "romanticized," as one scholar has put it, it was because language for him had become not just a fount of mythopoeic possibilities, but also a field of conversion —a domain of evangelical hope. In his reports on SNCC, Hayden bore witness both "to the wrongs of a fallen world" and to the Promethean efforts of activists to set it right. The activists had decided "not to protest but to transform as well"—to transform society, to transform their souls. The Deep South had become a moral testing ground, and Hayden tried to convey the challenge of the situation in his own impatient, impassioned prose. As he wrote to Haber, there was a "crazy new sentiment" growing in the South—that this was "not a movement but a revolution, that our identity should not be with . . . Negro predecessors but with the new nations around the world and that beyond lunch counter desegregations there are more serious evils which must be ripped out by any means: exploitation, socially destructive capital, evil political and legal structure, and myopic liberalism which is anti-revolutionary. Revolution permeates discussion like never before."[51]

Students who received these mimeographed letters from Mississippi still remember their feelings of vicarious excitement. "These reports were very important to me," says one; "that's really the reason I went into SDS." At the same time, Hayden was becoming a figure of considerable stature in his own right. On October 11, 1961, an assailant in McComb, Mississippi, dragged Hayden and Potter from a car and beat them. Hayden's image—cowering defenseless on the ground with his hands shielding his head—was captured by a photographer from The Associated Press and put on the wires. That winter a new left publication, the *Activist*, ran the picture along with one of Hayden's essays. In an editorial about McComb, *The Michigan Daily* summed up his unusual achievement in its headline: "Hayden Symbolizes Conflict."[52]

At the end of "Revolution in Mississippi," Hayden had quoted the Italian novelist Ignazio Silone: "I am convinced that it would be a waste of time to show a people of intimidated slaves a different manner of speaking, a different manner of gesticulating; but perhaps it would be worthwhile to show them a different way of living. No word and no gesture can be more persuasive than the life, and if necessary, the death, of a man who strives to be free . . . a man who shows what a man can be."[53]

By the end of 1961, Hayden was well on the way to becoming a figure like Silone's greatest fictional creation, Pietro Spina—an "insatiable" and "unquiet" rebel, a lapsed-Catholic-turned-maverick-Communist, a revolutionary forced to masquerade as a priest—the good-hearted hero of *Bread and Wine*, Silone's great novel of political ethics.[54] By living a life of principled nonconformity and devoting himself to the secular ideals of social justice and brotherhood, Hayden, like Silone's picaresque saint, would show "what a man can be." To many young students, Hayden already exemplified "a different way of living." In the minds of his peers in SDS, he was the archetypal new radical, the representative of a "new, natural party" arising innocently from the ashes of the old left. On the road in McComb, through the mirror of language, Tom Hayden, aged twenty-one, had found his calling. In the grandiloquent phrase that he used to close "Revolution in Mississippi," "the time for man has come."

PART TWO

TAKING DEMOCRACY SERIOUSLY

SOME MEN LOOK AT CONSTITUTIONS WITH SANC-
TIMONIOUS REVERENCE, AND DEEM THEM LIKE
THE ARK OF THE COVENANT, TOO SACRED TO BE
TOUCHED. THEY ASCRIBE TO THEM A WISDOM MORE
THAN HUMAN, AND SUPPOSE WHAT THEY DID TO BE
BEYOND AMENDMENT. I KNEW THAT AGE WELL; I BE-
LONGED TO IT, AND LABORED WITH IT. . . . BUT THE
DEAD HAVE NO RIGHTS. . . . THIS CORPOREAL GLOBE,
AND EVERYTHING UPON IT, BELONG TO ITS PRESENT
CORPOREAL INHABITANTS, DURING THEIR GENERA-
TION. THEY ALONE HAVE A RIGHT TO DIRECT WHAT
IS THE CONCERN OF THEMSELVES ALONE, AND TO DE-
CLARE THE LAW OF THAT DIRECTION; AND THIS DEC-
LARATION CAN ONLY BE MADE BY THEIR MAJORITY.
THAT MAJORITY, THEN, HAS A RIGHT TO DEPUTE REP-
RESENTATIVES TO A CONVENTION, AND TO MAKE THE
CONSTITUTION WHAT THEY THINK WILL BE BEST FOR
THEMSELVES.

—Thomas Jefferson
Letter to Samuel Kercheval (1816)

CHAPTER THREE

POLITICS AND VISION

W HILE TOM HAYDEN traveled through the South creating an image of courage and quiet charisma, Alan Haber sat in New York subsisting on packets of sugar filched from cafés, too driven by his vision of a renascent American radicalism to resign his post as SDS president and take a more sensible job. In the minds of those who were first meeting them, Haber and Hayden were like twins. Both talked tirelessly about a new form of politics —what they had begun to call "participatory democracy." Both suggested that the grass-roots insurgency in McComb, the protests over HUAC, and the rising militance of campus parties like SLATE and VOICE reflected a larger pattern of powerless people claiming a voice in public affairs. Both argued that the commitment of students could make a real difference in shaping the future.

It was hard to take them seriously. SDS was still tiny. In the fall of 1961, it claimed twenty campus chapters and only 575 members —hardly evidence of an incipient mass movement.[1] For all their talk about a new form of politics, Haber and Hayden in some respects were quite conventional campus politicians, aiming to build a conventionally structured student organization. The influence of SDS was nevertheless starting to grow. Haber was able to mail more than ten thousand free copies of an SDS newsletter to students and sympathetic adults, and Hayden's reports on SNCC reached a similar number of readers.

Ironically, the slowly gathering strength of SDS made the group a tempting target for criticism, particularly from rival radical groups vying for power within the hothouse world of student politics, where tiny groups of aspiring young statesmen argued furiously over the future of the world without cracking a smile. The chief charge against SDS, the kind of thing whispered at NSA congresses, was that the organization was "soft" on Communism.

In fact, it was not at all clear where Haber and Hayden stood on this issue. The ambiguity of their position was intentional: both thought that SDS should be an open, undoctrinaire forum for expressing the widest possible range of progressive political views. A ritual pledge of anti-Communism seemed to them to cut off debate, not encourage it.

Their position, however, aroused the suspicion not only of rival student groups, but also of SDS's adult sponsors in the League for Industrial Democracy. Before SDS could move forward, Haber had to answer the doubts of his critics in LID—a grueling and unglamorous process that began shortly after he arrived in New York City in June of 1960.

Democratic Analysis

Haber had come to New York imbued with his own sense of carrying on a great American tradition. By becoming the first president of SDS, he would be in a position to help renew the political legacy of Jack London, Upton Sinclair and John Dewey—patron saints proudly claimed by the League for Industrial Democracy. As Haber soon discovered, though, the legacy was more promising than the League itself. By 1960, LID had become an organization of socialists with long memories, faint hopes and an ingrained distrust of anyone offering a vision of sweeping social change—the treachery of the Communist Party had left them wary of political enthusiasm, popular insurgency, indeed almost any hint of militance or unabashed imaginativeness.[2]

At a meeting of the LID Student Activities Committee in December, 1960, Haber presented his plans for SDS. He proposed that SDS become "a national center for liberal activity," linked to the widest possible range of students involved with "civil rights, civil liberties, peace, campus political parties." Asserting that activists in each of these areas were "potential fodder for SDS," he urged the organization to tailor its educational materials "specifically to the people who are demonstrating." Haber wanted SDS to promote an understanding, which direct action by itself could not produce, of "the processes and goals of democratic reconstruction and the forces working for it."

Modest as this agenda might seem, it triggered a barrage of objections. One committee member thought Haber's plan wildly unrealistic: why should the LID squander scarce resources on some fantastic scheme to create a student organization dedicated to "democratic reconstruction"? Another committee member wondered whether SDS wasn't involving itself in "unnecessary organizational competition," since perfectly fine groups dedicated to civil rights, civil liberties and peace already existed. Besides, SDS would do well to steer clear of any undertaking "which clearly encourages mass activity of an agitational nature." For understandable reasons, LID did not want Haber's enthusiasm for direct action to jeopardize its own tax-exempt status as a nonprofit educational organization. As for campus political parties, "the trouble," sneered one committee member, "is that Haber conceives of every group which wants action, even on dormitory food, as an SDS chapter and would say that we should provide them with program materials."[3]

Behind the specific objections expressed at this meeting, though, lay a larger issue, involving the substance of Haber's vision. "They were within a trade-union model," says Haber of LID. "They wanted me to organize locals. I was within a more free-form university model, a seminar model. I wanted to organize people who could work together, I didn't care what they were part of. So I wasn't pushing membership. They wanted dues. I said, 'It doesn't matter how many members there are, it's who we're talking to and what we're connected with and where we're at.' They thought that couldn't be controlled. Because any Communist could come into a meeting and plant his seed. And these Communists would be in every meeting in every chapter, coordinated from headquarters— and we would all be just little nebishes out in Podunkland subject to their disciplined infiltration."[4]

Haber remembers one meeting with the LID board at which a member angrily tore off his shirt. "He showed me the scars on his back," says Haber, "where he was stabbed by the Communists at Madison Square Garden in nineteen thirty-ought in a fight over union organization. 'You can't trust them,' he said. 'They'll stab you in the back. I know.' I had a lot of respect for that. I could see their authentic experience. That they couldn't see *mine* was always my grief."

That the Communist Party was virtually a dead issue on America's college campuses in the early Sixties did not dispel the fears of LID. Indeed, their apprehension only increased when they met Haber's prize recruit, Tom Hayden. "The LID could barely deal with me," says Haber, "and my father was a member of the organization.

Tom they couldn't deal with *at all*. He didn't come from the same tradition"—in fact, he expressed a thinly veiled disdain for a legacy he considered "morbid." "They wondered who he was and what I had gotten him for. I had to keep justifying this guy to them."

In the spring of 1961, the tense relationship between Haber and the LID board blew up. On March 23, the executive committee voted to fire Haber. Haber pleaded with them to take a second look at "the kind of radical democratic organization I have projected." He also enlisted the support of his father, who wrote a long letter to LID in Alan's behalf: "I am sure he has a deep sense of responsibility and he has a deep sense of mission. In all fairness, you and I had it at his age and we cannot be too hard on young people who exhibit it at their age."[5]

In May, the LID executive committee reconsidered and decided to relent—they did not, after all, have other candidates of Haber's caliber beating down their door. In return, Haber agreed to skip holding a convention in 1961 and to commit to paper his organizational plans. For the rest of the year, he worked at devising a strategy for SDS that would reconcile the educational concerns and pragmatic caution of LID with the mood of impatient activism epitomized by Hayden.

"We must, in a phrase, start from scratch," wrote Haber in a memo that May. One by one, he ticked off the problems: SDS had no organizing leaflets, no speaker list, not even a bibliography of suggested readings; it had no office staff, no research staff, no reserve leadership. "We are without a functioning intellectual group at the center of the organization. . . . We do not have a banner of action, militancy, etc. to give us cohesion. . . . There is no common factor that gives compelling unity to the problems we focus on."[6]

To meet these difficulties, Haber again proposed that he devote his energies to turning SDS into a "source of stimulation, information and valuable associations." Given the doubts of LID, Haber was forced to walk a rhetorical tightrope: "We should not be an action organization," Haber flatly declared. "Our national office should, however, be identified as an intellectual center able to give educational service to action groups." The "militancy of the picket line" had somehow to be translated into "our educational activities."[7]

But how? Here Haber turned to the intellectual outlook that he had already used to recruit Jeffrey, Ross and Hayden. Although SDS "should encourage direct action," it should also constantly press its members to look beyond the immediate problems and issues raised by direct action. Precisely because American students were "suspicious of ideology," there was a need to provide them with "an integrating framework of values." The key, asserted Haber, was "democratic analysis." Given the American left's sad history of Stalinism—Haber here pitched his plan to LID—SDS should "maintain a program which stresses the integrating role that democratic values must play in any political formulation."[8]

It was not enough, however, simply to reaffirm received ideas about democracy. Although SDS of course retained a "commitment to the ideals and vison that have been the continual thrust of the radical movement: democracy, freedom, cooperation, planning, etc.," the organization in Haber's view had to face the real intellectual challenge posed by some of the new student activists: "They are concerned about the ability of democratic forms to meet the needs of underdeveloped areas, the real relevance of democratic forms to a non-literate population, the ability of democracy to [control] the private exploitation of public wealth, both human and material, and whether ruling interests don't really find techniques to insure an oligarchic tenure whatever might be the popular form of government." Such questions "force upon us a re-definition of values and goals. . . . They require us to understand the limitations, as well as the relevance, of constitutional liberal democracy."[9]

"All these concerns," wrote Haber in his most trenchant summary of the matter, "reflect a broader qualitative problem that students are coming to grapple with: democracy is based on the idea of a 'political' public—a body that shares a range of common values and commitments, an institutional pattern of interaction and an image of themselves as a functioning community. *We do not now have such a public in America.* Perhaps, among the students, we are beginning to approach it on the left. It is now the major task before liberals, radicals, socialists and democrats. It is a task in which the SDS should play a major role."[10]

To fulfill this task, Haber prevailed on LID to fund several specific SDS programs. He was allowed to send an SDS newsletter to an extensive mailing list that included student-body presidents, college editors, NSA coordinators and delegates, and the members of like-minded groups: SNCC, the Young People's Socialist League, Student Peace Union, Campus Americans for Democratic Action, the Young Democrats, American Friends Service Committee, Fellowship of Reconciliation. He planned a conference in the fall on "Democracy and the Student Movement" which turned into a conference on "The New Left: The Ideology, Politics and Controversies of the Student Movement." He organized a "Liberal Study Group" to represent the SDS position and recruit students at the NSA congress that August in Madison, Wisconsin. And he even persuaded LID to support an SDS "action project" in the fall.[11]

In the event, this "action project" turned out to be a matter of affiliating SDS with SNCC's efforts to register black voters in the South. As Haber and Sandra Cason explained in their memo justifying the project, the issue of voter registration was "fundamental," particularly from the perspective of a group devoted to "democratic analysis." "If the non-violent movement has increasingly focused on human dignity," they wrote, "it is nonetheless clear that to give dignity social content, the individual must find channels through which they can have influence within the broader community. Traditionally in a democratic system, participation in the political process, and specifically the electoral franchise, is chief among these channels. Political rights, ultimately, are the precondition for an equal footing in such areas as employment, housing, education, and welfare protection."[12]

If Not Now, When?

By successfully renegotiating his relationship to LID, Haber had won continuing financial support for a full-time organizer—Tom Hayden —and for projects like the SNCC voter-registration campaign. He had also won the freedom to recruit more aggressively on campus. "I looked for lists," he says. "I would get the list of people who signed petitions, the list of the people who were members of this chapter here or that support group there." He compiled "a core list" and a larger list—"in the range of ten thousand names and addresses of [those] who had been the activists in all the different sit-ins and all the campus support work and peace work."

Using his core list as "an acupuncture map of the body politic," Haber made the rounds of the different campuses, often with Tom Hayden at his side. "It was custom politics," says Haber. "I would say to them that what you want to do requires interacting with other people in other places who are doing the same thing you're doing, people who are doing related things, people who have some connection with a tradition that goes way back in America to 1905, people who are in touch with intellectual currents around the world, people who are writers, who have worked and looked at the situation that you're dealing with. Get in connection with these other people who are making history relevant; see that you are allied in a task. That will make your writing better, it will make the world you want better. You need an organization for that"—an organization like SDS.

Haber methodically went after the activists in the various campus political parties, attempting, in effect, to confederate the different groups under the banner of SDS. Besides SLATE at Berkeley and VOICE at Michigan, there were POLIT at Chicago, the Political Action Club at Swarthmore, the Liberal Study Group at Wisconsin, ACTION at Columbia, the Progressive Student League at Oberlin, TOCSIN at Harvard. He also contacted graduate students affiliated with the handful of new liberal and left-wing publications: *The Correspondent, Studies on the Left, New University Thought.* To the activists, he offered an intellectual framework, a vision of radical democracy; to the intellectuals, he offered a program linked to direct action. To all of them, he offered the sense that they could be partners in shaping their future: Haber's own freewheeling skepticism left plenty of room for creative contributions from each recruit. His vision of democracy was not a dogma, not even a clear-cut doctrine. It was the promise of political debate and shared discovery.

"Haber was an organizer like he was a writer," recalls Bob Ross: "Person by person, place by place, organization by organization. He knew what he wanted to do, he laid it out, and he did it. It was totally clear to him; he revealed all of his program to everybody he talked to. He had a talent not only for the conception but for the people. He found the right person in every organization, on every campus." [13]

At Swarthmore, for example, the right person was Paul Booth, who was just entering his sophomore year. The son of liberal parents who were involved in Americans for Democratic Action, Booth had been active in politics since grade school. His introduction to SDS came through one of the newsletters that Haber had sent to a college friend. His curiosity piqued, Booth made a point of meeting the SDS leaders when he attended the NSA congress at Madison, Wisconsin, in August of 1961. "They had something called the Liberal Study Group, through which they recruited people and established contacts," says Booth. "I remember one evening that William Buckley spoke outdoors in a driveway. Tom Hayden got into an argument with him. About two hundred people were watching. Hayden said, 'Everything you say takes for granted that an economics of exploitation is the foundation of all this.' And he pointed to a light bulb and said, 'that light bulb there, which allows us to have this meeting, was made by ordinary workers.' And Buckley said, 'The trouble with you liberals is that you have no eschatology.' I don't remember what else was said; I went running around trying to figure out what an eschatology was." [14] By December, 1961, Booth was an active member of SDS.

Sometimes Haber and Hayden used a more direct approach. Rennie Davis and Paul Potter were friends at Oberlin when they first met the SDS leaders. Potter had grown up on a farm near Champaign, Illinois, while Davis had lived on a farm in the Blue Ridge Mountains after the retirement of his father, an economics professor who had been a member of President Truman's Council of Economic Advisers. Inspired by the Southern sit-ins, the two of them had created a campus club, which they called the Progressive Student League. Davis recalls that first meeting: "We sat in our room together, feeling intruded upon, that it was kind of heavy coming in here, and that we had a nice scene going at Oberlin." Still, after Haber and Hayden had made their pitch for "a national communications network they called SDS," Davis and Potter concluded that they were "really opening our horizons. . . . By the summer, we had let go of our provincialism." In August, Davis joined the Liberal Study Group at the NSA congress; a few months later, Potter, who had become an NSA vice president at the same congress, accompanied Hayden on his journey to McComb, Mississippi. [15]

One by one, Haber and Hayden signed up members and sympathizers. Robb Burlage joined from the University of Texas, where he was studying economics. Gary Weisman came from the University of Wisconsin, where he was the student-body president. By November, Haber and Hayden had perfected their technique. A front-page story in *The Michigan Daily* described their Ann Arbor homecoming:

> While the Negro student has been struggling to gain his own and his people's civil rights, Northern students have failed to meet their responsibility, Thomas Hayden, '61, and Alan Haber, '60, told a meeting of the Political Issues Club last night. "The contrast is stark. The American student does not seem to realize the gulf between what is talked about and what is done," Hayden, a former Daily editor, declared. The Negro student is at the "cutting edge" of the civil rights movement, he added. White students do not sense its urgency. . . . A difference in background between the Northern student who leads a safe life and the Southern integrationist, a deadening horror of a

strife torn world on the individual consciousness, a lack of understanding of the real meaning of discrimination, and lack of feeling for another person's suffering were cited by Hayden as the main causes of this student failure. . . . Former Student Government council member Haber, now president of Students for a Democratic Society, said that students could identify with the democratic values of taking a role in the process of determining what affects his life. Hayden summed up the responsibilities of students with a quote from the Talmud, "If not for myself, who will be for me? If not for others, what am I? If not now, then when?"[16]

Political Stickball

Such language did not dazzle everyone. It left Steve Max, a native New Yorker and one of the most important new SDS recruits, absolutely cold. "Hayden was obsessed with the whole question of commitment," recalls Max. "I wasn't. I was born political. The people I knew had already made a commitment. The question was what to do next." Although he was just out of high school and one of the few SDS members who did not go on to college, Max had as much political experience as Haber and Hayden combined. His father, Alan Max, had been managing editor of *The Daily Worker*, the Communist Party newspaper, but had broken with the Party in the late Fifties. As a small child, Steve had handed out leaflets for Franklin Roosevelt, whose final campaign for the presidency had been endorsed by the Communist Party. Once a member of the Labor Youth League, a Party-sponsored youth group, he had left both the League and the orbit of the Party as a teenager: "It was clear that you couldn't function effectively in this country and still be connected with the Communists." While he was in high school, he worked as a community organizer, a trade-union activist, a free-lance agitator. In 1961, he was the leader of the Tom Paine Club, a New York City discussion group, and one of the editors of *Common Sense*, the club's newsletter.[17]

Max first met Haber and Hayden in the fall of 1961. Though Haber was the chief spokesman, it was Hayden who made an impression: "He really was a mesmerist," says Max: "He was soft-spoken and quiet. He was not a haranguer. When Tom spoke, the room got very quiet. Being soft-spoken at a time when a lot of the speech-making was more voluble and loud provided a striking contrast. He was very intense and deliberate, like he was thinking about every word, weighing it." The unique SDS blend of activism and intellectual analysis appealed to Max and his friends in the Tom Paine Club. But to sign them up, Haber resorted to a trick. "He took us to the SDS office," says Max, "and showed us this whole little room full of Addressograph plates. And he said, 'Well, this is our mailing list.' We were very impressed by that, and decided to affiliate. We didn't realize that the mailing plates went back to 1905."

Haber had good reasons for wooing Max and his club. Their newspaper, *Common Sense,* offered a ready-made conduit for SDS views. And their background—they were, as Haber recalls, "politically trained, Marxist, disciplined"—though unusual by college-campus standards, had prepared them admirably for coping with the sectarian politics typical of the left in New York City. Theoretical infighting "was just second nature to these people," says Haber. "They grew up in the streets of the big town—stickball." By recruiting Max to keep tabs on New York, Haber freed himself to focus on developments in the rest of the country.

Not coincidentally, a rival group of socialist students centered in New York was threatening to plunge SDS into an old-fashioned sectarian brawl. The key members of the group—Rachelle Horowitz, Tom Kahn and Richard Roman—all belonged to the Young People's Socialist League as well as to SDS. They also had ties to the LID leadership. Their mentor was Michael Harrington, a LID leader who was also an organizer for YPSL. What bound them together intellectually was fealty to the ideas of Max Schachtman. A Bolshevik heretic and former follower of Leon Trotsky, Schachtman had broken with his hero in 1939 in order to develop his own theory that the Stalinist bureaucracy was a permanent and totalitarian new class and not, as Trotsky had argued, a degenerate caste temporarily ruling in the name of the proletariat. By 1961, the "Schachtmanites," as they called themselves, had abandoned their once-fiery revolutionary rhetoric and joined the American Socialist party. Unlike those Socialists who still dreamed of building an American version of the Labor Party, the Schachtmanites hoped to advance the cause of democratic socialism through the two-party system. The strategy they favored was "realignment"—a scheme to turn the Democratic party into a left-leaning coalition of liberals and socialists by forcing the racist and conservative "Dixiecrats" out of the Party. They worshiped the labor movement with doctrinaire piety: as Murray Kempton once put it, Schachtman ran "the only school in America that can take someone young and turn his mind into an exact replica of every resolution passed at the 1948 AFL-CIO convention." Above all, the Schachtmanites were zealous anti-Communists. Their litmus test of loyalty to the socialist idea was unremitting hostility to Stalinists and "Stalinoids," as political naifs soft on Communism were called.[18]

"Harrington's plan," explained Max, "had always been that the YPSLs would take over SDS. They had a very concrete plan, which they told me about." At the time, Max himself was a proponent of realignment and, despite his family background, perfectly comfortable with expressions of militant anti-Stalinism. He nevertheless agreed with Haber that sectarian infighting was one cause of the political impasse on the American left. YPSL's Machiavellian plotting left him as cold as Hayden's florid moralism. According to Max, YPSL "wanted to get ahold of the budget. Their plan originally was that they would convert all of the YPSL chapters into SDS chapters, and thereby gain control of the two staff positions that were being funded."

But time was running out for the YPSL faction. With each passing week, Haber and Hayden were winning more and more converts to their own vision of a nonsectarian new left—from the Schachtmanite perspective, a vision that was dangerously vague about Communism. If they were to have any chance of success, Horowitz, Kahn and Roman would have to act soon.

Personal Ties

On December 11, 1961, the day of his twenty-second birthday, Tom Hayden addressed a dramatic letter to his comrades in SDS: "It is late in the afternoon," wrote Hayden, "about 16 hours since they confined us here. Eight of us, as probably you know, were on the 'freedom ride' to Albany [Georgia] Sunday which was met by police. . . . The cell from which I write is perhaps seven feet high and no more than ten feet long. The only light penetrates from a single bulb beyond the bars down the hall, and from the Negro quarters across the way. . . . This note is written on a smuggled piece of paper with smuggled pen—not just to give you a picture of the conditions, but to carry on my correspondence with you regarding the SDS meeting in Ann Arbor, Michigan, December 29–31. The implicit message of my earlier letter was, I hope, that it is imperative for people already committed to a struggle for humanism and democracy in the com-

mon life [to] come together now to ask themselves basic organizational questions: given that the SDS is office space, a little money,
and a somewhat amorphous program administered by a modest staff
at present, what direction do we want to give to it? how much do
each of us want to share in its shaping? what are we personally and
collectively prepared to give and produce?"[19]

Hayden hoped the December meeting would facilitate a "reflection on our total effort, past, present and future." SDS, he explained,
needed to work out a new organizational structure, in order to
"allow expansion of democratic control." At the same time, wrote
Hayden, SDS was "rooted in [a] tradition" that required "imaginative revamping in light of new realities, new needs, new goals." If it
was successfully to fend off liberal critics at NSA congresses as well
as skeptics within LID, SDS needed to clarify its distinctive political
orientation. Haber's memos and Hayden's letters were a start, but
their themes needed to be orchestrated, their variations sorted out.
The increasingly vociferous objections of the YPSL group had to be
addressed. At the same time, many of the newly recruited campus
activists had yet to be brought into the life of the organization.
Wrote Haber: "If what have heretofore been largely a set of personal
associations are to be transformed into an organizational entity having both vision and political relevance, then we must sit together in
serious discussion and attend to the job at hand."[20]

On December 29, 1961, 45 students and activists from around the
country met in Ann Arbor to discuss the future of SDS. To stimulate
discussion, Haber had solicited papers on different possible programmatic directions for the organization. The suggestions ran the
gamut. One paper urged organizing the poor, another pushed for
university reform; one paper defended campaigning for peace candidates, another (coauthored by Haber) argued that SDS should retain
its emphasis on support for civil rights activities in the South. The
YPSL partisans were meanwhile pressing for a comprehensive political statement: they wanted the organization to spell out just where
it stood on the great political issues of the day, from civil rights and
disarmament to alliances with Communists.

One of the avowed purposes of the meeting had been "to extend
and make more embracing our personal ties"—and in this it was a
stunning success. Students who had never met before became
friends, intimates, in some cases lovers. An air of erotic discovery
permeated the highly intellectualized discussions. "There was a
sense that we were really doing something brand-new," recalls
Sharon Jeffrey. "There was a great sense of making history, though
we never discussed that."[21]

In the preceding months, Haber and Hayden had both written about their yearning for face-to-face politics and their desire to be part of a public with common values and commitments. They longed for a vital sense of democracy, a living sense of community. Now, they were discovering it among themselves.

The debate over an SDS program continued into the evening of December 31. Finally, with no end in sight, Casey Hayden and Dorothy Dawson, a friend and fellow activist from Austin, Texas, broke out champagne and forced the group to stop talking.

Despite the inconclusiveness of the discussions, this impromptu celebration was a fitting climax. Several days later, Haber was happy to report that the group had agreed to work on "a political manifesto of the Left." A draft of this manifesto was to be prepared by Tom Hayden and debated at an SDS convention in June, 1962. "Projected as the first major assemblage of democratic and progressive forces on the student left in recent years, the convention," wrote Haber, "will lay out specific programs translating [into practice] the broad SDS concern with democratic ideals and its intermediate focus on political realignment." "The major debate of the convention," it was explained in a subsequent memo, "will center on a 'political manifesto' expressing the intellectual outlook of the organization, particularly a delineation of the concept 'democracy' as it applies in the contemporary world to such varied realms as industrial organization, the arts, education, colonial independence and economic development, etc."[22]

Hayden was the perfect choice to draft this manifesto. A few months before, he had proposed publishing a book of essays on similiar themes. Among a number of topics, he had suggested discussing the "role of the intellectual in marrying knowledge to power, in creating and informing a 'public,' in enriching the meaning of participatory democracy." "What is needed," explained Hayden rather elliptically, is "vision," a means "to bring back the public," "a way to connect knowledge to power and decentralize both so that community or participatory democracy might emerge, to be concerned with the problem of the individual in a time inevitably ridden with bureaucracy, large government, international networks and systems, etc. etc. etc."[23]

At the time, Hayden had remarked on the need for "a manifesto of hope." He now had the opportunity to write one.

CHAPTER FOUR

THE PROPHET OF THE POWERLESS

"**W**HERE DOES ONE begin thinking about manifestos?" wondered Tom Hayden in the spring of 1962. The existing political groups scarcely offered food for thought. "The socialistic parties are in a shambles," he wrote, "the working class etc. is just not the missionary force we can count on," the "civil rights leadership," though "more militant than most," was still oriented around a single issue. "I have the impression," wrote Hayden, "that we have been our own leadership to a far greater degree than most 'student radicals' of the past. . . . We are, like it or not, young intellectuals in an anti-intellectual society."[1]

As a "young intellectual," Hayden naturally turned for inspiration to books. By then, he had read all the titles on the recommended reading list that SDS had distributed the previous fall. These thirty-eight texts ran the gamut: from the Declaration of Independence to the Democratic Party Platform of 1960, from Karl Marx's *Economic and Philosophic Manuscripts of 1844* to Daniel Bell's *End of Ideology*, from John Dewey's *The Public and Its Problems* to Seymour Martin Lipset's *Political Man*, from Dostoyevsky's "The Grand Inquisitor" to Fidel Castro's "History Will Absolve Me," from the Sharon Statement of the right-wing Young Americans for Freedom to *Conviction* and *Out of Apathy*, two anthologies produced by the British New Left.[2]

Hayden found scant solace in most of what he read. "We are the inheritors and victims of a barren period in the development of human values," he wrote in March of 1962: "The old promise that knowledge and increased rationality would liberate society seems a lie." Given "the default of the politicians and the professors," to begin thinking about a modern manifesto was proving peculiarly difficult. "The real question," wrote Hayden, "is whether or not society contains *any* prophets who can speak in language and concept that is authentic for us, that can make luminous the inner self that burns for understanding."[3]

As so often, Hayden was exaggerating. He had, in fact, already found the prophet he longed for: C. Wright Mills. In an article on the new student politics for *Mademoiselle* magazine the previous summer, Hayden had singled out Mills as the one scholar with something to say to the student left. When SDS published its agenda for the December meeting in Ann Arbor, it opened with an epigraph from Mills. And when Steve Max joined SDS, he quickly learned that "you had to know C. Wright Mills"—to know not just the major texts and key concepts, but the personal anecdotes, the rhetorical style, the sweep of the man's political vision.[4]

The reason was simple: Mills was the master thinker behind a great deal of what Haber and Hayden were saying and doing. When Hayden in the spring of 1961 had written that "the University must work relentlessly at being a face-to-face, rather than a mass society," he was borrowing two phrases that Mills had made his own. When Al Haber declared in a memo that America lacked "a 'political' public," he was echoing a complaint that Mills commonly voiced. When Hayden spoke about "creating and informing a 'public,' " in order to enrich the meaning of democracy, he was using the master's own language to evoke Mills's vision of the intellectual and his proper task.[5]

"I was completely absorbed in his writing," says Hayden. "He was the inspiration for what I was trying to do."[6]

Outside the Whale

C. Wright Mills wrote in the age of the atom bomb and Eisenhower, the Cold War and McCarthy, at the twilight of Stalinism and the zenith of "The American Century." But even in the early Fifties, when many once-critical intellectuals were ready to sing the praises of America, Mills refused to celebrate. Instead, he excoriated the evils of modern American society. Like one of his favorite stylists, Thorstein Veblen, he grabbed his readers with hard-boiled prose and blazing slogans. America's "main drift," he declared, was toward a militarized, centralized, impersonally administered structure of "organized irresponsibility." A republic of alert citizens was being transformed into a mass of "cheerful robots." The ideal of Jeffersonian democracy had become a "fairy tale." "If we accept the Greek's definition of the idiot as an altogether private man," wrote Mills, "then we must conclude that many American citizens are now idiots."[7]

The immorality of power was Mills's great theme. But the powerlessness of intellectuals was his obsession. "Only when mind has an autonomous basis, independent of power, but powerfully related to it, can it exert its force in the shaping of human affairs," Mills wrote in a statement of purpose that became the epigraph for the SDS meeting of December, 1961. "Such a position is democratically possible only when there exists a free and knowledgeable public, to which men of knowledge may address themselves, and to which men of power are truly responsible. Such a public and such men—either of power or of knowledge—do not now prevail, and accordingly, knowledge does not now have democratic relevance in America."[8]

Mills was born in 1916. He grew up in Texas, first in Waco, later in Dallas. His father was an insurance broker, his mother a homemaker and devout Roman Catholic. Charles Wright, as she called her son, was a choirboy in the Catholic church of Waco. After graduation from Dallas Technical High School, he became a cadet at Texas A&M, a school that still embodies the provincial spirit of military spit-and-polish. He rebelled by becoming a student of philosophy. In 1936, Mills transferred to the University of Texas at Austin, where he studied philosophy and economics. In 1939, he went on to the University of Wisconsin, where he received a doctorate in sociology. From George Herbert Mead and Karl Mannheim, he learned to think of human nature as social and plastic. From C. S. Pierce and John Dewey, he took heart in "the power of man's intelligence to control his destiny." Wanting philosophy to be "impatient" and critical, he admired "Dewey's brave words: 'Every thinker puts some portion of an apparently stable world in peril.' "[9]

From an early age, Mills cultivated the image of a lone wolf and rebel. "I am an outlander, not only regionally, but down bone deep and for good," he once wrote. "In Orwell's phrase: I am just outside the whale and always have been." The summer after his graduation from Texas, Mills worked as an insurance clerk—only to shout out one day in disgust, as he later recalled his one-man revolt, "I am of the opposition!" Though he lived in New York and taught at Columbia University from 1944 until his death in 1962, Mills became legendary for his rough, unrefined manner—he usually wore boots and a motorcycle helmet and carried his papers in an Army-surplus duffel bag. When Mills liked someone, he would say, 'That guy's a real Wobbly.' "[10]

"He was like Rousseau coming from the country to Paris," his Columbia colleague and friend Charles Frankel recalled after Mills's death. "He was a Texan turned inside out." Frankel, who lived near Mills in Rockland County, New York, had commuted into Manhattan with him until Mills bought his motorcycle. "Getting his motorcycle," said Frankel, "was one way of cutting himself off. It was a way of showing contempt for the fraud and hypocrisy of polite society." It was also a way of expressing his love for superior craftsmanship; the proud owner of a BMW, he made a point of flying to the factory in Germany in order to learn how to repair the engine himself. The novelist Dan Wakefield, who was his student at Columbia, recalls watching a member of a small socialist sect solicit his signature on a petition requesting that the group be removed from the Attorney General's list of subversive organizations: "Mills obligingly signed, but then in discussing politics, as was his habit, he challenged all his visitor's beliefs and arguments until the poor fellow, pushed to the wall, said in frustration, 'Just what do you believe in, Mills?' At the moment Mills was tinkering with his motorcycle, and he looked up and said without a moment's hesitation: 'German motors.' "[11]

This kind of flamboyant style, combined with Mills's outspoken contempt for the routine canons of sociology—"the higher ignorance," he once called it—made many colleagues frankly hostile. It also made some students tremendously excited: here was a rebel and iconoclast in a world of button-down pedants! His legend gave added weight to his words. For in truth, Mills was more than an academic sociologist. In his key works, he hammered away at a handful of motifs and themes, almost all of them linked to a vision of America's lost democratic promise. An intellectual first and scholar second, he hoped to provoke, to alarm and, finally, to inspire—hopes borne out by admiring young readers like Tom Hayden.

Mills first revealed his ambitions and overarching political vision in a remarkable essay that he wrote in 1944 for the third issue of Dwight Macdonald's magazine *Politics*. The magazine's name was Mills's idea, and this was the first published work to bear the stamp of his distinctive voice; he was twenty-eight. In this essay, which he called "The Powerless People," Mills argued that intellectuals must respond to a "world of big organizations" where "grass-root democratic controls become blurred" and "irresponsible actions by individuals at the top are encouraged." The crucial fact about modern society was the "centralization of decision and the related growth of dependence. . . . More and more people are becoming dependent salaried workers who spend the most alert hours of their lives being told what to do. In climactic times like the present, dominated by the need for swift action, the individual feels dangerously lost. As the London *Economist* recently remarked, 'The British citizen *should be* an ardent participant in his public affairs; he *is* little more than a consenting spectator who draws a distinction between "we" who sit and watch and "they" who run the state.' "

The body of the 1944 essay represents nothing less than a preview of Mills's life project. He maintained that the intellectual as an "independent craftsman" was one casualty of the "world of big organizations": "The material basis of his initiative and intellectual freedom is no longer in his hands." As a hired hand in the "information industry," perhaps churning out pieces for a mass-circulation magazine, the intellectual found his prose "regulated by an adroit formula." As a salaried scholar in a university where research often depended on funds from private foundations and the government, the intellectual had to withstand a "vague general fear— sometimes politely known as 'discretion,' 'good taste,' or 'balanced judgment.' " Whether quarantined in the academy or trivialized in the mass media, the intellectual was cut off "from his potential public"—a public that Mills suggested had once flourished, thanks to the pamphleteering of republican writers like Tom Paine. In this situation, it was in the interest of the intellectual himself to resist the drift toward conformity and "to unmask and to smash the stereotypes of vision and intellect with which modern communications swamp us."

Knowledge was not enough. As pragmatism had taught Mills, "only through the social confirmation of others whom we believe adequately equipped do we earn the right of feeling secure in our knowledge. The basis of our integrity can be gained or renewed only by activity, including communication, in which we may give ourselves with a minimum of repression." The intellectual's private feelings of frustration and powerlessness should be linked to the big picture of society. The quests for personal happiness, truth and democracy, properly understood, went hand in hand; and the intellectual willing to speak truthfully about his own powerlessness was the natural ally of unhappy people seeking their fair share in decision-making.[12]

The Public in Eclipse

For the remainder of his life, Mills worked to clarify these ideas. In his great trilogy on the American scene—*The New Men of Power* (1948), on labor; *White Collar* (1952), on the middle classes; and *The Power Elite* (1956)—Mills animated with broad strokes and humorous vignettes a lively panorama of social types, from The American Salesman with his "theology of pep" to "the perfect candidate for the Presidency of the United States"—a farm boy from Ohio, ventured Mills, "of a sizable family, which arrived from England shortly after the *Mayflower*." In an effort to make his own knowledge relevant to the widest possible public, Mills used the wit of the satirist, the passions of the partisan, the imaginative attention to detail of the novelist—Balzac was one of his models. His ambition, he once suggested, was to create "a sociological poem which contains the full human meaning in statements of apparent fact." Later, in what Mills called his "pamphlets"—*The Causes of World War Three* (1958) and *Listen, Yankee* (1960)—he sharpened and simplified his rhetoric to arouse a mass audience.[13]

Mills wavered in his hopes for social change, as the gloomy picture of creeping totalitarianism in *The Power Elite* might suggest. In 1943, he proposed an alliance between intellectuals and labor as the only basis for "genuine democracy." The left he regarded as "a series of desperate attempts to uphold the simple values of classic democracy under conditions of giant technology, monopoly capitalism, and the behemoth state." Calling for workers' control of industry, Mills in 1948 avowed that "the left would establish a society in which everyone vitally affected by a social decision, regardless of its sphere, would have a voice in that decision and a hand in its administration." In the years that followed, however, Mills viewed the labor movement with increasing skepticism. By 1960 he had become convinced that Marx's "labor metaphysic"—his faith in the proletariat as the embodiment of freedom in world history—was a Victorian relic, especially in societies like America, where the working class had happily joined the political rearguard. He fixed on the intellectuals themselves "as a possible immediate, radical agency of change." Still, he never swerved from his basic idea—of the intellectual as an advocate for the powerless—which he had announced in 1944.[14]

In pursuing this political ambition, Mills remained committed to the methods of sociology. His books used the tools of empirical survey research and the "ideal type," as Max Weber called the pure models he abstracted from historical examples in order to classify different social phenomena. Both aspects of the sociological tradition come into play in another pivotal essay by Mills, "The Sociology of Mass Media and Public Opinion," an unpublished manuscript completed in 1950. This essay contains one of the earliest formulations of Mills's key distinction between "mass" and "public"—perhaps his most striking contribution to social theory and certainly the one that had the most profound influence on Hayden, Haber and the other young intellectuals in SDS.[15]

Though Mills again fondly evokes the lost world of Tom Paine, this particular paper, based on a study of opinion-formation in Decatur, Illinois, documents the enduring "independence and unpredictability" of U.S. public opinion in a midsize city. On the basis of interviews conducted with a representative sample of 800 of the city's 60,000 citizens, Mills concluded that "primary publics"—face-to-face groups of friends—actively responded to opinions expressed in the mass media, rejecting some, modifying others, arriving at their own, independent views through the give-and-take of "person-to-person discussion."

However, it was the theoretical frame for these empirical observations—and not the sanguine conclusions, which he subsequently modified—that Mills would return to repeatedly in his later works. In order to clarify the difference between opinions shaped by the mass media and those formed through face-to-face interactions, Mills defined two ideal types: the "mass ideal–type of 'public' in a mass society" and, by way of contrast, "the primary publics" typical of "the simpler democratic society."

In the democratic society, "Parliament, as an institution, crowns all the primary publics; it is the archetype for each of the scattered little circles of face-to-face citizens discussing their public business. ... So conceived, the public is the loom of classic, eighteenth century democracy; discussion is at once the threads and the shuttle binding discussion circles together."

In a mass society, by contrast, "institutions become centralized and authoritarian; and media markets gain ascendancy over primary publics. There is ... an historical parallel between the commodity market in the economic sphere and the public of public opinion in the sphere of opinion. ... There is a movement from widely scattered little powers and laissez-faire to concentrated powers. ... The mass media, as it were, expropriate from individuals in discussion the formulation of opinion." No longer a community of sovereign individuals, the mass public becomes the passive object of intensive efforts to control, manage, manipulate.[16]

Mills believed that these two ideal types highlighted conflicting tendencies in modern American society. His findings in Decatur confirmed that "the members of publics in smaller communities know each other more or less fully," thereby keeping alive some vestige of the simpler democratic spirit.

But Mills also worried that in larger cities, in suburbs and even in towns like Decatur itself, the democratic spirit was at risk. The decline of a truly independent middle class that he described in *White Collar* was destroying the basis for classical democracy. Jefferson's self-reliant yeoman farmer had given way to the buck-passing company man. Mills most memorably dramatized the baleful implications of this social and psychological transformation in his climactic chapter on "The Mass Society" in *The Power Elite*—a book that was closely studied by virtually every early leader of SDS.

"Man in the mass," declared Mills in *The Power Elite*, "is without any sense of political belonging." Despite "the folklore of democratic decision-making" in America, "the idea of the community of publics" had become the "assertion of an ideal"—"not a description of fact." In the "bedroom belts" and "one-class suburbs" surrounding America's great cities, residents were increasingly segregated into "narrowed routines and environments," losing "any firm sense of integrity as a public." Politics became a spectator sport. The support of voters was marshaled through advertising campaigns, not direct participation in reasoned debate. A citizen's chief sources of political information, the mass media, typically assaulted him with a barrage of distracting commercial come-ons, feeble entertainments and hand-me-down glosses on complicated issues. The self-reliant citizen who formed the bulwark of the simpler democratic society was being replaced by a depressing new breed of American: "He drifts, he fulfills habits, his behavior a result of a planless mixture of the confused standards and the uncriticized expectations that he has taken over from others whom he no longer really knows or trusts, if indeed he ever really did. . . . He loses his independence, and more importantly, he loses the desire to be independent. . . . He thinks he wants merely to get his share of what is around with as little trouble as he can and with as much fun as possible." One is reminded of Nietzsche's "last man," as "ineradicable as a flea-beetle."[17]

A New Moral Optic

"Often you get the best insights by considering extremes," Mills once wrote. His "ideal-type" of classical democracy was certainly an extreme: the perfect antithesis to his image of witless suburban conformism. But Mills's notion of democracy was more than a theoretical construct designed to throw into stark relief his empirical findings about the mass society he felt was emerging in modern America. His image of classical democracy also functioned implicitly in his work as what he called a "counter-symbol" or "moral optic"—a focus for moral outrage. In his first book, Mills had argued that simple deprivation could not, by itself, create a movement for social change: "With deprivation must come the rejection of the symbols and the myths that justify the authorities and the acceptance of counter-symbols that will focus the deprivation politically." In *The Power Elite*, by describing in detail the trends in modern America toward "manipulated consent" and then reminding his readers of the lost ideal of face-to-face freedom, Mills made outrage easy. Here is a town meeting animated by outspoken individualists. There is a clique of powerful politicians, tycoons and warlords, ruling over a herd of blank drones drifting vacantly through the shopping malls of America. Faced with that choice, most readers would not hesitate. His "ideal-type" of classical democracy was not simply a critical element in a clever piece of social theory. As a "counter-symbol," it was Mills's great ideological gift to the left in America.[18]

Throughout most of his life, Mills struggled to convey this democratic vision to a literate public. Not content with evoking the memory of a bygone world of zealous democratic thinkers, he set out to bend the mass media to his own ends, urging intellectuals "to make the mass media the means of liberal—which is to say, liberating—education." He struck up a partnership with Ian Ballantine, one of the pioneers of the paperback revolution in American publishing and a man keen to market John Hersey's *Hiroshima* as well as *Mad* magazine anthologies in cheap editions. Mills gambled his academic reputation to reach a larger audience, and in one sense, he won: *Listen, Yankee*, his polemical defense of Fidel Castro's Cuban Revolution, sold more than 400,000 copies as a Ballantine paperback.[19]

There is more to the story, though, than simple sales figures. To the small circle of young radicals who had gathered around Al Haber and Tom Hayden, Mills was a hero, an oracle, a model of the radical intellectual—particularly after he published his "Letter to the New

Left" in the fall of 1960 in the British journal *New Left Review*. Almost immediately, copies of this piece were circulated within SDS—it was one of the 38 titles on the recommended reading list that SDS distributed in the fall of 1961. "The Age of Complacency is ending," declared Mills. "We are beginning to move again." Answering the charge that the New Left was utopian, Mills stressed the need to analyze "the *foundation* of policies": "our work is necessarily structural—and so, *for us*, just now—utopian." Unlike some Marxists, Mills welcomed the new prominence of students: "Who is it that is getting fed up? Who is it that is getting disgusted with what Marx called 'all the old crap'? Who is it that is thinking and acting in radical ways? All over the world . . . the answer is the same: it is the young intelligentsia."[20]

"Mills was the first to see what was happening," says Hayden. "He saw that students, who hadn't played that much of a role in American history, were *doing* things. And that this opened a whole new period of history in which the left had to go from a belief in labor as the agency of change to students as an agency of change. Well, this just filled us with enormous confidence. It helped us make sense of what we were doing, and actually it made us feel as if we'd been *anointed*."[21]

"Mills was a model," says Paul Booth: "*The Power Elite* was Bible." Bob Ross recalls first reading *The Power Elite* in the winter of 1961. "I remember finishing it late one night and walking out into this cold, snowy dawn, crying. I was already in SDS, already was committed to this notion of participatory democracy, and this Leviathan had been portrayed to me. I walked the streets weeping. What can we do? Is this our fate?"[22]

In Mills, the young radicals found a theory of power, an image of democracy, a kindred spirit. Though none of the SDS leaders ever met him, Hayden, for one, knew all about his motorcycle. Mills's storied personal style—macho, blunt, impatient—had an impact. So did his distaste for Marxist cant and Cold War dogmatics. The students in SDS identified with his project of fostering a "free and knowledgeable public" and his eloquently expressed desire to conduct research with "democratic relevance." His belief that feelings of personal frustration and powerlessness ought to be connected to public issues was reiterated and developed by Hayden, becoming one basis for the characteristic assertion by the New Left (and later, by feminists) that "the personal" is "political."[23]

Taking It Big

Mills's influence on the young intellectuals of the New Left attests to the appeal of his political vision and the effectiveness of his rhetoric. By giving a fresh luster to the textbook image of democracy, he implicitly dared Americans to take it seriously. "Because democracy has never been fully realized," Robert Dahl has written, "it has always been and is now potentially a revolutionary doctrine."[24]

At the same time, Mills's approach to democracy suffered from weaknesses that would be aggravated and made palpable by the student movement he helped to inspire. His use of "ideal-types," for example, facilitated a highly imaginative reconstruction of the historical evidence. As Mills knew perfectly well, even revolutionary America had been a stratified and hierarchical society; at the very time he was completing *The Power Elite*, his friend Richard Hofstadter, the great historian, was dissecting the interlocking myths of the yeoman farmer and America's lost agrarian democracy. Mills's suppression of this kind of historical knowledge created a false aura of practical solidity around the image of classical democracy. To the extent that he created a countersymbol by using the sociological device of the ideal-type, Mills also avoided offering any independent argument on behalf of his ideal: though he saw clearly the need for an "indigenous political theory" on the American left, he produced no such theory and no original moral arguments. The only hint he gave as to what such a theory might look like was an admiring reference in 1948 to the Guild Socialism of G. D. H. Cole, who in turn relied on the philosophical premises of Jean-Jacques Rousseau. Unlike Rousseau, however, Mills never offered a systematic defense of his political principles; unlike G. D. H. Cole, he never made a sustained effort to demonstrate the feasibility of his political vision in the context of a modern industrial society. Instead, Mills allowed the ideal-type of democracy to function as a subversive exhortation disguised as a nostalgic typology.[25]

As a result, the implications of Mills's vision remained highly ambiguous. Despite his anxious description of the contemporary trends toward centralization and bureaucracy, he never really explained whether these trends might be reversed or somehow mitigated. Instead, he defended the virtues of a "genuine bureaucracy" staffed by knowledgeable civil servants. He also argued that "the centralization of the means of history-making itself" had created "new opportunities for the willful making of history." As his comments about parliament as the prototype of the primary publics may suggest, he seems to have held no reservations about the virtues of representative government. Although his romantic identification with Wobblies and his description of "the scattered little circles of face-to-face citizens" might evoke a decentralized democracy, other comments suggest that Mills was more realistic—and more interested in fostering within the modern nation-state an alert, knowing public able to appreciate the ideas of maverick thinkers such as himself. (As he once admitted in passing, "the theory of the public is, in many ways, a projection upon the community at large of the intellectual's ideal of the supremacy of intellect.") In an essay published in 1958, Mills's specific proposals for democratic reform are both vague and remarkably mild: he calls for the spread of "free associations" to act as a buffer between small communities and the state; "a civil service that is firmly linked with the world of knowledge and sensibility"; "nationally responsible parties"; and "an intelligentsia, inside as well as outside the universities, who carry on the big discourse of the western world."[26]

"Taking it big" was one of Mills's favorite phrases. He "loved 'tough-minded' writers and writing," recalled his friend Hans Gerth, "men of tall talk and 'no bones about it.' " But by the end of his life, his tough-minded approach to power and "tall talk" of democracy had taken on a desperate stridency. He was a more meticulous thinker than Tom Paine, his favorite pamphleteer, yet his edgy, staccato prose sometimes recalls the hard-sell slogans of an ad campaign. The support he gave to Castro was remarkably uncritical—maybe he considered him an example of "the willful making of history." It is no wonder that some readers felt bullied. To rouse his audience, he was prepared to sacrifice subtlety, nuance, the patient evaluation of contradictory evidence—in short, the virtues of dispassionate scholarship. His carefully cultivated image—the powerless intellectual as populist outlaw—masked an unresolved tension between an emotional sense of outrage and the conviction, inherited from the pragmatists, that reason ought properly to control man's destiny. He epitomized a politics of theatrical fury and mythomanic fervor, of high moral seriousness, savage social criticism and peculiarly blinkered self-righteousness.[27]

It is symptomatic that Mills, when he alluded to "Inside the Whale," Orwell's famous essay, turned Orwell's methaphor inside out. "Admit that you are inside the whale (for you *are*, of course)," wrote Orwell in 1940, justifying the "passive, non-cooperative attitude" of his friend the novelist Henry Miller: "Give yourself over to the world-process, stop fighting against it or pretending that you can control it; simply accept it, endure it, record it." This Mills could never do. To resist, protest, dream of alternatives—such was his daemon. If, as Orwell had warned in the same essay, "the autonomous individual is going to be stamped out of existence," Mills could not stand calmly by. A spiritual exile from the heartlands of America, he imagined himself to be "outside the whale." He wanted to harpoon the beast before it swallowed his public.[28]

The very shape of his career and nature of his influence on the New Left raise some hard questions: Is the middle-class intellectual a fit tribune for the powerless? Is the desire to win converts compatible with intellectual honesty? Is the self-dramatizing visionary a figure to be trusted?

Although he raised different questions, Tom Hayden was no blind disciple. "C. Wright Mills is appealing and dynamic in his expression of theory in the grand manner," Hayden wrote late in 1961 in "A Letter to the New (Young) Left"—the title itself, of course, was a kind of homage: "but his pessimism yields us no formulas, no path out of the dark." In the graduate thesis on Mills that Hayden started while he was still in Atlanta, he portrayed the sociologist as a loner whose spirit was finally crushed by his isolation. For Hayden, "community" was a synonym for "democracy." Mills, by contrast, once confided that of the three great goals of the French Revolution, he could appreciate liberty and equality—but not fraternity.[29]

Despite such reservations and differences, Hayden believed that the work of C. Wright Mills was the perfect place to begin thinking about a manifesto—particularly one that was designed for "a radical democratic organization." Writing under Mills's influence, Hayden incorporated the promise of face-to-face democracy into the document that he was drafting. As he explained in one of his notes, "I am primarily concerned about *the complete absence of an active and creative set of publics, people working in union to conform the structures and direction of events to their interests.*" In his notes, he did not shy away from one of the implications. "This is a central fatal fact about the United States," declared Hayden: "it is a republic, not a democracy, and nearly everyone wants to keep it that way."[30]

In 1948, at the close of *The New Men of Power*, Mills himself had spoken wistfully of the left in America. It was "powerless, distracted and confused." The ideas its intellectuals held were "less a program than a collective dream." Still, Mills cast his fate with that dream, pressing for a "more direct democracy of daily life," trying to "build a public," answering fears of futility with a defiant decision "to throw in with 'the little groups that cannot win.' " It was no wonder that Mills twelve years later became the first prominent American intellectual to embrace the fledgling New Left—after all, thanks in part to the success of his own "sociological poems," they shared the same "collective dream."[31]

CHAPTER FIVE

BUILDING A HOUSE OF THEORY

O N MARCH 20, 1962, while Tom Hayden was in the midst of
drafting the SDS manifesto, C. Wright Mills died from a
heart attack. He was forty-five. "It had a *terrible* effect on
me," recalls Hayden, who had completed draft notes on two sections
of the manifesto the day before. In his graduate thesis on Mills, he
described his reaction: "I remember my whole body hardening when
I came upon the obituary in *The New York Times*. It was as though
his own powerful physical system, thrown unrelentingly into the
grinding process of his mission, broke down in desperation and futility. For me, it symbolized the shattering isolation and collapse of
American radicalism against a fundamentally overpowering system." The martyrdom of the intellectual raised fundamental questions: "What kind of society so effectively destroyed radical protest?
Is the basis of protest and revolution really dead in America?"[1]

At the December meeting, Hayden had been instructed to circulate notes for the manifesto in order to allow other members to
register their opinions. The first two notes that Hayden completed
were three pages on possible themes for the introduction, plus six
pages and a bibliography on "problems of democracy."

In these draft notes and two others that followed shortly afterward, Hayden was trying to share his thinking about the manifesto.
But he was also doing something more, particularly in his comments
and questions on the idea of democracy: he was playing with ideas,
airing his political doubts, looking for the right words to express his
hopes.

In the previous year, he had vividly dramatized the role of the activist on the road in Tennessee, Mississippi and Georgia, risking his life for the cause of social justice. Now, writing in the shadow of C. Wright Mills, first in Atlanta and then in New York City, he could assume a different role. His sense of personal commitment confirmed by direct action, he could stop, and think. In solitude, surrounded by books and sitting at his typewriter, he was free to play the part of the radical intellectual, plumbing his political passions, examining his moral convictions, exploring different visions of what democracy could possibly mean.

He began his draft note on themes for the introduction with a fusillade of rhetoric, struggling to rise to the occasion. In by now familiar cadences, Hayden lamented the "moral uncertainty" created by "doubt, nihilism and despair." This situation, he complained, had been aggravated by the drift toward "value free" research in American universities. The resulting moral blindness reinforced political impotence: "We are too tightly confined to specialized roles to take up the citizen's role."

The alternative Hayden sketched with a quotation from Iris Murdoch, the British philosopher and novelist. "It is dangerous to starve the moral imagination of the young," wrote Murdoch. "Socialist thought is hampered and the appeal of Socialism is restricted, because our technical concepts are highly esoteric and our moral concepts are excessively simple and there is nothing in between. We need, and the Left should provide, some refuge from the cold, open field of Benthamite empiricism, a framework, a house of theory."

After interpolating another quotation, this time from C. Wright Mills on the responsibility of intellectuals, Hayden returned to Murdoch's metaphor. "The house of theory," he concluded, is "not a monastery. I am proposing that the world is not too complex, our knowledge not too limited, our time not so short, as to prevent the orderly building of a house of theory, or at least its foundation, right out in public, in the middle of the neighborhood."[2] The writing was clumsy, but Murdoch's metaphor fit: it was an image of what Hayden hoped that his manifesto would be.

Defining an Ideal

Hayden found the bricks for his "house of theory" in his bibliography on democracy. Besides C. Wright Mills's *The Power Elite* and *The Causes of World War III*, the twenty-seven titles included Robert Dahl's *Preface to Democratic Theory*, Robert Nisbet's *Quest for Community* and William Kornhauser's *The Politics of Mass Society*. Hayden read Erich Fromm's *The Sane Society*, with its frankly utopian plea for reintroducing "the principle of the Town Meeting into modern industrialized society," and also Robert Michels' classic *Political Parties*, with its pessimistic argument that an "iron law of oligarchy" condemned every organization, whatever its democratic pretensions, to bureaucratic sclerosis and rule by an elite. Two books by Reinhold Niebuhr attest to Hayden's interest in the theological dispute over original sin and its implications for political theory. The inclusion of Sheldon Wolin's *Politics and Vision* suggests his fascination with what Wolin called the "transcending form of vision"—a kind of thinking that could lead to "the imaginative reordering of political life." And the seven titles on the philosophy of education, including John Dewey's *Democracy and Education*, indicate Hayden's special interest in the pedagogical dimension of politics.[3]

His background in political philosophy of course gave him a head start in sifting through the arguments in these books. But his college course work had given him something more. The very phrase that he now adopted as a kind of beacon—"participatory democracy"— had first been used by one of his teachers at Michigan, Arnold Kaufman.[4]

In his 1960 essay "Participatory Democracy and Human Nature" —it duly appears in Hayden's bibliography—Kaufman had used the phrase to indicate a form of society in which every associate assumed a "direct responsibility for decisions." The "main justifying function" of participatory democracy, explained Kaufman, "is and always has been, not the extent to which it protects or stabilizes a community, but the contribution it can make to the development of human powers of thought, feeling and action. In this respect, it differs, and differs quite fundamentally, from a representative system incorporating all sorts of institutional features designed to safeguard human rights and ensure social order."

Kaufman used his distinction not to belittle representative democracy, but rather to suggest that increased participation would enhance the vitality of representative institutions: "participation is one of the most important ways of ensuring that those who vote will make their decisions intelligently." He examined in turn the somber views on human nature presented by Freud, Robert Michels and others, in order to defend the corrigibility of human character— through participation: "In modern industrial societies men can successfully assume responsibility for the direction of many affairs which today they regard as largely irrelevant to their lives because these affairs seem so remote."[5]

At the outset, Hayden's draft notes on democracy closely followed the argument of Kaufman's original paper. He began with a discussion of the ideal, "the participatory democracy." Like his teacher, Hayden linked the notion of democracy to the question of human nature. " 'Human nature,' is not an evil or corrosive substance to be feared or contained,"declared Hayden. "It represents a potential for material and spiritual development which, no matter how lengthily or rapidly unfolded, can never be dissipated." Because Hayden, like Kaufman, treated "participatory democracy" as a form of civic education that uniquely developed the human potential, he regarded it as a precondition of social justice: "Freedom is more than the absense of arbitrary restrictions on personal development," wrote Hayden. "For the democratic man, freedom must be a condition of the inner self as well, achieved by reflection confronting dogma, and humility overcoming pride. 'Participation' means both *personal initiative*—that men feel obliged to help resolve social problems—and *social opportunity*—that society feels obliged to maximize the possibility for personal initiative to find creative outlets."

So closely did Hayden follow his teacher that he concluded by reproducing his own version of Kaufman's argument that participation enhanced representative institutions. For Hayden as for Kaufman, "the participatory democracy" was an essential complement to representative institutions. It did not replace them.[6]

Doubts About Democracy

This preliminary "etching of the ideal that democrats seek to realize" was stilted, earnest and—on the face of it—naive. But after defining his participatory ideal in such halting terms, Hayden in his draft notes took a startling turn. "Our task," he declared, "is to examine, or better, find a way to examine in some detail the real meaning of these seductive moral statements." Organizing his discussion around six broad topics—human nature; the complexity of modern society; the structure of large corporations; mass society; totalitarianism; and Third World revolutions—Hayden raised doubts, posed questions, played the devil's advocate. The relative cogency and forcefulness of his prose leave a reader wondering whether Hayden was simply rehearsing possible objections to participatory democracy, or rather expressing some of his own feelings of ambivalence.

He began with the most basic question of all: What if the democratic ideal was based "on a false estimate of man's 'nature' "? If man by nature was evil, or self-interested, or "power-lusting" and "cursed by original sin," then a truly participatory democracy was "not only impossible to achieve, but misguided." Hayden pointed out that the political theorists who framed the American Constitution shared a fairly dim view of human nature and the potential for popular participation. Though he did not say so, he obviously knew that this was one reason why the Federalists had created "a republic, not a democracy." The Constitution thwarted "participatory democracy." By design, America was an "inactive democracy."[7]

Perhaps the Federalists had been right: the complexity of modern society certainly seemed to confirm their wisdom. Hayden summarized the account of modern representative democracy given by Joseph Schumpeter and the political scientists of "the Michigan school," among others. Though most citizens were apathetic and ignorant, their passivity scarcely mattered: a rational and orderly "circulation of elites" could perfectly well be accomplished "without participation of the mass of men."[8]

The feeling of participation was in any case susceptible to manipulation. Large corporations had shown an impressive ability to foster among otherwise powerless employees a keen sense of shared responsibility. Was such "organizational 'togetherness,' " wondered Hayden, "the perversion or perfection of participation?"[9]

And what would become of bold leadership in a "mass society" with democratic participation? An "undifferentiated mass" of separate, detached and anonymous individuals with "no social organization" and "no structure of status roles" might threaten the "creative elitist minority which nurtures and preserves the essence of culture." Whether he admitted it or not, "the democrat advocates implicitly the breakup of standards and moral direction for society."[10]

The experience of authoritarian regimes swept up in large-scale social change—Cuba and China seem to have been in Hayden's mind—raised still more questions: about privacy, about solidarity, about the ability of a democracy to satisfy the human longing for transcendence. "Surely there is considerable evidence," he wrote, "that dictatorships exist not only through total control of the means of violence . . . but also through sincerely expressed popular support. People in such a society can be mobilized by a sense of mission, an identity with some transcendent cause that appears to be attainable." These citizens "are not 'free' in any liberal or democratic sense." They "truly are separated from the means of decision-making." Yet they feel "a solidarity with their fellows." They are "happy, integrated into a group, purposeful, dedicated, sacrificing." What, wondered Hayden, were the moral issues involved in claiming that such "exuberant, creative" people "were not living 'the good life' "? Was there "anything innate in man that yearns for attachment to a consuming cause or a transcendent form of being? If so, how does the non-totalitarian society deal with that human yearning? Can a non-totalitarian society generate the same elan, mission, purposefulness? If totalitarianism involves an attack on privacy, what place do we give to privacy in our participatory society? And if privacy really has no place, if the really democratic political order is universal, how is it different from totalitarianism?" [11]

Finally, asked Hayden, "How are we to apply the idea of participation to a country engaged in the colonial revolution?" Was popular involvement in the transformation of social and economic institutions the primary concern? Or rather the existence of multiple political parties and a freely elected national government? Such questions, he wrote, "indicate the real inadequacy of our ideal theory and demand that we develop at least two instruments: 1) a theory of social change, 2) a scale of greater and lesser values." [12]

At this point, the draft notes on democracy abruptly stop: "It would be desirable to continue . . . but these notes already grow too long. . . . I hope they establish some basis for thought and correspondence about the meaning of 'Students for a Democratic Society.' " [13]

Hayden's unfinished meditations present a paradox. On the one hand, he explores a variety of doubts and questions with candor, curiosity and an obvious respect for objections and counterarguments. On the other hand, he never answers most of the questions that he so forcefully raises. In part, the unfinished form of the draft notes reflected a deliberate effort to spur controversy. Hayden and Haber shared an aversion to dogma. They wanted to keep the notion of participatory democracy tentative, provisional, open-ended. They treated the participatory ideal as an agenda for research and an invitation to act with humility as well as conviction.

As long as the goal was to avoid elaborating a formal doctrine in order to keep the participatory ideal "provisional," there was no urgency about giving reasons to justify it. On the contrary. But why should activists risk their necks for a political vision that might turn out to be a chimera? Why should intellectuals subscribe to a theory that apparently remained open to such strong objections? In Hay-

den's draft notes on participatory democracy, the barrage of unanswered questions leaves his response in limbo. By default, his
proposed political ideal appears as a kind of *credo quia absurdum
est*, as if the idea of participatory democracy ultimately rested not
on a reasoned argument, but rather on a leap of faith—a leap that
Hayden himself had already made through political action.

Theories of Action

As we have seen, Hayden was sometimes willing to argue that
"myths," even if they seemed "unrealizable," could have a "valuable, operative reality" as "standards." Writing under the influence
of Camus in his earliest essays, he pictured action as a proof of moral
resolve—of faith, against all odds, in an ideal "more real than reality." But at other times, he treated action as a kind of reasoned
experiment—the means by which a prudent idealist could dispel his
doubts by putting his vision to the test. His thinking throughout
this period is marked by a profound—and unresolved—tension between these two divergent theoretical approaches to political action,
as can be seen in the last two draft notes for the manifesto that he
wrote: a two-page memo on "Politics, the Intellectual and SDS," and
an eight-page note on "the issues."

His note on "the issues" consisted largely of a long list of the
topics that Hayden proposed to include in the manifesto, from
the arms race to "the bureaucratic structure, which . . . completes
the impersonalizing of life, creating a commodity again, not a citizen." But at the close of his list, Hayden laid special stress on the
significance of direct action. "The revolutions in the new nations
are important," he wrote, precisely "because they are trying to defy
the tendencies toward stultification by the hard assertion of individual personality." This was also true, he thought, of the civil rights
movement. It too consisted of "individuals who are their own leaders, whose courage is their own courage, whose human foibles are at
least their own foibles, whose passion to be at last creators instead
of simply creatures is authentic and truly self-constructed." The
manifesto ought not carp about the "intellectual faults" of the activists in these movements; rather, it should treat their "personally
willed participation" as "exemplary."[14]

Passages like this reflect Hayden's penchant for a kind of reckless
existentialism. "The hard assertion of individual personality" has a
rather ominous ring for anyone familiar with the fascist romantics

of the early twentieth century—or with the personality cults surrounding Communist dictators like Mao Tse-tung and Fidel Castro. The implication is that political ideals can best be realized through an unflinching application of the individual's will-to-power.

But in other passages, Hayden strikes a far more cautious note. "Life is too complex," he had declared a few months earlier, "for anything but a commitment to experimental procedure, built on a deep understanding of our presuppositions and the alternate presuppositions which we are rejecting. We must be continually willing to reconstruct our ideas as they prove inadequate in social conditions."[15]

The pragmatic tinge to Hayden's views is evident in his draft note on "Politics, the Intellectual and SDS." An obsession with intellectual clarity, he suggested, left the individual "in an ivory tower," while a preoccupation with practical results led to "a fear of big ideas." To resolve this classic political dilemma, Hayden proposed positioning SDS on the margins of established institutions, close enough to be "effective," remote enough to remain "honest." Warning against "myopic realism," he also declared that "SDS should not be content with visionary statements alone." It should "develop both intermediate ideals and consistent programmatic goals." For example, "if someone approves of socialized medicine as an ideal, then he should also advocate medical care for the aged as an intermediate ideal, and the bill which incorporates medical care into the national social security program becomes his programmatic ideal."[16]

Far from being reckless, this approach to political action seems irreproachably reasonable, if not downright timid. Perhaps that is because Hayden's argument for action in "Politics, the Intellectual and SDS" was aimed, in part, at Al Haber—the first sign of a difference of opinion that would slowly grow over the next few years into a bitter schism. "At this point," says Hayden, "Al was pushing the idea of building a mailing list and sending out theoretical documents; that's *all* SDS was. It was not a vehicle for action." The differences between the two had long been evident to those in the inner circle of SDS at the University of Michigan. "They had very different approaches," says Bob Ross: "For Hayden, it was what formulation would mobilize people to act. For Haber, it was what formulation was logically unassailable."[17]

In the spring of 1962, Hayden believed that theoretical problems had to be resolved through trying ideas out in practice—not through endless debate over theoretical documents. He wanted the members of SDS to participate in a wide range of political activities—from dangerous and exciting trips south to fight for civil rights to patient efforts at lobbying for progressive legislation. He was prepared to entertain a host of objections to the idea of participatory democracy —but he was not about to be paralyzed by doubt. He insisted that the members of SDS "should be protagonists for a political vision," not just intellectuals pondering the merits of that vision. The best way to settle doubts about the democratic faith was to show people in practice how their own political participation could effect real social change. A "house of theory" should be built "right out in public, in the middle of the neighborhood."

As Hayden put it in his draft note on "the issues," "The role of the intellectuals and of the universities (and therefore, I think, SDS) is to enable people to actively enjoy the common life and feel some sense of genuine influence over their personal and collective affairs." This meant persuading people to *act*. It also meant (as Haber had always stressed) "conscious efforts at personal and group introspection," "position papers and manifestoes of a tentative kind," "internal controversy." It meant "balancing direct action with scholarly investigation and social criticism, cemented by a concern with democracy"—a concern that was simultaneously passionate and prudent, tenacious and skeptical, "visionary and relevant."[18]

Hayden's apparent attempt to synthesize existentialism and pragmatism made for provocative rhetoric but tenuous theorizing. His understanding of political action remained ambiguous. But for now, the point of Hayden's rhetoric was clear enough: he was inviting readers to reinvent—and "to actively enjoy"—the world of politics.

A Re-assertion of the Personal

Hayden was a tireless advocate. In between working on the manifesto that spring, he took recruiting trips to Johns Hopkins and Temple, spoke at Sarah Lawrence, Buffalo and Oberlin, and also attended a SNCC conference in Atlanta.[19]

Above all, he composed a brilliant introduction to his credo called "Student Social Action." This text was originally delivered as a speech in Ann Arbor in March of 1962. It was distributed as a pamphlet by SDS at the 1963 NSA Congress. It was included in *The New Student Left*, one of the first anthologies of New Left documents. In 1966 alone, SDS printed ten thousand copies of it. Apart from *The Port Huron Statement* itself, it was one of the most widely circulated radical pamphlets of the Sixties.

No wonder: the text is an extraordinary performance, a virtuoso set of variations on many of the most important themes that Hayden was exploring in his draft notes for the manifesto. The ostensible topic is the doctrine of *in loco parentis*. But in the course of the speech, as Hayden unfolds his vision of personal freedom and political participation, it becomes clear that his real topics are democracy and moral courage: he is daring his audience to take democracy seriously.

Hayden began by describing an incident at a small Southern college. After a number of students had been involved in protesting segregation off campus, the college president expelled the protesters, giving as his reason their "general inability to adjust . . . to the pattern of the institution." Hayden treated the president's action as a revealing symptom of paternalism in American higher education.

Students generally lacked rights. Most student governments lacked real power. Such paternalism produced students molded in its own authoritarian image. Hayden cited the results of a survey: "three out of every four students believe 'that what the nation needs is a strong fearless leader in whom we can have faith,' . . . eighty-three percent saw nothing wrong with wiretapping. . . ."

"What are we witnessing here?" asked Hayden. "Surely it is the decomposition of democracy, if ever we had genuine democracy in this country." Most Americans felt powerless: "Less and less do we transform private troubles into public issues." To the extent that ordinary people participated in public affairs, "they participate with impotency. . . . There is no willingness to take risks, no setting of dangerous goals, no real conception of personal identity except one made in the image of others, no real urge for personal fulfillment except to be *almost* as successful as the very successful people."

The tragedy was that things could be different. The university could become a model of "education in a democracy." The structure of society could be changed, the destinies of students—and other ordinary people—transformed.

The challenge was simple: "We must have a try at bringing society under human control." The new student activists "are restoring the individual personality to a creative and self-cultivating role in human affairs." They identified with the civil rights militants in the South and revolutionaries of the Third World—"the masses of hungry, aspiring, utopian peoples intervening in history for the first time." Concluded Hayden: "The time has come for a re-assertion of the personal."[20]

Hayden first delivered this speech at the Michigan Union in Ann

Arbor. One of the people in the audience was Richard Flacks. "I knew that SDS existed and I was interested," recalls Flacks. At the time, he was completing his doctoral dissertation in social psychology. An ardent admirer of C. Wright Mills—he named his first son "Charles Wright"—Flacks was instinctively attuned to Hayden's language. The speech bowled him over. "There were other things that were exciting me," he says, "like *New University Thought* coming out of Chicago, *Studies on the Left* coming out of Madison, the Berkeley scene was producing some things; the language they were talking, the ideas, were all of a piece. But no one expressed it better than Hayden in that speech. He was putting into words what I had been feeling but had not been able to imagine articulating. Once I heard these words, I said 'I know I believe this.' "

Flacks returned home. His wife, Mickey, was already an activist in an organization called Women Strike for Peace. "Mickey," he said, "I've just seen the next Lenin!"[21]

Promoting Political Controversy

The sweep of Hayden's emerging views did not provoke universal enthusiasm, even within SDS. On April 26, mimeographed copies of his draft notes were belatedly mailed out. Several members were unhappy with what they read. Their reservations first surfaced at a meeting of SDS leaders held on May 6 and 7, after a conference on "Race and Politics" that SDS had sponsored in Chapel Hill, North Carolina.

The avowed purpose of this conference had been to clarify the political direction of the civil rights movement. After the violent events of the fall in McComb, SNCC had shifted its emphasis from direct action to voter registration, challenging the payment of poll taxes and running black candidates for Congress; in cooperation with other civil rights groups, it was joining in a large-scale "Voter Education Project." In a memo on the conference, Hayden applauded this shift. At last, he wrote, the civil rights movement was "entering the sphere of politics, insisting on adopting the role of *citizen* as defined long ago by Aristotle as taking part in the 'deliberative or judicial administration of the state.' " Still, "the moral clarity of the movement has not always been accompanied by precise political vision. . . . What is needed is the instillment of political consciousness, a will to publicly utilize the instruments of democracy." In effect, Hayden was complaining that the civil rights movement lacked an adequate understanding of participatory democracy. "In the context of Ann Arbor," says Hayden, "I was on the extreme end of taking action. But in the context of SNCC and the South, I was more in the middle, believing that some of the SNCC people were making too much of a mystique of action alone."[22]

Hayden's almost patronizing call for a "precise political vision" to guide the civil rights movement should help lay to rest the misconception that the idea of participatory democracy was a product of this movement. Though Hayden indeed admired the moral courage and political style of SNCC activists, his own approach to democracy, as we have seen, was relatively abstract, intellectual, bookish. At the time, his memo on the civil rights conference produced a tepid reponse. Poorly planned and sparsely attended, the conference itself was something of a fiasco.

After the conference was over, the inner circle of SDS met to discuss, among other things, Hayden's draft notes and the shape of the manifesto. Steve Max had driven down from New York hoping to drum up support for his political strategy of realignment. "Our analysis at the time," says Max, "was that you had to bust up the Dixiecrat coalition. The key was to work for civil rights, not just because it was good work to do, but because it would undermine those octogenerian committee chairmen in Congress. That would open the way for reform."

Given this analysis, Max could scarcely have been pleased by Hayden's draft note on "the issues." "Let [the movement] remain ambiguous in direction for a while," wrote Hayden: "don't kill it by immediately imposing formulas for 'realignment.' We have to grow and expand, and let moral values get a bit realigned. Then, when consciousness is at its proper stage, we might talk seriously and in an action-oriented way about solutions."[23]

For Max, who prided himself on a hardheaded approach to politics, Hayden's draft notes sounded like empty prattle. "I had never gone to college," Max explains. "We saw a very concrete series of tasks and never quite understood what Hayden and these guys were talking about. You had to know all these books. We didn't understand that very often it was the courses that students were taking and the books they were reading, by Mills or one of those people, that first started them thinking about politics. We thought you made a commitment because life became intolerable. So we literally couldn't make heads or tails out of a lot of this stuff."[24]

The minutes of the SDS meeting report that Hayden began by describing the disappointing response to his draft notes for the manifesto—only one letter so far. He went on to outline the form and content of the manifesto as he now envisaged it. Max and his ally Jim Brook then made a motion: they proposed that Hayden's drafts about "values" be treated as a separate introduction to the manifesto, and that they themselves complete the manifesto by supplying a political analysis based on the strategy of "realignment."

This deceptively mild proposal provoked an angry debate. At stake, whether or not all the participants fully grasped it, was the soul of SDS—Haber and Hayden's vision of a genuinely *new* left, defined by broad agreement about the value of participatory democracy.

Hayden vociferously rejected the idea of splitting the manifesto into two parts. Denying that there was any meaningful dichotomy between "values" and politics, he asserted that his values in any case might prove incompatible with Brook's particular brand of politics. After an acrimonious exchange, the committee rejected the motion to change the format of the manifesto. But later in the meeting, Max returned to the attack, complaining that the organizing efforts of SDS were suffering from its "excessive value orientation." This time, it was Haber who answered him. "SDS should promote political controversy and ideas around a commitment to democracy," he said. Otherwise, SDS would turn into a sectarian group like every other left-wing organization.[25]

Haber and Hayden carried the day, but they duly noted Max's objections. If they were serious about their own ecumenical, experimental approach, they would have to find some way to incorporate Max's point of view.

Shortly afterward, Haber circulated a short memo spelling out the conception of SDS that he had spent the last two years of his life trying to implement. "The image of the organization," he wrote, "must be integrated around democratic values rather than around a political or economic formulation." Though SDS should exclude "people opposed to a democratic form of social organization," it must, Haber stressed, at the same time "find a way to include various groups and tendencies on the left." The members of SDS ought to be freewheeling and open-minded—not dogmatic. "Our stress on democratic values," he concluded, "should be in terms of broad consensus rather than formal doctrine."[26]

The June convention promised to crown Haber's efforts. Discussion of the manifesto would provide an opportunity to forge the kind of "broad consensus" that he desired. But as the starting date of June 11 drew near, Haber had yet to find a site. On May 26, Robb Burlage wrote to Haber and Hayden: "I look forward to hearing from you further about . . . such details as WHERE THE HELL IS IT GOING TO BE?" With time running out, Haber turned to Sharon Jeffrey, who enlisted the help of her mother. Together, they persuaded the United Auto Workers to rent their camp at Port Huron, Michigan, for a fee that SDS could afford.[27]

The manifesto was still unfinished. At Chapel Hill, Hayden had promised to have a complete draft ready by the beginning of June. Living in New York City in a small railroad flat on West Twenty-second Street, Hayden locked himself in his room with his books and stacks of articles. Writing full time, he worked furiously, struggling to put the finishing touches on his "house of theory"—a framework that his colleagues, all of them, would be able to admire, use, call their own.[28]

CHAPTER SIX

PORT HURON

T HE IMMODEST PROCESS of setting "an agenda for a generation" was about to begin. Hayden finished his draft on June
1. The SDS convention was set to convene on June 12. As
participants from around the country began to converge on Port
Huron, those who had seen Hayden's draft already felt an air of
excitement. "I knew that we were going to produce something that
would define us," says Bob Ross: "I suppose that when political
people embark on such a venture, they always hope that they will
remake history. We thought the draft was hot stuff. I thought, 'If I
could get people to agree with this, I'd change America.' "[1]

As a group, they were full of hope. By talking and thinking and
arguing for a few days in the woods of Michigan, they were going to
create a document that crystallized the essential political possibilities of their era. By expressing their own utopian political vision,
they would inspire an entire generation. Elated by their sense of
newfound community, they were convinced of their unique destiny.
Says Sharon Jeffrey: "We were launching something that had not
happened among university students, ever."[2]

The turnout was disappointing—only 59 registered participants.
There were a few figures conspicuous by their absence: Paul Potter
and Rennie Davis, already important members of SDS, did not attend. But most of those who mattered made the trip. Eight of the
eleven functioning SDS chapters were represented, including delegates from Swarthmore and Johns Hopkins, Oberlin and Earlham.
The delegates representing the chapters in Ann Arbor and New York
City controlled the largest blocs of votes—21 percent and 38 per-

cent, respectively. At-large delegates, unaffiliated with any local SDS chapter, came from Harvard and Yale, Wisconsin and Indiana. Eleven people attended as observers, representing a wide range of fraternal organizations: the National Student Christian Federation, the National Student Association, the Young Democrats, the Student Peace Union, even by chance the German SDS—Michael Vester, a German who was a student that year at Bowdoin College in Maine, was also a member of the Sozialistischer Deutscher Studentenbund, the radical student group later led by Rudi Dutschke. The contingent affiliated with the Student Non-Violent Coordinating Committee included Casey Hayden, Chuck McDew and Bob Zellner, perhaps the most prominent white activist in that civil rights organization. In addition, LID, the SDS parent organization, sent Harry Fleischman, who was chairman of the LID executive committee.[3]

Some of the participants considered themselves liberals. Some were dedicated socialists. Some, such as Mary Varela, a Catholic, and Jim Monsonis, a SNCC activist and seminary student who admired the theology of Reinhold Niebuhr, had turned to political activism out of religious conviction.

Their expectations varied. Richard Flacks had arrived at the convention planning to cover it for the *National Guardian*, a weekly newspaper aimed at the independent Marxist left. "I thought something important was going to happen," says Flacks. "I was coming into contact with radicals of a kind I had never met before: namely, people who were radical coming *not* from New York, but from the South. You had Robb Burlage, coming out of Texas, you had Maria Varela coming out of this Catholic, Hispanic background. Bob Zellner grew up in Alabama—amazing. That was very inspiring. Because that was the first evidence that I had, I think in my whole life, that you could have a radical movement in the United States that wasn't tied to the specific urban, Jewish culture that I came out of."[4]

Steve Max, who had arrived with a carload of colleagues after an exhausting all-night drive from New York City, took a more jaundiced view, tempering any hopes with his characteristically droll sense of realism: "Here was one more student conference," he says. "We were relaxed about it. They were going to write a paper. Fine. I don't know about other people, but we certainly didn't think that this was going to make history."[5]

But that was precisely what most participants *did* think. "We knew that the student movement was a growing phenomenon," says Paul Booth. "Even though we weren't a political force yet—and we never dreamed of spawning a mass movement—we all thought we were making history. We thought we were writing a document that would influence thinking people. From the fringes of the main-stream institutions of society, we would speak truth to power. We would make intellectual history."[6]

Setting the Stage

Hayden's draft consisted of forty-nine typewritten pages divided into seventeen sections. It treated of politics, the economy, foreign policy, the colonial revolution, prospects for disarmament, civil rights, students, labor, values, the meaning of democracy. He had scrapped his previous outlines. The efforts at definition and open skepticism of his draft notes had all but disappeared. Although basic "values" such as the meaning of democracy had been the focus of Hayden's work throughout the spring, in the completed draft he condensed his thoughts on these matters into a handful of suggestive pages, buried in the middle of the text. Parts of the document had the bland assertiveness and plodding, plank-by-plank comprehensiveness of a conventional party platform. But other parts bristled with provocation: on the labor movement (its liberalism was "rote rather than radical"), on anti-Communism (it merely reinforced "public hysteria" and "paranoia"), on the Soviet Union (the United States might just as easily be charged with "military aggressiveness").[7]

Despite its uneven style, the document was impressive. It had passion and panache. It was bold, it was sweeping, it was long. It was almost too much.

"The draft," recalls Hayden, "was supposed to be about half, if not a third, of its final length. It had been mailed out only a week before the meeting, which almost destroyed the convention." Despite meetings by several local chapters to discuss the document, "people came unprepared. The first thing that had to be accomplished was to convince them to go forward."[8]

On Monday, June 11, the leadership of SDS, including Hayden, Haber and Ross, held a "preconvention meeting" at Port Huron to discuss the manifesto and to set a final agenda for the convention. At that point, the schedule called for an "educational conference" the next day, with a series of speakers and panels. The convention proper was not scheduled to begin until Wednesday morning. On Saturday, after the convention had elected officers, the new National Executive Committee was scheduled to meet. This schedule left just

three days for actually debating, revising and accepting the manifesto.[9]

"I remember people sitting around a room feeling really hopeless,"
says Hayden of the preconvention meeting. "To somehow transform
it, in three days, seemed impossible." Still, not to make the effort
was unimaginable. "I think it was sheer will," says Hayden, who
reminded the group of its higher calling: "forgive me for being late,
but what are we doing here if we're not giving birth to something?"

After some debate, the group agreed that the convention should
go ahead and make an effort to revise and ratify the manifesto. They
also agreed that the manifesto should be treated as a "living document." "That was very, very important," says Hayden. "One of the
things that got people committed was an agreement that whatever
we came out with would not be final, but that it would be offered as
a discussion paper to our generation. That seemed to relieve people
enormously. It meant that they could later disavow or amend it, or
even come back together for another conference and have at it
again."

The group next had to devise some practical way for the convention to work on the manifesto. "Obviously," says Hayden, "we
couldn't go through it as a committee of the whole." It was also
obvious that a group of 60 people could not rewrite the document in
three days. After a discussion of the problems, those at the preconvention meeting decided that the convention as a whole should try
to reach agreement on general instructions for revising the document, while leaving the actual work of rewriting to a "styles committee." This drafting group was to consist of Hayden, Al Haber and
Bob Ross. But as Ross recalls, there was never any doubt about who
was in charge: "Tom was The Writer. Everyone knew that he was
The Writer. That was something in between being a recorder of
people's ideas and saying to people, 'This is what you *really* mean.'
Tom was a genuine leader. He led because he really did express what
people wanted. Even at Port Huron, he was the architect, and the
rest of us were the carpenters, the clients in a sense: 'No, put the
porch over here.' "

To enable the clients to tell the architect just how to finish their
"house of theory," the preconvention meeting organized the convention itself into small groups that would convene after an initial plenary session. According to Haber's notes, there were to be eight
separate small groups. Each small group would discuss in detail a
different part of the manifesto: "themes" or values; students; American politics; economics; discrimination; Communism; the colonial

revolution; nuclear policy. The members of each group were expected to raise questions about the manifesto without trying to come up with new language. These questions would then be put to the group as a whole, according to a formula that divided issues into "bones," "widgets" and "gizmos." The major "bones" of contention would be allotted an hour of debate; minor points, or "gizmos," were to be handled in ten minutes or less; and "widgets," an intermediate category, were allowed perhaps a half-hour—as with so many aspects of the convention, many of the details remain unclear.[10]

Before adjourning, the preconvention meeting made two preliminary decisions about the substance of the manifesto. One involved Hayden's introduction, the other his discussion of values. Hayden's draft did not begin auspiciously: "Every generation inherits from the past a set of problems—and a dominant set of insights and perspectives by which the problems are to be understood and, hopefully, managed." It got worse: "We treat newness with a normalcy that suggests a deliberate flight from reality." The group instructed Hayden to complete a new introduction before the close of the convention—one of the few cases in which actual rewriting occurred at Port Huron.

The group also agreed that Hayden's two sections on "values" had to be moved. As they stood, these sections formed an awkward bridge between a diagnosis of the problems and a summary of the proposed solutions. Yet it was here that Hayden first discussed "participatory democracy"—the idea that defined the distinctive political vision of SDS. It was here that Hayden summarized all his thinking about the group's fundamental assumptions. The group decided to put the discussion of values and democracy at the beginning of the manifesto, immediately after the new introduction.

The stage was finally set, the agenda clear. On Tuesday morning, June 12, the SDS convention at Port Huron officially began.

Fathers and Sons

The convention opened with an all-day "educational conference." At the May meeting in Chapel Hill, it had been agreed that the speakers at this conference would discuss "modern liberalism from a critical point of view" and " 'The Intellectual Foundations of the Left,' an historical presentation of the ideas of the Enlightenment, radical Christianity, Marxism and Existentialism." In the event, few of these topics were specifically addressed by the speakers invited to the conference: Harold Taylor, Tim Jenkins, Roger Hagan, Arnold Kaufman, Donald Slaiman and Michael Harrington.

Taylor, the former president of Sarah Lawrence College and a LID member sympathetic to Haber and Hayden, had been invited to talk about his special interest, university reform (one of his books, *Education and Freedom*, had appeared on Tom Hayden's bibliography the previous spring). Jenkins, a SNCC activist in Atlanta when he was not attending Yale Law School, spoke about civil rights.

Hagan, from Harvard, was the editor of a newsletter published by the Committee of Correspondence, a coalition of academics and liberals dedicated to disarmament and the dissemination of fresh perspectives on social change (the newsletter's editorial board consisted of David Riesman and H. Stuart Hughes of Harvard and A. J. Muste from the Fellowship of Reconciliation). Hagan's area of special interest was the anti-Communism of Cold War liberals: in a symposium on "the young radicals" a few months before, he had expressed his sympathy for the new student left, explaining that "I have little to say or to learn from most socialists and fellow-travelers of the thirties. With a few exceptions, their recent function has been not to revive but to deny hope."[11]

Arnold Kaufman, the Michigan philosopher who had coined the phrase "participatory democracy," functioned as a kind of free-floating guru. Richard Flacks remembers a reverent audience gathered round a crackling fire: "Arnold spoke and people sat at his feet. At one point, he declared that our job as citizens was not to role-play the President. Our job was to put forth our own perspective. That was the real meaning of democracy—press for your own perspective as you see it, not trying to be a statesman understanding the big picture." Throughout the conference, Kaufman held forth in a small room on the philosophy of democracy. "I think he was reading a book he was writing," says Steve Max, who was rapidly becoming inured to what he perceived as certain oddities in the organization he had joined: "It was hour after hour. People drifted in and out. It was an interminable presentation."

The climax of the educational conference—and in some respects, the emotional climax of the entire convention—came Tuesday evening with the appearance on a panel together of Michael Harrington and Donald Slaiman of the AFL-CIO (the latter had been invited to appear in an apparent conciliatory gesture to the trade-union sensibilities of LID). The two, who were political cronies, had flown into Detroit together that afternoon. "I remember Harrington and Slaiman getting off the plane in a messy, disheveled state," says Richard

Flacks, "and driving all the way to Port Huron with them. That's how I got some insight into Slaiman. You've got to see this guy as an old-line Marxist who had joined the staff of the AFL-CIO and was living with it through a kind of bluster. I couldn't stand him. He seemed to me to be a caricature of a labor bureaucrat. He was big and fat."

Harrington—who quickly came to regret his behavior at the convention—remembers that he had pored over the draft of the manifesto: "I can almost see specific places where I marked it up." He had already been warned about the drift of SDS by Tom Kahn and Rachelle Horowitz, his allies in YPSL. Ironically, Harrington had no trouble at all with Hayden's larger political vision. The idea of "participatory democracy" fit comfortably with Max Schachtman's emphasis, which he shared with Trotsky in the late Thirties, on workers' control and socialism from the bottom up. Like a generation of left-wing Marxists, Harrington considered the original soviets of 1917 and their council form of democracy to be the very essence of the Revolution that Stalin had betrayed. But he was not so comfortable with other aspects of the manifesto.[12]

Hayden's draft, for example, decried a "crisis of vision" in the labor movement: "The general absence of union democracy finalizes worker apathy." Labor had grown "too rich and sluggish" to act as a leading agency of social change; that role had been taken over by radicals in the university. Hayden's comments on Communism were, if anything, even more provocative. The draft criticized the "policy-making assumption that the Soviet Union is inherently expansionist" and argued that "the savage repression of the Hungarian Revolution was a defensive action rooted in Soviet fear that its empire would collapse." A sober appraisal of the Soviet threat was made all but impossible by the climate of popular hysteria—a climate reinforced by left-wing intellectuals who indulged in ritual denunciations of Communism: "While the older radicals are indispensable for information and advice," wrote Hayden, "and while our sympathies parallel theirs on nearly every other domestic issue, they tragically coalesce with the less-informed, conservative and even reactionary forces in performing a static analysis, in making Russia a 'closed question.' "[13]

Such language was bound to irritate Harrington. Although *The Other America*, the book on poverty that he had just published, scrupulously avoided any mention of Karl Marx or even the word "socialism," Harrington took his Marx and his socialism very, very seriously, particularly in his dealings with an avowedly radical organization like SDS. As we have seen, loyalty to the socialist idea for Harrington entailed an unflagging hostility to Stalinism and the Soviet Union's brand of Communism. After he finished reading the draft, he fired off a sharply critical letter to the SDS office in New York.[14] By the time he arrived in Port Huron, he was prepared to tell the young students of SDS just where, in his opinion, they had gone off the rails.

His mood of righteous indignation was reinforced by the man whom SDS had chosen to be his companion in debate. Like Harrington, Donald Slaiman was a disciple of Max Schachtman. "Looking back," says Harrington, "Donnie was the key guy in moving Schachtman, Kahn and Horowitz to the right." Unlike Harrington himself, who went on to become an outspoken critic of the war in Vietnam, Schachtman and those who followed his lead became mainstream labor loyalists and staunch Cold Warriors. Kahn, for example, went on to become a top aide to George Meany of the AFL-CIO and, later, Senator Henry Jackson, both of whom advocated increased military spending and a hard line against global Communism. "At the time," recalls Harrington, "the Schachtmanite line was that Walter Reuther was the vanguard of the American working class and that George Meany was not, he was the traditional working class. Slaiman had just started working for the AFL-CIO. I'm not saying that he did it for venal reasons, but Slaiman was the first one to argue that Meany was the real leader of the American working class, and that Reuther wasn't serious. From a Marxist perspective, identifying the real leader of the American working class made a real difference."

Though nobody any longer remembers the details of what was said —the scholastic subtleties involved in declaring George Meany to be at the vanguard of the proletariat were beyond the ken of most of the delegates—almost everyone recalls the drama of Harrington's appearance at Port Huron that Tuesday night. "Harrington asked to say some things about the manifesto," says Richard Flacks. "He'd already read it, and he was angry about it. He felt that he needed to get certain things off of his chest." Harrington remembers ranging widely over a host of different topics: anti-Communism, liberalism, the labor movement, "the whole question of historical agency. I'm sure that came up at Port Huron. I would have been very critical about the idea that students were the vanguard."

At some point, Slaiman entered the fray. The critique of labor in Hayden's draft could not have pleased anyone in the AFL-CIO. Harrington also remembers Slaiman being attacked for "red-baiting"

SDS—for implying that the organization was soft on Communism. "He's a big guy," says Harrington, "a guy who is capable of getting very emotional, and he felt that his honor was being impugned." As Flacks recalls, Slaiman began to shout: " 'The American labor movement has won more for its members than any labor movement in the world! You people have some nerve attacking the labor movement! You people will stand for any left-wing Stalinoid kind of thing, but you have this double standard. George Meany, don't you attack George Meany! I've had as many fights with George Meany as anyone in this room—But!' You don't wash the dirty linen of the labor movement in public. That was our sin. There was nothing wrong with internal discussion—though where the 'internal' was, I couldn't figure out. Where would be inside enough?"

After a heated discussion, the group adjourned to the camp's dining room. There, over beer and cigarettes, the debate raged on. Harrington sat at a table while Hayden remembers perching himself on a countertop. The decibel level rose as more beer was consumed. ("I have an enormous capacity," says Harrington, "for drinking beer and talking about politics.") Harrington's position was supported by Harry Fleischman.[15] Hayden, seconded by Roger Hagan, fought back with a vehemence that startled at least one witness: "I couldn't believe that Hayden felt so strongly," says Richard Flacks. "He felt that he'd put too *much* anti-Communism into the manifesto already. The only reason he'd put any anti-Communism in was to please these people who were bigots and were living in the Cold War past."

Many of those listening were stunned. Michael Harrington was a friend, an ally, a model—just the year before, Hayden had cited Harrington as one of the two political figures young leftists admired (the other was Norman Thomas). "We were very fond of him," says Paul Booth. Harrington, in fact, remembers the discussion at Port Huron as "not unfriendly," perhaps because he loves the heat of political combat—years later, he still gets a twinkle in his eye when he recalls the old sectarian slugfests. But the students felt ambushed. "It was definitely a conflict," says Steve Max. "It may not have been a conflict in terms of the mode of discourse that Mike was used to— he came out of a much more rough-and-tumble atmosphere. But these kids came from households where nobody raised their voice. They had never heard people shout about politics."

"Although it was a purely intellectual debate," says Sharon Jeffrey, "there was an undertow of very heavy emotion." At the time, few people understood the reasons for the passion. As Jeffrey points out (and this would later become a complaint commonly voiced by other feminists as well), it was considered beyond the pale at meetings like this to discuss feelings openly. But one clue to the emotional heat of the debate was Hayden's critique in the manifesto of "older radicals." "This was *personal*," says Al Haber: "It was both an analysis and a personal statement. We were critical of labor and of liberalism out of a familiarity with some of its personages, by sharing dinner with them, and having them as fathers and mothers or whatever."

Hayden, in retrospect, has a similar view: "It was one of those unfortunate but necessary 'which-side-are-you-on' dynamics. We are trying to create a new student movement. Are you trying to hold it back? Are you really with us? From the point of view of his integrity, Michael had no real choices. To say nothing would have been slavish; to raise legitimate questions would have alienated us. He made the mistake of joining the argument about issues, when it was not about issues. It was about time. Here was a guy who still thought of himself as a student leader. But he was of a different generation. And these actual student leaders were creating an actual student organization. To the extent that you want to get Freudian about it, and there was some element of that there, he was the perfect guy for everybody to overthrow."

Says Harrington: "Here I was: I was thirty-four. I'd been a youth leader for so long that people were joking that I was 'the oldest young socialist in America.' It's personal autobiography: I'd always been the youngest at everything I'd ever done. I graduated from college at nineteen; I was the youngest editor of *The Catholic Worker*. My self-image was as a *young* person. Now, I'm in this Oedipal situation. Up comes this younger generation. I think that they are ignoring my honest, sincere and absolutely profound advice. And this struck at my self-image. I think that part of my emotional overresponse was there: I interpreted this as an Oedipal assault on the father-figure."

"It was a setup," concludes Hayden: "there couldn't be a more perfect setup. We were giving birth to some new force in American politics. And Michael, purely by virtue of being older and having other attachments, was being an obstacle in the delivery room."

The passions of the previous night were rekindled almost immediately the next morning. Harrington had to leave for another speaking engagement, so he instructed his allies in SDS—Rachelle Horowitz, Tom Kahn and Richard Roman—to monitor events and keep him posted. The first order of business of the first working plenary session of the convention was to clarify the status of the observers in attendance. These people were not members of SDS. How should they be treated? To extend to them speaking but not voting rights seemed fair enough. But one of the observers, a New York City high school student named Jim Hawley, was also a member of the Progressive Youth Organizing Committee, the Communist-sponsored youth group that had replaced the Labor Youth League. The questions debated the night before flared up in a new form. A member of a Communist group was asking to attend the convention. What should the organization do?

On one level, the debate was absurd. As Steve Max says, "Who's ever worried about seating *observers*? It's not something that most people talk about." Yet to the staunch anti-Communists within SDS —Horowitz, Kahn and Roman among them—allowing Hawley into the meeting would violate the long-standing traditions of the League for Industrial Democracy. "It was somehow tantamount to diplomatic recognition," says Max. "It was as if we were going to recognize Russia. Nobody could understand what they were talking about. It's like those countries where you only eat with your right hand—and then somebody comes to dinner and eats with their left hand, and you can't understand why you let your daughter marry them."

Despite his own family background, Max was uninterested in making a fuss over Hawley. "He was a fine guy, an old friend of mine. But getting the convention together was a very difficult and laborious act; and the idea that it might all blow up over whether Jim Hawley was there . . . it was taking up time that it shouldn't have." Hayden and Haber disagreed. For them, a principle was at stake. How could an organization that prided itself on its open-minded, nonsectarian approach to politics cave in to the most flagrant kind of Cold War prejudice and exclude an *observer*, simply because he belonged to a Communist youth group?

While the YPSL members argued with everybody else, Hawley himself drifted off, apparently embarrassed to be the center of attention. By the time the plenary decided that he should be seated as an observer, with the proviso that "this indicated neither approval nor fraternal relations," Hawley was gone—never to return.[16]

Despite the apparent absurdity of this debate, it was pivotal for some people. In the course of the morning, for example, Richard Flacks made the transition from interested onlooker to active participant: "During that debate, I said something and realized that I was now in it. That's really when I joined SDS." His wife, Mickey, had a similar experience. Like Steve Max, Richard and Mickey had both grown up in Communist families in New York. They had both gone to Communist summer camps, and had both come out of the Communist milieu of the Labor Youth League—like Steve Max, in fact, both had been instrumental in disbanding the League in 1956, on the ground that Khrushchev's revelations about Stalin and the Soviet invasion of Hungary had irrevocably discredited Communism. Still, the experience had left scars. In Ann Arbor, both the Flacks had been leery about joining political organizations, for fear that their past might be used against them, damaging the causes they wished to support. But SDS was different. "Here was an organization," says Mickey, "that wasn't red-baiting. And seeing Steve [Max], who I hadn't seen in two years, reinforced the idea that it was okay for people like us to be there."[17]

For other participants, by contrast, the debate over Hawley seemed like a bizarre hangover from another era. Perhaps for some of them it was even mildly titillating—here was a rare chance to flout one of the political taboos of the Fifties. At lunch that Tuesday, Flacks remembers talking to Roger Hagan, who had missed the debate: "He was the total, opposite pole from Harrington and the YPSL people," says Flacks. "When he heard about Hawley, he became very excited: 'Do you mean to say there was a *Communist* here?' I said, 'Yeah.' And Hagan said, 'Is he still here? I've *never* seen one.'"

The Spirit of Face-to-Face Politics

At last, the convention was ready to get down to business. After a general meeting where the format for revising the manifesto was discussed, the convention split up into smaller groups—here was Haber's "seminar model" of politics put into practice. Delegates were assigned to specific groups; Robb Burlage, for example, was in the "economics" group, since he was studying economics as a graduate student at Harvard. But there seem to have been no hard-and-fast rules, and delegates freely jumped from group to group. The convention quickly became a blur of talk, as each part of the manifesto was debated.

The talk extended far into Wednesday night. Richard Flacks remembers Hayden "in the middle of a meeting with a toothbrush in his mouth, talking about how it was so late that his teeth had fur on them."

On Thursday, the discussion continued. "We took our job very seriously," says Sharon Jeffrey. "I can see a picture of a small group of us sitting around on the grass on a sunny afternoon discussing issues. We knew the importance of what we were doing." As the talk went on, the details of the conversation for many people began to fade into a more general impression of exhilaration, intellectual stimulation, the joys of finding new friends.

"It's hard to know if there was a kind of mutual self-delusion going on," says Richard Flacks, "or if the people there were really that terrific. But I have rarely had the experience where I felt 'These people are *terrific.*' In that they were great, nice, wonderful people, plus brilliant—just that kind of feeling. I thought that I was pretty sophisticated; but suddenly I was dealing with a lot of new perspectives: I remember Mary Varela and Tim Jenkins discussing nonviolence and Christian radicalism, and that was the most interesting discussion of nonviolence I'd ever heard."

Something more than a manifesto began to crystallize during the discussions. Above all, a new *spirit* was becoming manifest. C. Wright Mills had written about "the scattered little circles of face-to-face citizens discussing their public business." "We do not now have such a public in America," Al Haber had observed the year before, adding hopefully that "perhaps, among the students, we are beginning to approach it on the left." Port Huron was bearing out Haber's hope: it was Mills's image of democracy come to life.

For those who lived through it, it was a kind of epiphany. "I feel like I know the people who were at Port Huron better than people who I've known much longer," says Richard Flacks. "I've thought about this a lot since. I'm not sure how many people I'm talking about—maybe only eight. But it really was one of the most *intense* things I've ever experienced with a group of people. How could this be? One thing is that if you're with people for twenty-four or thirty-six straight hours, that's actually, in amount of time, even though it's only a day and a half, in the actual amount of time together, that's a lot more time than you spend with most people over several years. And part of it was this mutual discovery of like minds. You felt isolated before, because you had these political interests and values and suddenly you were discovering not only like minds, but the possibility of actually *creating* something together. And it was our thing: we were there at the beginning."

Agenda for a Generation

Compared with the exhilaration of first experiencing the pleasures of face-to-face political debate, the specific issues so passionately discussed soon paled into insignificance. Few participants today remember much of what was said. But by comparing Hayden's draft of the manifesto with the final version published later in the summer, it is possible to itemize the major changes and to suggest the content of some of the major debates.

Surprisingly enough, some of the most striking aspects of the manifesto were scarcely discussed at all. Despite the contentiousness of the debate between Steve Max and Tom Hayden over what emphasis to put on "values" at Chapel Hill in May, this issue scarcely arose at Port Huron. The presence of Arnold Kaufman underlines the importance that Hayden and Haber attributed to the idea of participatory democracy; yet the notion was apparently never discussed formally in any detail, despite the host of fundamental questions that Hayden himself had raised in his notes in the spring. The strategy of "realignment," finally, was not one of the bones of contention. In his working draft, in a tacit concession to Max's group and the YPSL members, Hayden had simply summarized the gist of the realignment position in the section of the manifesto titled "Toward American Democracy."

Such concessions were more than cosmetic. Despite the confrontation with Harrington, conciliation was one of the defining themes of the convention. "They were ready to accommodate anything," says Max: "In the tradition I was used to, you sharpened the differences, you had a knock-down, drag-out fight, winners and losers. That's what made for a good conference. But this was a different kind of politics." Although the convention was run according to Robert's Rules of Order, with an elaborate apparatus of committees and votes, an informal effort was constantly being made to arrive at some kind of broad consensus. Making this effort seemed a good way to implement the group's nonsectarian credo.

For example, Bob Ross, who was in the "students" group with Rachelle Horowitz, remembers trying "to be responsive to her concerns. The issue was: Could students change society without labor? I knew that what Mills called the labor metaphysic was wrong to the extent that it led one to assume that whatever labor wanted was the agenda for social change. But I also knew that it was right in the sense that labor was the best-organized egalitarian force in society. I knew that Tom [Hayden] rejected that; but he didn't come from a home where anyone had benefited from the labor movement. And I knew that Rachelle had her own ax to grind. You could see where the grind was coming from: the LID was paying our bills. She had an interest in making labor central."

Ross made a diligent effort to arrive at some kind of compromise. His proposed solution, which Horowitz accepted, was relatively simple. Two paragraphs in praise of labor would be tacked onto Hayden's draft. ("A new politics must include a revitalized labor movement. . . . Middle class students, still the main actors in the embryonic upsurge, have yet to overcome their ignorance, and even vague hostility, for what they see as 'middle class labor' bureaucrats.") And two paragraphs would be added to soften the stress that Hayden had laid on the university as the locus of social change. ("We need not indulge in illusions: the university system cannot complete a movement of ordinary people making demands for a better life. . . . We must look outwards to the less exotic but more lasting struggles for justice.")[18]

Bit by bit, section by section, the general outlines of the rewritten manifesto began to take shape in the scattered circles of delegates discussing the different issues. Apart from the question of labor, the most difficult work on the manifesto involved the sections on Communism and anti-Communism. After the scene with Harrington, it was clear that Hayden's draft was going to have to be extensively revised if the organization was not to be summarily drummed out of the democratic left.

The obvious—and indeed, the easiest—concession was to preface the appropriate part of the manifesto with the necessary ritual pledge of anti-Communism. Richard Flacks, like Steve Max, saw no harm in such a statement. "It was not something I wanted to fight over," says Max; "I was probably more willing to concede than some of the people who came from liberal backgrounds." Flacks, who had similar sentiments, volunteered to help rewrite the anti-Communism section: "I was afraid that Hayden's mood, and Haber's, was 'We will not concede anything to the anti-Communists.' And I kept thinking, Well, there's a set of statements which should go into the manifesto which dissociate ourselves from the Soviet model. Let's just write them."

By late Thursday, the group on "Communism" had given the green light for Flacks to compose some new language, with Hayden looking over his shoulder—another rare instance in which actual rewriting occurred at Port Huron, in this case because the issue was so sensitive. The two of them set up shop in the dining room, with

Flacks at the typewriter. Hayden was still bitterly opposed to making too many concessions to Harrington.

Hayden's bitterness was rooted in his experiences in the South. Some of the most prominent older Southern civil rights activists were former Communists or people who had been active in one of the Communist popular-front organizations of the Thirties. Harrington shunned such people—a practice that struck Hayden as insane. He also had no patience with some of the criticisms made of SNCC: "They were seeing SNCC though the historical prism of the Russian Revolution," says Hayden. "And so somebody they didn't like always reminded them of Stalin. You know, some authoritarian black student leader is exactly like Joseph Stalin—even though he's in danger of going to jail, has no army, is regionally and racially isolated, and this is a democracy that is isolating him. Through the framework of the old left, everything was reduced to whether you were a 'Stalinist' or not. I cannot explain to you how exasperating this became to people who were full of life and itching to get going."

With Hayden watching, Flacks worked carefully to find the right tone. As the night wore on, Hayden, exhausted, slumped under the table, jogging himself awake periodically to check on Flacks's progress. Hayden's original denunciation of "unreasoning anti-Communism" remained in. But Flacks put a sharply worded paragraph at the beginning of the section on "Communism and Foreign Policy." "As democrats," wrote Flacks, "we are in basic opposition to the communist system. The Soviet Union, as a system, rests on the total suppression of opposition, as well as a vision of the future in the name of which much human life has been sacrificed, and numerous small and large denials of human dignity rationalized."[19]

In the early hours of Friday morning, Hayden, satisfied at last with Flacks's new language, threw his sleeping bag across the doorway between the dining room and the main meeting hall. The people walking over him on the way to breakfast would serve as his alarm clock. He did not want to miss a minute of the final plenary session.[20]

A New Beginning

On Friday, the entire group began formally to discuss the manifesto section by section. The agenda for the final meeting of the full convention was determined by the "bones" that had been picked by the small groups.

A sentence in the "values" section, for example, sparked a debate about human nature. Hayden's draft declared that "We regard *Man* as infinitely precious and infinitely perfectible." Mary Varela reminded the gathering of the doctrine of original sin and argued that it was wrong to overemphasize the perfectibility of man. Jim Monsonis, speaking from a Niebuhrian perspective, agreed. He also argued that it was a strategic mistake to retain the language about infinite perfectibility: it would only alienate Christian radicals. Convinced by such arguments (Michael Harrington too had objected to this language), the group directed the style committee to reword the sentence: "We regard *men* as infinitely precious and possessed of unfulfilled capacities for reason, freedom, and love."[21]

So it went throughout the day and into the evening. It was agreed that the sections on "Anti-Communism" and on "Communism and Foreign Policy" would be substantially revised, along the lines indicated by Flacks's new draft. The style committee was directed to rework the section on "Deterrence Policy," apparently in an effort to eliminate the clumsy and slightly flippant use of rhetorical questions in Hayden's draft ("Can international stability be pivoted around Doomsday weapons? How long?"). A paragraph was deleted that broached the vexed topic of support for authoritarian regimes ("because only mass participation in struggles against poverty and illiteracy will bring about the conditions for a democratic social order"). The sections on "The Economy" were recast freely by Robb Burlage, who presented his suggestions to the convention with a joke: "We accept the draft of Brother Hayden, with certain revisions by Brother Karl Marx."[22]

In addition to such major changes, a host of minor revisions were accepted, though it is not clear which, if any, of them came up for debate by the full convention. The printed version, for example, omits a passing remark that "private enterprise is not inherently immoral or undemocratic—indeed it may at times contribute to offset elitist tendencies."[23] Hayden's phrase conceded too much to the free market for some of the socialists in the group.

Even more interesting was the deletion of three sentences in Hayden's draft that obliquely alluded to the undemocratic implications of the U.S. Constitution: "Historically and currently, American politics are built on a desire to deploy and neutralize the 'evil drives' of men. . . . They have . . . tended to diminish general interest in citizenship and have encouraged the consolidation of irresponsibility at higher levels of government. Politics today are organized for policy paralysis and minority domination, not for fluid change and mass participation."[24] "I don't remember any specific discussion of this," says Richard Flacks, "but I can well imagine people saying, 'We don't need to tackle that.' We want to rest our premises on the U.S. Constitution. I think the broad point is that the first draft is Tom in the full flower of being a young intellectual and expressing himself more fully than he had ever done before, and therefore there are these personal touches. But he was really trying to write a manifesto for a generation. You had to make it broadly understandable, realizable, and he was very willing to play that role."

The convention continued into the early hours of Saturday morning. By now, even a blasé participant like Steve Max had been seduced by the ferment of talk and the sense that history was being made. Max remembers taking a walk outside after midnight and watching the aurora borealis: "It seemed *prophetic*—there was this enormous display going on in the sky over Port Huron."

At about five o'clock that morning, when the final sections, on foreign policy and Europe, came up for discussion, the group nodded a comatose assent to a set of revisions proposed by Michael Vester, the student from German SDS, concerning NATO and the Berlin Wall.

As the first rays of sunlight began to stream into the hall where the plenary was winding down its work on the manifesto, some delegates, half-delirious with fatigue, began to feel an almost supernatural sense of euphoria. "That was the climax of the whole week," says Richard Flacks: "the sun rising in the middle of the discussion. I thought it was very symbolic."

Hayden joked that he didn't know whether the sun was rising or setting. But the work of the convention was nearly done. Once all the "bones" had been picked over, the group voted to accept the manifesto as amended. Even though some of the final wording of what would become known as *The Port Huron Statement* remained unsettled for several weeks, the key ideas were in place and many of the crucial phrases already polished:

> We are people of this generation, bred in at least modest comfort, housed now in universities, looking uncomfortably to the world we inherit. . . .
>
> Americans are in withdrawal from public life, from any collective effort at directing their own affairs. Some regard this national doldrums as a sign of healthy approval of the established order—but is it approval by consent or manipulated acquiescence? [Here the manifesto offered implicit rejoinders to some of the questions that Hayden had raised

in his draft notes on democracy.] . . . Still others think that the national quietude is a necessary consequence of the need for elites to solve complex and specialized problems of modern industrial societies—but, then, why should business elites decide foreign policy, and who controls the elites anyway, and are they solving mankind's problems? Others, finally, shrug knowingly and announce that full democracy has never existed anywhere in the past—but why lump qualitatively different civilizations together, and how can a social order work well if its best thinkers are sceptics, and is man really doomed forever to the domination of today? . . .

The very isolation of the individual—from power and community and ability to aspire—means the rise of a democracy without publics. [Here was the stamp of C. Wright Mills.] With the great mass of people structurally remote and psychologically hesitant with respect to democratic institutions, those institutions themselves attenuate and become, in the fashion of a vicious circle, progressively less accessible to those few who aspire to serious participation in social affairs. . . .

In a time of supposed prosperity, moral complacency and political manipulation, a new left cannot rely on aching stomachs to be the engine force of social reform. The case for change, for alternatives that will involve uncomfortable personal efforts, must be argued as never before. The university is a relevant place for all of these activities. . . .

We are convinced that the first task of any new social movement is to convince people that the search for orienting theories and the creation of human values are both possible and worthwhile. [Here was the quest for "a politics of vision and relevance."]

The goal of man and society should be human independence: a concern not with image of popularity but with finding a meaning in life that is personally authentic; a quality of mind not compulsively driven by a sense of powerlessness. . . .

Human relationships should involve fraternity and honesty. . . . Loneliness, estrangement, isolation describe the vast distance between man and man today. These dominant tendencies cannot be overcome by better personnel management, nor by improved gadgets, but only when a love of man by man overcomes the idolatrous worship of things by man. . . .

As a *social system* we seek the establishment of a participatory democracy, governed by two central aims: that the individual share in those social decisions determining the quality and direction of his life; that society be organized to encourage independence in men and provide the media for their common participation.[25]

And so the SDS manifesto passed into history. The convention hurriedly held elections. Tom Hayden became president, Paul Booth vice president. Then, the group staggered into the sunlight. "We were exhilarated at the end," says Booth: "We really thought we had done a great job. We *knew* we had a great document."[26]

"I felt like I had been reborn, in the political sense," says Richard Flacks. "I thought that we had done something important."

"It was a little like starting a journey," says Bob Ross. "We all felt very close to each other."[27]

"I was excited," says Al Haber. "Since the organization got Tom to be president, I could get the hell out of there and go back to school. I'd done enough. I felt my work was done."

The group walked to the shore of Lake Huron and stood, some of them silently holding hands.

"It was exalting," says Sharon Jeffrey. "We felt that we were different, and that we were going to do things differently. We thought that we knew what had to be done, and that we were going to do it. It felt like the dawn of a new age."

CHAPTER SEVEN

BEYOND THE COLD WAR

T HE CONVENTION FINISHED, Tom Hayden and Al Haber returned to New York, Hayden to become president of SDS,
Haber to wrap up his official duties and begin preparing to
return to school in Ann Arbor. At the top of Hayden's agenda was
finishing the manifesto—the drafting committee had set a deadline
of August 15. Large stretches of Hayden's first draft had been virtually untouched. However, in the few places where extensive
changes had been mandated, they involved matters of the utmost
sensitivity on the democratic left, as the angry debates at Port Huron
had reminded the students.[1]

While the drafting committee of Hayden, Haber and Bob Ross
settled down to the task of rewriting, trouble was brewing in the
inner circle of the League for Industrial Democracy. Michael Harrington, for one, had departed from Port Huron in a blustery mood.
The SDS manifesto, he thought, was profoundly mistaken about
Communism, about the Soviet Union, about the labor movement,
about the role of students—none of them trivial matters.

As soon as he arrived back in New York, Harrington phoned Rach-
elle Horowitz to find out how the convention had gone: "I said,
'Were there any changes made in the draft?' and Rachelle said,
'No.' "[2]

Harrington blew up. "Here were these young people," he says: "I'd
worked with them, been loyal, helped and supported as best I could.
I'd given them my honest opinion. And then they didn't change a
single thing. I felt that I had been totally and completely ignored by
everybody there."

126

In fact, as we have seen, the group at Port Huron had tried diligently to meet Harrington's objections. The convention had even taken pains to accommodate Rachelle Horowitz. She had participated actively in the deliberations and decisions over revising the manifesto. So why did she now mislead Harrington?

Horowitz insists that she was being sincere: "I remember that some things were changed," she says, "but they were changed in a sort of opportunistic way, like 'Let's shut LID up.' On the substantial issues, we went down the tubes."[3] Harrington agrees: "From her point of view, it was true that the changes made at Port Huron were insignificant." Some of those on the other side, however, speculate that the young Schachtmanites in the YPSL faction, unable to win control by recruiting new students, had settled on a backdoor coup, hoping to destroy the new organization and capture its shell.

One thing is clear: Horowitz's report to Harrington virtually guaranteed that the full fury of LID would be unleashed against Hayden and Haber. "I was a godsend to the traditionalists on the LID board," says Harrington: "I was relatively young . . . and had been very active in the anti-HUAC fight, so I could not be dismissed as a redbaiting old fogey. I therefore became the spokesman for taking harsh organizational measures against SDS."[4]

Invitation to an Inquest

Egged on by Harrington, the officers of LID summoned the SDS leadership in New York to an emergency meeting on June 28. The purpose of this informal meeting was to review the convention and manifesto. Despite the lack of a revised document to stand on, Hayden, Haber, Bob Ross and Steve Max agreed to appear. Since Harrington was unable to attend, the questioning at the June 28 meeting was handled by Harry Fleischman, the LID chairman, and Vera Rony, the LID executive secretary. Tom Hayden did most of the talking for SDS.

According to the rough minutes of this meeting that were later circulated by LID, Hayden began by summarizing the gist of the manifesto. He did not think, he said, that SDS had taken either a "socialist or liberal doctrinaire position."

When Hayden turned from domestic to foreign issues, the meeting began to heat up. He suggested that the Soviet Union seemed "more disposed to disarming" than the United States, which had developed

"an economic commitment" to continuing the arms race. "I probably said the Soviets had more of an economic interest in reducing
the arms race because of their economic situation," he recalls.
Speaking on behalf of the group, Hayden was veering perilously close
to the kinds of sentiments that the convention had worked so hard
to qualify.

Fleischman grew testy: "Does the Berlin Wall show the desire or
possibility for disarmament?" Rony wondered why Hayden hadn't
applied his strenuous standard of democracy to the Soviet Union:
"Since your whole thesis is the importance of individual participation, is there in this commentary on the Soviets any comment on
the role of the individual as a free and active agent there?"

Hayden countered with a paraphrase of the revised manifesto's
unequivocal condemnation of Communism. But the longer he
talked, the more he let his guard down. He volunteered that SDS
was "critical of many domestic attitudes toward Communism."
Rony snapped back: "I understand the LID was included, which was
picturesque." (An explicit critique of LID never appeared in the draft
—a good example of how misinformation helped set the tone of this
meeting.) Hayden was beginning to feel cornered. Denying that SDS
had specifically criticized LID or the Socialist Party, he explained
that the group's concern was with "the continual use and misuse of
traditional categories of anti-Communism—rhetoric, epithets: 'Stalinoid,' 'Stalinist,' 'Trotskyist,' etc."

Fleischman objected: "Is there any analysis of how the Communists have brought general onus upon themselves?" Hayden could
no longer muster a solid defense. "That's not in the manifesto," he
conceded: "We put the blame on non-Communist America." He
explained that he had not met many people with firsthand experience of the Communists, and "would have to refer to your experience." Rony now pounced: "You wouldn't have to refer to Harry's
experience. [There are] countless books on this sort of thing. You
consider yourselves intellectuals; [you] could be expected to have
read some of these books."

Whether he knew it or not, Hayden was on the ropes. He struggled
to regain his composure with a succinct summary of what the Port
Huron statement was trying to accomplish: "What we want to do is
find a way to end the Cold War and increase democracy in the U.S.
and we think the two are related. We advocate universal controlled
disarmament, foreign-policy initiatives in strengthening of international organization, trying to do what will create political rather
than military foreign policy in the U.S. and Soviet Union."

His summary fell on unsympathetic ears. Rony called his comments "uninformed." Fleischman accused him of an unwillingness to apply the same moral standards to the Soviet Union and the United States. Rony: "If you don't think Moscow would be delighted with your document, you're wrong." Hayden: "[I] have [the] feeling I'm dealing with a Cold War situation in this room."[5]

It is not clear whether Hayden grasped the implications of the tone and the line of questioning in this impromptu inquest—twenty-two-year-olds sometimes lack political seasoning. "I don't know if Hayden understood how strongly the LID guys felt about Communism," says Steve Max looking back, and Richard Flacks agrees: "Tom was very new to the intricacies of political analysis from the left." It did not occur to him, for example, simply to keep reiterating the sinister and undemocratic character of the Soviet Union and the Communist Party, any more than it would have occured to him to declare Walter Reuther the leader of the vanguard of the American proletariat. Several days afterward, the SDS leadership reported that "although there was sharp debate, the meeting ended cordially with the expressed desire for further discussion."[6]

Convinced that fraternal discussion would continue, Hayden and Haber, with Vera Rony's blessing, left early on July 3 for Washington, D.C. They visited the White House and met with Arthur Schlesinger, Jr., and then went on to Capitol Hill to talk to liberal Democratic congressmen who had been outspoken in their support for new American disarmament initiatives. As Haber recalls it, they were in a congressman's office that afternoon when a phone call came from Steve Max in New York. "All bets are off," said Max. He had just received a memo from the LID executive board—and it contained yet another ultimatum.

The day before, the LID board had met to review the minutes of the June 28 inquest. Though Haber, as a nonvoting student representative on the board, was entitled to attend this meeting, he had not been informed about it. Alarmed by Hayden's performance, the LID board decided to question the SDS leadership in a more formal hearing later in the week. The LID memo that Max had received in New York directed Hayden and Haber to appear at a meeting on July 6 in order "to discover whether or not the officers of the SDS acted and plan to act in accordance with the basic principles of the parent organization. Until that time no materials, manifestos, constitutions, or other publications having to do with policy in any way, shape or form whatsoever may be mailed or distributed by the students under the identification of SDS, nor shall the LID pay for the preparation, printing and mailing or distribution of any such material."[7]

Hayden and Haber were stunned. They rushed back to New York City, where they spent the fourth of July writing two letters. One called the SDS National Executive Committee into emergency session in New York; the other informed the LID officers of their willingness to appear at the July 6 hearing. As the letter to the SDS committee makes plain, Hayden and Haber were finally clear about the threat they faced: LID, they warned, might attempt "to set conditions regarding the *content*" of the manifesto, or the "policy *status* of the adopted manifesto"; it might take "some form of punitive action toward Hayden, Haber and other staff members"; it might "dissolve all relations with SDS and discredit it within the liberal community."[8]

In their letter to the LID officers, Hayden and Haber managed to sound measured and calm. They expressed "concern"—about the arbitrariness of Haber's exclusion from the July 2 meeting; about the injustice of reviewing the work of the convention without reading the revised manifesto; about the unfairness of silencing the organization without warning. They nevertheless tried to put the best face on the situation: "It is our hope and belief that differences in approach and judgement can exist and are healthy in the organization."[9]

On July 6, a number of SDS members gathered at the national office and waited while Haber and Hayden faced members of the LID board. The room was packed with veteran trade unionists from the ILGWU (the International Ladies Garment Workers Union), officials of the Jewish Labor Committee, representatives of the Socialist Party. The board charged that the Port Huron convention was "unrepresentative of the organization, undemocratic in its operation and outside the basic principles of the LID in its actions."

What was new in this indictment was the charge of "undemocratic" procedures. At the hearing, Harrington explained: "There *is* no SDS as a functioning organization with a political life. It does not exist. So how can you get a representative convention from a nonorganization?" Since Hayden and Haber, like almost every other participant, had felt as profoundly *alive* politically at Port Huron as they had ever felt in their lives, it is hard to guess what sense they made of Harrington's simple and sublimely devastating proposition that SDS was a "nonorganization."

Warming to his task, Harrington went on: "Besides, this document of cosmic scope was *given* to the delegates—that's obviously not representative. It would require a year's discussion to get a really representative document. This can't even try to express the view of the people who were there—even *that's* not possible in such a short meeting. A founding convention should take ten days to two weeks and a year of discussion."

Hayden pointed out that the manifesto was "a living document" and an invitation to debate and reflection—not some pie-eyed tyrant's version of the Ten Commandments.

Harrington changed the subject. What about the case of the delegate from the Progressive Youth Organizing Committee? This group wasn't even a front—it was, Harrington shouted, "the *youth* group of the CP!" Did SDS seriously believe that LID would allow a *Communist* to be seated at this convention?

Hayden pointed out that the convention had decided simply to seat an observer, not to endorse the policies of the Communist Party.

"We should have nothing to do with such people," snapped Harrington. Harry Fleischman agreed: "Would you give seats to the Nazis too?" Harrington then hurled one of the most withering epithets in the Schachtmanite lexicon: *united frontism.* He accused SDS of committing the venal political sin of "accepting reds to your meeting. . . . You knew this would send LID through the roof. This issue was settled on the left ten or twenty years ago—and that you could countenance any united frontism now is inconceivable."

Hayden was at wit's end. "Just *read* the values section," he pleaded at one point. "We use a single standard. You have to *look* at the document."

Harrington was unimpressed: "Document shmocuments. Slaiman and I said that this was antithetical to the LID and everything it's stood for."

And so it went, for two grueling hours. Hayden and Haber were soft on Communism. Ferocious in their criticism of America, they were willing simply to tap the Soviets on the wrist. They had even let the convention elect Steve Max as the new Field Secretary—despite the fact that his father had once been managing editor of *The Daily Worker,* the notorious Communist newspaper, and that Steve Max himself had once belonged to the Labor Youth League, the notorious Communist youth group.

The meeting was adjourned after Haber pleaded for time to present written evidence that Harrington's objections at Port Huron had in fact been "taken to heart."[10]

The LID board, however, was in no mood for temporizing. Although they decreed that the formal decisions of the Port Huron convention should be allowed to stand, they announced their intention to fire Hayden and Haber, to censor all SDS materials leaving the central office and to appoint a new "student secretary" of SDS more responsive to the concerns and traditions of LID.[11]

Lockout and Appeal

The emergency meeting of the SDS national executive committee began in Steve Max's New York apartment on Sunday, July 8, and lasted, on and off, for nearly a week. Emotions ran high. "All of us felt our future careers were going to be ruined," says Bob Ross: "America's best liberals were on the lip of red-baiting us out of existence. We knew we weren't Communists, but the idea that our parent organization thought we were, was Kafkaesque." "We had the feeling we had been attacked from behind," says Paul Booth: "We were blindsided. We did not leave Port Huron thinking we were going to be in a war."[12]

The first issue before them was LID. Almost everyone agreed that their ties to LID had become a liability as well as an asset. Should they simply break these ties, or should they try to patch things up?

As Hayden wrote at the time, many members were worried about the viability of "future relations with the LID. There are hurt feelings, disagreements about political priorities, generational gaps which, along with serious interests in full autonomy and freedom to participate in political lobbying and action, constitute a powerful case for establishing an independent, though politically and organizationally cooperative relation with LID."[13]

Apart from the obvious disagreements over political direction, the LID tie sharply limited the possible scope of SDS action, for the simple reason that LID was a tax-exempt educational organization. "The LID was extremely nervous," recalls Max. "Mainly it was because of the Communism, but also it was because of their tax status. That they talked about endlessly." LID also distrusted figures like Hayden simply because they came from outside New York City. "The ILGWU for years had an 'out of town' department," explains Max. "Which makes perfect sense when you're in New York. But suppose you're in a local in Michigan? How would you feel about being a member of the 'out of town' department?"

There were good reasons, then, for leaving LID immediately. But there were other, more compelling reasons, the group agreed after discussing the pros and cons, for maintaining the tie and trying to set the relationship right again. Staying with LID meant two salaries, worth $120 a week, and office overhead; it meant being part of a ready-made network of links to the liberal and labor left in America. Leaving under a cloud in effect meant breaking these links, perhaps irrevocably, just at the time when SDS was trying to reach out to a broader public. It meant closing off numerous avenues for fund-raising, perhaps forever. It meant devoting a number of months, perhaps years, simply to putting an independent SDS back on a solid financial footing. In the process, precious time for organizing would be lost.

After a consensus had been reached to patch up the SDS tie to LID, the group resolved on a course of action. Since part of the problem was confusion over the content of the manifesto, the revisions mandated at Port Huron were to be completed immediately and the revised manifesto mimeographed by the end of the week. In addition, the group planned to compose a detailed "appeal," outlining their grievances against the LID board and clarifying the SDS position on the major issues.

After the committee wound up its deliberations on the night of July 9, Haber and a few others went to the national SDS office in downtown Manhattan. They discovered that the lock had been changed. "Well, this had happened to me once before," says Haber, who put his skill with tools to good use: "I picked the lock with a paper clip." They carted out the mailing plates that Haber had so laboriously compiled over the previous two years.

LID was playing hardball. The short memo that Vera Rony sent to the LID board announcing another emergency meeting on July 12 summarized the most serious of the charges against the students. They had "adopted a popular front position." They had "bitterly scored [American] foreign policy" and "placed the blame for the cold war largely on the U.S." while "making the merest passing criticism of Soviet actions." They had allowed a Communist to be "seated at the convention and given speaking rights."[14]

In the twenty-eight-page "appeal" that SDS composed in response, the young radicals defended themselves and accused LID of "falsehood, exaggeration and slander." The aim of the appeal was to restore the *status quo ante*—to keep Hayden and Max on salary, to keep the national office free of censorship and to keep the organization on a more or less autonomous footing.[15]

The manifesto that SDS had ratified at Port Huron, they insisted, was consonant with "the sentiments of liberal and radical democrats today." Although parts of the document were admittedly controversial, "democrats must raise issues in a sincere and public way." The manifesto was in any case never intended as the final word, as the frontispiece indicated: "This document is presented as a document with which SDS officially identifies, but also as a living document open to change with our times and experience. It is a beginning: in our own debate and education, in our dialogue with society."[16]

As the revised passages on Communism in the final draft of the manifesto clearly showed, the "excellent discussion . . . held with Mr. Harrington" at Port Huron had already led to changes in SDS thinking. "This is a perfect example of the way we wish to carry on relations with our elders in the LID—through discussion and dialogue, not through parental censorship or even compulsory arbitration." By opening the issues of Soviet policy and anti-Communism for fresh debate, SDS was simply trying "to avoid the unthinking hysteria about the expansionary mechanism of the Soviet system which freezes the United States into an automatic 'massive retaliation' policy and contributes to the patterns now found in the Cold War."[17]

"We share with the LID common values, constitutional ideals and democratic principles," concluded the SDS appeal. But "when one is attempting sincerely to understand what is happening in the dizzying New World of 1962, he cannot exercise his intellect with an Iron Curtain built in. . . . We must answer our own questions; in our own time; in our own way."[18]

This appeal, together with the distribution of copies of the revised manifesto, had the desired effect. It was hard to argue with the document. In addition, several influential friends and members of LID interceded on behalf of the students and in the name of common sense. Harold Taylor recalled how he "was impressed not only by the intelligence and forcefulness with which these young men of twenty-two made arguments which were essentially my own, but by the fact that they showed more faith in the power of democracy and in what they could do with it in political action than did their elders in the parent organization." And Norman Thomas, the elder statesman of American socialism, interceded in an effort to calm Harrington. As Richard Flacks recalls, Thomas took the long view: "He said, 'I've seen a lot of manifestoes in my day, and this one's no worse, nor no better. Give these kids enough rope, they'll either hang themselves or make something of it. You don't need to crack down on them; just go forward with them.' "[19]

Thomas became a mediator between the two contending parties.

LID, he declared, "is by no means a creedal organization." Although Communism was certainly an undemocratic social system and the citizens of the Soviet Union lacked basic political freedoms, "we share the hope of those who believe that there is some evolutionary progress in the USSR. . . . These views by no means prohibit dialogues with Communists or Communist sympathizers, but they do assert the traditional values of the LID."[20]

The LID board backed off, and tempers began to cool. By the end of July, LID had sent SDS the text of a "proposed LID–SDS agreement."

Growing Up Red

A year later, President Kennedy himself reopened the public debate over Communism and the Cold War by saying, in his famous American University speech in June of 1963, "Let us reexamine our attitude toward the Soviet Union." By the mid-Sixties, it was difficult to read the revised *Port Huron Statement* and to find in it anything radically different from the positions shared by many mainstream politicians: "Our paranoia about the Soviet Union," declared the students in 1962, "has made us incapable of achieving agreements absolutely necessary for disarmament and the preservation of peace. We are hardly able to see the possibility that the Soviet Union, though not 'peace-loving,' may be seriously interested in disarmament."[21]

The blind passion of Harrington's anti-Communism, by contrast, soon came to seem like an atavism—even to Harrington himself. "I should have had the maturity to understand that young people groping toward a political ideology were not to be treated as if they were old Trotskyist faction fighters following a line," says Harrington. "But on the other hand, coming out of the Schachtmanite movement, where *the* question was the Russian question—it was a line of blood. I knew people who knew Trotsky personally. The Communists were the people who had stuck a pickax in his skull. I'd been brought up on these emotions, and also on Catholic emotions. When it came to Stalinism and Max Schachtman, its emotional quality and the Catholic anti-Communism I had encountered when I was young had some similarities."

Steve Max recalls seeing Harrington in the mid-Fifties distributing newspapers outside a hall where the Labor Youth League was holding a festival. The headline on Harrington's newspaper read: "STA-

LINISTS, DID A MADMAN LEAD YOUR MOVEMENT?" "My God," says Max, "they printed a whole newspaper just to hand out to *us*. The Schachtmanites lived for this. They spent a lot of time harassing and heckling us—it was a very incestuous world they lived in. The best thing that ever happened to them was the dissolution of the Labor Youth League. That made them turn outward. That was when they discovered the Democratic party and the strategy of realignment."

By 1962, Steve Max and Michael Harrington in fact *agreed* on the strategy of realignment: they were in harmony on nearly every political point. Yet because of Max's background, Harrington shunned him. "Steve was coming out of a Communist family," explains Harrington, "and I was still being idiotic about his Communist past. He was not willing to say that the entire Communist Party had simply been an agent of Stalinism. He understood that it *had* been an agent of Stalinism, but that it had also been something else. I would say today that he understood some of the complexities a hell of a lot better than I did."

The term "red diaper baby" scarcely begins to convey these complexities. To grow up in a Communist milieu in the late Forties and early Fifties was to learn patriotic love and fear of the state simultaneously. For the parents of these children, it was a time of witch-hunts and blacklists. The Communist Party responded, in part, by stressing civil liberties and its commitment to the Constitution and the Bill of Rights. While they watched their parents hold hushed discussions about the Rosenberg case and Joseph McCarthy, the children were also taught to honor the America of Thomas Jefferson and Abraham Lincoln. As a Party slogan from the popular-front period of the Thirties had put it, "Communism is 20th century Americanism." In 1937, when the Daughters of the American Revolution neglected to celebrate Paul Revere's ride, the Young Communist League paraded in New York City with a sign, "The DAR forgets but the YCL remembers." Though such patriotic slogans were patently cynical—the Party abruptly stopped using them after the Nazi–Soviet pact was signed in 1939—a similarly fulsome "Americanism" was revived by the Party during World War II and the McCarthy era, shaping the Communist youth culture of the post-war period. Mickey Flacks remembers learning by heart Paul Robeson's "Ballad for Americans," a patriotic battle hymn. After reading a hagiographic biography written by the Communist author Howard Fast, Bob Ross came to revere Tom Paine. At the experimental Communist summer camp that Richard Flacks attended, a special effort was made to foster a climate of free expression and democratic participation.[22]

Different families reacted to the repression of the Fifties in different ways. Ross's parents withdrew from politics. Richard Flacks remembers the family throwing out its library of left-wing books and keeping copies of *The Daily Worker* hidden out of sight. Mickey Flacks, by contrast, remembers that *her* parents made a point of leaving *The Daily Worker* on the coffee table and cheerfully built up the family library of left-wing books from the discards of neighbors. "It was a very scary time," says Steve Max. "Everybody was getting hauled off to jail, the Rosenbergs were electrocuted, all the spy stuff was going on: you never knew from week to week exactly what was going to happen the next week. I never thought much about it. It was just the way life was."

Despite the variations from family to family, the experience of growing up in a Communist milieu had taught all these SDS members two indelible lessons. First, Khrushchev's revelations in 1956 showed them that the humane and libertarian ideals that they had learned to cherish growing up had been flagrantly violated in the name of Communism; Joseph Stalin had been one of the bloodiest butchers of the twentieth century. By the end of 1956, the SDS members who had once been involved in the youth politics of the Party had left, never to return. They were teenagers abruptly disabused of any illusions about Communism with a human face.

The second lesson this group learned, though equally powerful, was very different. They learned that America was not always the epitome of democracy and decency, that patriotic rhetoric was often empty prattle and that the official picture of Communists as immoral monsters was a lie. Bob Ross recalls that "the woman who taught me to drive a car was a red. Her husband, who worked as a salad-maker in a cafeteria his whole adult life, was a hero to me: he had fought in Spain, in the civil war against Franco. God knows they didn't understand about Stalin; they wanted to resist the bad news [of 1956]. But they were complete human beings. They were soft, gentle, caring people. I knew that they weren't Stalin—they were not a red terror. They were totally unlike what the newspapers and the teachers in school were telling me they were like." Indeed, such people showed a quiet courage in the face of terrible threats. Ross recalls the experience of his high school sweetheart, the daughter of prominent Communists: "She would tell me about the FBI watching her home. She told me about how the FBI approached her when she was in junior high school, before I knew her. They asked her whether she would like to talk about her mother and father." A state that asks an adolescent child to inform on her parents forfeits its moral authority.

Ignorance and Autonomy

In retrospect, it is easy to sympathize with the experience of people like Max, Ross and the Flackses. They had no interest in defending Communism; on the contrary. But they also had no interest in constantly apologizing for their past, or trying to keep it covered up. They came by their hostility to anti-Communism honestly: at stake was their political freedom.

It is also easy to see how Harrington's esoteric metaphysic of anti-Stalinism—a sophisticated Marxist variant of conservative Cold War dogmatics—had become a destructive obsession. Still, something important got lost in the blind passion that came to define Harrington's struggle with SDS. "To this day," says Harrington, "I think that the question of Stalinism was—and is—one of the central questions of politics. I believe that the worst thing that ever happened to socialism was Joseph Stalin. He did more than any other single person to discredit it, to caricature it, to destroy it, to subvert its moral stance."

In one of the many ironies of the episode, Steve Max and Richard Flacks—perhaps the two most prominent figures in SDS to come out of a Communist milieu—were also two of the figures most sympathetic to Harrington's point of view: they both knew from firsthand experience the kernel of hard truth in his hostility to Stalinism. Yet Harrington, by the sheer abrasiveness of his manner and the wildness of some of his charges, backed the young radicals into a corner. With his contumely fresh in their minds, many of them stubbornly embraced a kind of agnosticism about the history he brandished as a weapon of theological combat. A disregard of the past—a calculated innocence—became a perverse badge of their own political independence.

Tom Hayden, for example, today concedes that if the students in 1962 had been consistent in applying their moral and political principles, "those of us who were aroused about a cigarette butt being put onto the neck of a black student in the South would have been equally concerned about an ice pick being put into Trotsky's brain." At some point, though, the debate had ceased to be about principles, and had become instead a struggle over the autonomy of the younger generation. "For us," says Hayden, "the whole question of the Russian Revolution was mediated through what we perceived had become of the left. We had not been to Russia. We had not met Trotsky or Max Schachtman or any of the descendants of the various factions of the Russian Revolution. All we had met were people who were still entirely caught up in what we considered to be debates of fifty years' duration that were becoming quite stale. These people were out of touch with events in the United States. And these debates were confined to smaller and smaller groups of people in New York. And to understand what position you should take in the debate was tantamount to becoming a member of an Orthodox Jewish sect or the Catholic Church: you'd have to study the Talmud or the Catechism."

Scorned as a "catechism" that only craven acolytes could wish to master, the history of Communism in this century went largely unexamined. "The problem," says Bob Ross, "was to formulate ideas in a non-European way—and also in a way relevant to our times. There was this category in our minds, 'Old Left,' and that basically meant the Second, Third and Fourth Internationals and their wars, which we saw as unfruitful, uninteresting and irrelevant. In retrospect, of course, it turns out that one neglects this history at one's hazard. But for us there was a certain positive function: we wanted to be ignorant of all that."

Ignorant of history many of them defiantly remained. And seven years later the organization that they had struggled to set on an ecumenical and open-minded footing would pay the price. In 1969, after several dizzying years of anarchic grass-roots growth and increasingly arcane bickering over strategy among a new generation of leaders who were far more contemptuous of the past than the founding generation, SDS was successfully infiltrated and captured by the Progressive Labor Party—a disciplined cadre of self-styled Marxist-Leninists.

Perhaps that is why Alan Haber, looking back, speaks of the summer of 1962 so wistfully. "We shouldn't have been put under siege," says Haber. "The LID could have had a more generous attitude toward their offspring. Just as we were riding the crest of our new strength and making political connections in Washington, we were pulled up short. And it's hard to tell whether that was fortuitous in really galvanizing the organization that took shape at Port Huron, or whether it really turned us around in some negative way that didn't become apparent until some years later."[23]

An Uneasy Truce

As the summer drew to an end, SDS and LID negotiated the final details of a cease-fire. A LID proposal to retain Richard Roman as permanent SDS student secretary was shelved, while Steve Max was permitted to soldier on as the elected SDS field secretary. The revised SDS manifesto was circulated without censorship, and Michael Harrington wrote a letter in which he deplored the "confusion on all sides." For his part, Tom Hayden gave a qualified pledge of allegiance to the LID tradition: "If that tradition includes the development of social structure and individual character toward democratic community and personal freedom, respectively, then there can be no doubt of our roots. . . . But to be 'in a tradition' is not to be confused with being 'traditional.' "[24]

In September, after the NSA Congress in Columbus, Ohio, a new joint "Statement of Principles"—a formal armistice of sorts—was solemnly ratified by SDS and LID. For the occasion, LID sent a delegation that included Harrington and Norman Thomas.[25]

Still, relations remained tense. SDS members were forced to make a monthly donation to cover Steve Max's salary after LID refused to pay him. When Hayden prepared his "President's Report" for the first SDS membership bulletin that fall, LID insisted on censoring his draft, deleting a reference to "the smearing effects of the [LID] charges," among other passages. And when Michael Harrington approached Casey Hayden in Columbus, she said, "I know now what it must have been like to be attacked by Stalinists." "I had lost the confidence and trust of the young people," Harrington later wrote.[26]

In the mid-Sixties, Hayden recalled the episode with icy contempt. "It taught me that Social Democrats aren't radicals and can't be trusted," said Hayden. "It taught me what Social Democrats really think about civil liberties and organizational integrity."[27]

Years later, Hayden took a longer view: "This situation created a sense of 'them'—the old leftists—and 'us,' " he said. "Now we were embattled. They—not the right wing—were trying to prevent the growth of a new radical force. The names they called us reinforced our new left identity. . . . It was that positive communal experience at Port Huron, followed by this struggle for our own identity, that created such a sharp definition of ourselves. It's a unique experience to feel that you yourself are an agent of change. We felt, 'this is our destiny.' "[28]

CHAPTER EIGHT

PARTICIPATORY DEMOCRACY

I N JULY, 1962, the first mimeographed copies of the finished SDS manifesto appeared in New York, as part of the organization's effort to resolve its dispute with LID. Shortly afterward, copies were mailed out to members. At the end of the summer, SDS distributed the document to delegates at the annual NSA Congress in Columbus, Ohio. By then, it was being called *The Port Huron Statement*, to emphasize that it was a "living document." " 'Manifesto' sounds like 'Case closed,' " says Tom Hayden; " 'Statement' sounds like 'Take a look at this.' "[1]

"The effect of those ideas on other people was electric," says Hayden. "Whenever you handed it to someone who was in the civil rights movement," says Bob Ross, "you would have a positive response. People would read it and say, 'Oh yeah.' " At the NSA Congress that summer, a delegate from the University of Texas became so excited that she all but joined SDS on the spot. "By the time I started home," she wrote to fellow Texan Robb Burlage, "I felt a very real identity with the group, and found myself rather sad to be leaving. . . . Upon arriving here, I went over *The Port Huron Statement* in detail and now find myself more enthusiastic over the vision put forward therein to the point of effervescing these ideas to anyone even faintly inclined to have a comprehending ear."[2]

Speaking American

From the start, *The Port Huron Statement* had an almost mythic stature. Conceived with imagination and hope, it had been ratified through an exhilarating process of face-to-face debate. Its rhetoric was appealing, its moral tone urgent, its sweeping scope impressive. But it was rarely read carefully. Its analysis of domestic politics was quickly forgotten. Its critique of the Cold War, despite the furor it provoked in 1962, soon came to seem unexceptionable. Its section on "values," by contrast, was consulted for years afterward. And one phrase, above all—*participatory democracy*—came to capture the spirit of the convention, the soul of the document, the essence of the New Left. It became, literally, a catchword—used, over and over again, to recruit, to convert, to convince.

At first glance, the phrase seems virtually self-evident. It evokes an image that is both familiar and fresh. Let "the individual share in those social decisions affecting the quality and direction of his life." What could be more American? "Democracy" is a term that politicians and teachers routinely use to rouse audiences to stand up and salute the flag. But by taking such patriotic rhetoric and treating it as a transcendent political vision, Hayden presented the extension of democracy to new areas of social life as a matter of both home-spun common sense and political romance. A sign of hope, the notion of democracy became the object of a quest: "*We seek* the establishment of a democracy of individual participation."[3]

But what exactly were the young radicals in search of? How did the notion orient their quest? What, in short, did participatory democracy *mean*?

A consideration of these questions leads into a labyrinth. As a catchword, "participatory democracy" is remarkable for its *resonance*—its multiple layers of implied meaning, often communicated through allusions to authors like C. Wright Mills and Arnold Kaufman; its *elasticity*—the ease with which it could be stretched to cover a wide variety of different political situations; and its *instability*—a volatility caused, in part, by its range of different possible meanings and the implicit contradictions they contained.

At the time, it meant different things to different people. But in 1962 it did not yet mean what some subsequent historians have assumed that it meant—for example, that in the ideal "democracy of individual participation," some form of consensus would replace voting, hierarchy, and the traditional machinery of representative institutions. As we have seen, Hayden in 1962 followed his mentor Arnold Kaufman in treating participatory democracy as a *supplement* to representative democracy. This is one point on which virtually all the key participants at Port Huron agree. As Richard Flacks puts it, "Participatory democracy did *not* mean abandoning organizational structures of the usual sort, like elected officers and parliamentary procedure. We were thinking of participatory democracy at that time as a concept of social change, not as a set of principles for guiding the internal organizational life of SDS. We began as a small organization in which it didn't seem that much of a problem for leadership and membership to control each other, so to speak, and to interact with each other."[4]

To take another example, Michael Harrington has written that the students at Port Huron were "nonsocialists who took the formal promises of American democracy with deep and innocent seriousness." Such comments reinforce a widespread impression that they were naive reformers who grew more radical as they became disillusioned. There is an element of truth in this view. But as Paul Booth points out, the "deep and innocent seriousness" of *The Port Huron Statement* was "a *literary* style that we affected. There was no question that we knew that dramatizing the rhetoric versus the reality of democracy was politically efficacious as well as in harmony with our own feelings."[5]

These misunderstandings are a by-product of *The Port Huron Statement* itself. Compared with the systematic approach of Hayden's draft note on democracy, the discussion in the *Statement* is both lyrical and vague. This is not surprising. Manifestos generally place exhortation before analysis, and when it comes to "making values explicit," *The Port Huron Statement* is no exception, despite a caveat that "we have no sure formulas, no closed theories." Unlike Hayden's draft note, the *Statement* avoids any detailed discussion or definition of "participatory democracy"; nowhere does it seriously entertain doubts and questions. Its retort to the objection that "full democracy has never existed anywhere in the past" is revealing: "How can a social order work well if its best thinkers are sceptics?" As Al Haber wrote at the time, the "democratic values" of SDS were meant to support "broad consensus rather than a formal doctrine."[6]

To this extent, the ambiguity surrounding participatory democracy in *The Port Huron Statement* was deliberate: more than an empty slogan but less than a formal doctrine, it was an open invitation to embark on a shared adventure of political discovery.

A Conflict of Interpretations

The question remains. What did participatory democracy mean? What, specifically, did it mean in 1962? Here are answers given by some of the people who were at Port Huron:

To Al Haber, participatory democracy was "a model, another way of organizing society." But it was above all "a charge to action. It was how *to be*. To be out there doing. Rather than an ideology or a theory."[7]

To Tom Hayden, participatory democracy meant "number one, *action*; we believed in action. We had behind us the so-called decade of apathy; we were emerging from apathy. What's the opposite of apathy? Active participation. Citizenship. Making history. Secondly, we were very directly influenced by the civil rights movement in its student phase, which believed that by personally committing yourself and taking risks, you could enter history and try to change it after a hundred years of segregation. And so it was this element of participation in democracy that was important. Voting was not enough. Having a democracy in which you have an apathetic citizenship, spoon-fed information by a monolithic media, periodically voting, was very weak, a declining form of democracy. And we believed, as an end in itself, to make the human being whole by becoming an actor in history instead of just a passive object. Not only as an end in itself, but as a means to change, the idea of participatory democracy was our central focus."

Paul Booth: "If everything could be restructured starting from the SNCC project in McComb, Mississippi, then we would have participatory democracy."

Sharon Jeffrey: "On the one hand, it was a source of inspiration and vision and meaning: it was an idea that I could commit myself to from the depths of my soul. 'Participatory' meant 'involved in decisions.' And I definitely wanted to be involved in decisions that were going to affect *me*! How could I let anyone make a decision about me that I wasn't involved in? The other sentence that is essential to me is 'The goal of man in society should be human independence, finding a meaning of life that is authentic.' I think authenticity is something that we were deeply committed to discovering within ourselves. I had a very personalized sense of participatory democracy—but I could also connect it to black students, I could connect it to students in universities, I could connect it to the Third World."[8]

To Bob Ross, "The idea of democracy had embryonic in it the socialist idea. What you needed for America was to build on that. To the extent that European socialist ideals, even Marxist socialism, built on Rousseau, we had our own Jacobin tradition that had within it socialism—Tom Paine is not a bad example. Our problem was to find a way to talk about socialism in an American accent. To this day I know that this is what I meant and I thought it was what my colleagues meant by participatory democracy."

Richard Flacks: "It meant an exciting transformation of the meaning of socialism. Not just that it was another code word for socialism, it meant redefining the socialist tradition in terms of the democratic content of it. It meant extending principles of democracy from the political sphere into other institutions, like industry, like the university. I guess I had thought for years that if there was ever going to be a left in the U.S., it would have to reformulate its concepts and language in terms that fit American history and culture. Even though it was a cumbersome term—you couldn't call yourself a participatory democrat, that was too awkward—it was a very creative development."

For Steve Max, finally, it was a phrase that didn't much matter: "It sounded good. We were for it. You couldn't fault it. It didn't strike those of us who had more of a formal socialist orientation that it was really the key thing. We had always viewed it as somewhat superstructural, and that it was the relationships of production that really mattered and this other stuff would follow. It was a fine idea, but not one achievable under the existing economic relations. But since it was clear that you couldn't have participatory democracy without socialism, it was fine."[9]

These accounts raise as many questions as they answer.

Was participatory democracy a euphemism for socialism or an exciting transformation of the socialist idea? Was it an epiphenomenon of more fundamental social realities that would arise in due course once some form of socialism had replaced capitalism? Or was it a new form of political organization distinct from and irreducible to any form of economic organization? Was it simply a rhetorical device, a way to "speak American"? Or did participatory democracy involve elaborating a new social theory? Would such a theory emphasize "the political," in an effort to explain and counteract the eclipse of face-to-face publics by large-scale organizations? Would it focus new attention on political procedures, as a response, in part, to the tendency of socialist and Communist parties to develop into centralized bureaucracies? Or would such a theory emphasize "authenticity" and action, and explore the means by which human beings summoned the will to resist the blind onrush of events and, against all the odds, managed to seize control of their lives and make history? Would the appropriate intellectual approach to participatory democracy be through a new political theory? Through some kind of existentialism? Or through some form of Marxism?

The variety of possible approaches was, of course, a source of potential confusion. In the writing of Tom Hayden alone, there is a constant tension between civic republicanism on the one hand and existentialism on the other: when he follows Mills and his own teacher Arnold Kaufman, he depicts a world of orderly face-to-face discussion among responsible citizens; when he follows Camus and his own enthusiasm for the daring politics of direct action, he depicts a world of clashing wills and romantic heroes, mastering fate through the hard assertion of personality. It is by no means evident that these images can be reconciled. The will to act can easily be sapped by endless debate. And thoughtful discussion is rarely advanced through heroics.

The tension in Hayden's thinking suggests that the notion of participatory democracy involves not one, but two distinct political visions: the first is of a face-to-face community of friends sharing interests in common; the second is of an experimental collective, embarked on a high-risk effort to test the limits of democracy in modern life.

The vision of the face-to-face community is familiar from C. Wright Mills. It taps the mythology of American democracy: it is the image of the town meeting. In the minds of Mills and many of the young radicals, this vision was perfectly compatible with left-wing ideas about workers' control and socialism from the bottom up. It also has some affinity with Quaker conceptions of the "redemptive community." Since many of the young radicals had some knowledge of Quaker ideals—Casey Hayden through SNCC; Sharon Jeffrey through a summer spent at a CORE workshop; Al Haber through contact with conscientious objectors in Ann Arbor in the late Fifties; and Tom Hayden through his admiration for the solitary peace vigils held by Kenneth Boulding, the Quaker systems theorist —it is not surprising that their efforts to implement a participatory democracy would eventually turn for inspiration to Quaker practices. As the political philosopher A.D. Lindsay once pointed out, one of the prototypes for modern democracy was the congregation in a church, "a small community in which democratic practice is easy: in which individuals can be treated as individuals with their separate gifts and callings, with their separate message from God. Hence the exaltation of the small society in which the individual man in close community with his fellows can find shelter from the pressure of Leviathan."[10] As we shall see, when the young radicals fanned out into poor neighborhoods to organize the powerless and to establish communities of transparent freedom for themselves, they adopted such Quaker practices as rule-by-consensus—the directly democratic embodiment of the priesthood of all believers.

The vision of the "democracy of individual participation" as an experimental collective is less familiar. It has roots in pragmatism, but also in existentialism and in modernism. It grows out of Haber's interpretation of participatory democracy as a way "to *be*," and out of Hayden's emphasis on action and enthusiasm for Jack Kerouac. It is symbolized by the decision to treat *The Port Huron Statement* as a "living document." The guiding values of democratic experimentalism are spontaneity, imagination, passion, playfulness, *movement*—the sensation of being on edge, at the limits of freedom. "Everything for us had to be new," says Hayden. "We thought our vision lay in the traditions of the left, but that they had to be reconstructed all over again, in our time and place. That reconstruction was our mission." In pursuit of the new, the young radicals appropriated some of the themes by which modernism had come to define itself: "the glory of modern energy and dynamism, the ravages of modern disintegration and nihilism, the strange intimacy between them; the sense of being caught in a vortex where all facts and values are whirled, exploded, decomposed, recombined; a basic uncertainty about what is basic, what is valuable, what is real; a flaring up of the most radical hopes in the midst of their radical negations."[11] This is a quote from Marshall Berman's bravura interpretation of *The Communist Manifesto*. But of course Karl Marx and Friedrich Engels never intended to apply the precepts of modernism to politics; Marx himself, and classical Marxism in both its social-democratic and Leninist forms, stressed the deliberate cultivation of class interest, through the transmission of a formal doctrine of capitalist crisis and proletarian revolution, within a disciplined political organization. After rejecting these forms of political organization, some on the New Left were inclined to extend the vision of the experimental collective into a kind of anarchism. Spurning all fixed doctrines and forms, they exulted in discovery, improvisation, the drama of unpredictable innovation.

The implications of these two visions were contradictory. The experimental collective thrives on creative tension, constant upheaval, a hunger for fresh experiences, "the theme of permanent revolution . . . carried into individual experience."[12] The face-to-face community depends on trust, friendship, a stable set of rules for arriving at decisions. While the face-to-face community may foster a sense of profound personal responsibility, it is not at all clear what the experimental collective will breed—forever in the process of reinventing itself, it is more liable to induce vertigo than to pique conscience. The face-to-face community may be impractical in a large modern society, but at least it presents an image of political order. The infusion of modernist energies into politics affords no such solace, only the promise of a shared adventure—a promise of no small danger and no small appeal, particularly for anyone young, "full of life and itching to get going."

Beyond the Bewildered Herd

It would be misleading to overemphasize these conflicting visions; activists scarcely thought in such terms. Indeed, in its implications for strategy, the notion of participatory democracy may seem plain enough. As Tom Hayden wrote at the time, "I am primarily concerned about the complete absence of an active and creative set of publics."[13] United by a "broad consensus" on the value of participatory democracy, the members of SDS could cooperate in efforts to stimulate quiescent publics into action and creativity. But here again, a closer consideration of the issues at stake leads into a labyrinth.

In their attempt to mobilize "an active and creative set of publics," the participants at Port Huron were implicitly renewing a debate that had perhaps been most sharply joined forty years earlier, in an exchange between Walter Lippmann and John Dewey. Both had observed the negligible changes effected by such Progressive Era democratic reforms as the initiative, the referendum and the recall. Why had the Progressive enthusiasm for democracy yielded such disappointing results?

In *Public Opinion* (1922) and, even more bluntly, in *The Phantom Public* (1925), Lippmann had argued that any theory of popular government premised on the notion of "a public which directs the course of events" was premised on a delusion. "Primitive notions of democracy," wrote Lippmann, "such as rotation in office, and contempt for the expert, are really nothing but the old myth that the Goddess of Wisdom sprang fully armed from the brow of Jove. They assume that what it takes years to learn need not be learned at all." The development of a complex industrial economy and the rise of sophisticated techniques of propaganda, argued Lippmann, made the assumptions of the ardent democrat even more naive. "A false ideal of democracy," he warned, "can lead only to disillusionment and to meddlesome tyranny. If democracy cannot direct affairs, then a philosophy which expects it to direct them will encourage the people to attempt the impossible; they will fail, but that will interfere outrageously with the productive liberties of the individual. The public must be put in its place, so that it may exercise its own powers, but no less and perhaps even more, so that each of us may live free of the trampling and the roar of a bewildered herd."[14]

In *The Public and Its Problems* (1927)—one of the books that Hayden consulted while working on *The Port Huron Statement*— Dewey conceded the empirical accuracy of Lippmann's description of the public in contemporary America, only to insist on the enduring value of efforts to achieve a fuller democracy. "Democracy must begin at home," wrote Dewey, "and its home is the neighborly community," not a sleeker machinery of impersonal voting, as the fate of the Progressive reforms showed. "We lie," wrote Dewey, "as Emerson said, in the lap of an immense intelligence. But that intelligence is dormant and its communications are broken, inarticulate and faint until it possesses the local community as its medium." Whether the revival of "face-to-face relationships" and "direct give-and-take" in such "neighborly communities" was a practical possibility, however, Dewey did not pretend to show; he made "no attempt to state how the required conditions might come into existence, nor to prophesy that they will occur."[15]

That the participants at Port Huron, under the influence of C. Wright Mills, wished to put something like Dewey's hypothesis to the test—and thus refute Lippmann—seems clear enough. How they proposed to go about doing this, however, was anything but clear. On the one hand, *The Port Huron Statement* suggests utopian experiments in decentralization. On the other hand, it suggests that mere "protest" from the "periphery" fails to address "serious decision-making" at the level of Congress and the Presidency. (We have noted how C. Wright Mills's vision of democracy was marked by similar ambiguities.) In the section entitled "Toward American Democracy," the *Statement* called for a realignment of the two-party system, the revitalization of "mechanisms of voluntary association," the protection of peaceful dissent, "increased worker participation in management decision-making," the development of public planning, the abolition of poverty and squalor, and the extension of the right to vote to Southern blacks.[16] Some of these programs would require public decisions at a national level, but it was not clear how they were to be reconciled with experiments in decentralized, "neighborly" democracy.

The SNCC voter-registration project in McComb, Mississippi, which was regarded within SDS at the time as one paradigm of participatory democracy in practice, was marked by similar paradoxes. The organizers and the city's black citizens offered vivid evidence that an "active and creative" public could make its views known directly, through defiant acts of protest that brought people face to face. But the point of the organizing was to register *voters*: as a SNCC slogan at the time put it, "A Voteless People is a Voiceless People." In addition, the organizers maintained contact with the Justice Department. Although they were frustrated in their attempt to persuade the Kennedy administration to protect civil rights workers, they regarded the federal government at the time as a potential ally. Such an alliance was desirable because McComb contained more than one "public." The city's white supremacists were also "active and creative," particularly in their use of vigilante violence. Obviously, radical organizers had no interest in stimulating this particular public. But their lack of interest—and their readiness to appeal to the federal government—also suggests that a philosophy of democracy which emphasizes the virtue of community and face-to-face relations uneasily coexists with one that emphasizes equality, social justice and universal civil rights. In the community of McComb, moreover, the organizers were, literally, outsiders. At the outset, they were acting in effect as self-appointed tribunes for the powerless, hoping that their example would shatter the resignation and apathy of local blacks. "In its style, SDS was a group like the Jesuits or Bolsheviks," Tom Hayden says looking back. "It was a small band of true believers taking action to catalyze and convert."[17] This raises the specter of an elite cadre of intellectuals claiming to speak on behalf of a mute public—a strategy in evident tension with the final goal of stimulating "an active and creative set of publics."

A Muffled Tocsin

The members of SDS were not unaware of such difficulties. Their theoretical quandaries generated fruitful debate as well as confusion. Uncertain of the best way to work toward a fuller democracy, they explored a variety of different tactics, in keeping with their experimental approach. As they discovered the pitfalls of different tactics, they tried to improvise new approaches—finding an effective, noncoercive way to mobilize and educate poor people became, for example, one of their preoccupations. In the year after Port Huron, the intellectuals in the group expended a good deal of energy trying to clarify a strategy for social change that was both pragmatic and visionary. But the gravest difficulty facing them involved the nature of their final goal. Were they simply seeking reforms appropriate for stimulating quiescent publics? Or were they in fact proposing a revolution?

If a participatory democracy could not flourish within a capitalist system, as many of the students believed, then a radical transformation of the social and economic order was at stake. And there was more. It was by no means obvious that participatory democracy was compatible with the country's *political* system. As Tom Hayden pointed out, the United States was "a republic, not a democracy, and nearly everyone wants to keep it that way."[18]

In strictly historical terms, of course, Hayden was right. As the Progressive historian Charles A. Beard had reminded readers a half-century before, the framers of the Constitution had explicitly rejected "simple democracy." They had designed the Constitution of 1789 to inhibit popular participation in politics. As Benjamin Rush, one of the supporters of the Constitution, wrote in 1787, "It is often said that 'the sovereign and all other power is seated *in* the people.' This idea is unhappily expressed. It should be—'all power is derived *from* the people.' They possess it only on the days of their elections. After this, it is the property of their rulers." One of the great advantages of representative institutions, it was noted in *The Federalist Papers*, was "the total exclusion of the people in their collective capacity." In the terms that the Founding Fathers used themselves, America was a "republic, and not a democracy"—and the Constitution was specifically designed to keep it that way.[19]

Hayden in 1962 understood this. It is what he had in mind when he characterized America as an "inactive democracy." It explains an otherwise cryptic passage in his speech on "Student Social Action": "What are we witnessing here? Surely it is the decomposition of democracy, *if ever we had a genuine democracy in this country.*"[20]

But if what was at stake as a final goal was not only a radical social and economic transformation, but nothing less than a *political* revolution—the creation of a new, more democratic constitution for the United States—how did the reforms endorsed in *The Port Huron Statement* lead toward that goal? And how openly should the final goal be discussed? Hayden's oblique allusion to the constitutional problem was dropped from the final version of the *Statement* because, as he recalls, "it was simply too remote an issue."[21] It was also potentially explosive. It was one thing to "speak American" and to present "participatory democracy" as a star-spangled euphemism for socialism. But if socialism was a dirty word, talk of scrapping the Constitution was worse: a betrayal of America's civil religion, it was tantamount to treason.

In this situation, it was easy to fudge the radical implications, just as C. Wright Mills had done, and speak of the democratic ideal as if it marked the restoration of a lost American dream. But Hayden's disingenuousness at this critical juncture in the formation of the New Left would prove intellectually disastrous in the long run. It left a false impression of historical precedent and helped, as we shall see, to thicken rather than dispel the fog of rhetoric surrounding democracy. It fostered the illusion that fundamental issues of political theory had been addressed, and settled, when in fact matters of principle had scarcely been touched. It prompted the brightest young thinkers on the left in the years that followed to concentrate on strategy and economics and social issues, while the broader political vision of participatory democracy went largely unexamined. Because the vision was never codified and clarified and passed on as a formal doctrine of democracy, no shared approach to grappling with objections and difficulties was handed down. The final goal was left obscure. There was no emerging theoretical tradition to orient thinking and keep young activists from wandering up the same blind alleys over and over again, no clearly defined principles to forestall fundamental disagreements about what democracy ideally meant.

The Uses of Ambiguity

Hayden's effort "to speak American" in *The Port Huron Statement* crystallized in a phrase—and the phrase, we can now see, was hardly self-evident. Participatory democracy was a catchword. It became a cliché. It masked a theoretical muddle. It was a stick of conceptual dynamite. It pointed toward daring personal experiments and modest social reforms. It implied a political revolution.

These are a lot of tensions for one term to contain. The ambiguities of participatory democracy of course limited its value as an analytic tool. But they also help to explain its rhetorical power. "Participatory democracy" seemed pertinent to a variety of people for a variety of reasons. It combined a patriotic aura with a revolutionary ring. Because it remained open to different interpretations, it could unite people with different interests in a common political quest—and this, after all, had been one of Hayden and Haber's aims.

In the years that followed, as its popularity as a slogan grew, the meanings of participatory democracy multiplied, as we shall see. By 1964, it had indeed come to mean for many activists rule by consensus; by 1965, it was being widely discussed as a radical *alternative* to representative institutions. By then, the term had become a weapon of combat in a struggle against all forms of hierarchy and authority. As its connotations multiplied and its value as an analytic tool became patently questionable, new efforts were made to explain it, define it, justify it. Used both as an empty slogan and as a more or less clearly defined idea, the notion of "participatory democracy" became the lodestar of America's New Left. Contradictions and all, it defined what was *new* about this left.

The Port Huron Statement itself was reprinted and circulated in a variety of different forms. In 1964, twenty thousand copies of the complete document were printed. In 1966, SDS printed twenty-five thousand more copies, this time of excerpts (among the nine sections included were those on "Values" and "The Students"; among the eight sections omitted were those on "Anti-Communism" and on "Communism and Foreign Policy"). In 1966, there also appeared the first major paperback anthologies of New Left writing: *The New Student Left*, edited by Mitchell Cohen and Dennis Hale; and *The New Radicals*, edited by Paul Jacobs and Saul Landau. Both anthologies reprinted excerpts from *The Port Huron Statement*, including the section on "Values."[22]

By then, the language of participatory democracy had begun to crop up in other SDS publications. "Let the people decide" became a popular SDS slogan. An SDS "Letter to Young Democrats" closed with an invitation to join: "membership is open to all who share our commitment to participatory democracy." "Why SDS?" asked another leaflet from the mid-Sixties—and then answered with an uplifting and cheerfully misleading homily on the meaning of democracy: "Democracy is an integral part of the original American ideal. Very simply, Democracy means that the people are sovereign. This may seem like a very naive ideal to many of us. There are those who sophistically argue that we live not in a Democracy but in a Republic. The Students for a Democratic Society believe that a truer Democratic ideal is still attainable and that it is very much worth striving for."[23]

The most eloquent expression of such hopes remained *The Port Huron Statement*: "The search for truly democratic alternatives to the present, and a commitment to social experimentation with them, is a worthy and fulfulling human enterprise." It was a search "rooted in the ancient, still unfulfilled conception of man attaining determining influence over his circumstances of life." As the *Statement* conceded, the "values" at issue in this search were only "skeletal." Perhaps the notion of participatory democracy was too elastic and unstable to orient properly the search for a better way of life. Perhaps the effort was doomed to fail. No matter. As Hayden never tired of reminding his audiences, these were dark times. His generation had inherited a world of moral confusion and political stalemate. While the United States and the Soviet Union raced to arm themselves for a nuclear war, more and more people spent the most alert hours of their lives being told what to do. Never had the vision of democracy seemed of more pressing relevance. "If we appear to seek the unattainable," concluded *The Port Huron Statement*, "then let it be known that we do so to avoid the unimaginable."[24]

The quest for a "democracy of individual participation" was beginning. And for committed young radicals like Richard Flacks, Sharon Jeffrey, Paul Booth and Tom Hayden—the four Port Huron veterans whose hopes and struggles we will now look at in some detail—nothing would ever be quite the same again.

PART THREE

BUILDING A MOVEMENT

THE WORLD HAS NEVER FAVORED THE EXPERIMENTAL LIFE. IT DESPISES POETS, FANATICS, PROPHETS AND LOVERS. IT ADMIRES PHYSICAL COURAGE, BUT IT HAS SMALL USE FOR MORAL COURAGE. YET IT HAS AL-WAYS BEEN THOSE WHO EXPERIMENTED WITH LIFE, WHO FORMED THEIR PHILOSOPHY OF LIFE AS A CRYS-TALLIZATION OUT OF THAT EXPERIMENTING, WHO WERE THE LIGHT AND LIFE OF THE WORLD. CAUSES HAVE ONLY FINALLY TRIUMPHED WHEN THE RA-TIONAL "GRADUAL PROGRESS" MEN HAVE BEEN OVERWHELMED. BETTER CRUDE IRRATIONALITY THAN THE RATIONALITY THAT CHECKS HOPE AND STIFLES FAITH.

—Randolph Bourne
"The Experimental Life" (1913)

CHAPTER NINE

AN INTELLECTUAL IN SEARCH OF A STRATEGY

T HE FALL OF 1962 began quietly on most college campuses across America. The furor over *The Port Huron Statement* was confined to the tiny circle of students, intellectuals and organizers who followed debates on the left. The upsurge in campus activism that had begun in the spring of 1960 had subsided. The drama of the sit-ins and freedom rides was temporarily over. Though the struggle for civil rights continued in the South, on northern campuses there was little to do but hold meetings and distribute manifestos.

In Ann Arbor, Richard Flacks, together with his new friends in SDS, began to debate and plan the future of the New Left. At twenty-four, Flacks had been one of the oldest students at Port Huron. But the convention had been a turning point for him. Besides making new friends, he had experienced "a heady, exhilarated sense of intellectual breakthrough." His past had suddenly ceased to weigh on him. The young radicals at Port Huron, he thought, would "overcome 50 years of left-wing error, failure and exhaustion."[1]

At the end of the summer, Tom Hayden had left New York to rejoin the group in Ann Arbor. Although Hayden was the organization's new national president, he had decided to move back to Michigan while he completed his thesis on C. Wright Mills. The national SDS office remained in New York, under the supervision of Jim Monsonis, the group's national secretary. Hayden meanwhile was persuaded by the Ann Arbor chapter to rent an apartment that could double as a center for off-campus SDS activity. They found a two-story place with a separate entrance to a finished basement. Tom and Casey lived on the first floor, while the group converted the basement into an office.

"You could show up anytime," Bob Ross later recalled, even "three o'clock in the morning—and Tom would be in the basement, his shoes off, sitting in front of a typewriter, the phone next to him. He was constantly getting calls from the South about guys getting shot or arrested. You'd walk in and he'd say something like, 'Make these ten phone calls for me, get some food down to Mississippi, raise $100 to get this guy out of jail.' "[2]

Saturday mornings were set aside for group discussions in the basement. For many members, these meetings were the most memorable activity of the year. Dick Flacks joined Ross, the Haydens and Sharon Jeffrey in reading books and talking about where they were going. The group was a natural extension of Al Haber's "seminar model" of politics. Compared with the tedium and cramped format of most college lecture courses, the experience was exhilarating. Here education was treated, in Flacks's words, "as a process of free discussion of generally relevant issues in an atmosphere of equality and authentic search for answers."[3]

Their goals were daunting. "We wanted there to be a grand coalition of labor, minorities, progressives," recalls Flacks. "We wanted somehow to be a part of that coalition and envisioned ourselves as among the catalysts of it." But above all, the members of SDS hoped to redefine "the vocation of the intellectual." Years later, Flacks described the extent of their intellectual ambitions: "We wanted to find ways to connect intellectual work with the needs and realities of the disadvantaged and oppressed, . . . to expand the possibilities for effective social criticism, . . . to combine the analytic and reflective with engaged action, . . . to link the technical knowledge of some in the university to the programmatic needs of movements for social change, . . . to 'reform' the university so that it could be an arena within which the redefinition of the vocation of the intellectual could actually occur."[4]

To put it mildly, these were large goals for such a small group. In 1962, SDS was comprised largely of like-minded students—500 at most. But the members of SDS were, as Flacks says, "remarkable for their chutzpah." They were "unburdened by the terrible sense of futility, disillusionment and bitterness that afflicted leftists of all stripes who had gone through the disintegration of the Old Left."[5] Their innocence, their inexperience, their arrogance—in short, their youthfulness—allowed them to imagine themselves accomplishing the impossible: they would change America!

Although he was a newcomer to SDS, Flacks soon emerged as a leader. When Al Haber decided to focus his energy on finishing school, Flacks in effect took his place, becoming a mentor of the group in Ann Arbor, Tom Hayden's principal collaborator, and the chief architect of the first and most important sequel to *The Port Huron Statement*, the strategic manifesto called *America and the New Era*. To his new friends in SDS, Flacks seemed a model of the New Left intellectual—a scholar who struggled heroically "to combine the analytic and reflective with engaged action."

The Politics of Social Science

Flacks had first moved to Ann Arbor in 1958, in order to do graduate work in social psychology. The university's graduate program had been established in 1948 by Theodore Newcombe, a pioneer in social psychology whose reputation had been made by a study of how social and political attitudes were shaped by the interaction of students at Bennington, a small, experimental college in Vermont. "I was surprised at how liberal people like Newcombe were," says Flacks. "They had been left-wing students in the Thirties. After becoming politically disillusioned in the Forties, they decided that they could incorporate some of their values into a professional career, which is why they went into fields like sociology and social psychology. Then, in the Fifties, they began to believe that the real way to get what you wanted was not politics, but social science. They became part of a vast social science industry. From a purely Marxian point of view, they were all servants of corporate and state power. But from the inside, it was much more complicated. These were people who thought that what they were doing was the path to social enlightenment."[6]

The social psychologists at Michigan, like their colleagues at the Survey Research Center, taught the virtue of quantification. Their work was often narrow, austere, esoteric. But their continuing commitment to social reform was evident both in the missionary zeal with which they regarded the scientific method and their readiness to apply their findings in practice. Newcombe, for example, was convinced by his research at Bennington that involvement in an intimate community was an invaluable extension of the educational experience. The graduate program he developed encouraged students to participate in faculty deliberations. Later in the Sixties, Newcombe would become dean of the "Residential College" at the University—an experimental effort to simulate the conditions of a small educational community within the context of a large multiversity.[7]

Slowly, Flacks's wariness about politics began to fade. That the university should serve the cause of social progress was an article of faith that Newcombe had no trouble passing on to him. He became involved in research on disarmament and, under Newcombe's supervision, went to Bennington to write his dissertation on changing student attitudes.[8]

He also fell under the spell of C. Wright Mills. "*The Sociological Imagination*," he says, "hit me like a truck." Published in 1959, Mills's book was at once a polemic against the prevailing schools of social science and a plea for political commitment. In a situation where citizens were being turned into "cheerful robots," the duty of social scientists, argued Mills, was to confront the problem—not to conceal it beneath a welter of irrelevant numbers.[9]

"I thought that book was written for me," says Flacks. "It really changed how I viewed my work as an intellectual." As he later explained, Mills had helped him define the "core problem" of his discipline: "It seemed to me that, as Mills suggests, the central intellectual issue for our epoch is to understand why the eighteenth-century vision of the liberated individual has not been fulfilled, even though the democratic and socialist revolutions spawned by that vision have come to pass. Furthermore, as Mills suggests, the question is not only how to understand this failure, but also how to transcend it—how to find the terms of freedom in a postmodern, advanced industrial society."[10]

His intellectual interests led Flacks to pay close attention to the new student activism. He followed the progress of the Southern civil rights movement and avidly read Tom Hayden's articles and editorials for *The Michigan Daily*. His research on disarmament put him in touch with Ann Arbor's community of peace activists. Perhaps more important, he became involved in the city's bohemian fringe.

"Ann Arbor was really much more intellectually expanding than New York," says Flacks. "I have this principle: two percent of the population will believe anything. In New York, two percent constitutes a critical mass of support: you can spend your whole life there with other Trotskyists, or with other socialists, or with other Communists. Whereas in Ann Arbor, you *had* to associate with people who weren't exactly on your wavelength, because there weren't enough of you otherwise to constitute anything real." His own political reawakening perforce occurred in contact with beat poets, the experimental theater crowd and, above all, the local folk-music scene. With its artless broadsides and fantasy of uncorrupted community, folk music became Flacks's most passionate avocation. "To understand *The Port Huron Statement*," he says, only half-joking, "you have to understand Bob Dylan."

At Odds

Flacks brought formidable talents to SDS. He combined an aptitude for abstract theory with an insatiable appetite for information and left-wing debate. His files still bulge with yellowed newspaper clippings, Congressional testimony, labor union publications, articles carefully torn out from *The New Republic* and *The Nation*. Reared on Marxism, he was also a disciplined scholar, thoughtful and articulate, patient and reflective. Yet he was sympathetic to direct action, fascinated by the novelty of the New Left, and well equipped, by his training in social psychology and research on students, to make sense of the ferment on campus and to take seriously the "reassertion of the personal" that Hayden had called for.

As Flacks soon discovered, his enthusiasm for the New Left was by no means universal. During the summer of 1962, while his newfound colleagues defended themselves against the wrath of the social democrats in LID, Flacks tried to pique the interest of some members of the independent Marxist left. Their response was disappointing.

He had gone to the SDS convention as a correspondent for the *National Guardian*, a radical weekly still rooted in the revolutionary Marxist rhetoric of the Thirties. Earlier in the year, he had begun corresponding with the editors, taking them to task for their blinkered views on the Soviet Union. He had tried to convince them that the new generation of radicals was turned off by such apologetics. The article that he submitted on the Port Huron convention was glowing: SDS was opening new possibilities for the American left.[11]

The editors refused to run it. "I was enraged," says Flacks. "The paper ran only a short, rather sharp anti-SDS report. I called them up. They said that they really didn't trust the people who formed this group. They were going to wait and see. Therefore they weren't going to give the kind of glowing report that I had written. They perceived LID as a right-wing social-democratic organization. So how could their youth group amount to anything? One of them said, 'I give these people six months and they'll be back working for the establishment.' "

Flacks got a similarly lukewarm response from Leo Huberman, one of the founding editors of *Monthly Review*. In the Fifties, at a time when the magazine *Dissent* was sharply defining its differences with the Leninist tradition in Marxism, *Monthly Review* had kept faith with that tradition, in part by running sympathetic articles on the course of the global revolt against European colonialism and American imperialism; Castro's Cuba was proof that the dream of 1917 was not dead.

Flacks had met Huberman shortly after the Port Huron conference, at a friend's house on Martha's Vineyard. "I was excited to tell him about Port Huron," says Flacks, "and to give him material. But he was very skeptical, and basically uninterested. He said, 'Is this a socialist organization?' And I said, 'What does that mean?' And he said, 'Socialism is a government-controlled planned economy.' I said, 'How would you inspire American youth to such a vision?' And he said, 'Look, it's much more important whether Fidel Castro can defend his revolution than whether American youth think anything.' Furthermore, he said, 'the world will undoubtedly be blown up in a decade.' I couldn't understand why he would think that he had anything more to say to an American student organization after these remarks."

When *The Port Huron Statement* became available, Flacks nevertheless sent a copy, along with a letter, to Huberman, expressing his hope that *Monthly Review* would publish "a serious, critical appraisal of it done from a Marxist outlook." No review ever appeared.[12]

"It began to strike me," says Flacks, "that we were distinctive, there was something about our perspective that wasn't going to be shared by the Old Left. We were at odds with all of them. Which was great. Because we felt that we knew things better than they did. We had not only the belief that we could correct all their wrongs, but the further arrogance that despite the fact that they didn't understand or agree with us, they would sponsor us nonetheless. It seemed perfectly natural at the time that we'd know better than these old people. After all, they'd failed. It was obvious. And it somehow seemed intuitively right that if you were younger, you knew more than people who were older. Now that I'm older, I think that it's absurd."

Taking Stock

That fall, Flacks and other SDS members in Ann Arbor became involved in the congressional campaign of Tom Payne, a local Democrat supported by peace activists. SDS also developed close ties to the Center for Research on Conflict Resolution, which had been founded by Kenneth Boulding. The director of the Center, Bill Barth, was a freewheeling former graduate student who had wheedled a building and a budget out of the university administration. Barth believed in breaking rules. He welcomed the involvement of activists in the Center, and that fall put its facilities at the disposal of SDS.[13]

On Monday, October 22, the activities of SDS came to an abrupt halt. That evening, President Kennedy announced a blockade of Cuba until the Soviet Union removed missiles that, he charged, had been armed with nuclear warheads.[14]

To many people, World War III seemed imminent. In Ann Arbor, members of SDS gathered in Hayden's basement. While they nervously waited with the rest of the country to see what would happen next, they began to call up allies on other campuses. "We called people we were politically close to," says Flacks, "some of whom were in SDS, some of whom were not. We wanted to figure out some form of collective action."

The first major campus demonstration against the Cuban blockade occurred in Ann Arbor. Led by Hayden, the protesters acted in response to a telegram from H. Stuart Hughes, the Harvard professor who was running as an independent peace candidate for the U.S. Senate in Massachusetts. Hughes had urged "abandonment of unilateral action and negotiations through the United Nations." Hughes's position—and the SDS protests—did not arouse much sympathy. "It seemed to us," says Flacks, "that we were a tiny minority at Michigan. Fraternity guys surrounded us and pelted us with garbage and screamed at us." At Harvard, a meeting organized by SDS newcomer Todd Gitlin, among others, drew 2,000 students, most of them skeptics. At Berkeley, a "Hands Off Cuba" rally drew more hecklers than partisans. Meanwhile, Flacks and Hayden both went to Washington, D.C., to participate in a demonstration on Saturday, October 26, that had been hastily organized by a makeshift coalition of peace groups.[15]

That Saturday afternoon, while some 2,000 demonstrators outside the White House protested his handling of the crisis, President Kennedy ordered twenty-four troop-carrier Air Force Reserve squadrons onto active duty. When the maverick journalist I. F. Stone relayed the latest news in a speech to the demonstrators that evening in a church, the fears of the previous Monday night were freshly rekindled. Flacks recalls Stone saying that " 'Six thousand years of human history is about to come to an end.' Everyone believed it in that church"—including Tom Hayden, who thought that World War III had started. "Everyone was in utterly stunned silence," Hayden later recalled: "I—it's a very interesting feeling—at that point I felt my body detach itself from my mind, as if I had already given up everything but the spirit. I was marked for death and what I wanted to do was to be together with my closest friends who were there."[16]

The crisis quickly passed. Within twenty-four hours, it was clear that a confrontation with the Soviets had been averted. But the experience left a mark on both Flacks and Hayden. "That alienated us from the Kennedys," Hayden has recalled, "the idea that we should all die, people all over the world should be killed over this kind of question." Flacks agrees: "I think that generally we felt after the Cuban Missile Crisis that more confrontation with the Kennedys, the administration and those kinds of people, was going to be needed. They were not liberals of a kind that we wanted to work with. They had brought us close to nuclear war."[17]

When Hayden and Flacks returned to Ann Arbor, they decided to pool their thoughts on the meaning of the missile crisis for an article in Steve Max's newspaper, Common Sense. The article was the beginning of a fruitful collaboration. In many respects, Flacks was a perfect foil for Hayden. He was keenly aware of Hayden's brilliance. But he was neither cowed by his charisma nor bewitched by his rhetoric. He tempered Hayden's streak of impetuous romanticism with the careful attention to evidence and argument of a trained scholar.

"In the week of madness," wrote Hayden and Flacks, "we learned something about ourselves, as peace advocates . . . and about the political structure of the country." The nuclear threat had been made terrifyingly plain—and so had the impotence of the peace movement. "The priority today, as never before, is power. . . . Unless we can penetrate the political process, by direct participative means, then it is unlikely that even modest changes in foreign policy will be effected in the near future." Hayden and Flacks urged "serious research, sustained community education, direct demonstrations of sentiment"—but above all, they called with "desperate optimism" for "massive involvement by peace forces in local Democratic or even independent campaigns by 1964."[18]

After their experience in Ann Arbor with the peace candidacy of Tom Payne, Hayden and Flacks had good reason to call their optimism "desperate." Although no one had expected Payne to win, his SDS and VOICE campaign workers were dismayed by the paralysis that overtook their candidate once the Cuban missile crisis had begun. Peace activists considered Kennedy's behavior flagrant saber rattling. But a Democrat, unlike an independent such as Hughes, could scarcely speak out against a Democratic President. Flacks ruefully recalls Payne's appearance at a long-planned peace rally that by coincidence occurred in the midst of the missile crisis. Payne was tongue-tied. There was nothing he could say. He was reduced to making a feeble gesture: he announced that he had sent a wire to Kennedy deploring the suggestion, made by another Democrat, that the United States invade Cuba.[19]

After the euphoria of Port Huron, reality was crashing in. By the end of December, when the national council of SDS met in Ann Arbor, some members were expressing doubts about the structure of the organization—a preoccupation that would turn into an obsession in later years, as the frustrations of building a radical movement mounted.

At the December meeting, the national office reported that SDS had 450 "bona fide members paid since 1–1–62." It reported an income since November 1 of $250. Quite apart from the animosities created by the struggle of the previous summer, LID was itself in financial straits and could not provide much help. Independent fundraising was virtually nonexistent. Donations from the members could provide only a meager salary for Steve Max, who was the group's roving ambassador to the campuses—an odd job, as Max himself concedes, since he alone of the major members had never gone to college.

Two weeks before, Al Haber and Barbara Jacobs, a new member and Haber's new girlfriend, had addressed a long letter to their colleagues. In it, they complained about the group's numerous administrative slip-ups, its penchant for ad hoc actions such as occurred during the Cuba crisis, its amorphous criteria for local chapters, its "ingroupishness" (to a newcomer like Jacobs, the intense friendships of the core group felt cliquish), its sheer grandiosity: "intellectual humility as well as intellectual ambition" was needed, they said.[20]

Some parts of the letter had a rancorous and self-serving tone. The retired first president of SDS was implicitly passing a harsh judgment on his successor. Tom Hayden was clearly better as a publicist and bellwether than as an administrator—by moving to Ann Arbor, he had conceded as much. Bureaucratic routines bored him. Hayden could also be a cold and unfeeling person—it is striking how few colleagues believe that they ever really knew him. At the same time, Hayden's personal life was in a shambles. His single-mindedness and relentless drive were wreaking havoc on his marriage. The location of the Ann Arbor office in his basement did not help. For all of these reasons, Hayden throughout the fall had left much of the organization's work to the staff in New York.

Still, the substance of Haber and Jacob's letter touched on matters that went far beyond problems with a single leader. They argued that it was time "to transform SDS from a circle of friends into a membership organization," with a defined program, criteria for joining, a smoothly functioning central administration—in other words, an organization with the structure and some of the discipline of a conventional political party. Robb Burlage, in a written comment on the letter, agreed with many of these criticisms, but implicitly defended the functioning of the organization under Hayden. "THINK," wrote Burlage: "how many 'full-time' people does SDS have to run this colossal nation toward radicalism, realignment and rethinking?" In his presidential address to the December meeting, Hayden himself spoke wistfully of the need to create outlets for direct action. Otherwise members could "think as SDS people" but would perforce have to act under the auspices of some other organization.[21]

A series of reports at the December meeting showed that the situation was far from hopeless. Different members were pursuing a variety of different projects. Sharon Jeffrey described the tutorials on racial discrimination that she had given to some 50 students. Bob Ross talked about the four thousand pieces of anti-HUAC literature that he had helped distribute. Paul Booth reported that a reading group had been started at Swarthmore. Dick Flacks, speaking of the Saturday-morning meetings in Ann Arbor, said that outsiders were being attracted to SDS as a "result of combining activist and scholar parts of a number of individuals."[22]

This crazy-quilt pattern of activity—leafleting, tutorials, reading groups—was, in part, the result of a decision made a few months before. At a meeting in Columbus, Ohio, in September, after the NSA Congress, the SDS national executive committee had agreed to launch a number of different experimental projects on a decentralized, campus-by-campus basis. Some of these projects had come to fruition; many more had not.

But the chaotic pattern of activity also reflected the strategic ambiguities left unresolved by *The Port Huron Statement* itself. Some members wanted to stimulate a more coordinated movement of different local campus programs. Others, like Hayden and Flacks in the wake of the Cuban missile crisis, urged that an effort be made to "penetrate the political process" and to gain access to power on the national level.

In their letter, Haber and Jacobs pointed out the tension between these two approaches. One image of SDS was of an organization "directed *upward*, seeking to influence, through the core works of its leadership, the men and groups now significant on the national scene. The second image of the organization is one directed *outward* to the campus, whose strategy is to set up local groups to serve as a base for the first, embryonic inroads into the power structure."[23]

Jim Monsonis, in his report as national secretary, complained that "a decentralized program just does not get done." The members of SDS were united by what Monsonis rather grandly called a " 'revolutionary consciousness.' " But it had yet to create a coherent strategy. "Just how," wondered Monsonis, are "we handful . . . going to be influential in getting from here—the present state of American society—to there: the vision of the Port Huron Statement."[24]

In his presidential address to the December meeting, Tom Hayden clearly grasped the crux of the matter as a "mental problem—ambiguity on [the] strategic level," as a problem of "almost what to do next. More specific thinking needed." He offered a typically bleak assessment of the prospects. American politics suffered from an "anti-democratic" tendency to treat conflict as a "sickness" and to limit debate. The labor establishment had "supported invasion of Cuba if necessary." Though peace was not a liability in political campaigns, most people "don't like the idea of a radical alternative." They were interested only in "technique," not in "principles." The only hopeful signs Hayden found were in the civil rights movement, where SNCC was "broadening ideology in a leftward direction," and on the campuses, where students were "thinking about power."[25]

The national council agreed that the next national SDS convention in June, 1963, should receive "prime emphasis" in all SDS organizing activity during the coming spring.[26] Resorting to a device that had worked at Port Huron, the organization would focus on the intellectual dilemmas at stake in drafting the next chapter of the group's "living document." The new document would make an effort to resolve some of the questions raised at the meeting in December. One need was obvious: SDS had to devise a strategy for implementing its vision of democracy.

In Search of a Strategy

The task of preparing a sequel to *The Port Huron Statement* naturally fell to Tom Hayden. But Hayden had an important new resource: Dick Flacks. The two of them had already agreed to collaborate on an analysis of different strategies for the peace movement; Hayden had drummed up funding from the Canadian Peace Research Institute, with help from the Center for Research on Conflict Resolution. That spring, using the Saturday-morning SDS meetings in Ann Arbor as a sounding board, the two of them began their search for a strategy. In April, the SDS national executive committee formally asked them to draft a new convention document.

The familiar ways of approaching the issue of social change seemed highly questionable to both Flacks and Hayden. As its behavior during the missile crisis had shown, the labor movement was part of the problem, not part of the solution. Neither the peace movement nor the civil rights movement fit comfortably into traditional socialist accounts of the class struggle. "At the time," says Flacks, "we were very happy to be post-Marxist and pragmatic. John Dewey was relevant and pacificism was relevant and Marxism was nothing special compared to these things." This cheerful eclecticism was one of the most salient features of the early New Left—but a Babel of different theories did not make the quest for a strategy any simpler.

Hayden's frequent speaking engagements across the country and Flacks's voracious reading put them in touch with a variety of sympathetic intellectuals interested in social change. Some of them were socialists. Others considered themselves liberals. All of them offered food for thought.

One of the books that Flacks read carefully was *The Liberal Papers*. In the keynote essay in this paperback anthology, David Riesman and Michael Maccoby flatly declared that "as long as the Cold War goes on, we lack an uncorrupted public debate." But Riesman and Maccoby also saw signs of change. "Certain American elite groups," students among them, seemed to "be ready to give enthusiastic support to a far-reaching idealistic political movement that will provide them with a way of reasserting their faith in democracy." Marxists might scoff: "They see hostility rather than hope as the principal lever of political change." But "as higher education expands and as blue-collar work gives way to white-collar work, the often denigrated bourgeois idealist, the pilot fish of the Marxist theory of revolution, becomes a member of a class quite as large in number as the factory workers."[27]

Riesman was one of the editors of *The Correspondent*, a magazine that brought together disarmament liberals like Kenneth Boulding with militant pacifists like A. J. Muste. Another one of the editors was Marcus Raskin, who would found the Institute for Policy Studies in Washington, D.C., in the fall of 1963 with Richard Barnet. The Institute's commitment to "passionate scholarship" and its credo of "existential pragmatism"—a blend of Dewey and Sartre—was in obvious harmony with the SDS project as Hayden had defined it. One of the most prominent early fellows at the Institute, Arthur Waskow, became an SDS ally and political mentor.[28]

Although they were heartened by the support of such maverick liberals, Flacks and Hayden were groping toward a more independent position. In the wake of the Cuban missile crisis, they were increasingly wary of established liberalism. They read with sympathy the essays by Dave Dellinger and Paul Goodman on radical pacifism and anarchism in *Liberation* magazine.

As students of C. Wright Mills, they were also inclined to think that liberalism had "no theory of society adequate to its moral aims." Hayden's complaint about the lack of political debate over principles recalls Mills's observation that "piecemeal agitation is now the political substance of American liberalism." In addition, Mills had argued that the rise of a "democracy without publics" was, in part, a consequence of the triumph of New Deal liberalism. Franklin Roosevelt's attempt "to subsidize the defaults of the capitalist system," claimed Mills, had helped "move the society of the United States into a corporate form of garrison state." The innovations of the New Deal had issued in an oligarchy of "business and labor as systems of power," divorced from control at the grass roots.[29]

Flacks was influenced by a similar analysis of liberalism that had appeared in the fall of 1962 in the pages of *Studies on the Left*—perhaps the most important academic journal of the New Left. In an editorial on "The Ultra-Right and Cold War Liberalism," the editors argued that the chief obstacle to social change was not the conservative right, but the liberal establishment. "As the architects and custodians of the warfare state, the liberals have been the primary generators of the anti-democratic trends in American society."[30] Any coalition of radicals with liberals, such as that pursued by contemporary social democrats like Michael Harrington and by the Communist Party during its popular-front period, was therefore foolish and misguided.

At the same time, other analysts were suggesting that the New Deal coalition might be on the verge of breaking up. Flacks and Hayden were particularly impressed by the work of Stanley Aronowitz, a trade unionist and veteran socialist, and Ray Brown, a former union organizer who had become an economist for the Federal Reserve Bank. Predicting that automation would soon produce catastrophic unemployment, Aronowitz and Brown speculated that labor unions would not be able to rest content "with fighting for a larger share of the pie when the pie is rapidly being eaten away by automation." Although Aronowitz and Brown talked in terms of a "crisis," they were sanguine about the implications for social change: an army of the unemployed, in conjunction with newly militant labor unions and the peace and civil rights movements, might yet forge an effective new alliance that could move the Democratic Party beyond New Deal liberalism. The emphasis on automation also implicitly suggested that radical plans to restructure the economy could assume potentially limitless productivity and a society of abundance—a keystone of Marx's original utopian vision that seemed more plausible than ever before in the face of America's unprecedented postwar economic growth.[31]

The range of political opinions surveyed by Flacks and Hayden offers eloquent testimony to the intellectual ferment—and generally optimistic outlook—on the left in this period. That the opinions were so varied and contradictory also suggests the intellectual challenge facing them. First of all, they had to clarify their analysis of the system they were seeking to change; in particular, they needed to clarify their relation to liberalism. Then they had to decide how they were going to approach the different possible agencies of social change. Civil rights activists, pacifists, students, intellectuals, "bourgeois idealists," maverick liberals, the unemployed, independent labor unionists—the range of possibilities was promising. It was also potentially confusing.

History as a Way of Learning

At this point, Flacks consulted a book that gave him the germ of an idea for a new strategic synthesis: *The Contours of American History,* by William Appleman Williams.

Williams was a professor of history at the University of Wisconsin and the intellectual hero of the graduate students who edited *Studies on the Left.* In *The Contours of American History,* which was first published in 1961, Williams offered a sweeping reinterpretation of the national experience from the British colonization to the present. His aim was not archival. Williams rather treated history "as a way of learning" that "provided a method of discovering the essential features of existing reality." This reality he defined in terms of "corporation capitalism" and "syndicalist oligarchy."[32]

Williams described American development as a drama uniquely governed by the image of the frontier, a utopia of empty land and unlimited wealth. He argued that this utopia had "almost institutionalized everyman's propensity to evade his fundamental problems and responsibilities" by creating "a mirage of an infinity of second chances." Reformers in America, he wrote, "had asked the right questions" only when the *"frontiers of expansion were closed by foreign opponents or severe economic crisis"*—Williams mentioned specifically the Great Depression and the series of anti-imperialist revolutions in the Third World after World War II. "Such periodic shutting down of the frontier" forced Americans "to turn in upon themselves, face up to reality, and begin defining and analyzing the central issues in realistic terms."[33]

At the same time, Williams interpreted the history of the frontier in the context of an ongoing debate between two competing visions of "the Christian commonwealth" that had been broached during the English Civil War. Was this commonwealth to be based on private property, as the Calvinists believed, or on social property, as the Levellers argued? In this regard, the development of the United States exposed a paradox. Although the frontier was a utopia of private property that promised land for everyman, "by making escape so easy, it produced an unrestrained and anti-intellectual individualist democracy that almost destroyed any semblance of community and commonwealth." Siding with the Levellers and their hopes for a Christian commonwealth based on social property, Williams argued that abandoning the search for new frontiers would lead reformers logically to socialism. This "viable Utopia," he concluded, "holds very simply that the only meaningful frontier lies within individual men and in their relationships with each other. It agrees with Frederick Jackson Turner that the American frontier has been 'a gate of escape' from these central responsibilities and opportunities. The socialist merely says that it is time to stop running away from life."[34]

The Contours of American History suggested to Flacks a means of tying together a number of the different possibilities for social change that liberals and socialists were discussing. "Williams' whole idea," says Flacks, "was that you had two choices in American policy: internal reform, or the externalization of our problems. And that American leaders had always chosen to expand our frontier rather than to redistribute the common wealth. The idea that these were contradictory was very important. I sort of spun out that idea."

Under the leadership of Al Haber, SDS had already distinguished itself as a "multi-issue" organization. In *The Port Huron Statement*, the vision of the movement's final goal, participatory democracy, was meant to provide a common focus for a variety of different groups. Students, young intellectuals and blacks could all unite around the quest for a voice in the decisions that affected their lives. As Flacks recalls, Tom Hayden too "believed that the key to the forward movement of a political force was to have a political/ideological synthesis that tied as much as possible together."

"The only time I felt I had a synthesis," says Flacks, "was in 1963. It seemed to me that heightening grass-roots protest could entail fundamental policy changes. Simply demanding more help and jobs for poor people would affect the arms race—it wasn't just an economic demand. Some people argued the opposite: 'Well, if you create more disunity and conflict in the society, you're going to create the conditions for nationalism.' And we said, 'No, it looks to us like the people who are running the society are the corporate liberals. They want to stabilize, not repress. The real threat to the left is not the right wing, but a strengthened liberal center. That gives us a strategic lever. Because there are contradictions that the liberal center can't deal with: they can't simultaneously pursue an arms race and domestic reform. And since it's hard to get grass-roots support for disarmament, the peace movement should support civil rights and full employment and anti-poverty efforts, because that will move the country in the right direction.' That was the synthesis." Flacks in effect was proposing that SDS encourage disenfranchised and poor groups to tax the state with demands for change. By sharpening social conflict, SDS hoped to force the reformers committed to Kennedy's "New Frontier" to "stop running away from life."

At the same time, the grass-roots form of these protests would demonstrate in practice the meaning of participatory democracy—the alternative to the "syndicalist oligarchy" of the corporate liberals.

"We distinguished 'corporate liberalism' from 'liberalism,'" says Flacks. "'Corporate liberalism' meant reforms made by the power elite in the interests of social stability; 'liberalism' meant those groups that favored redistribution and social equality. I actually prefer to talk about liberal corporatism rather than corporate liberalism. Because corporate liberalism sounds like you're attacking Walter Reuther, when in fact the point was to attack the idea that Walter Reuther's role lay in meeting with General Motors and John Kennedy to hash out appropriate solutions for the society—that's corporatism. What the New Deal had accomplished was to take liberal groups, like the labor unions, and to bring them into a bargaining process in which their leadership was divorced from the grass roots. These groups had been separated from their real base of power. Meanwhile, their constituencies were not being educated or mobilized effectively. We used to talk about how, if the Kennedys fulfilled their program, it would be the end of democracy, because the whole thrust was toward technocratic, top-down control. And that was really what we were against. Not the more traditional targets of left-wing worry."

A New Era

In February, Flacks, with Hayden's help, had started up the Peace Research and Education Project—one of the first fully functioning SDS projects. Immersing themselves in the details of American military and foreign policy, Flacks and Hayden sensed that some form of détente with the Soviets was in the offing. Their prediction of an imminent thaw in the Cold War was the last important ingredient in their thinking that spring.

By May, Flacks had concluded that the Kennedy Administration "genuinely desires a test-ban treaty—in part, to maintain present U.S. nuclear superiority, in part, to limit the proliferation of nuclear weapons, and, in part, to further reduce tensions with the Soviets." A test-ban treaty, he wrote, would be "a major historical event." For the first time in years, Americans would be able to conduct "a wide-ranging national debate on the Cold War."

Of course such a development would present new opportunities for the left. But it would also present new challenges. Flacks argued that the Kennedy administration had learned "the lesson of Vietnam and Cuba"—"that counter-insurgency war cannot be effectively waged so long as the danger of escalation to nuclear war is great. A détente with the Soviets might free us, especially in Latin America, to prevent, forestall, or suppress revolution." The peace movement should therefore be prepared to change its focus from nuclear arms to conventional wars of counterrevolution in the third world.

"The *fundamental* debate of the coming years," Flacks concluded, "ought, then, to be between establishment liberalism and a new radicalism. The defining characteristic of the latter position will be the demand that immediate attention and full energy and resources be devoted to the problems of this society—that poverty be abolished, full employment established and racial equality guaranteed; this, in contrast to official liberalism's commitment to 'aggressive tokenism' and the 'long, twilight struggle' to preserve American power."[35]

By now, the gist of the convention document was clear. In an outline that was mailed to SDS members at the beginning of May, Hayden explained that the analysis would concentrate on unemployment, détente and "the emerging corporate establishment," which was "the most liberal . . . since the New Deal," but was "unlikely to offer programs which promote peace and democracy." In opposition to its "smothering paternalism" and "artificial politics of harmony," the document would recommend "the creation of local centers of conflict."[36]

As Hayden and Flacks refined their thinking, their friendship was deepening. Meanwhile, Hayden's marriage was collapsing. "Tom went through a considerable personal crisis," recalls Flacks. He drew closer to both Dick and Mickey Flacks. "We were the only married couple in SDS," says Flacks. "We had furniture, carpets on the floor, a television. And Tom looked to us as somewhat of an anchor."

Within the Ann Arbor group, the turmoil in Hayden's personal life cast a pall over preparations for the next SDS convention, scheduled to begin on June 15 in Pine Hill, New York. "It was very upsetting to me when Tom and Casey separated," says Sharon Jeffrey. "It was very upsetting to all of us. Because we were really committed to the integrity of relationships."[37]

A Living Document

Flacks assumed responsibility for completing a rough draft of the convention "American Scene Document," as it was now called, which was mailed out to members on June 8. The fifteen-page draft was divided into two parts: one devoted to "analysis," the other outlining a "program for action." Elegantly argued and dense with detail, the document offered a panoramic analysis and a flexible, multifaceted strategy for change. It was subtle where *The Port Huron Statement* was sweeping, concrete and pragmatic where its predecessor was vague and visionary. Although it was rarely read after 1965, it was one of the most significant—and original—documents that the American New Left produced.

Part one declared that "a new world is now in birth." The Cold War was moderating; technology was transforming the means of production and "a corporate-bureaucratic society" was emerging in which the use of "managerial integrative technique" limited "the democratic, active potential of human beings." The global scene was marked by the rise of newly competitive European economies; Third World states in revolt against colonialism and economic dependence; a growing rift in the Communist camp between China and the Soviet Union; and the growing irrelevance of America's nuclear threat in situations (like Cuba and Vietnam) "where an enemy power [i.e., Russia] is equally armed and the point of conflict was relatively minor in world political terms." The domestic scene was marked by a growing threat of unemployment, persistent poverty, racial strife, mounting signs of unrest among labor unions, and a reactionary Congress out of tune with the long-range interests of the liberal political elite in engineering new social reforms in order to forestall social conflict.[38]

This conjunction of global and domestic trends presented difficulties for the ruling elite—and new opportunities for spurring a popular movement for social change. While the domestic economy felt the pressure of automation, the country's traditional means of escape, the frontier, was being shut down by "the irresistible tide of national social revolutions," such as that in Cuba. The country's economic and political influence was being undercut by "the emergence of powerful competitive states across the world." Since "its massive military superiority could not be applied effectively to the new political-economic, and guerrilla-military forms of conflict," the "traditional keys to US power and prosperity—an open frontier for markets and investment, and an expanding mass-production economy putting men to work—were becoming impossible to maintain."[39]

"For those who seek new models of life based on commitments to democracy and peace, the shape of things to come is grim and there is a pressing need to ask: What are the roots of the present situation? What now are our possibilities as political and cultural actors?"[40]

In part two, an effort was made to address the second, strategic question directly. A new movement for social change would seek to abolish poverty, inequality, the spiraling arms race—and to realize, as its final goal, the vision of participatory democracy. In an era of "manipulated consensus, 'reform from the top,' and the degeneration of democratic participation," there was a need for "inspired, painstaking efforts to recreate democratic politics." Such efforts would unite voiceless citizens in an " 'insurgent' politics" that would demand "that social change be created through the conscious action of ordinary people." Depending on the situation, the new insurgent politics would take a variety of different forms: nonviolent direct action and voter registration in the South, protest against segregation in the North, electoral-reform efforts in large cities, campus community peace centers, tutorials for underprivileged children, discussion groups and research projects aimed "at analysis and exposure" of local and national conditions. In all of its forms, however, such a "new insurgency" would mark a return to the "first principles of democratic action."[41]

It would also put pressure on the liberal elite to reorder its priorities. "America would have to choose between devoting its resources and energies to maintaining military superiority and international hegemony or rechanneling those resources and energies to meeting the desperate needs of its people." At the same time, liberals would have to choose between "a style of politics which emphasizes cocktail parties" and social engineering, and a more democratic style of politics which emphasizes "protest marches" and popular mobilization—"the only conceivable ways by which liberal programs can be enacted." If "established liberals" decided to help the students explore democratic means for rechanneling the nation's resources, it "would be an occasion for much celebration (and surprise)." Still, the immediate strategic goal was, as Flacks later put it, "to inspire, catalyze, goad, and irritate the liberal and labor organizations," in the hope that they might sponsor truly democratic reforms—reforms that would set the stage for structural, and ultimately revolutionary, changes in the nation's political and economic life.[42]

The idea of a "new insurgency" was, like "participatory democracy," deliberately ambiguous. The document was designed, says Flacks, "to be open to being read in different ways, because part of our effort was to bring in different people. I remember thinking that the idea of a 'new insurgency' was a neat way of sidestepping the debate between people who wanted to realign the Democratic Party and those who favored an independent, third-party politics. We were essentially saying, 'We don't know what the best course of action will be, but meanwhile look what's happening, there's this grassroots insurgency and that's what we want to be a part of.' "

At the same time, the agnosticism implicit in the idea of a "new insurgency" indicated a break with the classical Marxist approach to interpreting history and analyzing social change. At this point, the intellectuals of the New Left felt no compulsion to search for a substitute proletariat—a class destined by the hidden hand of economic development to hasten the dawn of universal human freedom. "We took for granted," says Flacks, "that we were talking about social movements, coalitions and alignments, not classes. The 'labor metaphysic,' that phrase, was constantly reverberating for us. We didn't want to be guilty of it. And we weren't." The guiding influence remained C. Wright Mills—not Karl Marx.

Port Huron Revisited

The Pine Hill convention followed the Port Huron model. After an opening day devoted to outside speakers and educational panels, the group met to discuss the document and then split up into smaller workshops on specific subject areas. The outside speakers included James Weinstein, the editor in chief of *Studies on the Left;* A. J. Muste; Stanley Aronowitz and Ray Brown; and Arthur Waskow, who was then affiliated with the Peace Research Institute. Nearly 150 people registered to attend, roughly 20 percent of the total membership claimed by SDS at the time.[43]

The discussion at Pine Hill was spirited and specific. Flacks and Waskow argued about the significance of President Kennedy's landmark speech at American University on June 10, in which the President had first publicly signaled a thaw in the Cold War. Aronowitz and Brown differed over the importance of a missile-oriented military economy for the structure of unemployment. "There was probably more debate than at Port Huron," says Flacks. "Port Huron had a feeling of high consensus and mutual love. Whereas at Pine Hill there was more actual discussion." For all the discussion, though, and despite numerous drafts and extensive revisions before the "American Scene Document" was finally published later that summer as *America and the New Era,* the basic political outlook developed by Flacks and Hayden remained intact. "I was excited," says Flacks, "and I think other people were, that we had made some real intellectual progress, not on the level of vision, but in the actual diagnosis of what was happening right there in American society."[44]

For Flacks and many others, the high point of the convention came when Paul Potter spoke on "The Intellectual as an Agent of

Social Change." "For the first time," Potter declared, "there are alternatives for the intellectual other than service to the Establishment or isolation from society." The group that C. Wright Mills had once called "the powerless people" now had access to democratic power: "There is a new understanding, gained through direct participation in social movements, that power is something that can be created, that it can be generated at the base of the social structure; and that the intellectual can obtain power by involving himself in the emerging centers of power in society: the civil rights movement, the peace movement, the discussion of economic issues." Because intellectuals had found "a new home" in such "political action and agitation," their relationship to the university had changed: the university had become "a mechanism they can utilize, that they can manipulate to gain certain ends which they consider important." "What is happening," concluded Potter, is "a dropping out of the system. But what is critical about the new situation is that although people are dropping out, they are hanging on with one hand and are knocking the system for all it's worth. And they are getting away with it as well."[45]

To Flacks, Potter's speech "felt like a real breakthrough. It was neither against being in the university, nor endorsing it. There was this creative tension that he expressed"—a tension that Flacks himself embodied.

The meeting at Pine Hill, like that at Port Huron, was to end with the election of new national officers. Before holding these elections, the group agreed to implement the democratic principle of rotation: the SDS president would henceforth serve only a one-year term in office, in order to ensure a circulation of leaders and to check against a consolidation of personal power, such as routinely occurred in labor unions, for example. Todd Gitlin was elected the new president, while Paul Booth was reelected vice president.[46]

The convention closed with a "fund-raising orgy." "The scene," as Flacks later described it, "might have been written by Genet; it was worthy of filming by Fellini." Robb Burlage, "well clothed and well groomed but with his shirt collar open now, and his tie pulled down, shouted to the audience like an old fashioned revivalist. 'Come up,' he cried, 'come up and confess. Put some money in the pot and be saved!' And they came. The first youth, clutching the green pieces of paper in his hand recited for all to hear: 'My father is a newspaper editor. I give twenty-five dollars.' His penitence brought cheers from the assembly. The sin of the next young man was a father who was assistant director of a government bureau. He gave forty dollars. 'My dad is dean of a law school,' confessed another, as he proffered fifty dollars for indulgence.'"[47]

Radical Pluralism

As these confessions suggest, most of the young radicals of SDS came from prosperous professional families. Like it or not, they were *in*, even if they were not *of*, the middle class. Similarly, they were trying to be in, but not of, the university; in, but not of, mainstream politics. Like the bohemian writers, musicians and artists whom many of them admired, they were beginning to think in terms of "dropping out." Seeking to produce a "creative tension," they wanted to establish a certain distance between themselves and society. Through a kind of spiritual emigration similar to that undertaken by C. Wright Mills a generation earlier, they imagined themselves outsiders, even when they had influence and sought power. They were a self-styled intellectual avant-garde, performing experiments on the margins of established institutions. Testing the limits, they would probe the possibilities of modern democracy.

In the summer of 1963, as part of its ongoing effort to be "open," "experimental" and "decentralized," SDS sponsored a variety of different projects: Students and Labor, University Reform, the Southern Project and the project that Flacks supervised, the Peace Research and Education Project.[48]

"At the time," says Flacks, "I thought that it was really a good way to figure out how an organization should operate. You have your membership and chapters. And you also create these projects that have an unknown potential for growth. Instead of passing a resolution on everything, you say, 'There's a domain of work we want to do, let's create an intellectual basis for it, let's. make it an educational thing, let's just put out materials about it and let people learn about it, discuss it, and build from that.' It's like an experiment: you see where it goes. I always felt that SDS started to lose its way when it lost its understanding of this way of doing things."

As we shall see, SDS started to lose its way rather quickly, largely because its experimental modus operandi proved impossible to sustain in the face of rapid organizational growth and real political conflict. The almost ineffable *spirit* of early SDS also proved difficult to pass on to new recruits. Few young people were equipped either temperamentally or intellectually to function effectively in a political environment defined by deliberate amorphousness and "creative tension." In this regard, Flacks himself was unusual, though not unique. He was a model of the kind of intellectual that Paul Potter had described in his speech. He thrived on the tension between the skepticism of the scholar and the passionate convictions of the activist, and put the tension to good use in writing *America and the New Era*. But the role that Flacks exemplified was not easy to fill.

It was also not an easy role to maintain, even for Flacks himself. In the year after the Pine Hill convention, he supervised the Peace Research and Education Project on a seminar model of mobilizing students. Two years later, this model proved its political effectiveness when the Vietnam "teach-in" movement caught fire. Thanks to the groundwork laid by Flacks, SDS and a number of sympathetic faculty members at the University of Michigan, such as Kenneth Boulding and Arnold Kaufman, the first "teach-in" was held in Ann Arbor.[49]

Besides supervising the Peace Research and Education Project, Flacks offered behind-the-scenes advice to yet another SDS project, the Economic Research and Action Project. Favoring action as well as research in this particular project, he supported one of the earliest SDS efforts to organize the poor, in Chicago, and wrote one of the first reports about these efforts—a natural outgrowth of the notion of a "new insurgency."[50]

Once he had finished his Ph.D. in the fall of 1963, Flacks had plenty of free time to devote to these different political experiments. But he also had a wife. They were planning to raise a family. He needed to decide what he was going to do with the rest of his life.

Other members of SDS like Paul Potter and Todd Gitlin were postponing decisions about their careers by migrating to Ann Arbor and becoming graduate students, using the University of Michigan, like Flacks and Hayden before them, as a base of operation. The early New Left hymned the virtues of civic responsibility, but was rooted in a transitional period of life that demanded little in the way of domestic responsibilities. "There is a timeless quality about the movement," Flacks remarked years later. "It embodies an assumption that one always will be a student or an ex-student—leading the freelance, experimental, not-tied-down existence of youth."[51] Flacks reluctantly recognized that this phase of his life was drawing to a close.

After some hesitation, he made the decision to move on. In the fall of 1964, he began teaching at the University of Chicago. "Most of my comrades in SDS thought I would be better as a professor than as an organizer," says Flacks with a laugh. "Besides, my wife wanted me to take a regular job."

Blowin' in the Wind

Though his days as a leader were over, Flacks retained his ties to SDS. He remained one of Tom Hayden's closest friends. In his chosen field of sociology, he became one of the most prominent—and perceptive—scholars doing research on the causes of the new student activism. He played a part in the 1966 student protest at the University of Chicago—he was one of the students' principal faculty allies. He wrote several important essays advocating draft resistance. But he no longer shared in the total dedication, sacrifice and round-the-clock intensity that came to be hallmarks of the SDS experimental projects.

His most important contribution remained *America and the New Era*. This document made the vision of participatory democracy seem of immediate, practical relevance. A "new insurgency" would dare liberals to take democracy—and peace, and socialism—seriously. Between 1963 and 1965, SDS activity was guided by this strategy.

"I remember doing a lot of speaking for progressive groups," says Flacks, "with a strong confidence that we were on to some things that they hadn't really formulated, but that were going to be helpful for everybody to realize—whether it was participatory democracy, or the end of the Cold War, or the new insurgency, or the connection between economic issues and peace issues, or the connection between civil rights and disarmament, or the idea that the nuclear-test-ban treaty was very good but that it was going to help the U.S. wage war." The perspicacity of the political views that Flacks espoused—particularly the perception that America was liable to become involved in new wars in the Third World—helps to explain why SDS in 1965, after organizing the first major demonstration against the war in Vietnam, found itself at the center of a growing mass movement.

At the same time, ironically, the Vietnam War would starkly expose the weaknesses of *America and the New Era*. The document, as we have seen, includes a profound critique of the political forms and global implications of "liberal corporatism." Yet its key strategic assumption was that established liberals could be cajoled into changing their errant ways, rather as a tolerant, thoughtful father might be moved to respond to the urgent entreaties of an impatient, well-meaning son. This assumption was not entirely false. Some established liberals *were* willing to sponsor experiments in radical democracy—the initial funding for the Economic Research and Action Project came from the United Auto Workers. "We could talk about democracy per se," says Flacks, "because the issues of economic stability and traditional social-equality issues and *even* the Cold War issues were to some extent being raised by the established liberals themselves."

But the short-run success of the strategy merely concealed the deeper difficulties with it. It was never clear why, apart from succumbing to a fit of conscience, the liberal elite should promote experiments and reforms that were explicitly intended to diminish its power. The "strategic lever" that Flacks had described in *America and the New Era* depended on the existence of a strong, vital, almost monolithic established liberalism. Yet the same document's critique of liberal corporatism tended, by its very cogency, to *delegitimate* established liberalism. The radical implications of the critique became obvious when the established liberals began to delegitimate themselves, as it were, by escalating America's military involvement in Vietnam. At the same time, the growing war revealed that Flacks's central assumption—that a "new insurgency" could force liberals to choose between imperial ambitions and a commitment to domestic reform—had been mistaken. "If we had been right," says Flacks, "President Johnson should have avoided the Vietnam War in preference to stabilizing the domestic economy. He shouldn't have tried to do both at once. We were right that you *couldn't* do both at once. But I don't think that anybody expected that the war would go on and on and keep escalating."

In the summer of 1963, though, worries about war seemed remote. Despite the urgent rhetoric of *America and the New Era*, Flacks was full of hope. His new synthesis was bold; the strategy of a "new insurgency" seemed plausible. "You know," says Flacks, "the summer of '63 was a very, very optimistic moment, probably the peak moment for my generation. The nuclear-test-ban treaty was about to be signed. The civil rights movement was at a peak of exuberant pressure and protest. And Kennedy had made his speech at American University." The liberal agenda seemed open to change. Ordinary people were in political motion for the first time since the Thirties. Even the popular culture seemed full of portents. As Flacks and

Hayden rejoiced at the time, Bob Dylan's "Blowin' in the Wind" had become a top-ten hit.[52] By interpreting the grass-roots ferment as an opportunity for democratic renewal, perhaps the young intellectuals of the New Left could spark the liberal imagination. At least it was worth a try.

"It really felt like we were on to something," recalls Flacks. "We were going to be part of a larger process that was moving in a very good direction."

CHAPTER TEN

AN ORGANIZER IN SEARCH OF AUTHENTICITY

S DS WAS APPROACHING a crossroads. Though its intellectual influence was growing, its activities remained limited. "I was leaving college," recalls Sharon Jeffrey, who graduated early in 1963. "There was no place to go. If SDS was going to survive and have any lasting future for itself, let alone have an impact on things, it was going to have to change, from an intellectual to an action orientation."[1]

At the time, Jeffrey was one of the group's few accomplished organizers. She was happiest when she was picketing, protesting, passing out leaflets, tutoring ghetto children. Inspired by the ideas of authenticity and participatory democracy, and excited by her own firsthand experience of "the new insurgency," she was eager to translate the theories of the SDS intellectuals into practice. "I am a natural organizer," says Jeffrey. "I love talking to people and I'm fascinated by differences. I wanted the opportunity to work together and live with people different than myself." During the next two years, she played a central role in transforming SDS from a circle of intellectuals into an experimental avant-garde of ghetto organizers.

The chief vehicle for this transformation was ERAP, an SDS project established in September, 1963, in part as a means for testing the strategy of *America and the New Era*. The acronym stands for the Economic Research and Action Project. But the word, pronounced "ē-rap," soon became synonymous with direct action—and direct democracy. In the summer of 1964, some 125 members of SDS fanned out into the slums of nine American cities in an effort to organize the poor, pressure established liberals and stimulate "the new insurgency." Jeffrey became the first full-time staff member of the ERAP project in Cleveland. There she participated in perhaps the most utopian SDS experiment of all: the creation of a small commune dedicated not only to organizing the poor but also to testing the limits of democracy in the everyday life of the organizers themselves.

The *Vita Activa*

As we have seen, both of Jeffrey's parents were veteran socialists who remained active in labor-union and reform Democratic Party politics. She walked her first picket line at the age of five. "I experienced a lot of freedom in my family," she says. "I had total freedom within the boundaries, but the boundaries were much broader than for anybody else. So that the things I was doing—sympathy strikes, civil rights demonstrations, *The Port Huron Statement*—were applauded by my parents. It was very clear to me that although my parents' primary involvement was with the UAW and with the Democratic Party, they were always challenging these institutions. They were rebels. And I was a rebel."

Jeffrey's radicalism bears out a hypothesis that Richard Flacks proposed in one of his most trenchant scholarly essays. "In important ways," Flacks argued, "the 'new radicalism' is *not* new." His research suggested that its roots lay in the critique of the bourgeois family made by bohemians, cultural radicals and Progressives in the late nineteenth and early twentieth centuries. This critique, Flacks speculated, had been taken to heart by a number of parents who struggled to raise their children in a democratic and egalitarian environment, in some cases long after their own political passions had waned. "Young people raised in this kind of family setting," wrote Flacks, "are likely to be particularly sensitized to acts of arbitrary authority, to unexamined allegiance to conventional values, to instances of institutional practices which conflict with professed ideals." He concluded that "students who engage in protest or who participate in 'alienated' styles of life are often not 'converts' to a 'deviant' adaptation, but people who have been socialized into a developing cultural tradition."[2]

With the support of her parents, Jeffrey spent her student years mastering the art of the political agitator. In the spring of 1960, she helped Al Haber organize sympathy pickets in Ann Arbor for the Southern sit-ins. That summer, she went to Miami to attend a

CORE workshop on nonviolent protest, and met Martin Luther King. That fall, she helped Bob Ross recruit Tom Hayden to SDS. In the summer of 1961, she volunteered to work in Guinea, where she learned about Third World politics and the problems of underdevelopment in Africa. Back in Ann Arbor, she and Ross became the leaders of VOICE, the radical campus political party that Hayden had founded; both of them won seats on the student-government council.

In the summer of 1962, she joined an NSA project that was registering black voters in North Carolina. Her letters from this period attest to her enthusiasm for organizing. The black community, she complained in one, was "apathetic and complacent. To get them to move off of their front stairs to register is like trying to move a mountain without dynamite." Still, she wrote, "I am loving it. It is just what I want to do. And I am learning: the South is like a differentiation, customs, traditions, manners, everything is different from the North."[3]

"One of my best friends," she recalls, "was a black woman student. And one of the most profound experiences I had that summer was washing her hair—*touching* black hair, and discovering it was soft. Another profound experience was discovering anti-Semitism in the black community, even among the black students who were organizing. They told me about the 'Jew' who owned the stores. And I had to make a quick decision. They all liked me. So I said, 'Well, you know, I'm Jewish.' " It was a lie. But "the whole summer they thought I was Jewish. I wanted to make them confront their prejudice."

Since SDS at the time could not employ Jeffrey as an organizer, when she graduated from the University of Michigan early in 1963 she became "research director" for the Northern Student Movement (NSM). A group that had been formed in 1961 by religious activists inspired by SNCC, NSM sent white college volunteers into Northern ghettos, often as summer tutors, in an effort "to instill in people who live in depressed areas a new sense of social, economic and political awareness."[4]

"I'm living in a slum," she wrote in one letter from Philadelphia to Dick and Mickey Flacks. "Love people—hate conditions. People especially friendly. Fights, rapings, fires and bugs and dirt and toughs all around—it seems that the street is always in your window and people, lots of them, are always in the street. Ho hum, see you soon. Hope for some good talk, quietness, Joan Baez, cheese and crackers."[5]

Jeffrey felt strongly that SDS ought to be organizing the poor and voiceless, just like NSM. "They have captured the imagination of hundreds of college students and hundreds within the ghetto," she wrote to her Ann Arbor friends in February, 1963, shortly after going to work for NSM. "They['ve] got people and have done programs and actions. . . . Briefly, I think NSM activities raise many questions about [the] way SDS can—should—is thinking about forming an adult group to effectuate change."[6]

Jeffrey was not the only member of SDS who wanted the organization to become involved in political action under its own name. Tom Hayden had expressed a similar desire on numerous occasions. In the spring of 1963, in the midst of working on the "American Scene" convention document with Dick Flacks, Hayden wrote of his admiration for "the people working in liberal causes at the grassroots." "Can we spread our *organizational power* as far as our *ideological influence*," he wondered, "or are we inevitably assigned to a vague educational role in a society that increasingly is built deaf to the sounds of protest? . . . Can the methods of SNCC be applied to the North?"[7]

Because of its continuing financial ties with LID, SDS had to approach any course of action with caution. LID's lawyers had warned that the endorsement of a "new insurgency" by SDS in its 1963 convention document "would raise serious questions about the tax exempt status of the League for Industrial Democracy," which was under review by the Internal Revenue Service.[8]

Hayden meanwhile had written in March to Walter Reuther of the UAW, asking if the union would sponsor a student project devoted to economic issues. In early August, the UAW agreed to give SDS $5,000. Hayden was jubilant. "Maybe we're beginning to move," he wrote Todd Gitlin.[9]

Using the UAW grant as a springboard, SDS formally created the Economic Research and Action Project in September, 1963, at a meeting held in Bloomington, Indiana. Just days before, most of those present had participated in the March on Washington for jobs and freedom led by Martin Luther King. With King's stirring oratory and the image of an integrated mass movement still fresh in their minds, the group eagerly endorsed the new project.

Al Haber was named its director. Sharon Jeffrey joined Tom Hayden, Todd Gitlin, Paul Potter, Robb Burlage and three others on the executive committee. An undergraduate at the University of Michigan, Joe Chabot, dropped out of school in order to go to Chicago to start a pilot project immediately. In an effort to see whether a grass-

roots insurgency could influence the national liberal agenda, Chabot
was instructed to organize unemployed white youth on the Near
North Side of the city. A national ERAP office was opened in Ann
Arbor at the Center for Research on Conflict Resolution. There Dick
Flacks and the rest of the local SDS group—which now included
Gitlin, Potter and Rennie Davis—joined in discussions about the
best way to experiment with "the new insurgency."[10]

Shortly afterward, Jeffrey wrote to Hayden and Haber, reporting
that her mother "was very excited about the Chicago job." Her
mother had also passed on an insider's view of the prospects for
continuing UAW support. Although she said that "there is some
value in liaison with labor people," her mother had also stressed
that links with labor unions "shouldn't be a high priority." It was
surprisingly candid advice, particularly coming from a staunch
union activist.[11]

Meanwhile, events in Chester, Pennsylvania, coincidentally offered proof of the potential of grass-roots action. Located only two
miles from Swarthmore College, where Paul Booth had helped organize one of the most active chapters of SDS, Chester was a small
industrial town with a population that was 40 percent black. In the
fall, the local Youth Chapter of the NAACP had begun to organize
pickets, marches and petitions in conjunction with students from
Swarthmore. They acted in support of a thirty-seven-point platform,
which included demands for fair and full employment, new housing,
new schools, and fair police practices.[12] In November, more than 200
Chester blacks and 50 students were arrested at demonstrations before the city agreed to meet some of their demands and drop charges
against the protesters. In the aftermath, several militant neighborhood organizatons were established, again with the help of students.

The SDS spokesman in Chester was Carl Wittman, a Swarthmore
undergraduate with a flair for organizing and a taste for adventure.
After the November demonstrations, he went to Ann Arbor to talk
with Tom Hayden. They hit it off immediately and decided to write
a paper together.[13] The success of the militant coalition between
blacks and students at Chester filled Hayden with fresh hope. Why
couldn't ERAP organize similar coalitions in cities like Chicago?

An Interracial Movement of the Poor

Wittman and Hayden brought different agendas to their collaboration. Wittman was interested in developing a national strategy on

the basis of his experience in Chester. He believed that the one major failure of the Chester project had been its neglect of poor whites, who represented perhaps 20 percent of Chester's population and in coalition with blacks comprised a potential majority. "The realization that this group will have to be won over," wrote Wittman, "must be made by both students and Negroes, students so that they will begin to go into the white lower class neighborhoods to organize there, Negroes so that they can begin to adjust to a class, rather than race, approach to their problems."[14]

Hayden meanwhile had begun to voice doubts about the value of the university as a site for social change. "Intellectuals," he wrote, "are placed at vantage points which, described as seats of reason, actually function to immunize the senses and turn incoming truths into trickling, instead of tidal, currents." Only a few months before, Paul Potter had spoken of intellectuals "dropping out" of, yet "hanging on" to, the university as a place to pursue serious social criticism. By the end of 1963, though, Hayden had grown skeptical of the value of "hanging on." "It is sometimes foolish," he warned, "to judge the open mind, the questioning spirit, as ipso facto good"—an astonishing statement, particularly coming from a writer who, only the year before, had stressed the need for "experimental procedure" and "internal controversy." In no uncertain terms, Hayden now dismissed such a "liberal posture" as "an ideology of inaction and irresponsibility, pronounced from heights of shelter and sophistication." In a situation where "liberalism is defused, lacking a point of moral explosion," only bold and direct action could light a fire: "it will take extremism to create gradualism."[15]

Wittman and Hayden called their paper "An Interracial Movement of the Poor?" In it, they attempted to produce a new synthesis, connecting Wittman's analysis of Chester and Hayden's critique of the university with the account of automation, unemployment and corporate liberalism contained in *America and the New Era*. The economic crisis created by automation was going to open new possibilities for stuents to leave the stultifying confines of the campus, organize poor whites and help forge an explosive—and newly class-conscious—radical coalition. Perhaps their analysis would prove faulty. But, they wrote, "only in organizing will the proof be found. So it is organizing we intend to do. Too many people are hungry and kept down, and we are mad."[16]

As Paul Potter remarked a few years later, "An Interracial Movement of the Poor?" was "hardly the most refreshing document to come out of the New Left." Despite the question mark in the title, the tone of the text was doctrinaire. By stressing economic crisis and class analysis, the paper, in Potter's words, "substituted a kind of closed, vulgar Marxism for the more hopeful tentativeness of early SDS proclamations."[17]

"An Interracial Movement of the Poor?" nevertheless had its desired effect. In a style that made the proposal palatable to the group's intellectuals, it offered a rationale for turning ERAP into a full-scale experiment in organizing the poor. "In their minds," recalls Sharon Jeffrey, "there had to be a very strong theoretical foundation for this project. Otherwise it wouldn't have a chance of being adopted. Nobody knew if the analysis was true or not. But it sounded good, and it fit. And therefore we could justify doing these projects."

At the time, Jeffrey thought that Wittman and Hayden's position was perfectly logical. But looking back, she suspects that she embraced ERAP for a complex and contradictory variety of reasons. "There was a part of me that agreed with the analysis," she says. "Students were not quite radical enough, in my view; so there was a denial of myself, since my identity as a person, in terms of a social group, was still as a student. And then there was another part of me, the angry part, that was excited by the idea of toppling the American society. And then there was a part of me that just wanted to go out and organize. I wanted to organize people, I wanted to organize a movement. I mean, on some level, it was stupid: we were going to organize the 'lumpen,' it wasn't Marxist at all, we were going after people who were totally disenfranchised and disempowered and disorganized on a personal level. But we wanted to be independent. We wanted to have our own organization. We wanted to have a major impact on American society. So we had to carve out an arena in which there wasn't yet an organization."

One obstacle remained. Al Haber, the ERAP director, was dead set against Wittman and Hayden's new strategy. "Is radicalism," asked Haber, "subsisting in a slum for a year or two, or is it developing your individual talents so you can function as a radical in your 'professional' field and throughout your adult life?" Haber argued that "the first task in approaching any community is to understand what a radical perspective for the place is." This was an "intellectual job" that ought to "*precede* mass organization." Haber deplored the rise of an "unfortunate anti-intellectualism in SDS." Research had given way to a "fascination with the novelty and excitement of the new insurgencies." There was a lamentable presumption of "moral superiority for those who 'give their bodies.' " An action was not radical, insisted Haber, simply because it was "gutsy." The new "cult of the ghetto," he concluded, was "slightly sick."[18]

When the national council of SDS met in December, 1963, in New York City, the main issue facing it was the future of ERAP. A struggle ensued between Haber and Hayden. Despite the subsequent publication of a bland "priority proposal" that formally reasserted the group's commitment to education and to pluralism, Haber lost. He was replaced as ERAP director by Rennie Davis.

For Haber, it was a painful moment. The organization that he had nursed to strength had spurned his advice. It was embarking on a new course of action that would inevitably leave him behind. "On a personal level," says Sharon Jeffrey, "there was simply no way for Al to get involved in these projects. You see, it was easy for me to go into these communities. I was an organizer, that's who I was as a person. It wasn't easy for Al. So all of a sudden, he was going to be left out. He was no longer going to be a leader."

War on Poverty

During the meeting in New York, Bob Dylan dropped by and mumbled a vague benediction: " 'Ah don' know what yew all are talkin' about,' " one witness recalls him saying, " 'but it sounds like yew want somethin' to happen, and if that's what *yew* want, that's what *Ah* want.' "[19]

The new year brought fresh cause for optimism. In his first State of the Union address in January, 1964, President Lyndon Johnson (influenced, in part, by the impact of Michael Harrington's book *The Other America*) dramatically proclaimed that "This administration, here and now, declares unconditional war on poverty in America." After the assassination of President Kennedy in November, many liberals had been worried about the fate of domestic reform. Johnson was eager to prove that such worries were unfounded. In the days before his State of the Union speech, Johnson had told his aides that he wanted an antipoverty program that would "be big and bold and hit the whole nation with real impact." Of course, he had no intention of sponsoring a genuine redistribution of wealth; he would later make every effort to appease vested interests. But in his haste to make a splash, Johnson took what had been an experimental program and blew it up into a full-scale presidential crusade, inadvertently endorsing in the process several projects expressly designed by maverick policymakers to promote social change and to mobilize the poor themselves, under the slogan of "maximum feasible participation." SDS' newfound activism suddenly seemed like a legitimate counterpart to authorized government policies.[20]

"We are in a new state," wrote Dick Flacks in February: "It is tremendously exciting—one sign of it is that no one person can actually keep up with everything which is going on. . . . 'The times they are a-changing,' and we are part of it." The strategy of *America and the New Era* seemed more plausible than ever.[21]

Further evidence of its plausibility came several weeks later, when Tom Hayden and SDS president Todd Gitlin joined Michael Harrington, sociologist Gunnar Myrdal, economist Robert Theobold and a number of other prominent labor leaders and liberal academics to issue a "public memorandum" (a press release, really) on "The Triple Revolution." The document confirmed the gist of SDS thinking. It warned of a "cybernation revolution," which threatened unemployment; a "weaponry revolution," which threatened a nuclear holocaust; and a "human rights revolution," which threatened racial unrest at home and wars of national liberation abroad. The influence of SDS—and Tom Hayden—is perhaps most striking in the conclusion. An emerging era of abundance, the text declared, was creating at long last "the economic base of a true democracy of participation," in which "the unshackling of men from the bonds of unfulfilling labor frees them to become citizens, to make themselves and to make their own history."[22]

Heartened by the apparent resurgence of liberal idealism, the activists in SDS spent the spring preparing to wage their own war on poverty. Nine cities were picked to host ERAP projects, and a pamphlet was printed calling for volunteers. "We were all kind of sorting out where we would go and who we would go with," recalls Sharon Jeffrey. "You had Tom Hayden in Newark, and on some level I didn't want to be there. And Todd Gitlin was going to be in Chicago, and on some level I didn't want to be there. I did not want to be in a project that would be dominated by strong male personalities." Jeffrey decided that she would go to Cleveland with Paul Potter, with whom she was in a relationship. An introspective and soft-spoken leader with a finely tuned fondness for paradox, Potter had a flair for capturing on paper the creative tensions and ambiguities that, as much as any strategy or vision, defined the spirit of the early New Left. He also had a commitment to building a democratically managed project in which women were treated as equals.

At the end of April, Jeffrey drove to Cleveland, which had been picked as an ERAP site at the urging of Charlotte Phillips and Ollie Fein, a married couple who were both medical students at Case Western Reserve University. "I had my first meager meal with Ollie and Charlotte," says Jeffrey. "They had a very short time to talk with me, because they had to go to work at the hospital."

The planned location of the project was the Near West Side, an old inner-city neighborhood composed of traditionally ethnic enclaves occupied by a growing number of Puerto Ricans and Appalachian immigrants. Many residents lived in profound poverty; as an official government report issued in 1969 put it, "lack of education, lack of skills, and frequent lack of employment is an expected condition of life for a large number of Near West Side residents." Jeffrey, with help from Fein and Phillips, found a rambling frame house in the heart of a predominantly Appalachian part of the neighborhood. In 1965, a visiting journalist described the surroundings: "Poor whites from Southern Appalachia lived in squalid 'hillbilly havens,' in small, roach-infested apartments that rented for $25 a week. There was a WPA-vintage housing project nearby, with an unobstructed view of a clangorous barge-loading canal, and easy access to the city's most notorious rat-breeding grounds."[23]

After some discussion with Ollie and Charlotte, Jeffrey decided to rent a second apartment in the area, to house the unmarried women. Before Jeffrey's arrival, it had been agreed that the Cleveland project would be, among other things, an experiment in communal living. But the group also wanted, as Jeffrey recalls, "to be received positively by the community, and not be seen as a bunch of outside rebels." Though Jeffrey and Paul Potter were lovers, politics took precedence over romance. That summer, they would sleep separately.

During the rest of her visit, Jeffrey combed Cleveland for allies, gleaning information about the community and its problems. She made a special point of introducing herself and explaining SDS and ERAP to organizations already working on the Near West Side. The two most important service organizations within the area were a settlement house and a church ministry to the poor. "The church group," recalls Jeffrey, "was filled with fine, fine people. But the settlement house had people that I couldn't relate to. There was a funny man there, an Indian who wore a turban—it was very strange, you would see this guy with a turban walking around to help the poor. I had gone to talk to him to arrange a formal meeting with their board, in order to explain who we were and what we were going to do. I was told by the church people to be very careful in pronouncing his name; he had a name that was anti-something, it sounded like antibody. So I got up in the middle of this meeting and turned to him and said, 'Now, Mr. Antibody!' Here we are, not wanting to offend anybody, and I had *definitely* offended him. Antibody. And he looked like one."

At the beginning of May, Jeffrey dropped a note to Steve Max.

"Cleveland is coming along," she wrote. "I have learned lots about the white community in my short time [here] and about unemploy[ment]—but it is [hard] as hell to develop a program. The white poor represent [such] a minor part of the total city population, that a movement of the interracial poor is highly unlikely. Well, we shall see."[24]

This letter is revealing. More than a month before the Cleveland project had begun, Jeffrey understood that the strategy behind ERAP was probably not viable. Yet the possibility hardly fazed her. She wanted to test her mettle as an organizer. In addition, some of the most important aspects of the project scarcely depended on enlightening poor whites from Appalachia about the virtues of class conflict. "What we were really struggling with was what participatory democracy means," says Jeffrey. "At the time, it was all very exciting. It was exactly what I wanted to do."

Fragmentation

As June and the 1964 SDS convention approached, it was obvious that the organization was undergoing a sea change. In the span of a few months, it had been transformed from a kind of freewheeling seminar for young intellectuals into a ragtag army of activists preparing to invade the ghettos of nine American cities. While the number of SDS members had nearly doubled, some of the bonds of friendship formed at Port Huron had begun to fray. It was becoming hard to reach even a tentative agreement on the proper balance between thought and action, reason and passion, pragmatism and romanticism.

The high point of the convention came before it even started. The week before, some 100 people converged on Pine Hill, New York, once again the convention site, to attend the "ERAP summer institute." The institute included seminars on community research; the meaning of "radical organizing"; the appropriate relationship with other local groups such as churches, labor unions and social agencies; the role of public service in building a base of trust; the dilemma of being a "middle-class student radical in a working-class world"; the appropriate organizational forms for the project itself. On the agenda were a number of questions that would preoccupy ERAP organizers in the months to come: "Should we—have we the right to—impose our values and our vision on the community?" "Should there be a loose, informal structure [of decision-making within the project] which requires and permits all decisions to be made by the whole group, or is a more highly structured, more centralized system preferred, in which decisions tend to be made by an elected 'spokesman'? Is there some way of structuring things so as to utilize the advantages of both?"[25]

Privately, Tom Hayden was raising questions of his own. Dick Flacks remembers walking around the campsite with Hayden during the ERAP institute and listening together to the excited debate as the members of one project tried to come to a decision about the moral virtue of living at the subsistence level of a welfare mother. Said Hayden, turning to Flacks: " 'Dick, are we creating a Frankenstein?' "[26]

When the SDS convention formally opened on June 11, nearly half of those in attendance were still buzzing about the ERAP institute. The organization was planning to draft another chapter in its living document. It was also an election year, so there was talk of Barry Goldwater and the New Right, Johnson and the liberal resurgence— and above all, SNCC and the prospects for the "Mississippi Freedom Democratic Party" it was helping to organize, in order to transform the political lot of black citizens and challenge the state's lily-white Party regulars at the Democratic convention. For many, though, the ERAP institute made all the talk seem idle. They were impatient to get going on the summer projects.

More clearly than most, Paul Potter saw the opportunities—and the risks—in the ERAP projects. They had aroused enthusiasm, he wrote in a statement that he prepared for the convention, because they offered a "clearer direction and challenge" than other SDS projects. However, Potter warned that "we must set concrete goals for ourselves: . . . A program that cannot receive such definition is destined to frustrate those who pursue its image without any criteria to measure its reality." The group, he thought, would also do well to treat with skepticism the growing fascination with class struggle and distaste for the comforts of the campus. Potter conceded that "the objective conditions" analyzed in *America and the New Era* justified "some concentration on the problems of the dispossessed." But that fact did not diminish the importance of students. Instead of disparaging research and education, Potter urged the group to explore the possibility that "the community may prove a more effective place in which to *educate* students as radicals than is the insulated university." In any event, "the organization of the dispossessed was not enough." If "in fact a twentieth century American revolution is to be achieved," then the voiceless would have to become partners in a radical coalition that took seriously the "growing frustration of certain elements of the middle class." It would be a profound mistake to denigrate the shared discontents that, after all, had led Potter and his fellow students into a radical movement for social change: "It is through the experience of the middle class and the anesthetic of bureaucracy and mass society that the vision and program of participatory democracy will come—if it is to come." [27]

After a series of educational panels, three documents on organizational direction were duly brought before the convention, one by Dick Flacks, one by Steve Max and one by the Swarthmore chapter headed by Carl Wittman. In a long and rather turgid paper, Flacks defended a complex strategy designed to "develop popular opposition to corporate power, and popular consciousness of the desirability of participatory democracy." Steve Max, while conceding the value of community organizing—that, after all, was one of his personal talents—pressed for a coalition with liberals, trade unions and civil rights groups, stressing that the most dangerous obstacle to social change was not corporate liberalism (as some ERAP partisans argued) but the resurgent right wing of the Republican Party represented by Barry Goldwater. The Swarthmore chapter's paper, although conceding the value of electoral efforts to defeat right-wing candidates, emphasized creating "moral communities within an amoral society," modeled on the "agrarian revolutions of Cuba and China. . . . These islands spread by force of example or by guerrilla warfare until they control the whole country." After inconclusive debate, the convention rejected all three documents. By then, there was no time left to draft a new one. [28]

The next, crucial chapters of the "living document" begun at Port Huron would never be explained or summarized in a manifesto. Instead, they would be composed through the personal experience of organizers like Jeffrey. By default, some of their most revealing experimental findings would become the property of a small group of friends who to a large extent passed on their growing stock of knowledge orally. As we have seen, SDS had grown out of a conviction, modernist in its implications, that fixed doctrine was an evil to be avoided whenever possible—it inhibited growth, experiment, exploration. One unintended consequence was the gradual, all but unnoticed disappearance of a common fund of shared experience, a common sense of past accomplishments and future goals. The New Left would try to make a virtue out of this growing fragmentation, even as its own experiments in participatory democracy sought to create a healing sense of wholeness and community.

Chimes of Freedom

Sharon Jeffrey and Paul Potter left Pine Hill in high spirits. The convention had ended by electing Potter as the organization's new president. Despite the group's inability to agree on a new manifesto, the ERAP summer projects represented a bold step forward. "We were starting a very exciting adventure," says Jeffrey. "We had no idea what was going to happen. But we were really committed as a group to going through with this. We drove to Cleveland in a time warp. I don't mean that it took us longer or shorter to get there. I mean that we were out of normal reality. We were going to change the world! All ten of us in Cleveland. All one hundred of us at Pine Hill. And we were setting out to do it. We felt like Columbus."

The explorers arrived at their destination shortly before dawn on Saturday, June 20. After a few hours of sleep and some breakfast, an "outline of the day" was prepared, "and two committees appointed: the paint-up committee of the whole and the potato keepers—who prepare the menus and buy food." The group painted three rooms of the house. On Sunday, after sleeping late, the group discussed plans for its work in the community during the next week.[29]

These details are duly noted in the report that the Cleveland project filed on its first week of activity, a meticulous day-by-day diary, supplemented by detailed comments—eight single-spaced typed pages in all. "We were very conscientious people," says Jeffrey: "Our whole life was devoted to this, so we had plenty of time to do it." Although the first report was longer than those that followed, the Cleveland project for the rest of the summer sent detailed letters to the ERAP office in Ann Arbor, which compiled such reports in a mimeographed newsletter that was circulated among ERAP members, in an effort to link the different projects.

The group in Cleveland that summer consisted of 12 members. The core members, who would stay into the fall, were Jeffrey and Potter; Ollie Fein and Charlotte Phillips; and Ken and Carol McEldowney, political science majors who were both recent graduates of the University of Michigan.

"Everything we did was very consciously discussed," recalls Jeffrey. "The first thing we discussed was what our strategy would be within the community." The problem was simple: how could they most profitably approach the community? The idea of conducting a "survey" was rejected; since local welfare agencies had already compiled most of the relevant data, there seemed no reason to pester residents with more intrusive questions. Offering tutorials to local children was also rejected—according to previous surveys, the residents evinced little interest in education. That left voter registration: despite an antipathy to politics on the part of local residents and the lack of any appealing local reform candidates, there were a variety of community groups that were interested in voter registration. Undertaking such an effort would win the ERAP project goodwill with potential allies, and serve to introduce the organizers to the neighborhood.[30]

The group next discussed its internal organization. "The decision on how to organize ourselves," recalls Jeffrey, "was again made very communally. Each one of us would be responsible. We would have a communal lunch and a communal dinner. Men would be assigned to cook. If they didn't know how, they would learn. That was one of the significant early discussions: cooking was a learnable skill—and the women were willing to teach the men."

In addition to the "potato keepers," or cooks, the group appointed a "broom keeper" to be in charge of cleanup and household repairs; a treasurer; a "research keeper" (this was Paul Potter's job); and so on. The curious use of the term "keeper" marked a deliberate effort to avoid creating gradations of status in the assignment of different roles, as the first week's report explained: "The general internal functioning of [the group] could best be described . . . as 'loosey-goosey.' In many senses, authority is evenly dispersed thoughout the group. This concept is embodied in the notion of 'keepers' rather than directors. . . . This informal structure causes some rambling at times, but so far it is safe to say that no large problems have arisen because of it."[31]

"We deliberately chose our words," recalls Jeffrey, "to reflect our commitment to democracy. There wasn't any hierarchy. But there was respect for people's different talents. Everybody admired Paul as an intellectual. People really respected Ollie and Charlotte as genuinely committed, solid people. There was respect for Carol and me as organizers, and as women. There was just a lot of respect all the way around."

There was also a spirit of shared sacrifice. "The next major discussion we had," recalls Jeffrey of the project's first week, "was over how much food we could have each day. We were allowed just a little bit of orange juice, in little-bitty cups; and that's all you could have. You could have one egg every third day." After the first week, the group reported that "food costs for the week averaged $0.49/day/person. After having held back for the first four days, Sharon Jeffrey announced, 'I thought everyone was being polite. I've been starved all along.' "[32] A sense of humor helped the group to keep up its spirits—as did a sense of austere competitiveness with other ERAP projects. "One of the areas of competition between the different projects," recalls Jeffrey, "was to see how low you could keep your food budget. We were the king. Our proudest moment came when our food bill was down to 28 cents a day per person. We were very very proud of that."

One reason for such pride was practical: limited funding for ERAP meant that all the projects had to be run on shoestring budgets. There was also the fact that the organizers, as Jeffrey explains, increasingly thought of themselves as committed radicals—"and aren't radicals martyrs? Don't you give up everything and nail yourself to the Cross?" In her own case, there were personal reasons for this conviction. "I grew up with this underlying belief that I'm better than you if I am poor," she says, looking back. "My mother had come out of a poor family and a Catholic background, in which sacrifice was one component. My father came out of a well-to-do family, his father was a doctor, but he was the black sheep—my father was disowned by his family when he decided to work for labor unions. My parents conveyed—this was on an unconscious level—an underlying attitude that being a radical was about struggle and sacrifice."

Her own capacity for struggle and sacrifice helped make Jeffrey into a tenacious organizer, which was fortunate—the difficulties to be faced were daunting. "Every day," says Jeffrey, "we would go knock on doors and talk to people. That's what the work was. We would try to engage them in conversation." As the group quickly learned, this was no easy task. "They were basically disorganized people," says Jeffrey. "They were not well educated, not equipped with basic social skills. There was a lot of violence within families, and a lot of unstable families. To get them to a meeting was a major feat. To get them to discuss an issue together was next to impossible —particularly for the men."

In addition to canvassing door to door, the project during its first week approached potential allies and tried to gather information. Its schedule for the first two days was typical. On Monday, June 22, the ERAP group held a meeting with a social worker and a sympathetic local pastor; that night they attended a lecture by a staff member of the Cleveland Urban Renewal Department. On Tuesday, two members began work on a survey of unemployment compensation sponsored by CORE. Another group visited local churches to sound out ministers on their interest in inner-city social issues. A third group paid a visit to the welfare office and learned that Ohio mothers on welfare received only 70 percent of the standard for decent living established by the state.[33]

But the group had more on its mind than the plight of Cleveland's poor. On Tuesday night, a telephone call brought the news that Henry Cabot Lodge had been replaced as the American ambassador to South Vietnam by General Maxwell Taylor, formerly the chairman of the Joint Chiefs of Staff; and that three civil rights workers in Mississippi, James Chaney, Michael Schwerner and Andrew Goodman, were missing and feared dead. The change of ambassadors seemed to signal a new hawkishness in U.S. policy toward Vietnam, an area of the world that the group was following with close interest, since, according to the analysis of *America and the New Era*, American fortunes abroad would have a direct impact on their own efforts to reform the society at home. Even more depressing was the news from Mississippi. Just a few weeks before, SNCC, in cooperation with several other civil rights groups, had launched the Mississippi Summer Project, an ambitious assault on segregation that had brought almost a thousand volunteers, most of them white, to the state to help register black voters, teach in "Freedom Schools," establish community centers and work on building a new, integrated Mississippi Freedom Democratic Party. The disappearance of the three civil rights workers was an ominous indication that the volunteers in Mississippi were going to have to brave a racist reign of terror.[34]

The news also precipitated one of the first crises for the Cleveland project. "We had to decide," explains Jeffrey, "whether or not we were going to participate in a citywide demonstration of sympathy downtown. And there were high risks for us to do that. Because if we were publicly to demonstrate our support of the black civil rights movement"—particularly at a time when the project's support for the poor whites on the Near West Side had yet to be demonstrated —"we might be looked askance at by lower-class white Appalachians. Who were racist. Where were our loyalties? Where was our commitment? Who were we?" After long discussion, the ERAP project decided to participate in the demonstration. "Our conscience," says Jeffrey, "wouldn't permit us not to."

For the rest of the first week the time that was not spent in the field was filled up with discussions of internal issues, discussions of books on national affairs, discussions of local problems, discussions about organizing strategy—the talk often extended far into the night. "All these discussions have bound the group together," concluded the group's report on its first week; "perhaps, what is lacking presently, is informal discussion among project participants to build up the personal as well as the communal."[35] Then again, perhaps it was time that was lacking. There were only twenty-four hours in each day.

Experiments in Organizing

Throughout the summer, the ERAP project struggled to find a strategy for organizing on Cleveland's Near West Side. Several weeks after arriving, they had decided that the project "should be essentially an experiment in alternative modes of organization, aimed at getting a better idea of what might be most appropriate among [poor] whites."[36] Splitting up into different teams, the Cleveland project put three alternatives to the test: one group tried to create an organization of the unemployed; another group tried to establish a tenants' council at a local housing project; a third group tried to organize people who were on welfare.

According to the analysis of "An Interracial Movement of the Poor?," an organization of the unemployed had the greatest potential for raising fundamental questions about American society. But the Cleveland group soon learned that the strategy didn't work. The analysis was all wrong. "We were not met by armies of white unemployed," Paul Potter later explained, "and the unemployed we did meet were an extremely disparate group of people. There were winos, old people on relief and fixed pensions, young guys who still hadn't adjusted to the notion that they would spend their lives marketing themselves to factory owners, and older, steady workers who were laid off or 'temporarily out of work.' Making these people into one organization of unemployed to demand jobs from a cybernating economy that could not provide them was far and away tougher than convincing any group of them that black people were not their enemies. The fact that they were all unemployed or underemployed was a strange common denominator for one of the most variegated groups I can imagine. To top it all off, when the ERAP projects began, unemployment was actually decreasing in most of the cities we worked in."[37] By the end of the summer, the Cleveland project had given up trying to organize the unemployed.

For a time a promising alternative seemed to be the creation of a tenants' council. The constituency was relatively uniform, and the problems manageable: instead of trying to explain cybernation, the organizers could suggest concrete demands—for example, better supervision of the housing project's playground. Some ERAP members, however, doubted "the 'radicalness' of the issue, i.e., how directly does it seem to confront the basic problems of society." They feared that "degeneration into a neighborhood improvement association might be inevitable"—a problem, they added, "with all GROIN issues in general."[38]

The bizarre acronym GROIN—which had been coined by critics of the "neighborhood improvement" strategy, and stood for "garbage removal or income now"—had by then become a counter in a debate that raged throughout the summer at every ERAP project. The project in Chicago, which had developed into a union of unemployed workers, had been dubbed JOIN—for "jobs or income now." The proponents of JOIN defended the original ERAP strategy of organizing the unemployed. But the Cleveland project wasn't alone in finding an organization of the unemployed impossible to build. As Potter recalls, "the discrepancy between fact and analysis set off a rather forlorn, funny debate during the first summer, known as 'JOIN versus GROIN.' . . . People who took the JOIN position said we had to stick by our analysis no matter how difficult the organizational job, and make the basic demand, the Achilles' heel of the society, visible and militant. GROIN people, who were insulted by the tone of the acronym, defended themselves on the 'practical' basis that jobs just weren't the issue to move people on, and counterattacked against JOIN people for still not providing a scheme for organizing around jobs."[39]

In Cleveland, the tenants' council seemed to offer a " 'practical' basis" for organizing in a way that the issue of unemployment did not. The SDS organizers succeeded in mobilizing enough tenants to stage a meeting and demand more adequate recreation facilities. But the organizers soon ran afoul of the housing project's manager and the Cleveland police. The manager ordered the organizers to stay off the property, and ordered the tenants to stay away from the organizers. The group's participation in the demonstration of sympathy for the missing civil rights workers in Mississippi now came back to haunt them. Undercover police had taken pictures of the demonstration and passed them on to the sergeant in charge of the Cleveland subversive squad. The sergeant in turn paid a visit to the tenants of the housing project. "He would knock on their doors," recalls Jeffrey, "and show them the pictures of us in the picket line, obviously supporting civil rights activity. He said, 'I'm from the Cleveland police department, the Red Squad division. Do you know any of the individuals in this picture?' That scared the shit out of people."[40]

While the tenants'-council project was in the process of collapsing under this onslaught, the group working with welfare recipients was reporting modest progress. This was Jeffrey's pet project. "I discovered the welfare line," she recalls. The office where welfare checks were distributed was located in the heart of the Near West Side. "Here every Tuesday," says Jeffrey, "was a long line of people. As an organizer, I knew immediately that this was an ideal place. We had a captive audience; they were standing in line, having to wait for their welfare check, being humiliated—they *loved* having somebody to talk to." A local minister was interested in the welfare problem and willing to work with SDS. In addition, a militant, interracial organization called Citizens United for Adequate Welfare (CUFAW) had briefly flourished a few years earlier. By reviving CUFAW, the organizers were able to capitalize on the group's reputation—an invaluable asset.

But the most valuable asset of all, as Jeffrey soon learned, was the women on the welfare line. "They had life skills," she explains: "They were managing as mothers. They were coping with a houseful of children. The basic reality was that we were working in a community where there were matriarchal families. The husbands were going back and forth between Appalachia and Cleveland looking for a job. There was a lot of alcoholism. Men were not available to be organized. It was easier to relate to the welfare mothers, particularly for myself and Carol McEldowney."

At first, some members of the Cleveland project were skeptical about turning welfare into its main focus. On July 14 and 15, the group held two lengthy meetings to discuss the issue. SDS involvement in CUFAW was evaluated according to four criteria: 1) its potential for raising fundamental questions about American society; 2) its potential for developing local leaders; 3) its prospects of short-term success; 4) its chances for long-term survival. The welfare organization seemed likely to succeed, to survive and to develop local leaders—but did it raise the right questions about society? Was it even consistent with the group's political vision of "a full-employment participatory society"? Some members argued "that making this issue the keystone of organizing was at least a partial rejection of a full-employment society as a goal." Wrestling with these doubts led the group into a lengthy discussion of the welfare state. They reported that they had not found it easy "to imagine what a welfare system which recognized the work and dignity of the recipient

would look like. How does a dole become other than a dole?" At the
same time, the group's discussion revealed "our general lack of an
adequate conception of what a full-employment economy would
look like structurally and whether it was in fact a realistic or meaningful demand in a rapidly advancing technological society."[41]

The upshot of this discussion was typical. The group agreed to
carry on the effort to organize welfare mothers. And it also resolved
to use its internal education sessions to "discuss alternative visions
of a future society." Books by Gunnar Myrdal, Robert Theobald and
Karl Marx were the assigned reading.[42]

The complete published works of all three were unlikely to shed
much light on the practical problems of organizing the Near West
Side, however. In early August, the Cleveland project reported on
one of the first meetings of CUFAW, the resurrected welfare organization. Ten women and two men attended—by ERAP standards, a
respectable showing. At the meeting, after participants aired a chaotic array of personal complaints (a chronic problem), there was a
focused discussion of a specific issue—cause for cheer. The local
minister who was working with the welfare organization had proposed that the group stage a symbolic "stealing campaign." To dramatize the plight of the poor, they would descend on a local
department store and demonstratively "steal" a token piece of clothing. After excited debate, the plan was adopted. But afterward, Jeffrey
and her colleagues made a sobering discovery. The mothers hadn't
grasped the symbolism of the tactic. They thought that the group
was actually going to steal—surreptitiously—badly needed clothes.
Several of the women, considering themselves upright and honest,
had been upset by the idea. Intimidated by the articulateness of the
organizers, they had kept their misgivings to themselves. What had
seemed like an organizing breakthrough had in fact been a fiasco.[43]

In Search of Authenticity

As time passed, the reports filed by the Cleveland project appeared
more erratically, and their style became terse—silent testimony to
the frustrations of organizing. Yet for some months, the group's utopian enthusiasm scarcely waned. External difficulties stimulated intense debates within the group, offering a tacit reminder that their
hopes rested not only on the outcome of organizing but also on the
vitality and intensity of their own group process, and specifically on
the fruitfulness of their shared effort to find "a meaning of life that

is personally authentic." "Discovering authenticity was essential,"
says Jeffrey. "This was where my passion was." But few activists
were willing to talk openly about "authenticity," as she recalls: "It
wasn't considered legitimate—I couldn't have *said* that then and
gotten away with it." Some SDS members scorned the Cleveland
project as "touchy-feely"—a betrayal of the tough-minded, class-
conscious approach ostensibly embodied in the original ERAP strategy. "Their attitude," Paul Potter once explained, "seemed to be that
the 'Port Huron Statement' had simply been a kind of simpy, rhetorical exercise that had covered up or masked the hard, crisp, basic
economic analysis that was now emerging."[44]

The Cleveland group nevertheless remained fiercely committed to
their own experiment in participatory democracy. Their shared
quest for authenticity helps to explain their strenuous efforts to
embody a pure, direct, all-encompassing community of freedom
among themselves. By holding open-ended discussions, the group
endeavored to allow each member to participate in virtually every
decision that affected his or her life, from the way meals were
cooked to the kind of ideal society that should replace the welfare
state.

Despite its resonance for radicals like Sharon Jeffrey, the notion of
"authenticity" was never explicitly defined in *The Port Huron Statement*. In the speech on "Student Social Action" in which he had
called for "a re-assertion of the personal," Tom Hayden had linked
authenticity with "genuine independence" and "an intuitive alertness to that which is capable of occurring, to that which is not yet
realized, and a passion for the continuous opening of human potential." In his research on student protest a few years later, Dick Flacks
described it as an "acute sensitivity to hypocrisy, a wish for self-
knowledge and understanding, concern that one's own personal potentialities—as well as those of others—be realized, rejection of imposed standards of behavior, and acceptance of situational ethics."[45]

At once modernistic and moralistic in its implications, exalting
the flux of experience and simultaneously underlining the importance of a lucid sense of conscience, "authenticity" was obviously
not the clearest concept in the New Left lexicon. Still, for an activist
like Jeffrey the word had incalculable significance. "It was an ideal
that captured some deep meaning," she recalls, "and yet I wasn't
sure exactly what it meant. At that point in my life, it involved
dealing with social and political and philosophical issues. There was
a discrepancy between what I thought democracy meant on a personal level and the way people really operated. How could you in

fact create a democratic structure, and be committed to democratic politics, if your behavior and interaction with another human being was not open and honest? Somehow the way I'd been taught to relate, the way others related to me, was not real. There was some way in which I wasn't living in my own truth." Like C. Wright Mills, Jeffrey implicitly assumed that the quests for personal happiness, truth and democracy, properly understood, went hand in hand.[46]

In an effort to harmonize a shared quest for these varied—and difficult—objectives, the Cleveland project turned to the practice of rule-by-consensus. By striving for unanimity in their informal face-to-face discussions, the group encouraged each individual to ponder personal convictions in the light of collective concerns. Each felt a valued member of a larger whole. A sense of community was fostered through candor and critical thinking. Unlike parliamentary forms of self-government, finally, rule-by-consensus seemed flexible enough to tap what Hayden had called the "passion for the continuous opening of human potential."

Since the time of the Port Huron convention itself, SDS had made an informal practice of striving for a rough consensus. "Because our ideas were so new," says Jeffrey, "the only way those ideas would be implemented was if everybody in the room agreed to them and then went back to their campuses and recruited and organized people. Reaching consensus had relevance as a way of making a decision that was going to have a decisive impact." Similar practices had evolved at the same time in SNCC. A precedent was established.[47]

But what happened in ERAP was different. In 1962, SDS still observed parliamentary rules of order for electing representatives and voting on resolutions. During the summer of 1964, by contrast, in Cleveland and other projects a concerted and self-conscious effort was made to do without such rules. "A lot of our experimentation was on a personal level," says Jeffrey. "We got enthralled by ourselves and our own group process. That became more important than any other issue. It was much more of a Quaker norm in operation."

She recalls that Ollie Fein and Charlotte Phillips both had "strong Quaker backgrounds." Jeffrey herself had learned about the "Quaker norm" firsthand in the summer of 1960 in Miami, where, in her work as a CORE volunteer, she had absorbed that organization's emphasis on moral suasion through face-to-face discussion. Until agreement was reached, discussion continued. The requirement of consensus ensured that even the meek would be treated with respect within The Society of Friends, as the Quakers called themselves.

In Cleveland, rule-by-consensus became an article of faith. "We had a very strong feminine component," says Jeffrey, "and we had softer men. So that the Quaker norm really was acted out. Each individual did speak whatever they had to say."

When two sympathetic researchers visited the Cleveland project in 1965, they discovered what they called an "urban *kibbutz*." "At group meetings," the visitors reported, "their openness is apparent. They exhibit great tolerance, and no speaker is silenced, no matter how irrelevant or repetitious. And it is difficult to single out those who hold authority. Leaders, elected or *de facto*, hem and haw when they are called leaders, for traditional authority and arbitrary decision-making are incompatible with the values of the SDS staff."[48]

The result was exhausting. Marathon meetings became routine. "We worked *seven days a week*," says Jeffrey. "We had long, long discussions—twelve hours. Eighteen hours. Six or seven weeks into the summer, we had a twenty-four-hour discussion to decide whether we could take off *one* day and go to the beach. That was a big deal: to take off a day and go to the beach." In order to finance its organizing efforts, the group decided that each member should take turns getting a job and contributing the money earned to a collective kitty. The budgeting of these funds, says Jeffrey, led to "the next big discussion; I think it was in the fall, after the students had left. We decided to allocate a dollar per person per week for personal spending money. So you could buy some chewing gum."

In *The Social Contract*, Rousseau, perhaps the greatest philosopher of modern democracy, asserted that "the better constituted the state, the more public affairs dominate private ones in the minds of the citizens."[49] By this criterion, the constitution of the Cleveland project was very good indeed. "I never went to a movie," says Jeffrey. "I never went out to dinner. I didn't go to the beach. I didn't do any restful things. I didn't do anything on my own. Everything was with the group." The commune became her world. "This was my family. I never even thought about what I would do if I wasn't living and organizing in Cleveland with this group of people I loved. In the midst of individualism, we were trying to be very *group*. And yet we still were independent. Independent thinking was encouraged and supported. There was never any imposed limit on what could be discussed."

Several years after his participation in the Cleveland experiment, Paul Potter memorably characterized the kind of utopia that he and Jeffrey had tried to build. "I cannot conceive," wrote Potter, "of being in an organization . . . where internal and external are . . . easily distinguished. Or stated positively, the goals of an organization I would want to be part of would have to be goals that I could see as having flowed from or originated inside me and the other people in the organization." Such an organization would be open, flexible, transparent. It would allow individuals to show themselves to others as they really were. It would be directly democratic, and it would rest on the goodwill and sincerity of each participant.

"If these images correspond to any former image I have in my mind," continued Potter, "it is very definitely that of a church. Not of any church I have directly known or experienced, but of the church I have heard some churchmen talk about, the early revolutionary church, whose followers lived in caves and shared their bread, their persecution and their destiny. I say church, because in spite of what we observe them actually doing, churches stand for the salvation of men's souls, the salvation of humanity (frequently called Godliness) of its members. I say church because church stands for a belief in a radically different, spiritually liberated life which is thought to be so changed as to be unimaginable to people who live in this world. I say church because church stands for communion, and it is the church feeling of communion that I believe must be at the bottom of any organization we build."[50]

Nothing could be clearer—or more humbling. As the Cleveland experiment would show, maintaining a congregation of pilgrims in search of authenticity was even more difficult than mobilizing a community of disorganized poor people.

Reinventing the Neighborly Community

As the summer ended, half of the Cleveland staff went back to school, leaving the brunt of the work to Jeffrey, Ken and Carol McEldowney, and Dave Strauss, a native of Cleveland who had just graduated from the University of Michigan. Though Paul Potter remained, his duties as SDS president occupied much of his time. Once they were back in medical school, Ollie Fein and Charlotte Phillips could offer little more than moral support.

CUFAW, the Cleveland welfare group, was prospering. By November, it consisted of between 30 to 50 active welfare recipients. It circulated petitions urging Congress to make the food-stamp program nationwide; under the SDS slogan "Part of the way with LBJ," it helped 400 people on relief register to vote; it organized a series of community programs on the candidates and the issues; it set up a grievance committee to help people on welfare address their prob-

On a different track: Al Haber, Ann Arbor's resident student radical. (GEORGE ABBOTT WHITE)

Act now: Bob Ross exhorts fellow students at the University of Michigan. (1963 MICHIGANENSIAN YEARBOOK)

Radicals in student government: Bob Ross (front row, second from left) and Sharon Jeffrey (far right) on the University of Michigan Student Council. (1962 MICHIGANEN-SIAN YEARBOOK)

"He wanted to speak American": at twenty-one, Michigan Daily *editor Tom Hayden had panache, passion, a way with words.* (1961 MICHIGANENSIAN YEARBOOK)

The prophet of the powerless: maverick sociologist C. Wright Mills on his motorcycle. (PHOTO BY YAROSLAVA MILLS; REPRINTED WITH HER PERMISSION)

Revolution in Mississippi

Pam
68-2192

Special
Report
by
Tom
Hayden

20¢

A Students for a Democratic Society Publication

Witness to a revolution: Hayden's report on the SNCC project in McComb, published in January, 1962: (STATE HISTORICAL SOCIETY OF WISCONSIN)

"The time for man has come": Tom Hayden and assailant in McComb, Mississippi, October, 1961. (GEORGE ABBOTT WHITE)

Political stickball: Steve Max, from New York City, had grown up on Marxist infighting. (STEVE MAX)

*The seminar model of politics:
Paul Booth (rear) in Ann Arbor at
the December, 1961, SDS meeting
that decided to draft a manifesto.*
(GEORGE ABBOTT WHITE)

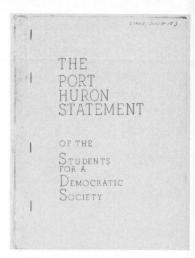

*Agenda for a generation: the
effect on young radicals was
electric.* (STATE HISTORICAL SOCI-
ETY OF WISCONSIN)

*A burning moral passion: 34-year-old
Michael Harrington was "the oldest
young socialist in America."* (ATELIER
VON BEHR)

*"We would make intellectual history": the dor-
mitories at the UAW camp at Port Huron,
Michigan.* (THE ARCHIVES OF LABOR AND URBAN
AFFAIRS, WAYNE STATE UNIVERSITY)

"It felt like the dawn of a new age": the main hall at the UAW camp, where The Port Huron Statement *was ratified on June 16, 1962.* (THE ARCHIVES OF LABOR AND URBAN AFFAIRS, WAYNE STATE UNIVERSITY)

In search of a strategy: Richard Flacks at the Pine Hill SDS convention, June, 1963. (GEORGE ABBOTT WHITE)

Dropping out but hanging on: Mary Varela (left) joins Rennie Davis (center) and Sharon Jeffrey (right) in her Ann Arbor apartment to help organize the ERAP projects, Ann Arbor, spring, 1964. (SHARON JEFFREY)

The new insurgency: the earliest known group portrait of SDS, taken at the September, 1963, national council meeting in Bloomington, Indiana. (From left to right: Tom Hayden, Don McKelvey, Jon Seldin, Nada Chandler, Nancy Hollander, Steve Max, Danny Millstone, Vernon Grizzard, Paul Booth, Carl Wittman, Mary McGroaty, Steve Johnson, Sarah Murphy, Lee Webb, Todd Gitlin, Dick Flacks, Mickey Flacks, Robb Burage, Rennie Davis.) (GEORGE ABBOTT WHITE)

"It will take extremism to create gradualism": Paul Potter (left) and Tom Hayden at one of the last ERAP meetings in Ann Arbor, spring, 1964. (GEORGE ABBOTT WHITE)

"We were going to change the world!":
Sharon Jeffrey going door to door on the
Near West Side of Cleveland. (SHARON
JEFFREY)

Democracy begins at home: Sharon Jeffrey
(right) with Lillian Craig, a local leader of
the Cleveland welfare-rights group that
SDS helped to organize. (SHARON JEFFREY)

'Freedom is an endless meeting": Sharon Jeffrey (center) presides over a discussion in he Cleveland project. (SHARON JEFFREY)

*"To me he appeared the quintessence of innocence":
SDS national secretary Paul Booth, fall, 1965.* (HARVARD
CRIMSON)

Democracy is in the streets: the first march against the war in Vietnam, April, 1965.
(UPI/BETTMANN NEWSPHOTOS)

The other side: Herbert Ap-theker (top), Tom Hayden and Staughton Lynd returning from Hanoi, January, 1966. (UPI/BETTMANN NEWS-PHOTOS)

The fire this time: National Guardsmen patrolling the streets of Newark, July, 1967. (UPI/BETTMANN NEWSPHOTOS)

Bringing the war home: Bob Ross (left) and Tom Hayden, on a visit to organize students at Michigan State University, 1968. (GEORGE ABBOTT WHITE)

"The communes are a better high than grass": a professor peers into a "liberated zone" at Columbia University, April, 1968. (UPI/BETTMANN NEWSPHOTOS)

The whole world is watching: police attack demonstrators outside the Conrad Hilton in Chicago, August 28, 1968. (UPI/BETTMANN NEWSPHOTOS)

Dare to struggle, dare to win: Tom Hayden in disguise during the Chicago protests, August, 1968. (MARY ELLEN MARK/ARCHIVE)

"Judge us not too harshly": Tom Hayden addresses the Weathermen as they prepare for the "Days of Rage" in Chicago, October, 1969. (UPI/BETTMANN NEWSPHOTOS)

lems; and it launched a campaign against the composition of the local War on Poverty committee, charging that its predominantly middle-class makeup did not meet the professed goal of "maximum feasible participation" by the poor themselves.

At the same time, the Cleveland commune continued to experiment with ways to extend democracy both within the group and within the neighborhood. With the experience of the summer behind them, they faced the task with few illusions. "What are the ways," they wondered, "of helping people shake off the adaptations they have made to the system and enabling them to burst free of the built-in restraints they have established over the years?"[51] It was going to be difficult indeed to forge an active, vital public out of the "bewildered herd" of poor whites on the Near West Side. The Cleveland group was nonetheless determined to try: as John Dewey had written, "Democracy must begin at home, and its home is the neighborly community."

Hoping to bring democracy home to the Near West Side, the Cleveland group tried out a variety of different devices. To help wean the welfare group from its dependence on her own leadership, Jeffrey instituted "rotating 'coordinators' for each meeting." In an effort to sidestep the disorganization and widespread lack of social skills among the residents of the Near West Side, the project discussed forming "clusters of people within a given area rather than depending upon weekly meetings. Specifically, a cluster would consist of groups of people, most of them friends, who live within the same immediate area. The same group which regularly meets for informal talks would meet to discuss substantive matters concerning the organization. This procedure would allow for more comprehensive discussions in which everyone might participate in a meaningful way, at the same time eliminating the negative aspects of the formal meetings." In October, after Cleveland had been picked as the site for an ERAP community-organizing conference to be held the following February, the Cleveland project proposed that the poor themselves, and not the ERAP organizers, be given the responsibility of planning the conference. "It was felt," explained Jeffrey in a letter, "that if the conference is really to be of the people from the community that we should aid it, not plan and run it."[52]

That fall, the need to raise money forced the Cleveland project to take stock of its strategy and explain its long-range goals in a grant application that was submitted to the Louis M. Rabinowitz Foundation and the New World Foundation, two of the liberal philanthropies that were giving financial aid to SDS in this period. As the members of the Cleveland project explained, a vision of civic education was at the heart of their organizing efforts. "Fundamental to the S.D.S. approach," they wrote, "is the contention that the problem of 'voicelessness' is of primary concern in dealing with poverty. No amount of attention from 'above' or good will from concerned and generous people can replace the impact of an aroused community of dispossessed people." But without a concerted effort at "political education," the initiative of poor people was likely to take the form, they warned, of "impotent, nihilistic fury." [53]

In speaking of "political education," the Cleveland project stressed that its understanding of both politics and education was broad. "We are looking," they wrote, "to the development of that quality which allows an individual to relate his personal problems to a broader community of concerns and to understand how, through organization and directed action, these concerns can be dealt with. We mean to include within that realm not only electoral politics but, more importantly, the comprehensive notion of politics as a process that allows individuals and groups to work as actors and positive agents of change in relation to a host of problems—be they the difficulties a mother has in receiving her welfare check or the problems a community has in making the poverty program deal with its perceived needs. Political education in these terms is an instrument for broadening the possibilities of democracy both within social movements and the nation as a whole." [54]

Education was desirable on several different levels. Among many of the poor, there was "little comprehension of the kinds of things that might be dealt with in a high school civics book." Most of them were mystified by the working of local and federal bureaucracies. In place of an understanding of how institutions really functioned, they had elaborated their own "fantasy and mythology about power and authority. Thus, for example, a popular notion in the housing project is that the project is controlled by a Chicago syndicate—an idea which quite aptly explains many of the inexplicable things that tenants observe." At the same time, there was an ingrained "cynicism about the possibility of collective action, a feeling that politics consists of knowing the right person, a lack of insight into the dynamics of neighborhood life" and a pervasive tendency to blame all failures on personal inadequacies, rather than to "deal with those problems in political terms." [55]

To flesh out its grant application, the Cleveland project listed some of the experiments in civic education it was planning or had already performed: neighborhood discussion groups, "to overcome people's reticence to admit ignorance"; field trips to institutions like the local welfare department; visits by promising local leaders to other organizing projects, to bolster self-confidence and to learn new techniques of leadership; meetings of the poor with middle-class welfare planners, where such planners could learn to communicate appropriately, without jargon, with poor people; speeches by distinguished visitors, as a means of building morale; the publication of a community newspaper, where residents might learn "to overcome the barriers to written expression." Above all, the Cleveland project stressed its commitment to open and honest face-to-face communication between organizers and the residents. The aim was to create a small-scale model of civic education that others might emulate.[56]

The Limits of Face-to-Face Politics

Cleveland was one of the most successful ERAP projects. While its experiment with "clusters" was soon abandoned and many of its educational programs were never implemented, its strenuous effort to develop local leaders bore fruit. So did its experiment with letting the poor themselves organize a national conference. The ERAP conference held in Cleveland in February, 1965, attracted 150 poor people and organizers from Baltimore, Boston, Newark, Chester, Hazard (Kentucky), Chicago, Detroit and Mississippi. It produced sermons, singing and weeping, in an emotional display of interracial solidarity. Jeffrey still fondly recalls how Fannie Lou Hamer, a hero of the Southern civil rights movement and a black, stayed at the home of Lillian Craig, one of the local white leaders of CUFAW on the Near West Side: "Here was this black lady sitting on Lillian's couch, chewing tobacco, spitting it in a can! They really got along. The conference was definitely a success." "At this conference," wrote one of the participating poor people, "one was allowed to see and feel the love that people have for another, even in this troubled and corrupted world. We were showed that regardless of color, race, or creed we all can live together as one. Just as God intended it to be."[57]

The Cleveland project had other successes to its credit. Welfare mothers won concessions from the board of education on school lunch programs. Several issues of a community newsletter were published, featuring contributions from local residents. The project helped challenge the overwhelmingly suburban, middle-class composition of the local War on Poverty commission, in part through a dramatic march to the steps of City Hall, where the demonstrators heaped carefully picked pieces of trash—broken furniture, tattered clothing, dead rats. Finally, at the request of local black activists, ERAP did some organizing in a black neighborhood while continuing its work on the Near West Side—this was about as close as any project came to realizing Wittman and Hayden's original scheme of "an interracial movement of the poor."[58]

Given the inexperience of many of the young organizers and the intractable problems of the community that they had entered, these results are not unimpressive. When the National Welfare Rights Organization was founded in 1966, it is no accident that Cleveland became one of its first strongholds. And the results of the ERAP experiment in Cleveland, though unique, were not unusual. The ERAP project in Newark, where Hayden was working, organized several successful rent strikes, won control of the local board of the War on Poverty and had some impact on local electoral politics. In Chicago, poor whites extracted a number of concessions from the local welfare system. The ERAP experiments were closely watched by SNCC, which increasingly borrowed the rhetoric of participatory democracy and followed SDS in shifting its focus from civil rights to economic issues and from electoral politics to participatory experiments in the wake of the Democratic Party's refusal to seat more than 2 token representatives from the Mississippi Freedom Democratic Party at the Party's convention in August. ERAP also attracted the attention of some liberals within the Johnson administration, such as Sargent Shriver and Frank Mankiewicz, who brought Hayden to Washington, asked him to give advice on mobilizing poor people for the War on Poverty—and, during one visit, even asked Hayden if he wanted to run a Peace Corps project in Latin America![59]

By the end of 1965, however, a number of the ERAP projects had been shut down. Though SDS organizers continued to work in Cleveland, Newark and Chicago, many participants came to regard the original ERAP experiments as a terrible failure. What had gone wrong?

Certainly the flaws in the original strategy had been harshly revealed. Because most cities did not have a problem of rising unemployment, a movement of the unemployed had proved impossible to build. Faithfully mirroring a key weakness of *America and the New Era*, ERAP projects oscillated between alliances with liberal institutions such as the Office of Economic Opportunity and hostile attacks on them. The most tangible victories of the organizers involved winning concessions from the established authorities. Yet the radicals increasingly saw themselves as would-be revolutionaries trying to build "counter-societies" and "counter-institutions." Local authorities sometimes treated them accordingly. In Cleveland, for example, officials unsuccessfully tried to have the ERAP project evicted from its house on trumped-up charges of violating the city's health code.[60]

The group's own quest for participatory democracy created more problems. There was a chronic tension between the exigencies of organizing poor people and the desire to live within a small community of perfect freedom. By 1966, the Cleveland project had decided to curtail its experiment in democracy. "We've come to realize," they explained, "that our very different style of life (a large coop house which houses a number of single young people) not only creates and supports a variety of rumors about prostitution, communism and bootlegging, but to the extent that we've related to the community as a communal group, we've restricted our opportunities to really learn about the community and become part of it."[61]

The quest for democracy produced even more difficulties at the national level. At a meeting of ERAP staff members in January, 1965, "organizers labored for eight consecutive days and nights," as one participant later recalled, "struggling for some way for intense experiences to be communicated honestly, searching for some means of comparing those experiences and basing national resource decisions on them. SNCC organizers were present at the staff meeting" —and SNCC remained a revered model, even when *it* was acting under the influence of SDS. The SNCC organizers, recalls this witness, "managed to impress ERAP with the image of an organizer who never organized, who by his simple presence was the mystical medium for the spontaneous expression of the 'people.' The staff meeting ended in exhaustion, with a feeling of trust between projects and a faith that the spirit would decide, that an invisible hand would enable all to be resolved if only honesty prevailed."[62]

In the spring of 1965, the national organization of ERAP was largely abandoned, in an effort to combat bureaucracy and to implement radical decentralization. As Paul Potter put it at the time, "given the complexity of the situations in which we work and the infinity of variables that alter and affect it, in the final analysis the decisions must be made through the intuitive sense of the people close to these situations." It was now thought presumptuous to suppose that the lessons of Cleveland, say, could apply to Newark, or vice versa. The group's distrust of formal doctrine pointed in a similar direction. In preparing for the ERAP summer institute in 1965, the Cleveland project suggested that time be allotted "for projects to meet and to maybe have a stream of consciousness description of what we started off doing, and this is what happened. . . ." This increasingly mystical reverence for raw experience threatened to render completely incoherent what was already a fragmented national experiment. After the summer institute in 1965, no two ERAP staffs ever sat down together to compare notes on their problems. Rennie Davis, who had been the national administrator for ERAP, moved from Ann Arbor to Chicago and joined the SDS community-organizing project there. Laboring in isolation, without any coordination or national visibility, organizers became demoralized.[63]

The final straw was Vietnam. The escalation of the war, and the urgency many within SDS felt about organizing against it, introduced a volatile new element into their relationship with their communities. As Jeffrey discovered during the summer of 1965, many poor people, though hostile to local police and welfare officials, clung to the American version of the myth of the Good King. After one community meeting to discuss the Vietnam War, she summarized the views of the participants: "THE government (the Federal government) somehow is honest, moral, and good. . . . If the US was involved in a war, then it must be for good reasons. . . . Given that the government fought only just wars and wars to prevent the spread of communism, it was wrong . . . to question the role of the United States in this war."[64]

Obviously, ERAP organizers had many good reasons to abandon their experiment. But their sense of failure cut far deeper. Their disappointment involved not just the strategy of *America and the New Era* but the vision of *The Port Huron Statement*. By trying to create for themselves miniature socialist commonwealths that embodied participatory democracy, they had explored what William Appleman Williams had called "the only meaningful frontier"—the frontier "that lies within individual men and in their relationships with each other." But now, whether they were ready to admit it or not, these self-styled pioneers on the frontier of politics had come face to face with the limits of their own utopian vision.

The collapse of ERAP as a national organization suggested the unsuitability of the "Quaker norm," even for a relatively small national group (ERAP at its height involved roughly 300 people nationwide). Even within the individual projects, it was impossible to sustain the levels of commitment and sacrifice necessary for a community of transparent freedom. "Freedom is an endless meeting," proclaimed one ERAP pamphlet—but endless meetings became oppressive. After a while, a trip to the beach seemed far more liberating than another interminable debate. At the same time, the very intensity of the friendships that sustained the group made it difficult for newcomers to reinforce flagging spirits. In a 1965 working paper, Ken McEldowney lamented how the quest for "community—soul— whole man" had led within SDS and the ERAP projects to "elite— isolation—in-groupism." A strong sense of community facilitated "the growth of people within the group," wrote McEldowney; it offered a preview of the group's ultimate goal—"it's the type of society we would like to live and operate in." Unfortunately, "community can also be defined in terms of who is in it and who is out." How could newcomers break into a circle of friends? "Exactly how is the community expanded? ... In broader terms, how does a counter-society grow?" It was a question that McEldowney—and the Cleveland project—proved unable to answer.[65]

The Cleveland project weathered reasonably well the everyday frustrations of community organizing. It proved less successful in riding out a series of internal crises that began in the summer of 1965. The sharpest blow came when the commune learned that Ken and Carol McEldowney were splitting up. "That was really shocking to all of us," says Jeffrey. "How could this be? How could our happy family be deluded? How could the two of them not be getting along? If they weren't getting along, how is it that we didn't know?" The incident starkly revealed how far short of "authenticity" the Cleveland group had fallen, despite the endless hours of discussion.

Though Jeffrey remained completely dedicated to the project, she slowly began to carve out a life of her own. For more than a year, she had been pursuing her relationship with Paul Potter in almost impossible circumstances. During the day, they were both working; in the evenings, they were tied up in group meetings. "Paul was asked to come and give a speech at Berkeley," recalls Jeffrey. "The group discussed two things. Could he leave? And could I go with him? There was a long discussion, endless hours. And finally it was agreed that yes, he could go; and that yes, I could go with him."

It was a momentous decision. After months of selfless devotion to the group, Jeffrey rediscovered some of the pleasures of privacy. Shortly afterward, Potter and Jeffrey decided that they would rent an apartment by themselves; after a lengthy meeting, everyone in the group agreed that this was acceptable. Although they all continued to eat together, the group was beginning to fall apart. Step by step, Jeffrey established more distance between herself and the group. When she took a full-time job, she decided to keep a part of her earnings for herself. Several months later, when Potter moved to Boston and Jeffrey decided to stay behind, she rented a new apartment for herself in the black neighborhood where she was working. She began to eat by herself. She finally left Cleveland altogether in 1967, to become the executive director of one of the most prominent community organizations in the country, the Hyde Park–Kenwood Community Conference in Chicago.

Four years later, Paul Potter summed up the ERAP experience. "People in SDS," he wrote, "had seen a chance to go directly for the jugular vein of the system. We leapt and missed and came up, not with a new society, but with a slightly different portion of the well-chewed piece of gristle so many American radicals had gnawed and choked on before."[66]

The ERAP experiments nevertheless had a decisive impact on the development of the New Left. Sympathetic journalists visiting the Cleveland and Newark projects in their prime were naturally impressed by the dedication and sincerity of the young radicals. Their enthusiastic reports introduced readers to a new world of political possibilities. Long after the experiments had wound down, it was possible to point to an example like Cleveland and say, "Look, *this* is participatory democracy in practice; *this* is the radical alternative." By the time the projects finally collapsed, the attention of journalists and radicals had shifted to the mounting protests against the Vietnam War. The image of participatory democracy survived untarnished. Of course, organizers who had lived through the experiments were in a position to know better. But many of them, though duly chastened, were reluctant to scale back their dreams. Besides frustration and failure, they had also experienced the joys of friendship and shared political discovery. Set beside the intensity of this experience, the routines of ordinary electoral politics, the mechanics of registering voters and counting votes, the cutting of deals and trimming of sails, seemed like a pale substitute, a poor excuse—an imitation of political freedom, and not the real thing.

In the decade to come, experiments in participatory democracy would be launched by thousands of young people in dozens of different situations. Health clinics, law communes, free schools, feminist collectives, underground newspapers, drug-crisis centers, food co-ops, radical theater troupes—all would try their hand at direct democracy and rule-by-consensus, sometimes with ingenuity and a surprising degree of success, sometimes with great difficulty and ultimately failure, but always with idealism and a sense of high hope.[67] For countless young people, the political adventure called the New Left was just beginning.

CHAPTER ELEVEN

A LEADER IN SEARCH OF LEGITIMACY

T HROUGHOUT THE SUMMER of 1964, while his friends in ERAP were experimenting with democracy and trying to organize the unemployed in slums, Paul Booth monitored international developments for SDS from an office at the University of Michigan. After graduating from college in the spring, Booth had replaced Richard Flacks as director of the SDS Peace Research and Education Project (PREP). At the time, PREP was housed at the Center for Research on Conflict Resolution, in a room near the national office of ERAP, run by Rennie Davis. "Those of us who were in Ann Arbor," says Booth, "basically were like a second national office of SDS. We would mimeograph whatever had to be mimeographed, and staple and collate whatever had to be stapled and collated. I'm sure I worked half-time on ERAP."[1]

On August 4, Booth's attention snapped back to foreign affairs. That evening, President Lyndon Johnson announced that Communist forces had twice attacked innocent American ships in the Gulf of Tonkin, off the coast of Vietnam. "Repeated acts of violence against the armed forces of the United States must be met not only with alert defense, but with positive reply," said the President. "That reply is being given as I speak to you tonight." U.S. planes were flying their first bombing missions over North Vietnam.[2]

So began in earnest America's longest war—a distant conflict that wreaked havoc on domestic political life. The war made mendacity, manipulation and lying into routine political practices. It helped to undermine the legacy of the New Deal, robbing Johnson's plans for "The Great Society" of initiative, money and popular support. By spurring inflation, it brought to an end an era of sustained growth and helped discredit establishment liberals as managers of the corporate economy. Above all, it triggered an outpouring of vehement protest, destroying the nation's foreign-policy consensus, tearing apart the liberal wing of the Democratic Party and bringing the New Left, ready or not, into popular prominence.

"We have been pulled powerfully by the escalation of the war in Vietnam," wrote Booth to his colleagues in SDS late in 1965. "In any country and at any time the moral quality of its Left is put to the test by the international adventures of its government."[3]

And so, he might have added, is the quality of its leadership. In the months after the Gulf of Tonkin incident, few leaders of the New Left were more intimately involved with the Vietnam War than Booth. He closely followed America's growing military commitment and supervised the first major public demonstration against the war in April, 1965. Helping to guide SDS through a period of turbulent growth, he was forced to come to grips with the practical limits of participatory democracy in a mass movement—just as thousands of new recruits were eagerly embarking on the quest for a "democracy of individual participation."

In the Tradition of Debs

At nineteen, Paul Booth had been one of the youngest participants at the Port Huron convention. Like Sharon Jeffrey, he was the politically precocious product of an uncommonly political family. "My folks were in the Socialist Party," he says. "They were from Chicago, but they went to Washington in 1935 to be in the New Deal."[4] His mother was a psychiatric social worker. His father, trained as an economist, worked in the government for some thirty years, becoming a section chief in the Labor Department's Division of Unemployment.

Twice elected SDS vice president, a post of largely ceremonial importance, Booth had proved his mettle by helping to build the Swarthmore SDS chapter into one of the biggest in the country. His special interests were political realignment, university reform and questions of war and peace—he produced substantial research papers in all three areas. During the summer of 1963, he had worked with Arthur Waskow in Washington, D.C., at the Peace Research Institute, a center for disarmament studies. There he became knowledgeable about "conversion"—the process of taking arms out of production and helping military workers shift to other industries. At the same time, he developed an extensive network of contacts among the left and liberal policy elite in Washington.[5]

Despite his research interests, Booth saw himself primarily as an organizer. His hero was Eugene Debs, the outspoken leader of the American Socialist Party at the height of its power in the decade before World War I. "Other people in SDS had a moral-witness starting point, or a philosophical starting point," says Booth. "My starting point was a commitment to mass organizing; that's why I admired Debs. He got votes, organized strikes and went to jail for protesting the First World War. He was both an effective organizer and a principled leader."

Booth tried to bring the same blend of virtues to the SDS Peace Research and Education Project. Under the direction of Dick Flacks, PREP had functioned primarily as an internal forum for foreign-policy analysis. But with the help of Todd Gitlin, PREP's new coordinator, Booth tried to give the project a more militant profile. "The whole institution was turning into activism," says Booth. "In order to compete with ERAP, we had to figure out how to have an activist foreign-affairs project." While ERAP activists invaded the ghettos of Cleveland and Newark, PREP in the summer of 1964 sponsored a program in Boston to organize defense workers threatened by plant closings.

"We were running around trying to show that we could develop a base among unemployed engineers," says Booth. "We even had one who was a member! But this kind of organizing wasn't so easy." It also lacked the romantic appeal of organizing the unemployed. It was hard to hymn the uncorrupted moral potential of the men who designed missile-guidance systems. Once Lyndon Johnson's foreign policy had begun to reinvigorate the entire "military-industrial complex," it became impossible.

The Secret of Vietnam

The President's Gulf of Tonkin speech hardly came as a shock to Booth and his colleagues. Six months before, Dick Flacks had urged SDS to watch developments in Vietnam with a particularly skeptical eye. "In a news conference this morning," wrote Flacks on February 29, "President Johnson may have provided further indication that a major expansion of the war in Vietnam is now being planned. The President declared that, just as Eisenhower had kept the plans for the Normandy invasion secret, he would not reveal the nature of current planning."[6]

The Gulf of Tonkin incidents seemed to bear out Flacks's speculation. Though in private the President joked about the second of the alleged Communist attacks—"Hell," Johnson told one aide, "those dumb stupid sailors were just shooting at flying fish"—in public his tone was grave. He swiftly sent to Congress a resolution that authorized him to "take all necessary measures" in Vietnam to "prevent further aggression." This resolution had been quietly prepared a few months earlier, in order to circumvent a formal declaration of war by Congress, as required by the Constitution. On August 6, 1964, Congress passed the resolution with only two dissenting votes, from Senators Ernest Gruening of Alaska and Wayne Morse of Oregon.[7]

Booth came to revere Gruening and Morse for their honesty and political courage. "I can remember standing in front of the mimeograph machine at three A.M.," he says, "reading every word of the *Congressional Record* on Vietnam, and cutting out Morse's and Gruening's speeches for other people to read the next morning." Booth also read carefully every issue of *I. F. Stone's Weekly*. "By this time," he says, "we had developed close ties with Izzy Stone. We depended on him to interpret all the events of the world for us. The moment his *Weekly* arrived, we devoured it."

At the end of August, Stone published a painstaking analysis of the Gulf of Tonkin incidents. As usual, Stone's first sentence went directly to the heart of the matter: "The American government and the American press have kept the full truth about the Tonkin Bay incidents from the American public." By examining in detail the testimony of Secretary of State Dean Rusk and Secretary of Defense Robert McNamara before the Senate Committee on Foreign Relations and Armed Services, Stone was able to bring out a series of inconsistencies and evasions that fully warranted his own conclusion, that the Communist attacks *"might have been provoked."*[8]

Galvanized by Stone's analysis and the dissent of Gruening and Morse, PREP swung into action. SDS ordered twenty-five hundred copies of one of Morse's speeches on the situation in South Vietnam. In the PREP newsletter that fall, the lead article declared that "We are on the brink of starting a full-scale war in Vietnam, a war which would put an end to the progress of the last two years on the American domestic scene." Given SDS hopes for democratic renewal, the implications seemed dire. "The growth of secret policy apparatuses" made "democratic relevance to decision-making even less possible in the United States." The PREP newsletter suggested holding campus conferences, creating informal discussion groups and sending out knowledgeable speakers to address "union locals, civic clubs, churches, and political bodies," in an effort to arouse "a forceful community of protest."[9]

At the time, the first, faint stirrings of such a community of protest were becoming evident. Arthur Waskow, Richard Barnet, Marcus Raskin and the other experts who were then affiliated with the Institute for Policy Study augmented I. F. Stone's reports with their own critical working papers on Vietnam. The Communist Party and various Marxist-Leninist splinter groups vociferously (and predictably) lamented the latest outbreak of imperialist aggression. And on July 3, 1964, veteran pacifists connected with the magazine *Liberation*, including A. J. Muste and Dave Dellinger, had proclaimed their "conscientious refusal to cooperate with the United States government in the prosecution of the war in Vietnam."[10]

The mainstream peace movement, led by the Committee for a Sane Nuclear Policy, or SANE, was by contrast far slower to respond. Founded in 1957, when Cold War passions ran high and memories of the witch-hunts of the McCarthy era remained fresh, SANE maintained a rigidly "exclusionary" policy—Communists could not become members. Fearful of dividing its liberal constituency and determined to avoid offering comfort to the Communists in Hanoi, SANE approached the war in Vietnam gingerly.[11]

Throughout the fall of 1964, Booth and Gitlin crisscrossed the country talking to students about PREP and SDS. They found scant interest in Vietnam. As the meeting of the SDS National Council in December approached, Booth helped prepare a set of proposals for PREP activities. In addition to expanding PREP's conversion projects into cities besides Boston, he hoped to stage a sit-in at a major New York bank that had investments in South Africa, in order to protest American support for apartheid. He was also interested in planning some kind of activity around Vietnam. But what? "Demonstration in Washington? Lobbying day? Combination? Other?" The PREP committee notes indicate uncertainty. Still, Booth and Gitlin wanted SDS to do *something*. Together, they prepared a "Draft Resolution on Vietnam," and invited I. F. Stone to speak to the SDS National Council on "America and the Third World."[12]

Zen Koans and New Recruits

That December, the SDS National Council met in New York City in an atmosphere of turmoil and expectation. The ERAP experiments, less than seven months old, continued to arouse enthusiasm

—and there was also fresh evidence of unrest on the campuses. In September, the Free Speech Movement had erupted at Berkeley. Though SDS had played only a minor role in the uprising, the organization's response was prompt. The national office and local SDS chapters helped arrange a tour for a number of leaders from the Free Speech Movement. Before the Berkeley rebellion, student protests had been largely limited to petitions, rallies and pickets. The Free Speech Movement suggested that more militant techniques, including sit-ins, the occupation of buildings and strikes, could be effective on campus. For young radicals, the sense of new possibilities was intoxicating.[13]

But at the same time, there were other, more unsettling developments within SDS. Though news of the ERAP experiments and the Free Speech Movement was producing a steady stream of new recruits, growth was proving to be a decidedly mixed blessing. "We now had a breadth that led to genuine debate," says Booth. For the first time, the word "faction" was being regularly used within SDS.[14]

At the National Council meeting that December, the most strident conflict between different factions concerned the Political Education Project, or PEP, which had been established at the last convention with Steve Max as one of its directors. PEP had helped organize SDS support for the reelection of President Johnson under the slogan "Part of the way with LBJ." Applying the analysis of *America and the New Era* to Johnson's candidacy, PEP partisans argued that a Democrat in the White House would check the growth of right-wing extremism and keep open the opportunity to pressure the President from the left. Besides, the Democratic Party platform was "superior to any passed by a major national party since the first New Deal."[15]

This may have been true. But to many activists it seemed increasingly irrelevant. It was boring to canvass neighborhoods for lackluster local candidates. Many SDS members were still angry at the refusal of the Democrats at their August convention to seat the Mississippi Freedom Democratic Party delegation that SNCC had organized as a challenge to that state's white Democratic establishment. Some were alarmed by developments in Vietnam. And those working in the ERAP projects had their own horror stories of hostility from local Democrats.

Tom Hayden, as usual, was a bellwether. In a paper written the previous spring, he had praised the "important gains of the new corporate society," such as arms-control efforts, desegregation and national economic planning. Scarcely six months later, in the light of his experience in the Newark ERAP project, Hayden was sounding a sharply different note. Scorning cautious reform efforts, he now called for a "revolt" that could express "emotion and anxiety as well as legislative demands; which finds a way to make a public and political issue out of alienation and abuse."[16]

"People who do community organizing," observes Booth, "are almost impelled to a sectarian attitude—I can speak without fear of contradiction, having done community organizing for many years myself. What makes community organizing viable is that you have a certain number of people willing to work incredibly long hours for almost no money, in order to be involved in something that they can totally mold. You have an overwhelming need as an organizer to justify your personal sacrifices by taking an ideological position that only doing exactly what you are doing is right and that everything else is wrong. That was the fundamental character of Hayden's attack against Max: 'I'm out here in Newark sleeping on a mattress, learning how to buy day-old bread and living communally. Either this organization is committed to being unconventional, or it's not.' That was the feeling."

In the past, the group had worked hard to paper over such differences. But not this time. After an acrimonious debate, Max's electoral strategy was decisively rejected.[17]

The struggle between Hayden and Max was complicated by the participation of new members, most of them unaware of the group's previous commitment to pluralism and experimentation, many of them resentful of the apparent lack of interest of the ERAP avantgarde in campus organizing. Most members of this new generation not only were inexperienced but also did not have the kind of political family history that had helped make SDS leaders like Max and Booth into such precocious activists.[18]

One newcomer was Jeffrey Shero, who would play a central role within SDS in the coming months. An Air Force brat who had helped desegregate toilets at the University of Texas with the memorable battle cry "Let my people go," Shero was a slim, bearded twenty-three-year-old who had worked in support of SNCC in several Southern states. "We are the first generation that grew up with the idea of annihilation," Shero explained to a reporter early in 1965. "In a situation like this, you have to go out and form your own religion." Finding his personal catechism in the "values" section of *The Port Huron Statement*, Shero brandished its rhetoric like a red flag of rebellion. "In Texas," he once explained, "to join SDS meant breaking with your family, it meant being cut off—it was like in early Rome joining a Christian sect—and the break was so much more total. . . . Your mother didn't say, 'Oh, isn't that nice, you're involved. We supported the republicans in the Spanish Civil War and now you're in SDS and I'm glad to see you're socially concerned.' In most of those places, it meant '*You Goddamn Communist.*' "[19]

Shero was certain that he wasn't the only middle-class student ripe for radicalism. "What thinking person cannot subscribe to democracy?" he asked in a paper on "Organization and the South" written shortly after he joined SDS. On conservative campuses like Texas, the group's democratic credo gave it an appeal that socialist groups lacked. At the same time, "the virtual autonomy of action that a local chapter can enjoy" permitted organizers to tailor their efforts to the special needs of each campus. By stressing the virtues of decentralization, newcomers like Shero accelerated the centrifugal forces that ERAP had already unleashed within SDS.[20]

These forces were further accelerated by a dramatic new style of leadership that was sweeping through SDS. Once again, Hayden was a bellwether. At meetings throughout this period, Hayden controlled the flow of discussion with non sequiturs presented as if they were Zen koans. For example: "What if we were to stay here for six years and not come to a decision?" "Suppose parliamentary democracy were a contrivance of nineteenth-century imperialism and merely a tool of enslavement?" "What would happen to bureaucracies if they had to be understood by the people they are supposed to serve?" "What would happen to professors if poor people could give lectures on poverty?" At one meeting around this time, Hayden refused to sit on stage and debate in front of an audience, instead taking a seat among the rank and file. "You're such a grass root, Tom," snapped his opponent, "that I don't know whether to debate you or water you."[21]

"This was imitation SNCC," says Booth. "It was such a thrill to have Bob Moses or Stokely Carmichael address a national meeting. I myself was infatuated with their personal style. While they talked, they would gesture and wave their finger around in a circle. It must have been funny to go to an SDS meeting and to see all these fingers moving around whenever anybody got up to talk."

Unfortunately, the new, ostensibly self-effacing style ill suited the increasingly sectarian tone of debate within SDS. Instead of being initiated into the tolerant and skeptical kind of radicalism that had been the birthright of SDS at Port Huron, new recruits like Shero were left at the National Council meeting to draw what lessons they might from histrionic displays of Socratic ignorance and moral humility—a humility that Tom Hayden, for one, belied when he vanquished a political opponent like Steve Max.

The Birth of the Anti-War Movement

It must have been a relief to hear the plainspoken I. F. Stone crisply marshal his facts and offer his arguments in his address to the National Council. Though his topic was "America and the Third World," Stone talked mainly about the war in Vietnam. He presented a brief history of the escalating military involvement in Southeast Asia, and eloquently argued that it was time for the United States to get out.

The National Council meeting resumed the following day to hear Paul Booth and Todd Gitlin present their proposals for the Peace Research and Education Project. After quickly approving a sit-in in March against the Chase Manhattan Bank to protest its investments in South Africa, the group opened debate on Vietnam.

Stone's speech had convinced a number of members of the need to protest the war—but there agreement ended. Gitlin proposed that SDS write and circulate a declaration "to this effect: 'I won't be drafted until the U.S. gets out of Vietnam.' " Jeff Shero suggested instead that SDS raise medical supplies and send them to the "Viet Cong by U.S. mails"—a bit of symbolic bravado that was typical of Shero's style and that duly alarmed Steve Max and his allies. The debate began to heat up. Was SDS pro-Communist? How could it endorse any action without first trying to educate its student constituency?

Discussion shifted to Gitlin and Booth's "Draft Resolution on Vietnam." Their resolution called on the President "to withdraw American troops from their undeclared war, and to use American influence to expedite a negotiated neutralist settlement in that beleaguered country." The group rejected the resolution, but then went on to discuss possible amendments. Gitlin reintroduced his "I won't be drafted" proposal, but it was defeated when Jim Brook, one of Max's allies, resorted to a bit of parliamentary subterfuge and introduced a substitute motion. He proposed that SDS sponsor "a march on Washington during spring vacation."

Some immediately rejected a march as too tame. Others argued that a march would be too difficult to pull off and that it would monopolize too much energy, jeopardizing the group's multi-issue approach and diverting resources that could be better used in the

ERAP projects. "In order to have a march on Washington," says Booth, "you obviously had to commit substantial resources. And that would put the organization on a dual trajectory, of having these community organizing projects, but also of developing the campus base."

At last Tom Hayden spoke. Summoning his best Zen style, he derailed the discussion with a series of sweeping questions, raising doubts about the wisdom of mounting a major anti-war effort. The matter came to a vote, and the proposal for a march was narrowly defeated.

The proponents of a march were unwilling to admit defeat. During a brief break in the meeting, while several ERAP partisans drifted away, those in favor of protesting the Vietnam War lobbied hard for support. They succeeded in persuading Bob Ross, who had voted with Hayden, to change his mind, and to reintroduce the motion for a march.

This time the proposal passed—barely. The meeting quickly agreed that SDS would be the sole organizational sponsor, but that any group could join—in explicit contravention of the exclusionary practices of SANE. Unable to reach consensus on a specific demand —unilateral withdrawal, negotiation and United Nations supervision were all discussed—the group finally approved a laconic statement: "SDS advocates that the U.S. get out of Vietnam. It so advocates for the following reasons: a) The war hurts the Vietnamese people; b) The war hurts the American people; c) SDS is concerned about the Vietnamese people and the American people."[22]

Responsibility for planning the march fell to Booth, Gitlin and the New York office of SDS. "All expectations are that it will be a big thing," wrote Booth a few weeks later. How big he could scarcely have guessed.[23]

Escalation

During the first week in January, letters went out inviting any interested groups to join the SDS march on April 17, Easter weekend. By the middle of January, I. F. Stone and Senator Ernest Gruening had both agreed to speak at the march. The smaller Marxist-Leninist groups quickly indicated their support. But mainstream organizations, including SANE, held back. In a series of meetings in January, A. J. Muste and other prominent older peace activists expressed their misgivings. They were unhappy that SDS had assumed sole sponsorship of the march, upset at the involvement of Marxist-Leninist groups and critical of the failure to present a clear alternative to the administration's Vietnam policy.[24]

While negotiations with SANE and the other mainstream peace groups dragged on, the significance of the march suddenly changed. On February 8, 1965, after an American air base in South Vietnam had been attacked by the "Viet Cong," as Americans called the guerrillas of the National Liberation Front in the South, U.S. planes began to bomb targets in North Vietnam. On February 11, the new U.S. policy of "sustained reprisal" was officially announced by President Johnson.

Across the country, small protests spontaneously erupted. In San Francisco, 300 students marched in front of the main branch of the post office, demanding a cease-fire and withdrawal of U.S. troops. In St. Louis, students staged a sit-in at the Federal Court House. At the University of Minnesota, the student government passed a resolution calling for U.S. withdrawal. In Washington, D.C., 7 people began a "fast for peace" in the George Washington University cafeteria, while on Capitol Hill, Senator Wayne Morse deplored a "black page in American history." In Cleveland, SDS President Paul Potter sent a telegram to President Johnson: "Sane men in capitals throughout the world today are hoping and praying that you will not escalate this mad war further." And in Berkeley, Paul Booth delivered an impromptu speech on the steps of Sproul Hall—he was on the West Coast scouting out the prospects for organizing defense workers and trying to bolster the profile of SDS in the area.[25]

Though Booth was preoccupied with planning the SDS protest against apartheid at the Chase Manhattan Bank on March 19 (the anniversary of the Sharpeville Massacre in South Africa in 1960), talk of Vietnam began to dominate his correspondence. "The number of spontaneous Vietnam demonstrations [is] very large," he wrote on March 5. "All the other peace groups are calling off their Easter Marches to support our demonstration. We are really the only thing moving, but we are moving very very rapidly."[26]

Relations between SDS and the mainstream peace movement remained tense. Early in March, representatives of the major groups met with SDS. In return for their support of the April march, they proposed that sponsorship of the march be transferred from SDS to an Ad-Hoc Committee—in effect, a temporary coalition. After lengthy negotiations, the SDS leaders accepted the proposal, subject to a poll of the SDS membership. Pending this formality, everyone agreed to act as if the Ad-Hoc Committee were a *fait accompli*. A new call for the April march went out endorsed by A. J. Muste, Norman Thomas and H. Stuart Hughes, among others.[27]

As votes trickled in from the SDS rank and file, however, it slowly became clear that no consensus in favor of the Ad-Hoc Committee existed. The proposed coalition was endorsed by only a slim majority. Some members objected to the way the vote had been handled. Fearful of setting an autocratic precedent, several national officers changed their minds. Less than a month before the march, SDS reversed itself and formally rejected the Ad-Hoc Committee, leaving its erstwhile allies understandably furious. It would not be the last time that the slow, cumbersome process of polling its membership caused the organization grief.

Meanwhile, anti-war sentiment on campuses around the country continued to intensify. On March 24, a group of teachers and students at the University of Michigan, including a large number of SDS and VOICE members, staged an all-night "teach-in" on the Vietnam War. The idea was widely imitated at schools around the country throughout the spring.[28]

The style of SDS agitation grew bolder. A poster showing a Vietnamese child badly scarred by napalm was printed with the message "WHY ARE WE BURNING, TORTURING, KILLING THE PEOPLE OF VIETNAM? . . . TO PREVENT FREE ELECTIONS." The national office mailed out a song sheet, with new lyrics set to civil rights songs: "And before I'll be fenced in," went one, "I'll vote for Ho Chi Minh, Or go back to the North and be free."[29]

Paul Booth moved to Washington to take on the task of coordinating the march. "My first job," he says, "was opening an office. What a mess that was. It was in the basement of the SNCC offices on Rhode Island Avenue. We spent hours cleaning out debris. We installed phones, negotiated with the National Park Police, coordinated all the logistics. I became one of the small number of people who know all the things you have to worry about when you organize a march on Washington."

Early in April, President Johnson committed more U.S. ground troops to Vietnam and ordered them to take the offensive. Although he tried to conceal these developments from the public, skepticism in Congress was mounting. Senators Frank Church and George McGovern came out against the war. Hoping to assuage his critics, the President directed his aides to draft a major speech.[30]

On April 7, 1965, Lyndon Johnson spoke at Johns Hopkins University. His text took a carrot-and-stick approach. The United States "will not be defeated," he declared—but he was ready for "unconditional discussions" with North Vietnam. Reaching into his pork barrel, he even offered to cut the Communists in on a U.S.-financed development project on the Mekong River. (In private, Johnson was more candid. "I'm not going to pull up my pants and run out of Vietnam," he bellowed at one liberal critic the day before his speech: "Don't you know the church is on fire over there?")[31]

The SDS response to Johnson's speech was swift, savage—and under the circumstances, remarkably shrewd. In a press release on April 8, the organization accused the President of "conning" the American people. It pointed out that Johnson had failed to offer a cease-fire, although the North Vietnamese had made this a precondition of any negotiations. It poked fun at his plans for building a "Mekong River TVA." It ridiculed his assumption that "push-button conspirators at mythical command posts" in Hanoi, Peking and Moscow generated revolutionary insurgencies in the Third World— as if "real and deep grievances" had nothing to do with it. Johnson's speech, the SDS statement concluded, was simply an attempt to make the administration's "obstinacy look like conciliation, its unreason look like reason, its war look like peace."[32]

Many older peace leaders were not yet prepared to draw that conclusion. Unamused by SDS ditties about Ho Chi Minh and appalled by posters of burnt babies, they found both the tone and the content of the SDS press release offensive. After all the backbiting and confusion of the previous weeks, some of them wanted simply to pull out and denounce the march; an attempt had already been made to dissuade Senator Gruening from speaking. Others wanted to lend the event carefully qualified support. After long debate at a last-minute meeting, several of the most prominent older peace activists, including A. J. Muste and Norman Thomas, finally agreed to issue a statement that expressed general sympathy with the SDS march, deplored "particular positions expressed by some of the elements in the march" and applauded the President's speech of April 7 for raising "the possibility of a healthy shift of American policy" in Vietnam. Despite its blandly conciliatory tone, this statement became the pretext for a caustic editorial about the SDS march which appeared shortly afterward in *The New York Post*—at the time, a bastion of liberal opinion. "Several leaders of the peace movement," declared the *Post*, "have taken clear note of attempts to turn the event into a pro-Communist production." But "especially in the aftermath of Mr. Johnson's call for unconditional negotiations, there is no justification for transforming the march into a frenzied one-sided anti-American show."[33]

The statement and accompanying editorial recalled the quarrel between SDS and the League for Industrial Democracy in the summer of 1962. Once again, two generations of the left were at odds. Once again, a series of misunderstandings had helped to poison relations. Once again, the issue was anti-Communism.

But this time, the conflict was out in the open, in full view of the mass media. This time, the old issue of "united frontism" was real: SDS *had* entered into a temporary alliance with Marxist-Leninist groups. And this time, a number of older radicals and liberals quickly leaped to the defense of SDS. As a result, SDS was in no danger of collapsing under an onslaught from its critics. On the contrary: popular support for the march continued to mushroom.

The First March

The march took place on a sunny spring day. Two weeks before, SDS had expected perhaps 10,000 people to participate. More than 15,000 showed up—some estimates ran as high as 25,000. This was no small circle of friends: this was the germ of a mass movement.

The day began with a picket outside the White House. "By 11:30," wrote Paul Booth in his report on the march, "the picket line completely encircled the White House." At 12:30, the crowd started to march toward the grounds of the Washington Monument. "As the marchers filed in," wrote Booth, "Phil Ochs, Bill Frederick, and the Freedom Voices sang about the war and what we would do with the peace if it could be won."

The first speaker was SNCC field-worker Bob Parris (Moses), who had recently stopped using his (real) last name in one of the most striking gestures of self-abnegating democratic (anti-)leadership in the Sixties. (He did not want to be regarded as a political messiah like the biblical Moses.) Parris maintained that the killing of peasants in Vietnam by American soldiers was morally and politically on a par with the killing of civil rights workers in the South by segregationists. "Use Mississippi not as a moral lightning rod," he said, "but if you use it at all use it as a looking glass."

I. F. Stone reminded the crowd that the British government in 1776 had considered the American Revolution a plot controlled from Paris; he also said that the men in charge of American foreign policy were "decent human beings" caught up in "monstrous institutions that have a life of their own." He urged the demonstrators to "go home and talk about these things, but not in tones of hatred and self-righteousness. We have to get out of this reign of hatred."

Staughton Lynd, a young Yale historian who had directed the Freedom Schools in the 1964 Mississippi Summer Project, talked about the activities of dissident faculty members around the country. He declared that he had refused to pay a part of his income tax, in protest against the war.

Senator Ernest Gruening criticized the Communist regime in Peking, but urged "the immediate cessation of our bombing in North Vietnam."

After Judy Collins sang Bob Dylan's "The Times They Are A-Changin'," a welfare mother recruited by the Cleveland ERAP project spoke. According to Booth's paraphrase, she said "that poor people in America are direct victims of the war in Vietnam, which is foreclosing the chances for a serious attack on poverty by wasting the money in Asia and by turning America into an armed camp."[34]

The formal program had been carefully planned to end with the speech of Paul Potter, who at the time was president of SDS. "What we must do," declared Potter, "is begin to build a democratic and humane society in which human life and initiative are precious"— it was the special burden of his speech to express the larger political vision animating SDS. "The incredible war in Vietnam," said Potter, "has provided the razor, the terrifying sharp cutting edge that has finally severed the last vestige of illusion that morality and democracy are the guiding principles of American foreign policy. . . . What in fact has the war done for freedom in America? It has led to even more vigorous governmental efforts to control information, manipulate the press and pressure and persuade the public through distorted or downright dishonest documents."

Potter climaxed his speech with a barrage of rhetorical questions. "What kind of system," he asked, "is it that justifies the United States or any country seizing the destinies of the Vietnamese people and using them callously for its own purpose? What kind of system is it that disenfranchises people in the South, leaves millions upon millions of people throughout the country impoverished and excluded from the mainstream and promise of American society, that creates faceless and terrible bureaucracies and makes those the place where people spend their lives and do their work, that consistently puts material values before human values—and still persists in calling itself free and still persists in finding itself fit to police the world? What place is there for ordinary men in that system, and how are they to control it, make it bend itself to their wills rather than bending them to its?

"We must name that system," said Potter, pausing for effect. Someone in the crowd yelled, "Capitalism." Others shouted him down. Potter finished his thought: "We must name it, describe it, analyze it, understand it and change it."[35]

The speech brought the crowd to its feet. As have few documents before or after, Potter's speech managed to capture the moral passion and restless questioning that constituted the heart and soul of the early New Left. "I talked about the system," he later wrote, "not because I was afraid of the term capitalism but because I wanted ambiguity, because I sensed there was something new afoot in the world that we were part of that made the rejection of the old terminology part of the new hope for radical change in America."[36]

"That may be true," says Booth. "But a lot of our discussion about Potter's speech was a lot more down to earth. We had hilarious debates about whether to name the system. Well, we all know this is capitalism, but should we say so? Maybe we should call it imperialism. Or maybe we shouldn't say." With the *New York Post* editorial fresh in their minds, the inner circle working on Potter's speech decided, as Booth recalls, "to leave it a mystery as to whether or not there was a capitalist system in the United States." Ambiguity had a tactical as well as intellectual value. If nothing else, it was useful for fobbing off liberal critics.

After Potter's speech, the crowd surged toward the Capitol, bearing a "Petition to Congress." "The problems of America cry out for attention," declared the petition, "and our entanglement in South Vietnam postpones the confrontation of these issues while prolonging the misery of the people of that war-torn land. You must act now to reverse this sorry state of affairs. We call on you to end, not extend the war in Vietnam."[37]

The form of the protest was orthodox—a group of citizens submitting a petition to their elected representatives. But the mood of the moment transcended its carefully calibrated symbolism. At a camp in Port Huron three years before, sixty people, after four days experiencing the pleasures of face-to-face political debate, had ratified a document calling for participatory democracy. In a handful of experimental projects in a few inner-city ghettos during the last twelve months, small circles of friends had probed the limits of democracy in practice, trying to change themselves, and to change America. Now they were marching with thousands of others on Congress. Walking 80 abreast, they clogged the Washington Mall. The vision of participatory democracy crystallized in a new experience, a new sense of power, a new sentiment of solidarity.

"It was unbearably moving," wrote Staughton Lynd a few weeks later, "to watch the sea of banners and signs move out from the

Sylvan Theater toward the Capitol as Joan Baez, Judy Collins and others sang 'We Shall Overcome.' Still more poignant was the perception—and I checked my reaction with many others who felt as I did—that as the crowd moved down the Mall toward the seat of government, its path delimited on each side by rows of chartered buses so that there was nowhere to go but forward, toward the waiting policemen, it seemed that the great mass of people would simply flow on through and over the marble buildings, that our forward movement was irresistibly strong, that even had some been shot or arrested nothing could have stopped that crowd from taking possession of its government."[38]

The first march against the war ended without incident. But for some young radicals, a new era of chiliastic hope had begun.

Revolutionary Symbolism

That night, 70 of the key participants in the march held a meeting in Washington. What was to be done next? The march had succeeded beyond their wildest dreams. Despite the fears of liberal critics, the tone of the event had been sober, its rhetoric finely shaded. SDS was now the undisputed leader of an anti-war movement that was growing far more rapidly than anyone had anticipated.

Perhaps the most astonishing proposal came from Tom Hayden. Resurrecting a device widely used during the American Revolution to protest the legitimacy of colonial institutions and to circumvent their power, Hayden suggested that SDS plan a national convention to create a new Continental Congress, and then stage some sort of demonstration within the Capitol—a symbolic gesture that would dramatize the political philosophy of the New Left to the rest of the country. Such a Continental Congress, Hayden later wrote, would represent "all the people who feel excluded from the higher circles of decision making in the country." It would become "a kind of second government, receiving taxes from its supporters, establishing contact with other nations, holding debates on American foreign and domestic policy, dramatizing the plight of all groups that suffer from the American system."[39]

Hayden was finally spelling out one of the revolutionary implications of participatory democracy. But apart from Staughton Lynd, who immediately grasped the historical resonance of the idea, most participants thought Hayden's proposal bizarre.

Meanwhile, there was growing sentiment for a break with the

League for Industrial Democracy, in part because LID's tax-exempt status inhibited the ability of SDS to engage in partisan political activity. The group debated a proposal to leave LID and move the national office from New York to Chicago. They agreed to move the office as soon as possible. But the final break with LID was delayed until October. Ironically, given the furious fight after the Port Huron convention, the divorce went smoothly. Many within LID were doubtless relieved to see SDS go its own way; SDS, for its part, left quietly. The issue of tax exemption gave both sides a pretext for a mutually amicable separation.

Much of the rest of the meeting centered on Vietnam. In the minds of most SDS members, including Booth, radical social change required more than simply protesting the war in Vietnam. The logic of their analysis of liberal corporatism had led them to the slums of Newark and Cleveland. And the success of the march, most agreed, should not divert them from their other goals. It is not surprising, then, that the group had difficulty deciding on a plan of action. A proposal to picket and leaflet military bases and induction centers was debated, and shelved, with an admonition that before such a risky plan was implemented, the membership should be polled. A proposal to send a delegation to Hanoi was submitted to a committee for further study. A newcomer to SDS, Carl Oglesby, a thirty-year-old technical writer and convinced anti-war activist who had helped Todd Gitlin draft press releases for the march, was hired to head a group that would gather "research, information, and publications," primarily on the war. It was finally agreed that a number of new full-time community-organizing projects should be created in the coming summer and should make anti-war organizing one of their priorities.[40]

At the time, Paul Booth was elated. "Throughout the weekend, the congressional opposition to the war began to come out of hiding," he wrote a few weeks later. "Chairman J. William Fulbright of the Senate Foreign Relations Committee announced opposition to the bombings of North Vietnam, and received backing from other committee members." The Gallup poll, he noted, indicated that 33 percent of the voters opposed the war. Even the hostility of the administration gave cause for cheer—better to be feared than dismissed as quixotic.[41]

Looking back, though, Booth is far less charitable. "We really screwed up," he says. "We had the opportunity at that meeting to make SDS *the* organizational vehicle of the anti-war movement. It was ours. We had achieved it. Instead, we chose to go off in all kinds of different directions—not including the direction of systematically organizing all the anti-war groups on all the campuses into our own network. The main thrust of anti-war activity was left unorganized by us."

Media Images

The tempo of events was accelerating. Just four months before, SDS had been desperate for media coverage, mailing out press releases to small magazines like *The Activist, New America* and *Liberation*. Now, suddenly, the national press was interested. In a Sunday front-page article a month before the march, *The New York Times* had run its first major story on SDS, sympathetically depicting a meeting of the group in Chicago: "the young men, in sports coats and without ties, and the young women, in skirts and black stockings, sat on the floor and talked about such things as 'community organization,' 'powerlessness' and 'participatory democracy.' "[42]

At the march itself, the *Times* interviewed Booth. "We're really not just a peace group," he stressed to the reporter, trying to get across the organization's other goals. "We are working on domestic problems—civil rights, poverty, university reform. We feel passionately and angrily about things in America, and we feel that a war in Asia will destroy what we're trying to do here."[43]

The liberal press gave mixed reviews to the march. "The word from inside the Administration," began a lukewarm editorial in *The Nation*, "is that the President, backed by his chief military and diplomatic advisers, looks on the rising peace drive with some alarm because of the encouragement it may be offering to Hanoi." *The New Republic*, by contrast, applauded the marchers' moderation: "their basic demand . . . was for a stronger 'will' to end the fighting; they would leave the specifics 'to the diplomats.' " It also sympathetically described the broader political views of the marchers: "They distrust Bigness and Bureaucracy; they fear the dehumanizing effects of automation. They are peaceminded, but not pacifist; repelled by any holy war against Communism, but not Communist; anxious to end poverty, but unimpressed by what our welfare state plans for the poor."[44]

Shortly afterward, both *The Nation* and *The New Republic* ran enthusiastic stories on SDS, by Jack Newfield and Andrew Kopkind respectively. Kopkind's portrait was so flattering that SDS reprinted it as a pamphlet. While Newfield, who for several years had been a

member of SDS, focused on the April march, Kopkind visited the
ERAP projects in Cleveland and in Newark, where he experienced a
kind of epiphany that was not uncommon among young liberals
coming face to face with the New Left for the first time. "Their
commitment to a common cause," wrote Kopkind years later, "cut
into the loneliness of work, which I had always assumed was inevitable. . . . In that intense mood, I fantasized an end to alienation,
despair, emptiness. I wanted to shout out loud." "More than anything," Kopkind shouted in the lead sentence of his piece in *The
New Republic*, "the new generation of students cares about democracy. They have talked about it, written about it, demonstrated
about it. Now they have begun to organize people to change their
communities into more democratic forms." At the end of the year,
when Newfield published another long story on the New Left in *The
Nation*, he struck a similar (though less original) chord; he started
with a quotation from *The Port Huron Statement*: "We seek the
establishment of a democracy of individual participation. . . ."[45]

As new members began to pour into SDS, it is no wonder that
democracy became one of their obsessions. Whether or not SDS
chose to make the war in Vietnam its main focus, opposition to the
war was attracting recruits in unprecedented numbers. The ideas of
The Port Huron Statement were disseminated through writers like
Newfield and Kopkind, and slogans like "Let the people decide."
Every eighteen-year-old, draft-eligible kid knew that he had not
shared in the decision to fight in Vietnam. It was not even clear that
Congress had shared in that decision. To many young radicals, the
war was a shocking example of a democracy in decay. Thousands
now embarked on the quest for "a democracy of individual participation."

Anti-Politics

In June, some five hundred people gathered for the annual convention of SDS at a camp near Kewadin, a small town in upper Michigan. Paul Jacobs and Saul Landau, who attended the convention in
order to gather material for a book on the New Left, described the
scene: "Sleeping bags were crowded together in small rooms or on
the cold ground outside. The food was cheap, badly cooked, and
insufficient to feed the crowd. But no one expected anything better.
Despite the lure of the lake, the warm sun, the empty tennis courts,
most of the people spent their energy in workshops, discussing the

issues that had brought them to the convention: program, policy and strategy, the election of officers and the exchange of information."[46]

Of these functions, the exchange of information was the most crucial. By the summer of 1965, the group's disdain for formal doctrine had become so pronounced that, as Jacobs and Landau noted with some amazement, "the primary source of information is conversation." There was certainly a lot to talk about. In the last six months, the number of members, by one estimate, had nearly doubled. "The majority of the newer SDS members," reported Jacobs and Landau, "are not well read in Marxism or in other radical literature." Rival groups on the left had traditionally recruited adherents to an ideology as well as an organization. But from the beginning, SDS had been different. Even *The Port Huron Statement* was considered "a living document," open to revision in the light of changing circumstances. In the wake of the ERAP experiments, the meaning of its key concept, participatory democracy, was in flux. "Today in SDS," observed Steve Max a few weeks later, "there is no predominant theory of any permanence which guides the organization—it rapidly becomes what its members are and its members change with events." Since the organization was thriving, its intellectual drift did not bother most members. After all, you didn't need a weatherman to know which way the wind was blowing. You could just listen to Bob Dylan—by this time, a central influence on SDS. Or you could listen to Tom Hayden. "Power in America," he explained at the convention, "is abdicated by individuals to top-down organizational units, and it is in the recovery of this power that the movement becomes distinct from the rest of the country and a new kind of man emerges."[47]

A new kind of radical had already emerged. The endless meetings and gentle persuasion pioneered by ERAP projects like Cleveland had given new meaning to Hayden's old call for a "re-assertion of the personal." "For many members," reported Jacobs and Landau, "SDS is more than an organization: it is a community of friends." Long hair was becoming common, and the sweet smell of marijuana hung in the air for the first time at an SDS convention. "A raid on the . . . Convention would have resulted in the arrest of two-thirds of the active core of the organization," complained Steve Max in a letter to Paul Booth: "If God had meant us to be anarchists we would have been born with beards."[48]

Before the convention began, it had been agreed that no effort would be made to draft a sequel to *The Port Huron Statement*. Instead, the convention was organized around a series of workshops devoted to discussing papers that had been written on a variety of different topics—on foreign policy, on "democracy and organizational structure," on the university, on "alienation from American culture," on the idea of "counter institutions" that had been generated by the ERAP experiments.[49]

Paul Booth, in a paper that coolly analyzed the alternatives for anti-war organizing, from mass demonstrations to burning draft cards, closed with a dialogue between "Carl," a despairing militant ("The whole world feels sick"), and "Paul," a voice of reason, hope —and tactical discipline. "Your commitment," says Paul to Carl, "is redeemed by the force it can mount when joined with the commitment of other people. . . . [That] commitment demands that we act, and that means to me that we act in a way that holds the most promise."[50]

Many of the other working papers contained shrewd observations about the direction of what virtually everyone by now was calling "the Movement." Paul Potter, in a characteristically terse one-page statement, questioned the kind of defiant identification with the Viet Cong that was becoming common. In an "Open Letter to Tom Hayden," Paul Cowan criticized Hayden's idea of creating a Continental Congress, deploring "the exaggerated attachment some people in the movement are developing to symbolic politics itself." Dick Flacks pointed out the tension between "two types of goals," one involving "a redistribution of wealth and power in the society," the other an "attempt to achieve 'community,' to reach levels of intimacy and directness with others . . . to be self-expressive, to be free." Flacks worried about investing too much energy in "personal salvation and gratification," only to realize "that these possibilities are, after all, limited"; he also warned that when "the necessary distinction between the public and the private self breaks down, either the community is undermined, or personal freedom is sacrificed."[51]

It is not clear what impression any of these papers made. The talk at most workshops was informal, unstructured, meandering. Paul Booth's most vivid memory is of a group marriage. "We all got together," he says, "and functioned as the priest. I remember personally not being up to figuring out how the national organization should evolve. This whole period after the march on Washington, I lost my sense of what made sense. I skipped some of the sessions and just wandered around gossiping."

By now, the self-abnegating style of Robert Parris (Moses) and Tom Hayden had become *de rigueur*. And an (anti-)leader in action was far more striking than any working paper. Jacobs and Landau described the performance of one (unidentified) speaker: "Leaders mean organization, organization means hierarchy, and hierarchy is undemocratic. It connotes bureaucracy and impersonality, said one of the speakers at the plenary session of the Kewadin, Michigan, convention. He described his project, in Hoboken, New Jersey, as a non-project. One of his speeches, about forty-five minutes long, was an example of a kind of spasmodic sincerity, an inarticulate, highly gesticulating presentation which emphasized 'gutting with people.' . . . If there was to be a transformation in values, the spokesman for the Hoboken non-project felt, it had to come through personal relationships. Throughout his speech, he spoke of alienation, the quality of human life produced by the bureaucratized society."[52]

Internal Democracy

This speech was symptomatic of the growing hostility within SDS to "elitism," hierarchy, structure—almost anything that anyone might perceive as an obstacle to free will. The convention proved unable to agree on any substantive matter, apart from reiterating the commitment of SDS to "nonexclusionism"—the refusal, on principle, to rule out joint action with Marxist-Leninist groups. The only other issue that aroused passionate debate was "internal democracy"—the question of what political structure, if any, SDS should have.

Although this issue was an old one in SDS, it had assumed a fresh cogency in the wake of the ERAP experiments, the April anti-war march and the subsequent influx of new members. Despite its deepening experimental commitment to direct democracy, SDS could not guarantee that participation would be equally open to every member. Veterans like Hayden and Booth naturally commanded unusual prestige within the growing organization—and the increasing size and informality of SDS meetings only enhanced their authority. The agenda for a convention workshop on "Democracy and Organizational Structure" indicated some of the questions that now arose: "How do we achieve the kind of democracy and participation we want within a dynamic social movement? What do these questions mean for SDS in particular? How does consensus democracy relate to traditional formal approaches? What is the role of the ideologue or leader in a democratic movement? Is there a dichotomy between a movement and an organization? How do we increase participation and communication?"[53]

One of the most ardent advocates of creating a more democratic structure for SDS was Jeff Shero. He had earned respect at the convention by jousting with the most renowned SDS (anti-)leader of all, Tom Hayden. "I thought he was a smart dude, but I wasn't in awe of him at all," Shero later recalled. The two crossed swords at a workshop over the relative importance of poor people and middle-class students. Claiming that "the middle class worker not only sells his labor . . . but his mental allegiance as well," Shero argued "that many middle class business employees are even more alienated than working class men" (as if "working class men" had no "mental allegiance" to sell). Hayden defended the radical potential of the poor. After the workshop was over, both agreed to continue their debate before a plenary session of the convention. "I got a little scared," Shero has recalled. "But then for some reason Tom decided not to argue: he got up and gave about a five-minute somewhat Zen speech, and sat down, and didn't come head to head against me."[54]

In the working paper that he had written for the convention, Shero had proposed creating a "Movement for a Democratic Society." Including adults as well as students, "A Movement for a Democratic Society," explained Shero, "would elect representatives from all parts of the organization. . . . A national MDS conference . . . would be the first truly democratic organization, representative of America, since World War I. Because the MDS program would be initiated from the bottom, rather than by an organizational elite determining policy, these meetings bringing together people on an equal basis from all stations of life would be a radically new concept in American political organization."[55]

At the 1965 convention, the organization willy-nilly plunged in a new, ostensibly more democratic direction. Members like Shero increasingly viewed veterans like Hayden with suspicion: the "old guard," as leaders like Hayden had come to be called, seemed to represent an "organizational elite" at odds with the ideal of participatory democracy. A determination to root out "elitism" and bureaucracy swept through the convention. In a report shortly afterward, Steve Max parodied the prevailing mood: "Structural democracy is an obvious fraud; out with it! Representative government doesn't really represent anyone; out with it!" Some workshops debated whether or not to have a chairman. To supervise the plenary sessions, which usually consisted of more than 250 people, members were picked at random. "Convention credentials went unchecked," complained Max, "and some key votes went uncounted. What constituted two-thirds, a majority, or a quorum of the delegates remains a mystery to this day." The Convention discussed the virtues of being a movement rather than an organization, debated abolishing national officers, and refused to hire a new national secretary—traditionally, the group's chief administrator. The abolition of the national office was halted only by the decision to hold a referendum—everyone agreed that such a democratic end required the use of a properly democratic means. And that was not all. The convention also ordered the national office to hold a referendum on any program (such as draft resistance) that entailed legal risks—the idea was that the membership should be able to vote on, and veto, any dangerous program.[56]

Steve Max, for one, thought these reforms were insane. Deploring the prevailing "confusion between lack of structure and democracy," he issued a prescient warning: "To destroy formal structures in society is unfortunately no small task," he wrote, "but to do so in one's own organization is not only possible but easy."[57]

Most of the "old guard," however, were in no mood to argue with Young Turks like Shero. Before the convention, some members of the Ann Arbor clique had approached Booth about accepting their nomination to become the next national secretary. Booth adamantly rejected the idea. Writing privately to Todd Gitlin, he explained that SDS needed "to make national guys like me into regional and local-based guys, and make the new generation of local-regional people into national people. . . . Here the point that I have vast contacts is part of a self-defeating syndrome—the people in the middle *always* have them. NEW BLOOD!!"[58]

At the close of the Kewadin Convention, the delegates elected Jeff Shero vice president and picked Carl Oglesby as the new president. Though older and more experienced than most members, Oglesby was certainly not part of the "old guard"—he had been a member of SDS for less than four months! Oglesby was naturally a little bewildered by his sudden ascent. As he bunked down that night, he remembers asking Paul Potter, the outgoing president, why he thought the convention had chosen him. Potter, says Oglesby, "just turned over on his bed and faced the wall and wouldn't say a thing." As Oglesby came to realize, Potter's silence was an implicit expression of his democratic convictions. Like Cincinnatus returning to his fields after serving the Republic in war, Potter was preparing to return to the ERAP project in Cleveland. His silence left Oglesby to guess for himself the meaning of his office—and the secret of being a truly democratic (anti-)leader.[59]

Getting Attention

His stint as PREP director drawing to a close, Booth was eager to become involved in a community organizing project. Interviewed by Paul Jacobs and Saul Landau at the convention, Booth explained that "Our most important experiment now, I think, is ERAP. I think we have made some breakthroughs. . . . I'm going to Oakland to help set up the project there. I feel comfortable in the role of a student organizer, and I think SDS can out-organize the other [campus] groups because it is more in tune with the mood of students. The mood? It's searching, honesty, democracy, like we have inside SDS."[60]

On his trip to the West Coast, Booth had recruited a nucleus of sociology graduate students to supervise the Berkeley SDS chapter and to scout out an appropriate neighborhood for a Bay Area ERAP project. Targeting West Oakland, the group followed the Cleveland model. "We found a house to rent," says Booth, "that had enough room, if you stuck everybody into various corners, for everybody to sleep in, and to live in communally." It was taken for granted that the Oakland project would be run by consensus. "There wasn't any authority exercised," says Booth. "That meant that some important decisions were not made effectively. We had a problem with our house not being in conformance with the building code. Because nobody was really in charge, the problem just persisted." Still, the commune's democratic structure did not hamper its ability to organize—and Booth did not feel any serious reservations about the value of rule-by-consensus.

"We proceeded to survey the neighborhood," says Booth. "In fairly short order, we pulled together a very large public housing tenants' organization." The Oakland project also tried to get local kids to file for C.O. status, in hopes of "clogging up the draft system"—this was Booth's main focus. In addition, Booth and the other members of the commune participated in the most important anti-war protest in the Bay Area that summer, an attempt by demonstrators to blockade troop trains in Berkeley and Emeryville. "It was a confrontation with the real enemy," wrote Booth afterward, "the war machine incarnate carrying helpless draftees off to kill and die. For a flickering moment the movement regained an understanding that characterized the 1960–1962 peace movement." As Booth himself conceded at the time, the troop-train protests made little political sense. They alienated more people than they attracted. The action nonetheless spurred the moral passion of the protesters. "It was pretty exciting," says Booth. "It was a burgeoning movement. And we were getting a lot of attention." For the moment, that seemed satisfaction enough.[61]

Chaos

In Chicago, meanwhile, the SDS national office was in a state of mounting chaos. Applications for membership and letters asking for literature deluged an office in the midst of conducting "an experiment in office democracy," as Jeff Shero called it. In an effort to root out "elitism," it had been agreed that all staffers would share responsibility for processing the mail; the person who sent the last copy of a document would be responsible for mimeographing, collating and stapling another batch. But nobody liked to mimeograph, collate and staple. Nobody liked to stuff envelopes. Consequently, nobody did these things. Elitism was routed—but virtually no mail was processed.[62]

As the chaos grew, so did alarm among the veteran members. As the summer drew to a close, two letters to the national office, one from Al Haber, the other from Dickie Magidoff, another veteran of the Ann Arbor days, helped to crystallize a shared sentiment that something needed to be done—and quickly. Magidoff posed the key question bluntly: "Is SDS, as a national organization, worth preserving in any recognizable form? If so, what is to be its structure?" The group, in his view, had a choice: "On the one hand we can choose to see SDS as the developing and growing organizational manifestation of the movement. If this is the case, we should exert every effort to integrate its parts, to relate them one to the other, to formalize its operations, to make sure that it is . . . truly representative. . . . On the other hand, we can see the movement as something growing way beyond SDS, that is being molded on its many local levels by different forces, different ideas; that at present its greatest needs are commitment, initiative, motion, not any kind of organization. . . . If this is the case, then the above organizational questions are not immediately relevant, and we should recognize that by ending the pretense that the National Council or the Convention is a decision-making body."[63]

The crisis came to a head in September at a meeting of the National Council in Bloomington, Indiana. Representatives of the old guard wanted to cut back the summer experiment in office democracy. Jeff Shero wanted to expand it.

Shero was forced to admit that the " 'democratization' of office work" had so far been a disaster. But he argued that the organization had "a theoretical commitment to certain ideals." The ideals were fine, it was the experiment that had been flawed. As Shero saw it, the mess in the national office had been caused by cramped living quarters and meager salaries—not by too much democracy. He urged the group to phase out the national office entirely, and create instead a new, more democratic and decentralized federation of regional offices.

The debate left Carl Oglesby, for one, a bit puzzled: "Why now are we stressing [the] problem of identity with [the] world as it is?" While SDS dithered over its definition of democracy, leadership of the anti-war movement was slipping from its grasp. Why weren't they discussing Vietnam? "We are not in [a] position," someone replied with disarming candor, "to discuss politics when we don't really understand our basic ideas and rhetoric." Bob Ross agreed: the "most impor[tant] thing," he said, "is to get change in America— but change is meaningless without [an] end in mind."[64]

The debate dragged on, in part because the difficulty of agreeing on a democratic structure for the national office implicated the final goal of participatory democracy, as the group fully appreciated.[65] Difficulties that *The Port Huron Statement* had managed to gloss over now came back to haunt the young radicals. Would a different internal structure make democracy feasible? Was the goal of participatory democracy impractical? What, in fact, did "participatory democracy" mean? One man, one vote? Responsible leaders held accountable in regularly scheduled elections? The informed and active involvement of every citizen in local and national political affairs? Direct action as well as voting? Rule-by-consensus in a face-to-face circle of friends? Honesty and authenticity within a tight-knit community? Abolition of all traces of hierarchy and the division of labor, abolition of elections and all representative offices?

These questions could obviously not be resolved by the National Council. So the group agreed to organize a special conference, to be held in December, devoted to reflection and debate—a meeting that might rekindle the intellectual spark of *The Port Huron Statement* and perhaps clarify the group's democratic credo. In the interim, in a stopgap effort to cobble together some kind of anti-war program, the National Council endorsed the "International Days of Protest" that were scheduled to begin October 15, urged local chapters to protest the war locally and asked the national office to prepare a referendum on anti-draft organizing, as stipulated by the convention. By a slim margin—the final vote was 14 to 12—the National Council also decided to hire a new national secretary, which the convention had refused to do. The group then unanimously elected Paul Booth to the job—he was as able an administrator as SDS could muster.[66]

Booth got the call in Oakland. "I was an easy guy to tap," he says. "I was very much into doing what was needed. I wasn't so deep into the ERAP project that I couldn't extricate myself. I didn't seek the job; but I didn't resist it, either. I was easy to convince."

Little did he know that he was wading into a political swamp.

Conflict

In the fall of 1965, the SDS national office was located on the South Side of Chicago. A reporter from *The New York Times* described "a warren of dank second-floor offices, badly lighted and in wretched repair." On the walls were posters: a Picasso design for the Italian Communist Party; a charcoal drawing of Eugene Debs; IWW stickers; a SNCC poster; a print by Ben Shahn; a Jules Feiffer cartoon; newspaper photographs of Bob Dylan; and the slogan "Make love, not war."[67]

Despite the difficulties of the summer, the office staff were still carrying on their experiment in democracy. They continued to live in the same apartment and eat together. Each was paid $12.50 a week. A great deal of time was spent discussing living arrangements.[68] The national office in effect was striving to emulate the ERAP experiments. Of course, the participants in this particular experiment were elected officers and clerical workers, not a self-selected circle of friends. As a result, the group in Chicago conspicuously lacked the esprit de corps that characterized the ERAP organizers in Cleveland and Oakland.

Paul Booth's arrival only made matters worse. From the outset, he and Jeff Shero were at odds. Shero considered Booth a free-lance bureaucrat: "I perceived the National Secretary's role as coming to straighten out the office and get it running smoothly again." Booth interpreted his office more broadly. He assumed that he had been hired to use his Washington connections, strategic savvy and smooth style to increase the impact of the organization. "My job," he told Jack Newfield, "is to politicize the organization and give it some form, and to make sure there is real internal political education . . . SDS has to be more than just an outlet for personal frustrations. It has to have a tangible effect on the society."[69]

One of Booth's first priorities was to get news circulating within the organization again. For a start, he proposed instituting a "key list" mailing. "This was a big list at this point," says Booth: "it included all the chapters and all the ERAP projects." But some members of the national office objected that the term "key list" was elitist. A lengthy debate followed. "So we called it a 'worklist' newsletter," says Booth, wanly smiling at the memory. "And then there was the question of production. Who was actually going to process the incoming membership applications? Who was actually going to correspond with people who wanted to set up chapters?"

Booth's sense of frustration quickly began to mount. It was one thing for the Oakland ERAP project to avoid repairing a rented house; it was something else again for the SDS national office to let requests for membership sit around unanswered. " 'Within the new left,' " Booth told a reporter for *The New York Times Magazine* that fall, " 'you know, we work for consensus, but how can you get consensus if there is an already committed bloc?' He shook his head regretfully, saying, 'The self-destructive forces within the coalition really shouldn't be underestimated. Outside of meetings, though, things work O.K.' " Within SDS, Booth was more candid. "What is amazing," he complained at the end of the year, "is that the organization refuses to admit the fact that it plays an important role in American politics, and as a consequence, refuses to create responsible mechanisms from week to week." The longer he struggled to get the national office smoothly functioning, the clearer his convictions became: endless meetings conducted according to the Quaker norm of democracy were no way to run a national organization.[70]

Shero by contrast was unflagging in his zeal for avant-garde democratic probes. He feared that any consolidation of bureaucracy would rob the Movement of its cutting edge. "Some people have personalities that allow them to work well in offices and enjoy it," wrote Shero that fall. "The problem is that if the natural dynamic is for power to flow to the bureaucracy, then those people who best thrive in a bureaucratic situation, exercise it. This is probably the key. The men who make the revolution"—Shero evidently counted himself among them—"are usually not thrilled by or adept at office work."[71]

Late in 1965, Shero wrote privately to a friend in Texas. His friend had asked for comments on an essay about C. Wright Mills and the face-to-face "public" as the model of true democracy. Shero wholeheartedly agreed that Mill's "public" was the image of an ideal democracy. But in his reply, he passed quickly from issues of political theory to the situation in the national office. "One of the great causes of my alienation here in the office," explained Shero, "has come from people who espouse expedient answers to our problems. . . . Booth for example sees us as applying our total political force through a focal point, the National Office, so [as] to have the greatest effect. On the short term his method is correct. It is hardly revolutionary though, and it doesn't build the large 'public' that you speak of." Years later, Shero charged that Booth had turned him into a "psychological wreck"—he had been cowed by Booth's barbed wit, articulate convictions and impressive network of contacts.[72]

Booth managed to restore the SDS administrative apparatus to some semblance of working order. He drew up a program for anti-draft organizing and sent it out for a referendum, reminding members that encouraging draft evasion was punishable by up to five years in jail and a $10,000 fine. He also fired off letters to a variety of foundations, looking for a grant to support the December conference. "The phenomenal growth of SDS in the last year has taken no one by surprise more than it has SDS itself," wrote Booth. "Two years ago we viewed ourselves as the 'intellect of the student left'; to have foreseen a year in which SDS would come to be identified with the Berkeley revolt, a March on Washington, and community union organizing projects in Northern ghettoes was impossible for those of us who had self consciously dedicated ourselves to our 'roles of intellectuals in social change.' . . . Where two years ago the model SDS personality was someone doing a master's thesis on C. Wright Mills, today he is a college dropout. . . . But it is not surprising that an organization with the traditions of SDS could not hold its pendulum for too long at such a non-reflective extreme." Like many other veterans of Port Huron, Booth hoped that the December conference would resolve some of the philosophical and strategic problems that now plagued the organization.[73]

Red-Baiting

That fall, with the "International Days of Protest" coming up in October, the news division of CBS television decided to do a piece for the evening news on draft resistance. The field producer for the piece, Stanhope Gould, was sympathetic to the anti-war movement, but above all committed to the drama of the story: middle-class kids in rebellion against the government. In conjunction with the piece, he decided to profile SDS. Booth was a perfect peg for the story. (Carl Oglesby, the organization's president, was not readily accessible: in keeping with what had become an unwritten SDS tradition, he was living in Ann Arbor.) Gould persuaded CBS to do the piece in part by stressing the fact that Booth was intelligent and articulate. He was also, as a reporter from *The Harvard Crimson* put it, "a most unlikely-looking revolutionary. The press has described him as 'clean-out with shocks of curly, sandy hair and blue eyes,' and to me he appeared the quintessence of innocence." Boyish in suit and tie, Booth on camera would shock viewers by confounding the stereotype of the radical agitator. Though cooperative, Booth hoped to use the CBS broadcast to get across the nuances of the SDS position. Gould remembers arguing with Booth that "you can only get one symbolic idea across, to get people's attention."[74]

On October 11 and 12, the CBS evening news ran Gould's piece in two parts. For the first time, an audience of millions learned about SDS. Though Jeff Shero would complain a few weeks later that press coverage had been pursued at the expense of "internal democracy," at the time he was enthusiastic. "We in the office view the publicity as the greatest *opportunity* the anti-war movement has yet had," wrote Shero. "All reports indicate that SDS has grown fantastically in the last few days."[75]

Unfortunately, students were not the only viewers struck by the CBS report. The broadcast occurred in the context of a mounting outcry in Congress and the media over the anti-war movement. On October 13, Senator Thomas Dodd of the Senate Internal Security Subcommittee published a report asserting that control of the anti-war movement had shifted from moderate elements "into the hands of Communists and extremist elements who are openly sympathetic with the Viet Cong." On October 14, the syndicated newspaper columnists Rowland Evans and Robert Novak asserted that SDS had a master plan to sabotage the war effort and that it was urging young men to "clog up draft boards." On October 15, Senator John Stennis called on the administration to crack down on the anti-draft movement, saying that the CBS broadcasts had revealed "deplorable and shameful activity on the part of those who have no regard for duty, honor, or their country." Suddenly SDS and Paul Booth were at the center of a fire storm of negative publicity fed by half-truths and false assumptions.[76]

On the day of Stennis' diatribe, a reporter from *The Chicago Sun-Times* approached Booth for an interview. He seized the opportunity to set the record straight. Carefully explaining that SDS had not yet endorsed *any* plan of draft resistance, Booth gave the reporter a copy of the referendum text. This was a mistake. The next morning, the

Sun-Times carried the front-page headline "U.S.-WIDE DRIVE TO BEAT DRAFT IS ORGANIZED HERE." Though the details in the story were completely accurate, the tone was breathless, the implicit message alarming: traitors were stalking the streets of Chicago![77]

Later that day, the attorney general, Nicholas B. Katzenbach, in Chicago for a speaking engagement, held a press conference at which he revealed that the Justice Department had started a national investigation of groups involved in the anti-war movement. Asked about Communist influence in the movement, he said that "you are likely to find some Communists involved." Asked specifically if Communists were leaders in SDS, the attorney general replied, "By and large, no." *The New York Times* report on the Katzenbach press conference focused on the charges against SDS. It ran under the headline "U.S. INVESTIGATES ANTI-DRAFT GROUPS—Katzenbach Says Reds Are Involved in Youth Drive."[78]

The bad news about SDS was traveling fast. The Chicago D.A. said SDS might be treasonous. Illinois Senator Everett Dirksen demanded an investigation of SDS. And on Monday, October 18, President Johnson announced his intention to press the Justice Department investigation. On October 19, the lead story on page one of *The New York Times* was headlined, "JOHNSON DECRIES DRAFT PROTESTS—PRESSES INQUIRY/He Fears Enemy Will Doubt Nation's Resolve and Fight Harder, Prolonging War/CONGRESS ALSO CRITICAL.[79]

As the storm clouds gathered in the daily headlines, Paul Booth and Carl Oglesby decided to hold a press conference, hoping to get across the group's position and stave off more negative publicity. They flew to Washington, D.C., where Booth had rented the Grand Ballroom of the National Press Club for the occasion. A text was prepared by Booth, acting, he explained a few weeks later, "in consultation with about a dozen local SDS people, and with some sampling by long distance with chapters Tuesday night."[80]

"I knew I was in uncharted waters," he says. "Once the initial mistake had been made [with the *Sun-Times* reporter], subsequent decisions were pretty sound. Some decisions were made without proper consultation: what we should have done is polled the national executive committee. But we had the intelligence to realize that you don't try to hide from publicity, that only makes matters worse. While you have the attention, you try to make some points. Which we did."

The press release that Booth read on October 20 was headlined "Build, Not Burn." "We are anxious to advance the cause of democracy," declared Booth. "We do not believe that cause can be advanced by torture and terror. . . . Our generation is not afraid of service for long years and low pay; SDS has been working for years in the slums of America at $10 a week to build a movement for democracy there. We are not afraid to risk our lives—we have been risking our lives in Mississippi and Alabama, and some of us died there. But we will not bomb the people, the women and children of another country. . . . Let us see what happens if service to democracy is made grounds for exemption from the military draft. I predict that almost every member of my generation would chose to build, not burn."[81]

A letter that Booth wrote the next day indicates that he was deeply worried about the impact that the news coverage of SDS had been having on liberal opinion. "There is not the slightest doubt in my mind," he wrote, "that the repression that's beginning has its roots deep in the need to enforce consensus behind a war policy for which the people are unenthusiastic at best. The need to attack the war, from vantage-points which appeal to liberals, is highly important. That's why at our press conference we emphasized a catchy proposal. . . ."[82]

In effect, Booth was unilaterally trying to prop up the strategy of *America and the New Era* for a progressive coalition of insurgent radicals and populist liberals. In the short run, he succeeded. Although *The New Republic* printed an editorial deploring the apparent indifference of SDS to the dangers of Communism, Booth's decisive action and the moderate language of his press release apparently helped to turn the tide of liberal opinion. "Among faculty, liberal lawyers, and a lot of others, it bolstered our allies," reported Booth several weeks later. "People in the Peace Corps started advocating the alternative service plan. . . . The Build Not Burn theme received an extremely favorable audience among church people."[83]

In Search of Legitimacy

Within SDS, however, a fresh crisis was brewing—and Booth's press conference was the reason. "TONE OF STATEMENT DEPLORABLE," wired Ken McEldowney from San Francisco on behalf of the Western region of SDS: "NEED INDICATED TO REEXAMINE ROLE OF NATIONAL APPARATUS. PARTICIPATORY DEMOCRACY BEGINS AT HOME." Jeff Shero criticized Booth for his failure to "adhere to strict notions of democracy" when he used the word "we" in his press release:

"Surely this was a surprise to members . . . to find out that they had just gone on record supporting programs *without any kind of representation.*"[84]

Perhaps the most poignant letter of protest came from Texas. "Last year our Texas chapter was a real 'community,' " wrote one member. "We were excited—we were constantly involved in *something that mattered;* we had a real alternative to the present American society. This wasn't a structural thing; it wasn't even an ideology—it was a feeling toward people. Without verbalizing it, somehow we all felt it was necessary to treat people as individuals, not things; that in order to achieve our goals we had to, as much as possible, live them as we were fighting for them." Booth's press conference struck this member as a flagrant instance of undemocratic leadership: "I do not understand. Maybe your goals . . . are different from mine. If so, I would like to know what you see as the *spirit* of the society you are working for. Explain to me how you can change America at the same time you accept her methods."[85]

Booth had run out of patience with his critics. To one irate member who had complained about the "growth of the bureaucratic mentality" in the national office, he shot back a snide reply: "give us a more careful look before you go joining the young peoples front for community and love."[86]

The whole sorry episode came to an ironic conclusion on November 16, when The Associated Press called to find out whether it was true, as rumored, that the SDS membership in its referendum had in fact *defeated* the draft-resistance proposal that had caused so much controversy in the first place. Once again, Booth made, in his own words, "a series of on-the-spot administrative decisions." When AP called, ballots had been trickling in for weeks; the tally stood at 233 for the draft-resistance proposal and 266 against. Apart from offering evidence of apathy—only 500 participating voters in this most democratic of organizations!—the tally suggested that the anti-draft program faced likely defeat. Booth decided to "spill the beans," as he put it, hoping to have some influence on how the story was reported. Afterward, he urged local chapters to counteract any impression of faintheartedness by issuing "a steaming blast at the war policy." Above all, he stressed that "SDS is internally democratic."[87]

As the December conference approached and the outcry over his leadership continued to mount, Booth tried to sort out the issues at stake. "What was disappointing," he says, "was that 'Build, Not Burn' became a proxy for the discussion of the other administrative issues." The problem was both simple and hard to see. Through its experimental quest for a "democracy of individual participation," SDS had in effect evolved "an informal system of nonmandated representation," as one student of the New Left's organizational forms has put it: members who held positions of power in such a system perforce represented "the interests of the others without being formally accountable to them."[88] Though the problem was simple, the solution was not. To admit that power was unequally distributed within SDS, and that administrators like Booth were *de facto* representatives of the larger group, entailed admitting that SDS, as a large national organization, had fallen short of its professed ideals of "authenticity," neighborly community and rule-by-consensus. To some militants, that seemed tantamount to conceding rule by an oligarchical elite—the very antithesis of "participatory democracy."

For his part, Booth had become convinced of the need to reform SDS' organizational structure. "I wanted," he says, "to force a decision to re-create accountability mechanisms inside the organization." Reinstituting procedures to give officers a formal mandate to act on behalf of the group would also in theory make it easier for the group to instruct its representatives and to hold them explicitly accountable. Unfortunately, as Booth recalls, "it was easy to deflect the points I wanted to make by saying, 'Well, what about "Build, Not Burn"?' I would say to people, 'Look, if we had had accountability mechanisms, then you all could have been satisfied with the decision-making process'—an incident like 'Build, Not Burn' was a reason to *have* accountability mechanisms. But they would say, 'No no no, if you have accountability mechanisms, then the bad guys' "—and critics like Shero clearly meant guys like Booth—" 'are going to control them to do things that the true membership really doesn't want to have done.' "

In one especially revealing letter from this period, Booth summarized some of his thinking about the forms of democracy appropriate for a large national organization. "I think we are now too large to proceed along the lines of consensus," he wrote. "We have to begin to structure debates in the organization to make conflict possible, and articulate, and educational. Have votes, even. Otherwise we do two bad things—one, we muddle issues, and two, rank-and-file people tend to judge questions on the basis of whether they trust the people arguing, not on the merits of the case. That is, we have created a dependence on demagogy. . . . We have to learn the value of creating permanent institutions to embody the movement. We tend to believe in the false view that structure in itself is harmful—and we should learn how, throughout the movement, to create structures to which people will feel confident in attaching themselves. This also includes the question of leadership. . . . People wish for some confused reason that leadership didn't have to exist . . . and 'abolish' it, by abolishing the formality but not the function. They use this as a license to abandon the responsibility of leadership." Booth recalled the confusion that had set in after the Swarthmore SDS chapter abolished officers. There was "no argument about political direction—nobody felt the responsibility for formulating a point of view. But there was a whole lot of community. Love that community!"[89]

Like a Rolling Stone

The spirit of open-minded tolerance that had once characterized SDS was dead. Booth's sarcasm was one sympton of the change; Jeff Shero's doctrinaire hostility to "bureaucracy" was another. The new spirit rising within SDS—and within the avant-garde of the youth culture—was impatient, raw, hard with anticipation. The song of the moment was "Like a Rolling Stone," not "Blowin' in the Wind." Bob Dylan wasn't strumming an acoustic guitar and singing broadsides in the artless manner of Woody Guthrie any longer; now, he was shouting over a welter of amplified instruments, plunging headlong into dreamlike poems of betrayed love and apocalypse with the fevered, deranged conviction of a rock-and-roll Rimbaud.

In Chicago and elsewhere, the police had started to harass anti-war activists. "They're really following us, day and night, now," Booth told one reporter with a mixture of pride and paranoia. "I traveled bearing messages of bravado and fear," wrote Todd Gitlin in a poem, called "Movement," which he published that November: "Rattle the door but don't bother waiting/It locks from inside/Tonight the radio speaks of Nationwide Demonstrations/All my friends are desperate/We go on making plans."[90]

At the end of November, SDS participated in another major anti-war march in Washington, this one sponsored by SANE. Before the march, an ad hoc meeting of New Left groups called the "National Coordinating Committee" convened to discuss anti-war strategy. For the first time in the decade, the born-again Marxist-Leninist sects turned out in full force—there were Trotskyists, Maoists, Castroites, even some old-fashioned Communists. When Booth addressed a plenary of the convention and suggested two or three questions that the Movement ought to be thinking about, a delegate was overheard saying, "There's the SDS line." It was, of course, true that Booth's own political convictions in the heat of political conflict had become more pointed and sharply defined. Looking back, Booth harshly criticizes himself for clinging with myopic tenacity to the vision of an experimental, multi-issue, radically democratic Movement. But it was also true that the freewheeling and antisectarian traditions of SDS remained a complete mystery to most outsiders. As one veteran radical complained at this meeting, understanding SDS was "like digging Bartok or Bird when you've been listening to Bach all your life."[91]

On Saturday, November 27, 30,000 people participated in the biggest demonstration yet against the war. In the midst of a soporific program, Carl Oglesby, the sole representative of the New Left on the podium, delivered a speech that electrified the audience. "We radicals know the same history you liberals know," said Oglesby, "and we can understand your occasional cynicism, exasperation, and even distrust. But we ask you to put these aside and help us risk a leap. . . . Help us shape the future in the name of plain human hope."[92]

SDS now claimed some 10,000 members. It had never seemed more important. It had never been more confused.

An Ending

The December conference, which was planned to resolve the confusion, succeeded only in confirming it. The meeting convened on December 27, at Champaign, Illinois. Numerous papers had been produced for the conference. Many of them discussed participatory democracy.

One paper commended the Yugoslavian model of workers' self-management. Another cited the ancient Greek *polis* and quoted both Hegel and Herodotus on the virtues of positive freedom. One paper defended the role of experts in society, arguing that in a modern democracy "technocrats should be responsible to their utmost ability to make popular demands technically feasible." Another paper urged abolishing the executive offices of president and vice president within SDS, in order to combat the concentration of power and maximize grass-roots participation. Echoing the complaint of one writer that "political knowledge is transmitted in SDS like folklore," Paul Booth argued that "a test of the strength of an institution is its ability to pass on accumulated experience" and that "only an

institution with the paraphernalia of structure, tradition, administrative procedures that translate needs into responsibilities that people expect to assume, etc., will be successful." Reiterating a proposal
presented at the last SDS convention, Jeff Shero called once again for
SDS to decentralize, and to reorganize itself into a Movement for a
Democratic Society (MDS) that would embrace "faculty groups, Free
University projects, and MDS affiliate motorcycle clubs, plus affiliated MDS chapters of the aged!"[93]

A terrible fog had stolen over SDS. Bewildered about its direction,
the group instinctively turned toward the ideals of *The Port Huron
Statement*. But the old ideals shed no light. The shared faith in
"participatory democracy"—a phrase that had never been defined by
any clear principles—was one of the reasons they were confused.

Paul Booth: "*We* understand democracy to be that system of rule
in which the people make the decisions that affect their lives." Jeff
Shero: "That there is no staff democracy makes workers feel that
they have no control over the decisions that affect their lives."
Booth: "It is shocking that out of a misplaced commitment to 'participatory democracy' young organizers force community people to
sit through intricate procedural discussions." Shero: "To argue that
democracy is a workable ideal within the internal structure of SDS
is at times considered a most radical statement." One is reminded
of two boxers, swinging wildly, knocking each other down with
accidental punches.[94]

Paul Booth was right to stress the need in a democratic national
organization for structure, orderly administration and responsible,
representative leadership. But his own leadership was no longer representative. Unchastened romantics like Shero and a new generation
of members, staking their own claim to power within SDS, wanted
to quicken the quest for a politics purged of deceit, authority, hierarchy. Honesty, guts, local initiative—these would keep the Movement going. Not discipline. Not leaders. Not a new political party of
the left. It was time to cut the bureaucratic crap.

Few of the older veterans of Port Huron wanted to swim against
the tide. In part, they were handcuffed by their own ideology: power
struggles weren't part of their democratic credo. They also did not
want to be considered old fogeys—they were proud to be part of a
radical avant-garde. Besides, the organization that they had created
was *Students* for a Democratic Society. Nobody wanted to be the
next Michael Harrington.

The mood at the December conference was generally bleak. "Because we'd set it up as a series of seminars and discussions," says

Booth, "you couldn't get consensus on anything. I couldn't even get sustained attention to the points that were in my working paper." The talk at most workshops made it clear that the group's old sense of intellectual community had been hopelessly shattered. Bob Ross recalls attending an "ideological workshop of about fifteen persons. . . . The span of participants' views covered free market anarchism to technocratic planning. Not a single participant had read S.D.S.'s strategic 1963 document, *America and the New Era*, and none had read C. Wright Mills' 'Letter to the New Left.' "[95]

At the same time, the December conference revealed new tensions within the Movement. The most striking debates focused not on democracy, but on the role of women. Sharon Jeffrey still recalls the shock waves set off when the women convened a special workshop and closed the doors to men. "One of the biggest problems," wrote Jeffrey and Carol McEldowney in their notes summarizing the workshop, "is teaching women to accept ourselves, to accept our limitations, abilities and needs, as WE define them, and not as men define them." The women criticized the highly intellectualized style of the male SDS leaders, deplored the sexual exploitation many of them felt they had suffered and reiterated their own "expectations that a revolutionary organization has revolutionary forms of relationships." Tired of a "participatory democracy" monopolized by men, particularly when so many ERAP projects depended on skilled organizers like Jeffrey, the workshop demanded a "re-assertion of the personal" among women—and so helped to launch the modern women's movement.[96]

The feelings of high consensus and hope that had buoyed the group at Port Huron were long gone. The veterans of that meeting had gone on to become pioneers. They had pressed the quest for a "democracy of individual participation" to its logical and practical limits. They knew the power of the vision. Now they understood some of its pitfalls.

Port Huron for them had been a new beginning. For many of them, the December conference was a kind of ending. "I had lost the sense," says Paul Booth, "that the house could be put back in order."

The vision of political freedom that had once inspired their enthusiasm and moral confidence now was mired in paradox and contention. Many newcomers regarded the SDS tradition of open-minded experimentalism as an invitation to anarchy; a growing number of women charged that most Movement men, for all their radical posturing, were manipulative and overbearing hypocrites; the prevailing hostility to elites, bureaucracy and political structure made the creation and preservation of institutional safeguards against the abuse of authority by elected officers perversely difficult; and a growing mood of militance made sober discussion of such issues all but impossible. The experiments with democracy in the ERAP projects and in the national office had in fact usefully demonstrated some of the dilemmas of participatory democracy; they suggested the unsuitability of rule-by-consensus for a national organization marked by conflicting interests; but they had also undermined the national organization, making it difficult for the implications to be widely appreciated. Failing to transmit in any coherent form what they had learned, the veterans of Port Huron were bequeathing to their heirs in SDS an ambiguous and volatile legacy. "In its beginning as a mass organization was its end," remarked Todd Gitlin years later: "the internal frailties that were to undo the organization were already built in at the moment of its greatest growth and vigor."[97]

At the time, such internal frailties scarcely seemed to matter. Brandishing slogans like "Let the people decide," the new generation of student radicals gamely resisted the resurrected Marxist-Leninist sects and their stale ideological certainties. *The Port Huron Statement* remained a touchstone. In 1966, it was reprinted, appearing along with the first paperback books on SDS and the New Left: *A Prophetic Minority*, by Jack Newfield; *The New Radicals*, a report with documents by Paul Jacobs and Saul Landau; and *The New Student Left*, an anthology of documents edited by Mitchell Cohen and Dennis Hale. It was easier than ever before to learn about the New Left and the quest for participatory democracy.

Although he removed himself from the national office that spring, Paul Booth remained active in SDS until the 1966 convention in Clear Lake, Iowa. At Clear Lake, he was swept from power along with the rest of the "old guard"—he was twenty-three. Settling in Chicago, he became a leader of the city's anti-war movement and an activist in a variety of dissident local grass-roots political groups. He participated in an abortive effort to launch an adult version of SDS, and an equally abortive effort, through the National Conference for New Politics, to create a radical third party. Forsaking his old organization and its increasingly shrill Marxist rhetoric, he became a labor-union organizer. While his erstwhile comrades in SDS sank deeper and deeper into ersatz proletarian posturing, Booth committed himself to the slow, arduous process of changing the political convictions of some of the real members of America's real working class.[98]

SDS continued to grow. In 1968, it would claim some 100,000 members. The war in Vietnam grew, too. By 1968, nearly 500,000 American military personnel were stationed in Vietnam. In both cases, the impressive numbers masked strategic defects. But until the end of the decade, the escalation of the war kept the idea of participatory democracy alive. In city streets and on college campuses across America, in scores of demonstrations and marches against the war, in situations tense with anxiety and chiliastic hope, fantasies of revolution flared. Old political premises collapsed. To young radicals, anything seemed possible—including, certainly, a "democracy of individual participation."

CHAPTER TWELVE

A MORALIST IN SEARCH OF POWER

O N DECEMBER 28, 1965, while his old friends vainly grappled with the dilemmas of "participatory democracy" at the SDS conference in Champaign, Illinois, Tom Hayden, twenty-six, was on a plane headed for Hanoi. Gazing out the window as the plane flew low over the Chinese border into Vietnam, Hayden marveled at the landscape. "Below rolled miles of delicately manicured fields," he later wrote, "a countryside developed with obvious care by generations of people." Stepping off the plane, he was warmly greeted by a delegation of officials. "Little girls dressed colorfully approached us hesitantly, with flowers and salutes." Driving from the airport into the city, he saw checkerboard rice fields "tended by people working actively in the huge paddies." Their faces, he thought, were without fear: "If they were the quaking targets of the U.S. Air Force, it did not show. . . . In fact, if anyone was feeling an emotional shock, it was ourselves as we entered this little world forbidden to Americans, so unknown to our people and so exposed to our military power."

Here was "the other side." It seemed to be populated by brave citizens, not immoral monsters. The officials he met treated him not as an emissary from a belligerent power, but as an honored dignitary—a representative of the uncorrupted conscience of his nation. Hayden felt a growing sympathy for these stalwart Communists: "After all, we call ourselves in some sense revolutionaries," he wrote shortly afterward. "So do they. After all we identify with the poor and oppressed. So do they."[1]

In Hanoi, the apostle of participatory democracy discovered a fateful new symbol of moral and political resolve: an armed people in the throes of a guerrilla war. Hayden's own identification with the poor and oppressed had already led him from student life in Ann Arbor to ghetto life in Newark, New Jersey. His identification with the Vietnamese Communists—and his experience in the ghetto of Newark—would lead him in the future to talk of "bringing the war back home." Wishing to create an American movement of fearless activists, he hoped that a new kind of man would pave the way for a new kind of society.

In December, 1965, such fantasies seemed farfetched. Three years later, they had become one of the defining features of a burgeoning radical subculture that drew strength from the growing hostility among students and intellectuals to the Vietnam War. Inspired by teach-ins and marches and defiant acts of draft resistance, a growing number of previously apathetic young people passionately debated the right of civil disobedience, the wrongs of government policy, the duties of citizenship, the limits of authority, the possibility of revolution. In these debates, the spirit and often the language of Port Huron lived on. And in the minds of many of the participants, as well as those who were watching as the talk of revolution spread, Tom Hayden became a spokesman, a symbol, finally a celebrity.

As he traveled from Newark to Hanoi and back again, the progress of his own political pilgrimage was carefully attended by those who knew him and, through his writing and interviews, by those who knew of him. "Many of us," Bob Ross told a reporter in 1968, "spend a lot of time worrying whether Hayden would approve of what we're doing." "When pondering a political or existential decision," journalist Andrew Kopkind later recalled, "I would flash on Hayden and guess what he'd say, or think, or do. I'd sometimes confuse him with [Bob] Dylan . . . : in their obviously different ways, they seemed to express the tones, shades, colors of a generational spirit that others could merely put into words."[2]

A Wager

In the summer of 1964, Hayden finished perhaps his last major piece of sustained intellectual work, his thesis on C. Wright Mills, with an imaginary monologue written in the style of Mills—a soliloquy that revealed the dimensions of Hayden's own revolutionary dream. Most of the thesis was dense with definitions, exegesis, a defense and some criticism of the great sociologist. But in the final two pages, struggling to express what Mills might have said had he lived to lead the New Left, Hayden tried his hand at imitating Mills's hard-boiled lyricism, his "distant, but personally revealing, monologue form." For a moment, Tom Hayden *was* C. Wright Mills—and the prophet of the powerless was expressing Hayden's own fondest wish: that a new era of democratic hope was at hand.

"What experience we have is our own, not vicarious or inherited," wrote Hayden/Mills. "We keep believing that people need to control, or try to control, their work and their life. Otherwise, they are without intensity, without the subjective creative consciousness of themselves which is the root of free and secure feeling. It may be too much to believe, we don't know."

The old radical credos, above all Marx's metaphysic of labor, had proved sterile: "All the old premises are questions. . . . There is no country, no class, no vanguard to count on for freedom." The vision of democracy might well turn out to be an intellectual mirage: "We don't know if there is a base, a real community of people who need this freedom and the sharing of power and responsibility which it will mean. It will take a long time to know, if we ever do, because the greatest resources of most people are contained, unused, far beneath their daily unobtrusive doings."

Still, there were signs that a different way of life was possible. "You can see freedom surfacing, now and then," continued Hayden/Mills, "in demonstrations, in serious conversation, in love-making, in hard work, in mass meetings, in letters, pictures and even glances." These signs were scattered enough to warrant humility: "We don't know if freedom will break her chains, much less the invisible constraints holding her." The possibilities for democratic renewal were ambiguous: "This may not be a revolutionary time, as they say, but more importantly, we may not be capable revolutionaries."

But "there is no way in theory to find out. Work, and some patience will create an evidence of its own." The best hope lay in direct action—a wager on the future: "We'll see what happens. It's so obviously a better goal than money or winning the Cold War."[3]

Let the People Decide

Between 1964 and 1968, Hayden lived in the Clinton Hill section of Newark, New Jersey. He had come there with an SDS ERAP project; he stayed on long after most of the other SDS experiments in community organizing had wound down.

The Newark ERAP project had located itself in Clinton Hill under the misapprehension that the neighborhood had a mixed racial composition. In fact, Clinton Hill was largely populated by black home-owners, most of them middle-class. The grass-roots liberal organization that had invited SDS into the neighborhood, the Clinton Hill Neighborhood Council, included many activists whose chief concern was preserving property values. Wanting to make the streets cleaner, safer, better lit, they had become adept at lobbying Town Hall.

Preserving property values, of course, was not quite what Hayden and the other SDS organizers had in mind. They hoped to inspire "ordinary people" with their vision of direct action and democracy. Once they had sized up the situation, the ERAP organizers moved to the lower part of Clinton Hill, where the people were poorer and the housing dilapidated. "Our place is at the bottom," reported the Newark ERAP group at the end of its first summer. Creating the Newark Community Union Project (NCUP), they began to organize tenants and welfare recipients, most of whom were not registered to vote. These people could be united by a demand for democratic participation; they had little to lose and something to gain through direct action. The NCUP motto, later adapted by SDS, was "Let the people decide!"[4]

"Students and poor people make each other feel real," declared Hayden in perhaps his most widely read essay from this period, "The Politics of 'The Movement.' " The alienated student could instill self-respect and a sense of democratic possibilities in the poor. The poor, in turn, could "demonstrate to the students that their upbringing has been based on a framework of lies." Because radical students and poor people shared "a common status"—they both felt power-less—they had a common interest in the quest for participatory democracy. Still, the poor had a unique role to play in this alliance. By the very fact that they remained on the margins of the emerging system of "universal conformity," they preserved an estimable measure of "honesty" and "insight." The tenants in the Newark Community Union readily resented "a manipulative clique" or "anyone displaying marks of snobbishness or privilege." Among poor blacks in the South, "the worth of men is likely to be measured by what they do, not as much by the labels and organizational imagery they project." By concentrating on the ordinary, everyday problems of the materially dispossessed, and by building a movement where "everybody is a leader," students could absorb some of the uncorrupted virtues of the poor and prepare themselves for those extraordinary moments of rebellion, "when people transcend their pettiness to commit themselves to great purposes"—purposes beyond the blinkered values of rational self-interest and material well-being enshrined in Marxism, liberalism, and middle-class mores.[5]

Hayden's scheme for democratic renewal, conveyed in speeches and articles published in 1965 and 1966, won few converts. "Rousseau was not a cotton picker," sniffed one old lion of the civil rights movement. Orthodox socialists were unwilling to give up on the working class. Others wondered why Hayden—even after the Free Speech Movement in Berkeley—showed so little interest in organizing a mass movement of students. To unsympathetic outsiders, he looked more and more like a crafty worker-priest scheming to lead a cabal of insurgent mendicants.[6]

Hayden himself had become increasingly peremptory. He wrote derisively of "traditional leftists" who were "limited fundamentally by their job and family situations." He upheld a punishing standard of sacrifice and scorned those who did not meet it. "We are going to drift and experiment for some time to come," he declared. But under the impact of his experience in Newark, his convictions were hardening. "You have to pursue a goal like that with extreme passion and force of argument," says Hayden looking back. "You pay a price, because you oversimplify, you polarize your own friends. I regret it. But that's easy to say looking back."[7]

The Other Side

Hayden was only marginally involved in the early months of protest against the war in Vietnam. Though he had initially voiced doubts about staging the SDS march against the war in April, 1965, he of course attended it, bringing along a delegation of poor people from Newark. But his picture of Vietnam remained fuzzy—most of his attention was still focused on Newark. "I thought [Vietnam] was fundamental," he says, "but that didn't mean that I had any projection of where it was going or what would be revealed by it or anything of that sort."[8]

That fall, Staughton Lynd approached Hayden about traveling to Hanoi. Lynd had been asked to make the trip by Herbert Aptheker, a Communist historian who had been invited by the North Vietnamese to visit Hanoi and bring along two distinguished colleagues who were radicals, but not Communists. Lynd's outspoken refusal to pay taxes had made him one of the best-known critics of the war, particularly in academic circles. A Quaker and declared pacifist,

Lynd was horrified by the escalation of the war. On election day in November, his acquaintance Norman Morrison, in protest against the bombing of children in an unprotected South Vietnamese village, had set himself on fire and burned to death in front of the Pentagon. Convinced that stopping the war was a moral imperative, Lynd told Aptheker that he would go to Hanoi, provided that he be allowed to pick the third person. "I don't remember all the details," says Hayden, "but the point finally was that Staughton asked me if I wanted to go."[9]

Lynd's invitation put Hayden in a quandary. The group would be defying a State Department ban on travel to North Vietnam, and Hayden worried about the possible impact on SDS and the ERAP project in Newark. But he finally agreed to join Lynd and Aptheker. The group left New York on December 19, 1965. After a stop in London, they flew on to Prague, Moscow and Peking.[10]

For Hayden, the trip was a revelation.

"Well, I was a native American boy from the Midwest," he later recalled, "and my furthest travel and contact with other peoples had been a year in the South and in the Newark ghetto. . . . [While] I didn't accept any Cold War rhetoric[,] I had no idea of what was going on. . . . In the space of one month, I was in China for five days and I was in Vietnam for two weeks, and it was the other side of the world."[11]

At several points during this trip, Hayden felt phrases from his own prose spring vividly to life. In Czechoslovakia, he visited a museum in Lidice, a small village that the Nazis had wiped out in 1942; a stone there was engraved with the names Lidice, Coventry, Hiroshima, Nagasaki. Many of the women in the village had survived the Ravensbrueck concentration camp. As a college senior in Ann Arbor, Hayden had written melodramatically of "the nearness of total war." Now he surveyed its ravages, and felt a visitor in "the cemetery of an era." "Perhaps my experience is too small to embrace what happened here," he later wrote.[12]

Socialism, too, till then had been a kind of rumor to Hayden. "I'd never been in a socialist society," he says, "where people actually are producing for themselves, building for themselves, educating themselves." Despite his outspoken contempt for anti-Communism, he was still startled to find China and Vietnam populated with people who were energetic, gentle, apparently happy. "I realized," he explained in 1968, that "we were part of a broad movement to limit America's power and role in the world, to fight against capitalism and bureaucracy." (The abstract schematism of this remark, the suggestion of boilerplate Marxism, the faint evocation of an epochal Manichean struggle reveal as much about what Hayden learned in Hanoi as the overt message of cosmopolitan commitment.) "It's a very strange thing to realize your country is bombing the city you are in," he added, coming to the emotional heart of his experience: "I can never forget the faces of the people living under the bombs of the American Air Force."[13]

Hayden was determined to share his experience. He wanted others to see and feel "the faces of the people living under the bombs." He came home convinced, as he recalled in 1972, that "the U.S. was being defeated, that the Vietnamese people *could* preserve their freedom and independence and that the Vietnamese people had special qualities, which I'm still trying to understand, that made them the most extraordinary people now living in the world, setting a standard of morality and sacrifice for the whole world."[14]

A Socialism of the Heart

In collaboration with Lynd, Hayden decided to write a book. In many ways, Lynd was an ideal partner. The son of Robert and Helen Lynd, the authors of the classic sociological study *Middletown*, Lynd had briefly flirted with Trotskyism, spent several years in a cooperative commune in the Fifties and done some community organizing in Manhattan before taking a job teaching history, first at Spelman College in Atlanta and then at Yale. As his career demonstrated, he was sympathetic to the idea of experimentation in politics. He was also sympathetic to the ideas of Tom Hayden. Since 1963, Lynd had admired Hayden's rhetoric of participatory democracy; as a trained scholar of American history, he was one of the few outsiders who fully grasped that it *was* a rhetoric, one that Hayden had largely invented, rather than something that he had found ready-made. After the April SDS anti-war march, as we have seen, Lynd was one of the few people openly enthusiastic about Hayden's plan to convene a new Continental Congress. He also shared Hayden's enthusiasm for Camus, and for Ignazio Silone's novel *Bread and Wine*. Though Lynd was a Quaker pacifist and Hayden was not, they shared a similar set of religiously tinged, vaguely "existential" moral sentiments. Lynd finally could compensate for Hayden's ignorance of socialist history. In an essay published in 1963, Lynd pointed out the richness and diversity of the possible historical antecedents of "participatory democracy." He argued that the idea could define a new sense of the radical tradition, uniting figures as disparate as Robert La Follette and Rosa Luxemburg, and linking political innovations as different as the French anarchist "syndicat" and the American progressive "direct primary."[15]

Unfortunately, Lynd (unlike Dick Flacks) reinforced rather than tempered Hayden's deep streak of romanticism. Two images dominate *The Other Side*, as they called their book: Norman Morrison in flames; and the North Vietnamese in tears. By the time Lynd and Hayden arrived, Morrison had already been canonized by the North Vietnamese as a political saint. "Morrison's suicide," says Hayden looking back, "vindicated the Vietnamese belief that the American people were essentially good, and that only the U.S. government and its policies were bad. Morrison's act of self-immolation was akin to the Buddhist self-immolations in South Vietnam, and seemed to show that Americans potentially could identify with the suffering of a distant, non-white people." In their book, Lynd and Hayden reported that "the leading Vietnamese poet had cried while writing a poem in tribute" to Morrison. The manager of a factory in Hanoi, speaking of Morrison and Abraham Lincoln, "broke down, and several of the workers became moist-eyed"; Morrison, said the manager, had "sacrificed himself for justice, not for economic self-interest.' " "The strength of emotion," Lynd and Hayden confessed, "left us dazed."[16]

Their experience convinced them that Vietnam at war offered a nearly ideal model of social and political organization. "Guerrilla war," they wrote, "means, to begin with, that in the process of taking over the state one creates a replica of the larger society one hopes to build in the microcosm of a remote rural 'base.' . . . The twentieth century guerrilla finds himself forced by circumstance to live out even before the 'first stage' of socialist construction many relationships which Marxist theory prescribes only for the Communist 'final stage': equality of income (food is scarce, and everyone eats from the same pot); a blending of manual and intellectual labor (Mao kept a garden at Yenan); an emphasis upon the power of human will to overcome objective difficulties." Describing the "constant dialogue" encouraged by Communist guerrillas in village meetings, Lynd and Hayden praised the Vietnamese for their "rice-roots' democracy." "We suspect," they ventured, "that colonial American town meetings and current Vietnamese village meetings, Asian peasants' leagues and Black Belt sharecroppers' unions have much in common." Above all, they admired the Vietnamese for creating a *"socialism of the heart,"* which was evident "in the unembarrassed handclasps among men, the poetry and song at the center of man–woman relationships, the freedom to weep practiced by everyone—from guerrillas to generals, peasants to factory managers—as the Vietnamese speak of their country."[17]

Lynd and Hayden did not make all this up. The morale—the patriotic passion—of the Vietnamese Communists was perhaps the decisive factor in their victory over American forces with superior firepower. Though still committed to the "dictatorship of the proletariat" and the discipline of a one-party state, the Vietnamese Communists had in fact developed their own brand of Marxism-Leninism, which emphasized the virtues of "revolutionary morality"—sacrifice, heroism and hope. Furthermore, Lynd and Hayden visited Hanoi at a point when the Party was keen on mobilizing the population in village and military councils in order to withstand the total war unleashed by the Americans. In an effort to harness the will of the people as a weapon of war, popular enthusiasm and intense political participation became prized features of revolutionary organization. As one American military expert has put it, "the amount of this Party-led activity during the Vietnam War years was staggering. . . . Steadily for years—daily in many of the 2,500 villages of South Vietnam—cadres organized and staged demonstration after demonstration." The same expert, though stoutly anti-Communist, nonetheless concedes that these village meetings "carried a sense of political participation, and the individual Vietnamese usually felt he got something out of it." "Theory and practice therefore produced a fresh synthesis," the left-wing historian Gabriel Kolko has concluded. "Whatever else the Party accomplished"—and whatever its ultimate political aims—"its efforts helped minimize the bureaucratic excesses which marked all other Marxist-Leninist parties in power."[18]

The heroic courage and political improvisations of Vietnam's peasant guerrillas profoundly resonated with Hayden's own moral vision of ordinary people making history. Three years before his trip to Hanoi, in his notes on democracy for *The Port Huron Statement*, he had speculated on the paradoxical possibility that an authoritarian, even a totalitarian, regime might foster some form of participatory democracy. "People in such a society," he had written, "can be mobilized by a sense of mission, an identity with some transcendent cause that appears to be attainable." "Is there anything innate in man," he wondered, "that yearns for attachment to a consuming cause or a transcendent form of being? . . . Can a non-totalitarian society generate the same elan, mission, purposefulness?"[19]

Before his trip to Hanoi, Staughton Lynd had expressed somewhat different views. In 1963 he had invoked the legacies of democratic socialism and progressivism, citing the names of La Follette and Rosa Luxemburg. It is hard not to believe that *The Other Side* would have been a better book if Lynd had reconsidered Rosa Luxemburg's caustic comments on Bolshevism in the context of Vietnam. Shortly after Lenin seized power in Russia, Luxemburg had remarked that "socialist democracy . . . does not come as some sort of Christmas present for the worthy people who, in the interim, have loyally supported a handful of socialist dictators." But no criticism of "socialist dictators"—and no skepticism about the possibilities for spurious participation in a one-party state—blemished the revolutionary pastorale produced by Lynd and Hayden. Their "socialism of the heart" conspicuously lacked that unflinching realism which may be Karl Marx's most precious gift to social criticism.[20]

"I didn't see the whole truth," says Hayden looking back. "I think I was too motivated by anger at feeling excluded, and so I overidentified with the really excluded, like the Vietnamese. It skewed my judgment as to what was possible, or even necessary. I made the Vietnamese more than human. At the time, the key question for me was: Can human beings overcome the raw mechanical firepower of advanced technology? What kind of world are we living in? Is it controlled by those who control the machines? Or is human energy a primary factor? I presumed because the Vietnamese were superhuman under the American bombing that they were superhuman in fact. That didn't turn out to be the case. There was a significant element of Stalinism in the Vietnamese Communist Party.

"But what I saw was true, in the sense of real. I wasn't fooled. I saw people in a state of epic transformation, making an ultimate sacrifice against apparently invincible odds. The war was a military epic; it was one of the most phenomenal struggles in the history of the world. And since I wasn't interested in respectability at the time —if anything, I was interested in *not* being respectable—I didn't have any fear in describing what I saw. That's a great feeling."[21]

Ambition Unbound

Once he had finished writing *The Other Side,* Hayden hit the college lecture circuit to spread the news about Vietnam. "I did a lot of speaking at a lot of teach-ins," he later recalled, "but I stayed in Newark partly on the grounds that I thought people had to be rooted in the community and partly on the grounds that I thought it was important that the different wings of SDS, the community organizing and the anti-war, be bridged, and partly, I think, because I was personally unresolved about what to do."[22]

In Newark, Hayden shared in the sacrifices demanded of a community organizer. But he lived in a world apart. "Everybody is a leader," he had declared in 1965. But not everybody traveled to Hanoi. Not everybody published books. Not everybody gave lectures. Certainly not everybody had Hayden's aptitude for visionary leadership. In an essay on problems in the Movement published in 1967, Al and Barbara Haber pointed out that most people did not have the ability to become "freelance intellectuals or charismatic leaders." These roles, they wrote, were "a viable possibility only for those with extraordinary talent, intelligence, self-confidence, sense of opportunity, autonomy and self-mythologizing ability."[23]

Hayden had never made a secret of his conviction that it was sheer willpower that, above all else, enabled men to make history. But for several years, Hayden's personal ambition—his own will to power —had been contained within the experimental democratic forms that he had helped to create. By rotating leaders and, later, through rule-by-consensus, SDS and the ERAP projects tried to regulate the clash of wills and (in Rousseau's terms) forge a "general will." "Looking back," says Hayden, "what I really think is that you had an organization with a lot of very strong male egos. And leadership tendencies and ambition. And having a one-year check on leadership and automatic rotation prevented certain kinds of rivalries. You really cannot exaggerate the degree to which this movement was a rebellion against middle-class careerism. Skip the view that consensus came from the Quakers or that it was based on a value differentiation from hierarchy. I think it was the perfect organizational formula for the suppression of middle-class ambition. Because it means that the ego of the individual has to be submerged in the group as just one ego among many. And it worked, to an extent. Because it made you harness your own conditioning."[24]

Hayden's political harness, however, was slowly coming undone. Like other veterans of Port Huron, he drifted away from SDS, dropping all formal ties to the group. In Newark as in Cleveland, the ERAP experiment in participatory democracy slowly fell apart. "The problems of operating a staff of 45 in a democratic manner are much greater than anybody seemed to realize at first," reported the Newark project in the summer of 1965. "Although many of us regard voting as undemocratic, there is a real question about whether we can afford to take 8 hours to attain a consensus on every issue."[25]

"In the end, it became very difficult," Hayden later recalled, "because we took over the poverty program. It was the only poverty program in the country that had community elections, and we were the only organized group of poor people, so it was fairly easy to use the electoral process to take over the poverty program in a certain area. But then what happened was they changed the poverty program. They eliminated the democratic structure, and eventually people were faced with the problem of whether to stay outside the poverty program and go on in a situation where they did not have an economic base . . . or stay in the poverty program and try to work from within as a progressive force." For the poor themselves, the choice was obvious: they would try to consolidate the political power they had won, and continue to work within the bureaucracy.[26]

Hayden commanded a growing political power of his own. When *The New Republic* or *Dissent* or *The Evergreen Review* needed an essay or a comment from an authority on the New Left, it naturally turned to Hayden.

In a bitter passage written in 1970, he complained that "only males with driving egos have been able to 'rise' in the Movement or the rock culture and be accepted by the media and dealt with seriously by the Establishment. . . . The first step in this power syndrome is to become a 'personality.' You begin to monopolize contacts and contracts. You begin making $1000 per speech. With few real friends and no real organization, you become dependent on the mass media and travel in orbit only with similar 'stars.' "[27]

Once he had drifted away from SDS, it may well be true that Hayden had "no real organization." But he had long cultivated ties to the media. His skills as a writer allowed him not only to reach a relatively large audience with his opinions, but also to refine and polish his own political image.

Ever since The Associated Press had circulated a photograph of Hayden shielding himself from racist vigilantes in McComb, Mississippi, in 1961, he had symbolized to many in the Movement "a different way of living." In the words of Ignazio Silone that he quoted shortly afterward, "no word and no gesture can be more persuasive than the life, and if necessary, the death, of a man who strives to be free . . . a man who shows what a man can be." But as Hayden's fame grew, and the restraints on his ambition weakened, the gap between his actions and the various images he tried to project became impossible to hide. At the height of his commitment to self-renunciatory leadership, he dominated SDS meetings and freely threw his weight around. He participated in endless meetings, but was impervious to criticism. In his writing he frequently reiterated the need for daring, boldness, courage and risk-taking; yet he hedged his own political bets, keeping lines of communication open to mainstream reform Democrats well after he had embraced the image of the guerrilla warrior. He espoused a "socialism of the heart" and had called for a "re-assertion of the personal." But a surprising number of acquaintances, both close and casual, perceived him as cold and remote.

When the women in SDS caucused at the December conference in 1965 and complained about domineering male leaders, Sharon Jeffrey recalls that Hayden was considered a "prime culprit." When Al and Barbara Haber deplored the influence of leaders with "self-mythologizing ability," Hayden was clearly one of their targets. Dick Flacks recalls how some members of SDS resented the shame and guilt they felt in Hayden's presence, as if they could not measure up to his total commitment to politics. And Irving Howe, like many older intellectuals on the left, developed a profound antipathy for Hayden's single-mindedness. "Pinched in manner, holding in some obscure personal rage, he spoke as if he were already an experienced, canny 'political,' " Howe has recalled. "In Hayden's clenched style —that air of distance suggesting reserves of power—one could already see the beginnings of a commissar. All through the sixties I kept encountering Hayden, each time impressed by his gifts yet also persuaded that some authoritarian poisons of this century had seeped into the depths of his mind."[28]

"I'm a divided person," says Hayden, "who has good and bad qualities. The elfish side of me gets pulled toward hostile reaction. I got a certain fiendish satisfaction out of Irving Howe attacking me; at one time, that was all I needed to know that I was on the right path. But I also did not anticipate having to play a role as a political leader. I had no training for it: I was an understudy to no one. I was basically a raw human being who had a zest for life. At the same time I was attracted to politics and to these roles. Politics is like a razor that cuts into your personal life and makes demands on you to be someone you're not—and I mean *all* politics. I had a problem: being a leader in a leaderless movement, and having conflicts myself over whether to be a leader. I mean, part of the conflict with being a leader is not wanting to be friends with everybody who wants to be friends with you. Part of the uncontrolled feeling I've always had about that is that I push that kind of person away—it bothers me. In political relationships, too, you break out of it when a person is no longer of use to you. And there is another problem, I think, for me: so far in life I seem to have an unbreakable ego. And if I can name the problem with an unbreakable ego, it's called *pride*. A lot of people, during a lot of encounters in my life, have wanted to humble me. I'll take a step, but there's something in me that says I won't survive unless I continue to go my own way. Some of it is original endowment. I was a little Catholic guy in a Protestant neighborhood, and pugnacious—a competitor like you've never seen. If you want to be psychological, my mother was driven almost crazy by the pressures she thought I was under in the Sixties and therefore that she was under. And the fact that my father was a conservative who wouldn't speak to me throughout this whole period does tend to make you skeptical about how much love there is in society.

"But then there's the impact of society—there's the outside world."[29]

The Fire This Time

On July 12, 1967, the black ghetto of Newark, New Jersey, erupted in a riot. The violence lasted for five days. The residents systematically looted and smashed the windows of white-owned businesses. The National Guardsmen brought in to "keep peace," poorly disciplined and terrified of snipers, staged a riot of their own, charging down streets, shooting up black-owned businesses, killing innocent bystanders. Twenty-four black residents were left dead; scores more were injured.[30]

The uprising came as no surprise, least of all to committed young radicals. Since the Watts riot in Los Angeles in August, 1965, ghetto rebellions had occurred with increasing frequency. By official count, 43 racial disorders occurred in 1966; 164 more occurred during the first nine months of 1967. The year before, Stokely Carmichael had become chairman of SNCC, publicized the slogan "black power" and rejected the ideal of racial integration "as a subterfuge for the maintenance of white supremacy." After the Mississippi Freedom Democratic Party fiasco at the Democratic Convention in 1964, SNCC had led the way in moving young black radicals toward a vision of international struggle. While some members of SNCC briefly embraced the rhetoric of participatory democracy and rule-by-consensus, others—after the Watts riot, a majority—supported some more disciplined form of revolutionary socialism. Spurning SNCC's original moral commitment to nonviolence, Carmichael declared that the "days of the free head-whipping are over." The rash of urban riots made it plausible to suppose that such sentiments were shared by a growing number of black Americans.[31]

When the violence in Newark broke out, Tom Hayden was play-

ing football in the street with his lawyer. For three years, he had
been working with the Newark Community Union. He had helped
the residents win control of the local poverty program. The Union
had helped prevail on the city to build a new neighborhood playground. But the root problems—of chronic unemployment, bad
housing, high crime, poor health care and a glaring lack of political
influence and power for the black majority—had scarcely been
touched. Just days before, Hayden had been quoted in a radical newspaper as saying that "urban guerrillas are the only realistic alternative at this time to electoral politics and mass armed resistance."
"The riot was going to happen," Hayden wrote afterward. "The authorities had been indifferent to the community's demand for justice; now the community was going to be indifferent to the
authorities' demand for order."[32]

After the violence started, Hayden circulated through the city,
gathering information, courteously helping the newsmen he met
while cruising the streets in his Volkswagen. "It was one thing for
most Americans to read about ghetto rebellions in newspapers," he
later recalled. "It's another thing to live in a black community and
observe it take place. . . . The repression, the use of military force
. . . one look at that, just the five days of looking at the streets of
violence, was really radicalizing. . . . We used to go and sit on a roof-
top at night and watch these guys. It was straight out of Vietnam.
They'd come down the street with bayonets, with automatic guns,
pushing people around, shooting, and they couldn't subdue the people for five days."[33]

After midnight on the fifth day of the riots, Hayden was summoned to a secret meeting of top state officials by an aide of New
Jersey Governor Richard Hughes, an Irish Democrat who regarded
himself as a progressive liberal. A car filled with state troopers
whisked Hayden to the riot command central: "They jumped out of
the car at full attention, guns pointed at the rooftops, pointed at the
trees and ushered me into the building as if at any moment the
guerrillas would come crashing down on the car." Inside, he was
introduced to Hughes, who greeted him with a smile and a warm
handshake that struck Hayden as incongruous—outside, the city
was burning. The Governor asked Hayden's opinion about what
he should do. Four years later, Hayden recalled his reply: "You are
the outside aggressor. There is no justice in your position. There is
nothing for you to do but get out. . . . The troops are gonna
massacre more people, and you're going to go down in history as
one of the biggest killers of all time. . . . Your repression will breed

resistance, which you will then have to repress, which will create more resistance, and you will be destroyed in the process. You have to withdraw troops unconditionally." Looking back, Hayden now says that "the discussion was far more polite and aimed at persuasion."[34]

Whatever the tone in which it was offered, Hayden's advice struck the State Police commander as dangerous. Some of the Governor's aides tried to devise a compromise position. After several hours of debate, with the Governor's course of action still unresolved, Hayden was dismissed. "He made no commitments," Hayden later recalled, "thanked us very much like a good Irish politician, took a card with his name on it out of his wallet . . . wrote 'Good Luck, Tom' on it—said he really hoped to see me again sometime, and we left." The next morning, Hughes withdrew the troops, and the rioting ended.[35]

His dramatic late-night meeting with the Governor did nothing to dampen Hayden's growing interest in the idea of guerrilla warfare. Newark's "streets of violence" had convinced him that the conditions were being created for "an American form of guerrilla warfare based in the slums." As he explained a few days later, "I decided the most important task for myself was to suggest to 'the outside world' a way of understanding the violence that took place."[36]

Hayden accepted an assignment to write about the riots for *The New York Review of Books*. A young publication already at the zenith of its influence, *The New York Review* had become the most prestigious outlet in America for serious social criticism. By printing a growing number of essays by young radicals and critics of the Vietnam War, it was linking the New Left to a large audience of academic readers.

In his article, which he later expanded into a short book called *Rebellion in Newark*, Hayden adopted a style of dry documentation: "The author of these pages is a white man who has spent the past four years in the Newark ghetto organizing around issues of housing, welfare and political power." His intention, in part, was to convey the logic of the violence, rather than dismissing it, as many liberal commentators did, as utterly chaotic or "senseless." But the essay was also in effect a sequel to "Revolution in Mississippi." Once again, Hayden aimed "to make facts real," trying to illuminate the moral urgency of the situation in order to "evoke not reader interest but productive commitment."

Though he explicitly cautioned against "radical illusions about 'revolution,' " Hayden scoffed at liberal and conservative critics of ghetto violence. "A riot represents people making history," he wrote. For many participants, it was "the celebration of a new beginning. People felt as though for a moment they were creating a community of their own." To those involved, "the riot is far less lawless and far more representative than the system of arbitrary rules and prescribed channels which they confront every day."

But while "violence can contribute to shattering the status quo," Hayden added that "only politics and organization can transform it. The ghetto still needs the power to decide its destiny on such matters as urban renewal and housing, social services, policing and taxation." For Hayden, the final goal remained participatory democracy. "People need to create self-government," he concluded. "We are at a point where democracy—the idea and practice of people controlling their lives—is a revolutionary issue in the United States."[37]

To pick up Hayden's piece, *The New York Review* sent to Newark journalist Andrew Kopkind, who was working on a piece of his own for the magazine. Kopkind met Hayden in a coffee shop on the outskirts of the burned-out neighborhood where the riots had occurred. Curious about the mechanics of arson, Kopkind asked Hayden if he knew how to make a Molotov cocktail. Using a napkin for the purpose, Hayden drew a diagram. Kopkind brought the napkin back to New York and showed the diagram to the editors of *The New York Review*, who decided it would make a splendid cover image (though David Levine, the staff artist, refused to draw it).[38]

"I think I was in a bind," says Hayden looking back. "Either I was a new romantic hope, or I was a person to be dismissed, by Irving Howe and others, for not living up to ideological expectations. And the editors of *The New York Review* have a romantic fantasy about Molotov cocktails that begins and ends with drawing something on the cover of their magazine. They didn't *make* any. I don't know if they ever got gas on their fingers in their lives. I did. I mean, I saw people dead, I saw horrible things. So I was an object of fantasy—'Let's talk to Hayden, we can't talk to the blacks, but we can talk to Hayden, he went to college, he read Mills and all these people, and he talks like us, so he can interpret for us what's happening. He's the white Stokely.' It was an invention."[39]

Perhaps. But it was also an "invention" that Hayden at the time did nothing to correct. And whatever his private reservations—if, indeed, he so clearly felt them at the time—Hayden's growing fascination with guerrilla warfare was directly and indirectly entering the mainstream of America's intellectual culture.

Fantasies of Revolution

Less than a week after the end of the Newark insurrection, Detroit erupted in the worst American riot of the century. It left 43 dead, 7,000 arrested, 1,300 buildings destroyed and 2,700 businesses looted.

A growing number of black radicals, embracing, like Hayden, the image of guerrilla war, felt that the ghetto uprisings were a preview of the armed struggle that must inevitably engulf America. H. Rap Brown, who had replaced Stokely Carmichael as the chairman of SNCC, argued that black America was an internal colony; he suggested that the colony consider August 18, 1965, to be its day of independence, since that was the day that "the blacks of Watts picked up their guns to fight for their freedom." In August, 1967, Carmichael, whose advocacy of "black power" had made him internationally famous, attended a conference in Havana, Cuba, to discuss the call, made by the Latin American guerrilla Che Guevara, to create "two, three, many Vietnams." Carmichael declared the solidarity of black Americans in the international struggle for liberation. The Havana conference passed a resolution calling on "the Negro people of the U.S. to answer the racist violence of the U.S. imperialist government by increasing direct revolutionary action."[40]

While Detroit and Newark burned, American planes continued to rain bombs on Vietnam. By the middle of the year, North Vietnam's capacity to generate electricity had been cut by 85 percent; the country had suffered well over $200 million in damage. These statistics were meaningless. The American bombing campaign paradoxically bolstered the morale of the Vietnamese Communists, and rekindled their revolutionary zeal.[41]

In a kind of surreal counterpoint, radio stations and stereos throughout Europe and America ceaselessly played the Beatles' *Sgt. Pepper's Lonely Hearts Club Band*, a rock album that sought to express—and, for a generation, succeeded in defining—a heady, epochal spirit of euphoria, adventure and joy. "The closest Western Civilization has come to unity since the Congress of Vienna in 1815," wrote the rock critic Langdon Winner in 1968, "was the week the *Sgt. Pepper* album was released. . . . For a brief while the irreparably fragmented consciousness of the West was unified, at least in the minds of the young." The avant-garde bohemianism that a decade before had been confined to Greenwich Village, North Beach and a handful of university towns, where radicals and artists had to make do with the same coffeehouse and bookstore, was now everywhere. So were drugs: hashish, marijuana, above all LSD. "Turn on to the scene, tune in to what is happening, and drop out," urged Timothy Leary, who six years before had argued (against the aristocratic reservations of Aldous Huxley) that LSD should be made widely available as a tool of democratic spiritual enlightenment.[42]

While the psychedelic circus-music of the Beatles' "Lucy in the Sky with Diamonds" hung in the air like a hologram of bliss, images from "the other side" streamed into the lives of millions of middle-class kids nightly through television. Pictures of Vietnamese in flight from American bombs, their faces gaunt with terror, their skin burned by napalm, blended seamlessly with scenes from the urban inferno in Newark and Detroit, creating a collage of crisis and collapse. Viewed through an increasingly thick fog of drugs by a generation half-convinced by *Sgt. Pepper* of its world-historical destiny, these images of injustice made the idea of revolution weirdly credible. "Two, three, many Vietnams." Of course.

We Are All Viet Cong

In September, Tom Hayden flew to Bratislava, Czechoslovakia, with a delegation of American activists to meet with a group of Vietnamese. In the wake of the summer's riots, he felt compelled to abandon community organizing; as a white trying to organize blacks, he was especially vulnerable to criticism from the advocates of black power. Becoming more involved in efforts to stop the war in Vietnam offered a graceful way out.

Hayden had arranged the meeting in Bratislava with the help of Dave Dellinger, the veteran pacifist and anti-war leader. The purpose of the meeting, says Hayden, "was to open lines of communication between Americans and Vietnamese." By inviting representatives of the new cultural and political insurgencies in the United States and bringing them face to face with "the other side," Hayden hoped to promote a deeper, more visceral sense of solidarity between American radicals and the Vietnamese. The Vietnamese contingent of 35, which included several prominent Communist officials, was one of the highest-level delegations to meet with Westerners outside North Vietnam since the signing of the Geneva Accords in 1954—Bratislava was, in effect, to be a dress rehearsal for higher-level contacts with the U.S. government. The American delegation, as Andrew Kopkind later quipped, was "30 friends of Tom

Hayden, chosen at random": journalists, religious leaders, civil rights militants, "one verifiable welfare mother . . . and several stoned underground newspaper editors."[43]

Hayden had taken special pains to coax Rennie Davis into leaving his community-organizing project in Chicago in order to make the trip to Bratislava. "Rennie could make things happen that I could only dream about," says Hayden. "He was an organizational balance for me, like Dick Flacks was an intellectual and personal balance. Now, Rennie had made a life commitment to community organizing: he wished the war would go away, because it was destroying all of our plans for domestic social reform. My goal, the only thing I thought would convince Rennie to help me organize against the war, was to get him out of Chicago and into Vietnam. Rennie was a people person. If he saw somebody covered with napalm burns, he would get the point." Still boyish and clean-cut at a time when long hair and scruffiness had become badges of cultural independence, Davis was the picture of innocence. "What happened to Rennie is really an amazing story," says Hayden looking back: "He was the All-American boy, and he turned into an avenging angel."[44]

Starkly attired in black and all business, the Vietnamese used Bratislava as an opportunity for communicating their views on the course of the war. They declared that they were on the verge of final victory. They distributed the new program of the National Liberation Front. They reiterated their demand that American troops be withdrawn. They handed out rings made of scrap aluminum from American planes shot down over North Vietnam. Afterward, one American delegate complained that Hayden had rigged the conference: "We were supposed to go as individuals, but from the beginning he tried to move the group into cohesion. He wanted a clear expression of solidarity with the Vietnamese." But Hayden did not need to twist many arms. Most of the participants were overwhelmed by the Vietnamese. Several young cadres from the National Liberation Front reported that their trip out of the South had taken weeks, and they had often traveled under harrowing circumstances. One of the Vietnamese described launching a mortar assault on a U.S. air base; another volunteered comments on a recent piece on Vietnam in *The New York Review*. Here, it seemed, were serious intellectuals who were also serious guerrilla warriors. After meeting privately with one Vietnamese official as part of an unsuccessful effort to be allowed to report on the war from behind Communist lines in the South, Kopkind, as he later wrote, was filled with fantasies of radical fraternity: "I was to be appointed a master spy, I was to visit the Liberated Zones, I was to receive the Revolutionary Word."[45]

It was Hayden himself, however, who created perhaps the biggest stir at Bratislava. In a speech that Kopkind, for one, recalls as an emotional high point of the meeting, Hayden talked about the meaning of solidarity. "I related the story of the Roman slave Spartacus," says Hayden. "The Roman soldiers were looking for him in a crowd of slaves. To protect him, one slave said, 'I am Spartacus,' then another, and another, and so on. Similarly, I said, the U.S. has dehumanized the 'enemy' into a shadowy, conspiratorial 'Viet Cong,' has unleashed their full firepower on them, and expects everyone else to save their skins by stepping out of the way. The test, I said, is whether we as Americans can identify enough with the suffering and ordeal of the Vietnamese people to feel what they feel, and not turn away. So that when the Pentagon carries out a search-and-destroy mission and demands to know where are the Viet Cong, we will be able to step forward and say, 'Here we are, take us instead. . . .' "[46]

The media, predictably, took Hayden's speech and boiled it down to his punch line: "We are all Viet Cong!"[47]

The world was beginning to spin with dizzying speed for Tom Hayden. From Czechoslovakia he flew first to Phnom Penh, Cambodia, and then on to Hanoi (again ignoring a State Department ban), bringing along Rennie Davis and five others. In Bratislava, the North Vietnamese had asked Hayden to help arrange the release of three American soldiers who were being held prisoner by the National Liberation Front—a gesture, Hayden speculates, that the Communists hoped might pave the way for peace talks. "They didn't want it to appear that they were entering into a formal relationship with the government that was bombing them. So a peace activist was a channel." Hayden and his party stayed in Hanoi for two weeks. They then flew to Paris with promises but no prisoners. There Hayden stayed by himself—and waited. Finally receiving word from the Vietnamese, he flew back to Phnom Penh, Cambodia. Again, he waited.[48]

"I lived there for days," he says, "never knowing when I would find out anything. I would have lunch and dinner with Cambodian officials and American correspondents in these lovely outdoor restaurants—and the war would be sixty miles away; you'd see huge flashes of light on the horizon. I developed a view, right or wrong, of Cambodia as a pastoral island in the middle of all this, which really haunts me. Because I assume that all of the people I met are now skulls in a museum somewhere."[49]

On November 10, after weeks of waiting, word finally came that the prisoners would show up in two hours. "I went to the NLF compound in Phnom Penh," says Hayden. "The prisoners had been driven straight in from the war zone. Three hours before, they'd been prisoners in some kind of mobile prison gang—this is the first war, I believe, where prisoners were kept alive by guerrillas. They did not know who I was, and now I was proposing that they go with me to the United States. They were suspicious, but they decided to say yes; they had been living day by day, and calculated that this was no more of a gamble than what they had gone through in the previous days."[50]

With the help of the Cambodians, the Australians (who had been acting as surrogates for the American government) and a CIA agent, Hayden arranged to fly with the freed Americans from Phnom Penh to Beirut, stopping only for refueling. In Beirut, the flight was interrupted. After spending a night in the U.S. embassy in Beirut, Hayden and the POWs resumed their flight in a plane filled with CIA officers, with New York the destination. "It was quite an experience," says Hayden. "One of the prisoners was very sympathetic to me, another was very hostile and the other was very sick. The entire process had taken weeks. It was the longest I had ever been outside the United States."[51]

Rituals of Confrontation

While Hayden was negotiating the release of the first prisoners of war to be freed by the Vietnamese Communists, the anti-war movement in the United States had entered a tumultuous new phase of militance. In the middle of October, Rennie Davis and the rest of Hayden's party had left him in Paris and flown home just in time to rush to Washington, D.C., to participate in the biggest—and most dramatic—anti-war demonstration yet: the March on the Pentagon.

Organized under the auspices of a "National Mobilization Committee," a broad coalition of pacifist, religious and radical groups, the March was an attempt to synthesize "Gandhi and Guerrilla," as Dave Dellinger, one of the organizers, put it. Rather than simply petitioning the government, some demonstrators were going to try a new strategy, of "asserting and acting out the power of the people," by staging isolated acts of disruption and challenging symbols of authority and power. The change in nonviolent tactics was marked by the slogan "From protest to resistance." To choreograph this symbolic assertion of popular sovereignty, Dellinger brought in

Berkeley activist Jerry Rubin, who had pioneered the tactic of "resistance" in the Bay Area troop-train blockades of 1965. Envisioning a
dramatic confrontation between "the people" and "the warmakers,"
Rubin suggested that the Pentagon rather than the Capitol become
the destination of the demonstrators.[52]

On October 21, 1967, the day of the march, some 100,000 demonstrators besieged Washington. Prominent among them were a handful of intellectual celebrities, including Norman Mailer, whose
account of the event, *Armies of the Night*, perfectly captures the
sense of wild excitement—and fear—that would soon come to punc-
tuate the lives of young radicals with an ecstatic, disorienting series
of exclamation points. "It is safe to say that the beginning of this
confrontation has not been without terror on either side," wrote
Mailer of the moment when the marchers finally reached the Pentagon. "The demonstrators, all too conscious of what they consider
the profound turpitude of the American military might in Asia, are
prepared (or altogether unprepared) for any conceivable brutality
here. On their side the troops have listened for years to small-town
legends about the venality, criminality, filth, corruption, perversion,
addiction, and unbridled appetites of that mysterious group of city
Americans referred to first as hipsters, then beatniks, then hippies;
now hearing they are linked with the insidious infiltrators of America's psychic life, the Reds! the troops do not know whether to expect a hairy kiss on their lips or a bomb between their knees. Each
side is coming face to face with its conception of the devil!"[53]

Pacifists urged restraint. Militants evoked the memory of Che
Guevara, who had been killed a few weeks before. A small "Revolutionary Contingent" stormed the walls of the Pentagon, and succeeded in scaling them. A group of pranksters led by New York
radical Abbie Hoffman tried to levitate the Pentagon. Viet Cong flags
waved. Scores of demonstrators were arrested. Some were beaten.
"There was no leadership," said one participant; "that was what was
so beautiful." The power of the people was acted out—and the result
seemed to be a kind of benign, joyous anarchy. After midnight, as
the arrests and beatings ended, an uncanny sense of calm crept over
the crowd. Stars filled a clear fall sky. Outside the Pentagon, people
began to sing "Silent Night."[54]

In Search of Power

The March on the Pentagon left Rennie Davis, like most young
radicals, elated at the prospects for creating a mass movement of

protest to force an end to the war. At the same time, his trip to Hanoi had convinced Davis that such protest was a moral necessity. "Rennie flew out of Hanoi," recalls Hayden, "clutching an anti-personnel bomb, which he carried with him everywhere and which he showed to everyone: this evil little bomb that is made of these clusters that break open, creating little fragments that penetrate the skin, so you can't get them out." Hayden's original plan had worked like a charm: Davis' pilgrimage to Hanoi, much like Hayden's own trip two years before, had turned his world upside down.[55]

"I think for him it was a religious conversion," says Hayden. "In Hanoi, he was hit by destruction like he'd never seen. He felt like he was on a mission to tell the American people all about this. He wanted to confront America with the fact that we were killing people by barbarous means—that we were doing things that he had never *dreamed* in his childhood that Americans would have anything to do with. Napalm. Phosphorus. Fragmentation bombs. All these things designed by scientists to kill people painfully, to mutilate them, to scar them for life."[56]

In December, Hayden and Davis attended a meeting of the Administrative Committee of the National Mobilization to discuss what action to take the next summer at the Democratic Convention in Chicago. President Johnson seemed bent on escalating the war. The committee all but unanimously agreed that some kind of national action should be organized—but there agreement ended. Committed pacifists worried that the mounting enthusiasm for confrontation was bound to increase the potential for violence. Advocates of aggressive direct action were openly contemptuous of mere rallies: as one militant had pointed out after the March on the Pentagon, a handful of people could more effectively resist the war machine by stalling and burning an automobile on every road leading to the Pentagon. Liberals were as wary as ever about consorting with sympathizers of the Viet Cong. And to make matters worse, a new government antiriot statute made the organizers of any demonstration that produced acts of violence liable to long prison sentences, even if they were not directly responsible for such acts.[57]

Hayden hoped that a large-scale protest on the model of the Pentagon march would make visible "the political drama that's going on in the country." He spoke of "bringing our cast of characters to confront theirs and having confidence that in that confrontation the truth would not be lost either on us or them." In part, such a demonstration would be another piece of street theater, designed to "act out the power of the people." But Hayden also believed that through such a demonstration, participants "could make entry into a net-

work of forces and have an impact and almost become the determining factor in the situation." He still had dreams of sparking the
liberal imagination.[58]

Sensing that Hayden and Rennie Davis had a deep commitment
to organizing a demonstration at the Democratic Convention, and
impressed with their skills, Dave Dellinger of the National Mobilization Committee authorized them in February, 1968, to open an
office in Chicago and prepare a prospectus for "an election year
offensive."

"Election year 1968 will be a fateful one for American democracy," their prospectus began. Millions already opposed the war in
Vietnam and racism in the United States. "But the deeper crisis is
the failure of democratic and representative government to work."
The war had made a "mockery of democracy." The country's foreign
policy was "dominated by a 'national security complex' whose decisions are subject to only the most feeble democratic review." To
protest the nation's undemocratic drift, Hayden and Davis proposed
"a campaign" to dramatize "the right of people to know the truth,
to control their own government, to use politics to solve their problems. We should demand self-determination in Vietnam, the ghettos, and in the boring, insecure life of the ordinary white citizen who
pays taxes and blood to a political system that shuts him out of
meaningful participation." In order to appeal to pacifists and disgruntled liberals as well as to militant radicals, "the campaign
should not plan violence and disruption against the Democratic National Convention. It should be non-violent and legal. The right to
rebellion is hardly exercised in an effective way by assembling
300,000 people to charge into 30,000 paratroopers." As Dave Dellinger later recalled, the original idea was to stage "a loose countercon-
vention, decentralized and diversified in contrast to the rigid,
overcentralized, and authoritarian convention of the Democrats." If
successful, explained Hayden and Davis in their prospectus, such a
demonstration would "delegitimate the Democratic Party while
building support for an independent people's movement."[59]

Hayden and Davis' scheme did not meet with universal acclaim.
The leaders of SDS were openly skeptical, in part because the group
had veered sharply away from its original commitment to nonsectarian radicalism. For more than a year, SDS had been the target of a
takeover attempt by the Progressive Labor Party, a Marxist-Leninist
cadre of Maoists. With its disciplined, puritanical style and dogmatic
commitment to create a dictatorship of the proletariat in America,
the Progressive Labor faction stood against most of what once had

defined the New Left as new. The Party's show of revolutionary rigor nevertheless had a profound impact on the intellectual climate within SDS. "Sitting in an SDS gathering," complained two veterans, had become "a hellish agony," with "intellectualization and parliamentary manipulation" replacing "a sharing of experiences and consensus decision-making." This was putting it mildly. SDS meetings all too frequently degenerated into a farrago of sectarian speeches, with one person liable to quote Herbert Marcuse on the vices of liberal tolerance while another quoted Joseph Stalin on the nationalities question. Marxism became a tool seized on by both sides, not only as a theory for interpreting the world, but as a weapon in an internal power struggle. The new leaders of SDS, who had never developed a coherent strategy to replace that of *America and the New Era*, developed instead a penchant for dramatic posturing: to remain on the cutting edge of the Movement required the appearance, at least, of being a revolutionary—preferably a *serious* revolutionary. One consequence was an increasingly hermetic debate over agencies of social change: Would "the revolution" be led by factory workers? By a "new working class"? By an "internal colony of blacks"? Or by a "revolutionary youth movement"? Another consequence was a growing disenchantment with the idea of participatory democracy. A truly "revolutionary organization," wrote one SDS leader unconnected with the Progressive Labor Party, required a "responsible collective leadership," not "long formless mass meetings."[60]

In this context, Hayden and Davis' plan seemed hopelessly old-fashioned. Critics in SDS scored its potential for triggering more government repression. They warned that some demonstrators drawn to the convention might find their revolutionary ardor dampened by proximity to seductive liberal leaders like Robert Kennedy and Eugene McCarthy, who was campaigning against President Johnson as an anti-war candidate in the Democratic primaries. Spurning the planned demonstration at the convention, the leaders of SDS urged instead that "draft resistance should be the primary focus of our work in the coming months."[61]

Davis and Hayden's plans were complicated still further by the "Yippies"—a group formed, in part, out of disgust with the growing solemnity of SDS. Founded in December, 1967, by Jerry Rubin and Abbie Hoffman, the Yippies (for "Youth International Party") planned to stage their own "Theater of Disruption" in Chicago, "blending pot and politics into a political grass-leaves movement." As an "international party," the Yippies were nonexistent; but as impresarios of the new symbolic politics, Rubin and Hoffman were nonpareil. Picking up where his effort to levitate the Pentagon had left off, Hoffman began constructing a "vast myth" out of a relentless barrage of outrageous threats and non sequiturs: "We will burn Chicago to the ground!" "We will fuck on the beaches!" "We demand the Politics of Ecstasy!" "Acid for all!" "Abandon the Creeping Meatball!" When the National Mobilization Committee met in March to discuss the prospectus prepared by Hayden and Davis, Hoffman interrupted the meeting to announce that the Yippie program for revolution included a demand for the abolition of pay toilets.[62]

The Yippies' hidden agenda was no joke, however. Rubin and Hoffman both wanted to foment aggressive street actions in Chicago. If Hayden, Davis and the Mobilization were squeamish about violence, then so much the worse for the Mobilization. As one Yippie slogan reminded Hayden, "Everyone is a leader."[63]

Shadow Ambassador

Hayden viewed such slogans with increasing skepticism. "Participatory democracy," he explained to a reporter early in 1968, "points out what is essentially wrong with places like Newark—the absence of self-government. But as a pure organizing tool, it left a lot to be desired. It didn't explain how leadership could be exercised or how bureaucracy could be used. It didn't anticipate factional conflicts and how to resolve them." Hayden still trumpeted the old phrase. Participatory democracy still defined his vision of the final goal; he was still in principle committed to building a pluralistic and decentralized framework for the Movement, as witness his plans for the Democratic Convention. But Hayden, although he left his precise views shrouded in ambiguity, had by the beginning of 1968 become convinced of the need for structure, organization—and visionary leaders. "It would be a mistake to say we don't need leaders," he explained a few years later. "That would ignore the fact that every new act is preceded by the preparation of public opinion, the prior examples of martyrdom and sacrifice, the writing of books that somebody has read and passed on. . . . The organizing is not for the sake of building a bureaucracy with an elite at the top. The function of organizing is to create continuity from one generation to the next, from one person to the next, to summarize experience."[64]

Hayden himself was now leading a split existence. In his speeches and essays, he presented himself as an uncompromising outsider—

an impassioned, defiant insurgent anxious to "delegitimate" the Democratic Party. But as his friends knew, Hayden also functioned behind closed doors in Newark and Washington, D.C., as a curious kind of insider—an improbable shadow ambassador, unelected and unappointed, from the international left to liberal America. "And the thing is," said a Hayden associate interviewed for a *New York Times* "Man in the News" profile in November, 1967, "he doesn't talk about love and community and all. He talks about votes. He's very practical."[65]

The *Times* profile was occasioned by Hayden's dramatic announcement in Phnom Penh, Cambodia, on November 11, 1967, that the Vietnamese Communists had freed three captured American soldiers, whom he would be escorting back to the United States. The State Department had privately cabled its thanks, and in one confidential telegram noted that "HAYDEN COOPERATED FULLY WITH EMBASSY OFFICIALS." On his return, Hayden met with Ambassador-at-Large Averell Harriman. Since these were the first POWs to be released by the Vietnamese Communists, the ambassador wanted to learn how Hayden had succeeded where he had failed. They discussed the possibility of future prisoner releases. Harriman reminisced about the Cold War. The unrest that had recently broken out in Czechoslovakia was heartening to him, he told Hayden, because it suggested that President Roosevelt's dream of closer ties with the Communists might still be within reach. While they talked, aides scurried to get coffee and cake for the Ambassador-at-Large, who was celebrating his seventy-sixth birthday.[66]

This was not Hayden's first meeting with a key member of the liberal establishment. Earlier in the year, journalist Jack Newfield had arranged a meeting between Hayden and Staughton Lynd and New York Senator Robert Kennedy. After reading *The Other Side*, the Senator had asked to meet its authors. At the time, Kennedy was preparing to deliver a major speech criticizing the war in Vietnam; he was also weighing the possibility of running against President Johnson in the 1968 primaries. "Tom was wary," recalls Newfield. "He was in a radical, even a revolutionary phase. Robert, for his part, was very tentative about making this break with Johnson. It was very Freudian and Shakespearean for Robert to attack a war that his brother had started, and a President whom his brother had picked as Vice President." To the Senator's surprise, Hayden and Lynd advocated not unilateral withdrawal but an unconditional bombing halt. "Tom always was a good politician," says Newfield, "and so was Robert. They were both looking for some common ground. The issue was finding some way to initiate negotiations." After the meeting, Hayden told Newfield that he thought Kennedy superior to conventional liberals. "He identified with the alienated," says Hayden looking back. He was impressed by the Senator's willingness to consider opposing the war, and impressed, too, by the Kennedy charisma: here, after all, was a strong-willed leader who had already sparked popular hopes for social change. Still, Hayden was ambivalent. Kennedy, he said in 1972, "seemed very isolated by his wealth and power, and not sure of what was really going on [in Vietnam] and still thinking in terms of Cold War categories."[67]

Hayden visited Washington—and Robert Kennedy's home—several times over the next few months. "I was in a situation where some people thought I was flirting with guerrilla warfare," he says looking back, "and other people"—particularly skeptics on the left, including the militant vanguard of SDS—"thought I took liberalism too seriously, and believed in Robert Kennedy. All of these suspicions were accurate. I tried to think in terms of multiple possibilities. One was that a revolution, or a period of violent revolutionary activity, was beginning. I thought that was a definite possibility that ought to be taken seriously and prepared for. And then there was a possibility that by working through the liberal wing of the Democratic Party and by having large, peaceful demonstrations, we could pull out of Vietnam and get back on the road that John F. Kennedy had started on. I thought that was too hopeful, but not impossible. I explored all those possibilities, not knowing which was most real. Even if you thought we were approaching a revolution, it was best to approach it with the broadest possible base of support, to try all the options. And I really wanted the Vietnam war to end. So it didn't seem inconsistent to talk to the Vietnamese in Hanoi, to Harriman in Washington, to Kennedy."[68]

In addition, as Hayden and his liberal allies discussed at the time, their political hopes for a figure like Kennedy had some historical precedent. In 1954, after the Vietnamese Communists had scored a strategic victory at Dien Bien Phu over the French, who were struggling to keep control of their old colonial possession, Pierre Mendès-France, the left-wing leader of the centrist Radical Party and an outspoken critic of the war, became Prime Minister of France with a mandate to negotiate a peace settlement—which he promptly did. If the Vietnamese Communists could produce a military victory over the Americans like Dien Bien Phu, then, Hayden reasoned, an American Mendès-France might emerge triumphant—perhaps Robert Kennedy, perhaps Eugene McCarthy.

In February, 1968, as Hayden watched history in the making not from the "streets of violence" but from the corridors of power, such hopes seemed more plausible than ever. At a meeting early that month in Washington to discuss the war with officials at the State Department, Hayden was stunned to learn that Washington could not communicate with its embassy in Saigon. A few days before, the Vietnamese Communists had launched their Tet Offensive. Nearly 70,000 Communist troops had assaulted more than one hundred cities and towns in South Vietnam, including Saigon, where commandos had attacked the U.S. embassy. The breakdown in communications seemed to Hayden like the handwriting on the wall. Could Tet be the beginning of an American Dien Bien Phu? [69]

Facing Reality

Tet changed everything. It had been planned by the Vietnamese Communists in part to shatter the political complacency of America —and in this it unquestionably succeeded.[70] A growing sense of crisis gripped the country. Television coverage brought the battle for Saigon to vivid life nightly. An American defeat, unthinkable days before, suddenly seemed possible. Each passing week seemed to bring fresh tidings of disorder and uncertainty.

On March 12, Eugene McCarthy came surprisingly close to receiving 50 percent of the votes in the New Hampshire Democratic presidential primary—and Lyndon Johnson suddenly seemed vulnerable to an anti-war challenge.

On March 16, Robert Kennedy announced that he too would challenge Johnson for the Democratic nomination.

On March 31, President Johnson announced that he would not run for reelection.[71]

Four days later, Martin Luther King, Jr., was killed by an assassin in Memphis, Tennessee.

As the news of King's death spread, blacks across America took to the streets. Uprisings occurred in Boston, Detroit, Chicago, Philadelphia, San Francisco, Toledo, Pittsburgh. And for the first time in the decade, Washington, D.C., went up in flames, as three days of rioting reduced miles of the inner city to a blasted landscape of smoldering rubble.

Hayden watched the riot out of a State Department window. He had come to talk again to Averell Harriman. "The city was burning," Hayden later recalled. "Out the window you could see that Washington was on fire. We had a hard time getting into the building, because the blacks were burning down the center of the city. . . . And here in the State Department you could . . . talk calmly with [Harriman] regarding the state of affairs regarding American prisoners, and not detect the slightest hysteria in him about the fact that the capital of the US behind him was on fire. Luminous red flames [were] coming up from the business district. The only people who seemed hysterical were the secretaries, who were wondering whether the children would be all right, how they were going to get home—you know, ordinary people who had to go out there and get in cars and buses and face reality."[72]

But what indeed was the "reality"? The spectacle of the nation's capital in flames? The apparently unflappable confidence of the country's liberal leaders? Imminent defeat in Vietnam? Civil war in America?

And who was the real Tom Hayden? The practical politician who talked about votes? The prophet of participatory democracy? The shadow ambassador enjoying backroom power? The apologist for guerrilla warfare? Or did all of these apparently contradictory roles represent, at least in Hayden's own mind, different aspects of a coherent strategy to end a cruel and barbarous war?[73]

Bringing the War Home

On April 23, a group of radical students at Columbia University, led by members of the campus SDS chapter, took a dean hostage, seized a building and issued a set of six demands. "I was in a meeting with Stokely Carmichael in New York to discuss Chicago," recalls Hayden. "The black students and the SDS chapter asked me to come as soon as possible to the campus, where a confrontation was developing." Hayden, who had been preparing to move from Newark to Chicago, rushed instead to Morningside Heights. "It would be terrible," he quipped to one reporter, "if the revolution actually started and I was driving across the country."[74]

Among other things, the Columbia rebels demanded the right to demontrate inside university buildings; they demanded that the university stop work on a gymnasium opposed by local residents; they demanded that the university disaffiliate from a defense institute involved in research on the Vietnam War; they demanded amnesty for all protesters. As the week progressed, more buildings were occupied and individual "communes" were established. The members of each commune "ate, slept, discussed, debated, fought, got busted together," explained Mark Rudd, one of the Columbia SDS leaders, shortly afterward. "This was one of the first times in our experience," said Rudd, "that 'participatory democracy' had been put into practice. . . . For many it was the first communal experience of their lives—a far cry from the traditional lifestyle of Morningside Heights, that of individuals retiring into their rooms or apartments. One brother remarked to me, 'The communes are a better high than grass.' "[75]

Shortly after Mathematics Hall was seized by students in the early morning hours of April 26, Tom Hayden emerged as one of that commune's leaders. As rumors flew that the police were preparing to storm the building, Hayden calmly readied his charges for the worst. "My reason for being at Columbia was more accidental than strategic," he says looking back. "Once I got into the place, it became difficult to walk out and abandon the students. It was hard to know what you were getting into. And by the time I'd been there two days, it became impossible to leave. My life froze. So I participated in the strike, and tried to give some advice to the leadership; and I took responsibility for trying to keep sanity in one building." In the chronicle of the occupation compiled by reporters from the *Columbia Daily Spectator* afterward, Hayden was described as "a maestro of participatory democracy" who conducted the mass meetings in Math Hall with deft skill.[76]

The police attack did not materialize the first night. For the next four days, Mathematics Hall was turned into a "liberated zone" behind barricades. In lengthy meetings, the students discussed the nature of American society, the failings of the university, the role of revolution. "I was in Columbia," Hayden recalled four years later, "living with people who felt such international solidarity with people around the world and such solidarity with students across the US and such revolutionary pride in their ability to live together communally for a week under such danger." Here was Al Haber's old seminar model of radicalism and Hayden's moral model of a community of shared risk combined in a few heady days of political adventure: Danger! Defiance! Democracy! So *this* was what politics was really all about! That this was in fact what politics meant only at its limits, in situations where matters of life, liberty and death seemed to converge—and that the Columbia student strike was only a trumped-up simulacrum of such a situation—was easy to ignore in the excitement of the moment.

Despite the euphoric sense that "participatory democracy" had at last been realized, the student strike organization was a disciplined hierarchy. And Tom Hayden, although literally an outside agitator, was one of a few people with power at the top. "Most of the students," a participant wrote afterward, "were politically undereducated; they had never experienced anything comparable; they were confused and easily led." In all his mythic glory, Hayden was an especially intimidating figure. During the occupation, the poet Stephen Spender, who later wrote about the rebellion, bumped into Hayden and was startled by his politeness. "A friend," said Spender, "had warned me that it would be useless for me to talk with Tom Hayden . . . because he had nothing to say to anyone over thirty. . . . I still felt too uneasy, though, to talk, but I keep my impression of him—with his slightly scarred complexion and his light eyes—as a general visiting a battlefield." [77]

In the early morning hours of April 30, as police massed for their long-awaited invasion of the campus, a knot of literary celebrities gathered outside Mathematics Hall to watch. Among them were Jack Newfield, the cartoonist Jules Feiffer, the editor and writer Jason Epstein of Random House and a handful of editors from *Ramparts*, a slick monthly that had become the most widely circulated journalistic voice of the New Left. Shortly before dawn, the police arrived. They tore down the makeshift barricades and began to beat students and drag them from the building to a waiting paddy wagon. Hayden walked. As the police pushed him forward, he flashed a grin, raised his arm and gave a V-for-victory sign. [78]

"The goal written on the university walls was 'Create two, three, many Columbias,' " wrote Hayden shortly afterward in the pronunciamento he produced for *Ramparts* magazine: "It meant expand the strike so that the U.S. must either change or send its troops to occupy American campuses. At this point the goal seems realistic. . . . The students' protest constantly escalates by building on its achievements and legends. . . . American educators are fond of telling their students that barricades are part of the romantic past, that social change today can only come about through the processes of negotiation. But the students at Columbia discovered that the barricades are only the beginning of what they call 'bringing the war home.' " [79]

Tears of Rage

On June 5, 1968, minutes after claiming victory over Eugene McCarthy in the California presidential primary, Robert Kennedy was shot and killed in Los Angeles by a deranged Arab nationalist named Sirhan Sirhan.

On a trip to San Francisco the week before, Hayden had accidentally met Kennedy in an elevator. "His hands were bleeding," recalls Hayden. "Something like that gets to you subconsciously. It was at the height of the California campaign, with admirers mobbing him everywhere. His palms were cut." Kennedy asked Hayden whether he was planning to campaign for him. Hayden said that he personally supported him. But Hayden also knew that the radical anti-war coalition could not afford to be dragged into what had become a bitter and divisive struggle between McCarthy and Kennedy for the chance to challenge Vice President Hubert Humphrey, President Johnson's heir apparent. Hayden told Kennedy that he would not be campaigning for any candidate, but that he was planning to focus his energy instead on organizing a peace demonstration at the Chicago convention, which he hoped might be of some help to him.[80]

Hayden, who was free on bail after his arrest at Columbia, was preparing to leave for Chicago on the day when Kennedy's body arrived in New York. That night, he went with Jack Newfield to St. Patrick's Cathedral, where a funeral Mass for the slain Senator was planned for the next day. As he entered, the dimly lit cathedral seemed to him to be empty. He sat down in a pew, holding a green cap from Cuba. Slowly he became aware of the preparations around him for the funeral Mass the next morning. He watched workers erect scaffolding for the cameras that would televise the service. He noticed the faces of the Kennedy staff, "which were absolutely gray and wasted," he recalls, "showing how for them the only reality was in this person."[81]

Kennedy the man Hayden had known only briefly. But the myth had long fascinated him. The Kennedys had symbolized the promise of the Sixties: youthfulness, change, liberal renewal. Finally, Hayden noticed the coffin.

He later recalled the turbulence of his emotions: "This person who was inflated larger than life and who could pick up a telephone and wield power and write a check for any sum of money and affect millions and millions of people with the statement of a few words, was now nothing, an unnoticed body in a coffin in the corner of a vast room which was to be the last scene, the last spectacular scene of his life."[82]

By reputation, Robert Kennedy had been a man of large passions, driven by ambition. If he had lived, perhaps he would have mastered his pride, perhaps not. Now his martyrdom—and his pending media apotheosis—made his sins seem to Hayden irrelevant: "You could just tell that he was nothing now, but he was going to be elevated to the level of sainthood and focus all the grief of people who were hoping for reform," recalls Hayden. "That really moves me to tears." Sitting in the pew, Hayden began to weep.[83]

"While I could never explain it by ideology," Hayden later wrote, "there was something compelling about the odyssey of Bobby Kennedy. . . . He was loved by the poor. He was at least trying to understand our realities, those of poverty and racism and war around the world. . . . What really drew me towards him, however, was his personal place in the [worst] collective shock of my life: the murder of his brother. I felt that that single horror had to acquaint Robert Kennedy with the absurdity of life . . . and had to teach him the frailty of power, plant in him a knowledge of the mad violence lurking in the culture and make him realize that there were guns between any reformer and the achievement of the reformer's goals."[84]

Hayden finally turned to Newfield: "I asked . . . if there shouldn't be something done in respect for the dead, instead of just waiting for the big spectacle tomorrow. In a few moments, the Kennedy aides motioned to me, and a few of us stood silent vigil by the casket. It must have been a strange sight. 'On to Chicago' kept repeating itself in my mind."[85]

Afterward, Hayden was invited to ride on the train that would carry Kennedy's body from New York to Washington. He refused. "I would not have been comfortable there," he says. "The whole government was going to be there." "The people on the train," he explained in 1972, "had not proven any interest, as far as I could see, in the grass-roots people who cared about Kennedy."[86]

The next day, Hayden flew to Chicago and went to the apartment of Dick and Mickey Flacks on the South Side. Bob Ross, who was then doing graduate work in the sociology department at the University of Chicago, dropped by to visit. Together, the old friends from Ann Arbor gathered round a television set to watch the progress of the train that was bearing Kennedy's body from St. Patrick's Cathedral to the nation's capital. While they watched, Hayden spoke of Kennedy and the lost promise of liberalism. He spoke of Kennedy as the last politician able to unite poor whites and blacks. Again, he wept.[87]

Six years before, these friends at Port Huron had been full of hope that their democratic idealism and direct action might spark the imagination of liberals like Kennedy. That dream had died in Vietnam; now, Kennedy's death dashed any lingering hopes that it might be revived. "I shared with a lot of other people," says Hayden, "these feelings of loss and despair and grim, grim days ahead."[88]

Democracy Is in the Streets

The plans for Chicago were in disarray. The events of the spring had left the anti-war movement badly split. Lyndon Johnson's withdrawal had robbed the protesters of a villain of truly demonic stature. Although Hubert Humphrey professed loyal support for the administration's foreign policy, his garrulous "politics of joy" was easier to ridicule than vilify; indeed, some liberals held out hope that Humphrey, once a shining knight of the liberal Americans for Democratic Action, might, if elected, negotiate a settlement with the Vietnamese. Activists who had supported Kennedy in the primaries were bitter at Eugene McCarthy for not withdrawing. McCarthy loyalists resented the fact that Kennedy had belatedly entered the race. Many young radicals, emboldened by the strike at Columbia and events that spring in Paris, where a general strike sparked by radical students had briefly paralyzed the country, now scorned liberals from all the camps; their goal was revolution, *now*: "two, three, many Columbias."

The point of the Chicago protests had become murky. The Yippies were still eagerly planning to provoke street violence. Hayden himself no longer held out much hope for reform: "Our strategy for change," he wrote, "is based on direct action and organization outside of the parliamentary process. . . . We are in the streets because no institution is changeable from within." But Hayden still hoped to stitch together a coalition, uniting the mildest liberal critics of the war with the most militant members of SDS, in an effort to win the broadest possible support for "an independent people's movement." Arguing for a balance between "militance and breadth," he urged radicals to maintain ties to supporters of both McCarthy and Kennedy. As Rennie Davis later recalled, "our idea of Chicago was a rank-and-file walkout of ordinary Democrats, spearheaded by the campus, but much, much broader than that."[89]

Meanwhile, Mayor Richard Daley made it clear that he was going to turn Chicago into an armed camp. He announced that the city's 12,000-man police force would be placed on twelve-hour shifts during the week of the convention. Three hundred members of the force would be armed with helmets, service revolvers and shotguns and assigned to areas of possible unrest. Six thousand Army troops and 5,000 National Guardsmen would be on call in case of an emergency. Daley's actions earlier in the year had demonstrated his willingness to crush dissent by force if necessary. During the riots after Martin Luther King's death, the Mayor had ordered officers to "shoot to kill arsonists and shoot to maim looters." In April, the city's police had broken up an anti-war rally with brutal efficiency, banging the heads of demonstrators against paddy wagon doors. Despite months of tortuous negotiations that involved the Justice Department and the White House as well as Mayor Daley, the city of Chicago agreed to grant the Mobilization committee only one permit—for a daytime rally in Grant Park on Wednesday, August 28, the day that Hubert Humphrey was to be nominated.[90]

As it became clear that coming to Chicago would be potentially suicidal, estimates of the turnout began to plummet. Hayden and Davis had originally hoped for a crowd of 300,000. This was sheer wishful thinking; in the event, they were lucky to draw 10,000.

Relations grew strained within the Mobilization. Dave Dellinger no longer trusted Davis and Hayden's declared commitment to tactical nonviolence. "Both of them," as Dellinger later described his worries, "were strongly committed to the idea that in the long run the movement would have to move to violent resistance and armed struggle. They couldn't totally resist the temptation to prepare for the future (which didn't seem all that far away to Tom, whose eyes would light up at the prospect, whereas Rennie would look sad but determined) by making occasional contemptuous remarks about pacifists and bourgeois liberals who refused to face up to the necessity for violence. . . . Some of the now disillusioned leaders of the early New Left found it hard to move from protest to resistance without adopting some of the cynicism and *realpolitik* of the society we were resisting."[91]

Early in the summer, Hayden flew to Paris to confer with the North Vietnamese, and to meet again with Averell Harriman. Certain that ending the war was an absolute moral imperative, he had become a *de facto* go-between for the Communists in Hanoi. But his behavior was growing erratic. The assassinations of Kennedy and King had left him haunted by the fear that his own end was near. "Kennedy's death," he says, "made me feel in a paranoid sense that this was going to be my year. There had been so many killings, it was so wanton, and the people who were the best hope for reforming the system seemed to draw the most violence. That, combined with the number of people they were killing in Vietnam, made you think, 'Well, maybe there's some kind of genocidal instinct that's getting out of control here.'"[92]

The pressures on Hayden continued to mount. Early in August, the Chicago Yippies withdrew their request for a permit to stage a rock festival during the convention, warning in an underground newspaper editorial that "Chicago may host a Festival of Blood. . . . Don't come to Chicago if you expect a five-day Festival of Life, music and love." On the afternoon when Abbie Hoffman and Jerry Rubin tried to change the mind of Abe Peck, the Chicago Yippie who had written the editorial, Tom Hayden was called in to mediate the dispute. He arrived wearing slippers, apparently still groggy from a nap. His manner, Peck later recalled, "suggested that he was not thrilled to be out mediating a dispute between two sets of *freaks*." Hayden sat impassively. After the two sides had rehearsed their arguments, they turned to Hayden. Staring at Jerry Rubin but talking about Peck, Hayden rendered his verdict in three letters: "CIA."[93]

Hayden's fears, though without basis in Peck's case, were by no means completely irrational. The FBI tried to foment confusion by spreading "disinformation" among the young radicals. As the convention approached, the protesters' ranks began to swell with undercover agents and police provocateurs. A CBS Television News special broadcast in 1978 attributed to Army sources the claim that in Chicago during convention week "about one demonstrator in six was an undercover agent." One of the agents, disguised as a long-haired biker, became Jerry Rubin's bodyguard and at one point helped pull down an American flag. Other agents used a different tack. Both Rennie Davis and Tom Hayden were shadowed by beefy Chicago police agents who periodically muttered threats. "I woke up one day," recalls Hayden, "with guys parked in front of the apartment and guys parked in back, with their revolvers conspicuously on their hips, who wouldn't identify who they were. I felt like I was in the presence of my own murderer."[94]

Convinced that he was being pushed into a life-and-death struggle, Hayden resolved to resist, to fight back, to baffle and confuse and terrorize his tormentors at every possible turn. He suggested "practicing the tactic of being 'everywhere and nowhere.' . . . Make them find us everywhere they go. . . . We should continue to break through their security networks. . . . This will psychologically shake up the security forces. . . . We are forced into a military style not because we are 'destructive' and 'nihilistic,' but because our normal rights are insecure and we must be able to survive in the jaws of Leviathan."[95]

In a series of declarations that he published on the eve of the convention, Hayden's rhetoric rose to a new, feverish pitch of violence. "We are coming to Chicago to vomit on the 'politics of joy,'" he wrote, "to expose the secret decisions, upset the night club orgies, and face the Democratic Party with its illegitimacy and criminality. American conventions and elections are designed to renew the participation of our people in the 'democratic political process.' But in 1968 the game is up." With the convention hall behind barbed wire and Chicago swarming with armed troops, it wasn't necessary to read C. Wright Mills to figure out the truth about American democracy. "The American reality is being stripped to its essentials," declared Hayden: "Our victory lies in progressively de-mystifying a false democracy, showing the organized violence underneath reformism and manipulation." Chicago would be a showdown between "a police state and a people's movement."

"At the very moment they seek to renew complicity in their system and confidence in their authority," warned Hayden, "we will be saying No from the streets. . . . many of us will not be good Germans under the new Nazis." At the same time, "by creating a popular upsurge we can experience an alternative kind of politics to those of the establishment, a politics of unrepresented people taking authority back into their own hands, voting with their feet, bodies and free minds, talking among themselves without Robert's Rules." The protesters would reassert the sovereignty of the people; they would covertly strike through "small guerrilla surprise acts" and make their numbers visible in mass demonstrations. "Democracy is in the streets," blared the headline of one of Hayden's preconvention manifestos. Hayden himself quoted Chairman Mao: "Dare to struggle, dare to win."[96]

The Struggle Begins

By Sunday, August 25, the attention of the world's press was riveted on Chicago. After the chaos of the spring, interest in the convention was uncommonly high. The spectacular threats of the Yippies had grabbed the attention of the media, as had Eugene McCarthy's pleas for anti-war demonstrators to stay away, in order to avoid bloodshed. Unlike previous anti-war protests, which had been over in a day, the drama of the Chicago protests was all but guaranteed to build as the week went on. Television coverage would be live. And there were already signs that Daley's heavy-handed tactics had alienated the mass media. On Sunday, the leaders of the National Mobilization Committee met in a mood of near-euphoria. Some of them had just finished watching a correspondent on NBC News conclude that democracy was being impaled on the barbed wire around the convention site—"the most chilling sight of the decade." "One hundred percent victory in propaganda!" exulted Hayden.[97]

But when the Mobilization leaders turned to the question of tactics, the tensions of the previous weeks flared up again. There was disagreement over how seriously to take the armed troops in the city. There was disagreement over how to handle the small turnout. Hayden argued that the numbers didn't really matter. Above all, there was still sharp disagreement over the basic political questions: Why were the protesters there? What did they expect to accomplish? Some thought the point was simply to bear witness, militantly but nonviolently, to the outrage of "Democratic Death" in Vietnam and the state of siege in Chicago. Others, led by Hayden, argued that "registering discontent" was no longer enough. Daley's refusal to grant the protesters permits and the threat of police violence, Hayden argued, had left the demonstrators with no choice but to "turn the Convention upside down." He was eager to create in the streets of Chicago a community of risk like those he had seen in McComb, Hanoi and Morningside Heights; he wanted the New Left to forge a stronger sense of moral resolve—a bolder will to power—under the stress of the guns and tear gas of a police state. "People have to be faced with the existential question of giving their lives," he said; they had to be "forced into a moral squeeze, forced to decide whether they're chickenshit, asked what they are willing to do to stop the war."[98]

After hearing rumors that some protesters were practicing such measures as throwing body blocks against police, some in the meeting argued that the Mobilization should not endorse any plans that might provoke confrontation. "Somebody could easily get shot," commented one participant: "We can't feed the [Daley] Machine's preparations." The meeting ended inconclusively. But later that night, the Chicago police—who had succeeded in infiltrating the Mobilization's inner circle—helped make doubts about the wisdom of confrontation moot.[99]

At 10:30 P.M. that Sunday, police ordered protesters to leave Lincoln Park on the city's North Side, where the Yippies were staging their "Festival of Life." The police were met by a volley of taunts: "Fuck pigs, oink, oink!" "The parks belong to the people!" Rocks and bottles flew. Forcing the crowd from the park into neighboring streets, the police began to hurl epithets of their own: "Kill the Commies!" "Get the bastards!" Through clouds of tear gas, officers —some without their badges displayed—began to club protesters and bystanders with blind fury. "What had happened outwardly," wrote one participant, "was that a bunch of people had gotten pushed around by a bunch of cops. . . . But inwardly, what had happened to a lot of people . . . was that they had understood somehow that they were locked into this thing with the cops (and there was even a sense that it was a kind of drama—though real drama), and that this was the beginning of it and that it was going to go on and get worse and be very ugly."[100]

On Monday, the day the convention formally began, Tom Hayden was arrested twice, once as he sat under a tree in Lincoln Park, the second time as he tried to enter the Conrad Hilton Hotel, where both Humphrey and McCarthy had their headquarters. On his first ride to the police station, a plainclothesman said, "You motherfucker, we're going to wipe you out. We're going to kill you. . . . We're going to take you into a dark alley and you're never going to come out." Rennie Davis led a march of 1,500 people to Chicago police headquarters to protest Hayden's arrest. After posting bail, Hayden was released. But that night, after he was invited by some friends who were McCarthy supporters to join them in the Conrad Hilton, Hayden was assaulted by another plainclothesman, again without provocation. The policeman grabbed him from behind, wrestled him to the ground and, after kicking him, placed him under arrest. After midnight, Hayden was released on $1,000 bond. Embarking on a series of complicated forays through the back streets of downtown Chicago with Jack Newfield, Hayden tried to dodge his police tail—who issued another threat to murder him. At 3:30, Hayden finally caught a taxi, and disappeared. He promptly went underground, assuming a variety of disguises in an effort to shake off the police agents shadowing him.[101]

Earlier that night, a crowd of between 2,000 and 3,000 demonstrators had skirmished again with police in Lincoln Park. As they charged into the defiant crowd, the police chanted, "Kill, kill, kill!"

On Tuesday, the daily "Wall Poster" that *Ramparts* magazine published during convention week carried a front-page editorial on Hayden's arrest: "We can only call on free people everywhere to keep fighting in the open—in the parks and the streets—for the right to get together on their own terms." *Ramparts* quoted Hayden: "The man is on our back . . . and he is killing us. We have to get him off our back." The poster-paper published by SDS, which had belatedly endorsed the Chicago demonstration, was even more explicit: "We don't need symbolic marches. They took Hayden; we should take the streets. Instead we marched right past the jail yelling how much we hate the pigs while walking legally and safely on their sidewalks. Our words have to fit our actions, or they're just words." That night,

Bobby Seale of the Black Panther Party, an independent black organization with links to SNCC and a commitment to armed struggle,
addressed the throng in Lincoln Park. "If a pig comes up and starts
swinging a club," advised Seale, "then put it over his head and lay
him out on the ground." By now, the nightly skirmishes between
the police and the protesters in Lincoln Park had become a kind of
grim team sport. That night, the street fighting occurred on schedule, yielding 93 arrests, 9 damaged police vehicles and 7 injured
policemen.[102]

After midnight, a crowd gathered in Grant Park opposite the Conrad Hilton Hotel. Although they were allowed to stay, they were
soon joined by 600 National Guardsmen bearing M-1 rifles, carbines,
ammunition and gas masks. Shortly before dawn, Hayden briefly
materialized to address the demonstrators in the park. "Now that
the pig is on the collective back of all of us," he was quoted as
saying, "we are going to find a way to go underground."[103] And then
he disappeared again.

Obsessed with outwitting the police, Hayden had by now embarked on a reckless course of confrontation by remote control. "I
was worried about what they were going to do if they found me
again," says Hayden. "I didn't want to do anything visible that
would indicate where I was. Because each time I did, I was arrested.
I didn't want to spend the week in jail, and I didn't want to back
off." Donning an endless variety of costumes that caught even old
friends unaware, he joined in the debates in Lincoln Park and Grant
Park about how best to sow confusion and spread disorder. "We
talked about all kinds of things," he recalls. "I mean, people were
going into hotels with butyric acid to try and create stink bombs."
In one of the strangest incidents in what had become a very strange
week, Hayden arranged to have a tape recording of his voice broadcast from an upper floor of the Conrad Hilton, in order, as he recalls,
"to make the cops think they were outwitted and to get more people
to figure out ways to get into the hotel." The plan was foiled at the
last minute when his accomplices refused to play the tape, fearing
that the crowd that had gathered across the street might storm the
hotel and create a bloodbath. "It was a crazy ploy," admits Hayden.
"It was a psychological-war thing. It was living by your wits. There
were all kinds of subplots going on—I was running around in a
football helmet. But I think the main thing about those several days
is: What was going on with the police? The things that they were
doing were bizarre."[104]

Indeed they were—and there was more to come.

The Whole World Is Watching

Wednesday was the big day: the one day when the Mobilization Committee had been granted an official permit to hold a rally at a band shell in Grant Park. By now, there was every indication that the confrontation between police and protesters had assumed a life of its own, divorced from any clear plan or rational calculus on either side. Even as the day began, organizers within the Mobilization remained sharply divided over how to proceed. Dellinger wanted to make an effort to march to the convention site. But nobody knew quite what to expect from Daley's police force next. Most nervously endorsed tactical nonviolence, though what this might mean under the circumstances had become obscure. Dellinger proposed that if the police, as threatened, prevented a march, then marchers should sit down in protest, and wait to be arrested. Hayden felt that the only course of honor that remained was to defy Daley's police-state tactics, by taking to the streets by whatever means possible, in order to do whatever had to be done to bring the confrontation to the attention of the country. (The Chicago police informer at the meeting later testified that "Hayden said that if the city doesn't give in to our demands, there would be war in the streets, and there should be.") In a final, democratic flourish, Hayden also offered the novel (and completely impractical) suggestion that marshals at the rally circulate through the crowd to get some sense of what the people who were actually there wanted to do next.

Fear filled the air. The streets leading into downtown Chicago were jammed with jeeps, tanks, armed National Guardsmen. As the rally began early in the afternoon, the crowd—there were perhaps 10,000 in all—milled restlessly. As the speakers droned on, an attempt was made—some say by an agent provocateur, though this has never been proved—to remove the American flag from a flagpole adjacent to the rally site. When the police charged toward the flagpole, they were met by a volley of debris. Rennie Davis waded into the melee, trying to restore order. He was attacked by a policeman, who clubbed him unconscious.

Till then, Hayden had been watching from the rear. "I'd come semidisguised," he says. "I was in the back, standing on a bench." When he saw the police charge, he rushed to help Davis. By the time he arrived, his friend was lying on the ground. "I didn't know how badly he'd been hurt," says Hayden. "It turns out he wasn't too badly hurt. But his head was split open," his face covered with blood; "he was knocked out—and this was my best friend in the world at the time."

While Davis was carried away on a stretcher to an ambulance, Dave Dellinger, the chairman of the rally, pleaded with the crowd: "Be calm! Don't be violent!" The melee continued. Police continued to attack and beat protesters. Some protesters tried to resist. After twenty minutes of confusion, the police cleared the area in front of the shell and the rally resumed.

Meanwhile, a scuffle had nearly broken out among the rally organizers. "I thought we were all going to be arrested," says Hayden. "I thought they were going to try to nail us in Grant Park, gas us, beat us, put us away before the nomination of Humphrey. I didn't want them to round us up and beat the hell out of us."

He threatened to seize the microphone unless he was allowed to issue a call for some show of resistance to police brutality. Sidney Peck, a rally leader and veteran anti-war activist who feared that such a call would simply provoke more violence, was ready (in his own words) to "physically remove" Hayden. Peace was restored only after it was agreed that Dave Dellinger and Hayden would each address the crowd separately.

By then, armed National Guardsmen had moved into position alongside the rally area. National Guardsmen could be seen on the rooftops of neighboring buildings. Military helicopters circled overhead, making it hard to hear.

Dellinger proposed that the group attempt a nonviolent march to the convention site.

Then Hayden spoke. "This city and the military machine it has aimed at us won't permit us to protest in an organized fashion," said Hayden. He cautioned the crowd not to "get trapped in some kind of large organized march which can be surrounded," suggesting instead that people break up into small groups: "We must move out of this park in groups throughout the city, and turn this overheated military machine against itself. Let us make sure that if blood flows, it flows all over the city. If they use gas against us, let us make sure they use it against their own citizens. . . . [Make] this whole city be so disrupted it begins to charge around like a dog gone mad. . . . Remember Rennie Davis!"

In the confusion of the moment, Hayden's speech was too garbled to have much impact. To some people listening, it was unclear what, exactly, he was proposing they do.

Hayden vanished. The crowd milled around while Dellinger made a last-ditch effort to negotiate permission to march to the convention site. After his efforts had failed, he instructed the crowd to regroup in the patch of Grant Park opposite the Conrad Hilton Hotel.

People began to move toward the Hilton, but nobody knew how to get there. Armed troops blocked most roads to the hotel area. Leaderless, the crowd swarmed through the park looking for a path. Along the way, skirmishes with the police broke out, filling the air with tear gas. Discovering an unguarded escape route, demonstrators began to stream toward the hotel. There they were met by a line of police.

The sun set. Klieg lights were switched on. Television cameras recorded the action. The marchers stacked up outside the hotel, pressing against the line of police. Suddenly, without warning, the police attacked. With nowhere to go, the crowd collapsed on itself. A plate-glass window shattered beneath the weight. Tear gas and the muffled thumps of wood pounding on flesh filled the air, as police methodically peeled protesters one by one from the crowd. The floodlights were blazing. Fused by panic, rage and pride, the crowd began to chant: "The Whole World Is Watching! The Whole World Is Watching! The Whole World Is Watching!"[105]

Incognito

After exhorting the throng in Grant Park, Tom Hayden had dashed into a waiting getaway car. With him was a reporter from *The New York Times*. Speeding south to the Hyde Park neighborhood where Hayden was hiding, the car successfully shook off its police tail. Bringing the reporter with him, Hayden climbed a fire escape to the apartment where he was staying. "Mr. Hayden got out a woman's wig and brushed the brown hair into a close approximation of a hippie's unkempt locks," reported the *Times*. When he came out of the front door, the reporter still in tow, he looked like a "junior size Fidel Castro." They raced back to Grant Park, where Hayden incognito melted into the crowd marching toward the Hilton. "Occasionally he spoke to friends," reported the *Times*. " 'My God! Tom?' said one, on hearing his voice."[106]

Hayden was elated by the confrontation. "We should be happy we came here, fought and survived," he told a crowd in Grant Park the next day. "When they injure us, we will be warriors. When they smash blood from our heads there will be blood from a lot of other heads."[107]

"People came to Chicago," he explained in an interview in a radical newspaper shortly afterward, "not in the superficial way that they had come out to previous mobilizations where they participated for a few hours. The people who came to Chicago came with a serious commitment, having considered the risks that were involved." The chief problem, he thought, was "not so much the tendency toward adventurism, to running out in the streets, as it is a tendency in the opposite direction—to look for ways to achieve social change without pain, without loss of life, without prison sentences." "We're going to create little Chicagos everywhere the candidates appear," Hayden boasted to *The New York Times*.[108]

On one level, the Chicago demonstration had indeed been a spectacular success. As planned, the protest, despite the small turnout, had left the Democratic Party badly bruised, if not quite "delegitimated." The demonstrators in the streets, blooded in battle, had forged a new sense of courage, daring and community. They had sparked a new interest among countless young people in protest—in dissent, confrontation, the passionate expression of moral outrage at a war that was, after all, morally reprehensible and unjust in its brutality, as well as strategically mistaken.[109] By raising the specter of civil war, the protesters in Chicago had also dramatically raised the costs of prolonging that war. And the saturation coverage on television had brought the existence of the New Left inescapably to the attention of all America.

But what had America seen? Was a crowd helplessly chanting in the midst of a police riot the image of participatory democracy? Was street fighting the seed of "a people's movement"? Was this really what a generation's moral revulsion against the Vietnam War and idealistic quest for "a democracy of individual participation" had come down to?

Hayden was headline news. The media became his megaphone. But in his preoccupation with the drama of "resistance," he had let his larger sense of political purpose melt away.

Most Americans, after all, scarcely appreciated the moral weight of his rage at the war any more than they understood his broader vision of democracy. Television had shown them a mob of long-haired kids—spoiled brats, they seemed to some—hurling curses and chanting slogans and waving Communist flags. A lot of people thought Hayden a firebrand and rabble-rouser. Period.

There are two revealing moments in Hayden's testimony before the House Un-American Activities Committee in December, 1968. Called before the committee to answer questions about the events in Chicago, he had spent much of his time blaming Richard Daley for the violence in Chicago, explaining his views on guerrilla war and evading the implications of his various calls throughout convention week for confrontation with the police.

"Mr. Hayden," asked the HUAC counsel near the end of his testimony, "is it your present aim to seek the destruction of the present American democratic system?"

Hayden: "That is a joke."

HUAC counsel: "I am asking you, sir."

Hayden: "Well, I don't believe the present American democratic system exists. That is why we can't get together, to straighten things out. I mean, I believe you have destroyed the American democratic system, by the existence of a committee of this kind."

Hayden might as well have been a Man from Mars. The committee members hadn't the faintest clue what he meant by "democracy."

"You have indeed a very strange philosophy, sir," commented a Congressman from Michigan a few minutes later. "You say that you don't care about electing a President. You don't care about a President at all. What kind of government do you want?"

Hayden: "I want a democratic government. My views on that are spelled out—not so very well, perhaps, certainly not in my opinion, but they are spelled out in exhaustive detail in all kinds of things that I have written. . . ."[110]

What Hayden had previously written scarcely weighed in this balance. Before the convention, he had talked about turning "the streets and parks into schools for education-through-action." "There's coming a time," he declared shortly afterward, "when the American movement will become more violent for defensive and survival reasons." But that was the problem: the growing violence of the Movement was defensive, reactive, without constructive purpose. Defiance in the face of brute force and passionate expressions of moral outrage have a certain nobility—but they make a poor substitute for strategy and tactics. Years later, Hayden accurately described the essence of what had in fact happened in Chicago: "You get driven into a corner," he said, "and you react like an animal."[111]

That is exactly what most Americans had seen; that is all that most of them understood.[112]

Lost

That fall, Hayden moved to Berkeley. Deliberately fleeing from the old centers of his power, he hoped "to remake myself into a normal human being." Seeking to atone for his ambition and vanity—the sins of celebrity—he joined a collective. "The need to overcome our inbred, egoistic, middle-class character," he declared, "has to become a foremost part of our consciousness." Unconvincing as an "anti-leader" five years earlier, he was unconvincing as a meek egalitarian now.[113]

His fantasies of revolution grew bolder. He suggested creating "Free Territories in the Mother Country"—the enclave of radicals in Berkeley was one example—where citizens could mobilize support for struggles in the Third World, engage in "constant confrontation" with the police, learn skills of survival and self-defense, and engage in utopian "cultural experiment." Though Hayden had earned something of a reputation as an uptight square among the psychedelic daredevils of the counterculture, he now pitched his utopia to the partisans of better-living-through-chemicals: "Drugs," he solemnly declared, "would be commonly used as a means of deepening self-awareness." Within the Free Territories—a variation on his old plan for "counter-institutions"—collectives would offer models of the "new, humane and participatory system."[114]

"The coming of repression will speed up time," wrote Hayden, "making a revolutionary situation . . . more likely." Why repression should accelerate time—and why this acceleration of time, which many young radicals experienced, should hasten "revolution"— were questions that Hayden characteristically left unexamined. "If we look at the last ten years"—he repeated his assertion—"we see that history is moving faster and calling us to become a new generation of American revolutionaries." Alarmed by a rash of shoot-outs between the police and Black Panthers, and half-convinced that Armageddon was imminent, Hayden organized target practice, teaching young radicals how to handle guns.[115]

When he thought to produce a broader justification for such action, he adverted—in listless, mechanical prose—to the principles he had embraced a decade before. In "a pure democratic state," he explained, "the people can make their needs known to officials and, if those needs are not met, replace their officials through elections. In this mythical rational system, the people supposedly form opinions freely, with the certainty that these opinions will be influential"—Hayden here reproduced from memory a rough sketch of C. Wright Mills's ideal-type of democracy. "But when the democratic system is less than pure, when in fact it is corrupt"—the experience of a decade had convinced Hayden that this was true—"then citizens have to return to the *origins* of the First Amendment and rediscover their own sovereignty. The root concept of the American Revolution was and still is: power to the people." As the decade ended, he still entertained hopes of convening a "revolutionary Continental Congress."[116]

Hayden's talk of revolution was sheer bravado. Like most other young radicals, he was disoriented, confused and (though of course the thought was taboo) defeated. "On August 28, 1963, the President welcomed civil rights leaders and 250,000 people to Washington for a sort of joyous celebration," said Hayden in a rare moment of sober reflection shortly after the Democratic Convention. "On August 28, 1968, we were gassed in front of the Conrad Hilton and both Kennedys were dead. The difference between those two things, although they're only five years apart, are too staggering to sort out and fully understand right now." A few months later, Hayden admitted that "we were as unclear as anyone else about the whirlwind toward which we were plunging."[117]

In March, 1969, Tom Hayden, along with Rennie Davis, Dave Dellinger, Abbie Hoffman, Jerry Rubin, Bobby Seale and two others, was indicted on charges of conspiracy to incite a riot in Chicago during the Democratic National Convention. The indictment conveniently ignored the fact that before and during the convention, many of the "conspirators" had argued bitterly among themselves. But the new administration of Republican Richard Nixon, who had narrowly defeated Hubert Humphrey in the presidential election of 1968, was determined to squash the anti-war movement. "It is not too strong a statement," said President Nixon in a speech on student rebellion, "to declare that this is the way civilizations begin to die." That summer, the President warned demonstrators that "we have the power to strike back if need be, and to prevail."[118]

Hayden, along with the other defendants, was swept up in a new maelstrom, this time of interviews, speaking engagements, publicity. He became a center of attention and privilege, a pampered pop aristocrat on a par with Bob Dylan and the Beatles. "You become addicted to the media environment," confessed Hayden a few years later. "Your identity gradually becomes so involved in that that you don't know who you are except in relation to technology, media and crowds."[119]

The conspiracy trial began in Chicago in September, 1969. At the time, Hayden spoke of the "need to expand our struggle to include a total attack on the courts." He declared that he and his codefendants had come to Chicago "as participants in the creation of a new society in the streets . . . with its own natural laws, structures, language and symbols." But as the trial proceeded and the judge, Julius J. Hoffman, expressed his own unbridled hostility and contempt for the defendants, Hayden, like his comrades, sank into exhaustion and despair.[120]

Sometimes he feared the worst. "Things happened," he says. "Like one night, we were in a crazy mood and we went out with Nicholas Ray"—the director of the James Dean film *Rebel Without a Cause*, who was shooting a movie based on the trial. "He had us act out a parody of the whole trial. I played the judge, sitting on a ladder eighty feet above the defendants, drinking wine. This is the way we got rid of the tension in the courtroom. We got home that night at two or three in the morning and were sleeping on the floor when the phone rang—it was five in the morning. It was our lawyer, saying that Fred Hampton and Mark Clark had been murdered, sleeping in their beds, by the police. Hampton was a sweet guy, he'd come to the courthouse every day, he was Bobby Seale's best friend. This was just one incident. It was a totally absurd situation, permeated with violence and threats of violence."[121]

In an inadvertently revealing metaphor, Hayden likened the defendants on trial to "survivors of a shipwreck getting to know one another because we shared the same raft." "My personal relations shriveled to nothing in Chicago," he later wrote. "The trial had to be the most alienating time of my life."[122]

Never had he been more famous. Never had he been more isolated. During the protests in Chicago, he had pushed himself—and been pushed—beyond the pale of respectable dissent, embracing a defiant, often apocalyptic kind of rhetoric that left some erstwhile liberal allies feeling bewildered and uneasy. Years before, he had forfeited his credentials as an intellectual, preferring the excitement of direct action to the discipline of making an argument. Slowly, insensibly, irrevocably, he had also discredited himself as a moral model in the eyes of many fellow radicals: long fascinated by power and willing to manipulate his own image, he had become enmeshed in the kind of hypocrisy commonplace among politicians, but unseemly in an advocate of "authenticity" in social relations. Now, even as he urged others to join him in the revolutionary task of creating a new society, he had to admit that he had never quite succeeded in harnessing his own ambition and egoism. "I have always been more of an independent catalyst than equal member of any collective or group," he painfully confessed to his readers. "Hayden was a candidate," jibed Murray Kempton with cruel accuracy, "but he had no party."[123]

The New Left meanwhile was approaching the peak of its numerical strength—and hurlting toward self-destruction. Hundreds of thousands of young people, excited by the televised spectacles of the Columbia uprising, the showdown at the Democratic Convention and street fighting in Berkeley, came to consider themselves radicals too. Many of them expressed their alienation by growing long hair, getting stoned, listening to rock and roll, and informally pledging allegiance to the prevailing radical myths and celebrities—Tom Hayden was a star in this galaxy. Few members of this vast and now utterly amorphous youth movement actually *did* much. But when they acted, their deeds were sometimes spectacularly destructive. The radical avant-garde in SDS set the tone with slogans like "The future of our struggle is the future of crime in the streets." Hayden chimed in with speeches about "revolutionizing youth" through "a series of sharp and dangerous conflicts, life and death conflicts." To take "direct action" now meant to taunt the police, destroy a car, burn down a bank (as students did in Santa Barbara). As they circulated through the national media, these images of violence became stereotyped models of revolutionary zeal. "People were becoming consumers of something that didn't even represent them and they couldn't control," Hayden obliquely admitted in 1972. The New Left had become inextricably part of the "mass society" it had set out to transform.[124]

Hayden himself remained in the eye of a storm that still seemed to be gathering strength. On February 20, 1970, Hayden was sentenced to five years in prison for his role in the Chicago demonstrations of 1968—news that sparked a spate of marches, demonstrations and riots on college campuses across the country. On April 30, President Nixon went on national televison and stunned the nation by announcing that U.S. troops were being sent into Cambodia. More protests erupted across the country. Stanford saw the worst riot in its history, and students at Kent State University in Ohio burned down the ROTC building. In New Haven on May 3, in the midst of addressing a Black Panther rally at Yale, Hayden, who was free while his conviction was being appealed, was handed a slip of paper: reading it to the crowd, he announced that more than one hundred colleges were supporting a nationwide student strike, to protest Nixon's invasion of Cambodia.[125]

The death knell for the Movement sounded the next day. On May 4, 1970, National Guardsmen opened fire on students demonstrating on the campus of Kent State University. The bullets were real. The days of revolutionary fantasy were over. After a last, tremendous outpouring of protest—five hundred campuses and 4 million students went on strike to protest the Cambodian invasion and the death of 4 students at Kent State—the New Left collapsed, plummeting into cultural oblivion as if it had been some kind of political Hula-Hoop.[126]

SDS had collapsed the year before. In June, 1969, the Progressive Labor Party had formally taken over SDS, leaving what little was left of its original spirit to a rump led by a group that called itself "Weatherman," after a line in a Bob Dylan song. Their style was paramilitary, their strategy—though they kept their precise plans shrouded in secrecy—a matter of wanton violence. They took heart from the skirmishing between protesters and police in Chicago during the 1968 convention; the violence in Chicago, they declared, had done "more damage to the ruling class . . . than any mass, peaceful gathering this country has ever seen." Professing their admiration for Che Guevara and steeling themselves for guerrilla warfare, the Weathermen hoped to become outlaws in enemy territory: America was irredeemably lost.[127]

On the night of October 8, 1969, Hayden had addressed the Weathermen as they prepared to launch their first surprise guerrilla attack, again in Chicago. Armed with helmets, baseball bats and apparently bottomless reserves of arrogance and self-loathing, the Weathermen had assembled after nightfall in Lincoln Park, nerving themselves to smash through their bourgeois inhibitions and "tear pig city apart" in a "national action" they called "The Days of Rage."[128]

Hayden had debated joining them. "They had started, characteristically, as idealistic and benign people," he says looking back. "And then something happened. Some of it was a response to events, in which moral suasion of the power structure seemed to be an obsolete idea. And this was augmented by a psychological thing: in existential terms, it became a matter of whether or not you were a man, which was measured by how outrageously subversive you were willing to be."[129]

At the time, Hayden was on trial. One night, Hayden took a walk with Bernadine Dohrn, Terry Robbins and two other Weathermen. " 'Tom,' " Hayden recalls them saying, " 'this trial is going to end and you're going to be jailed. You're not going to get a conviction overturned in the higher courts, because Nixon is quickly changing their composition. And you will be killed in a prison riot.' " They urged him to jump bail and go underground. "We had such painful arguments," he recalled in 1972. "They would say that I was not seizing the time, that I was not willing to risk everything."[130]

This was Hayden's kind of talk, come back to haunt him. He

fancied himself a fearless revolutionary. How could he resist a fresh dare? For nearly ten years, he had been on the cutting edge of the Movement, in the vanguard, ready to risk everything. But Hayden had reached his limit. "I didn't want to cross that line," he says.[131]

Why? Had his courage finally failed him? Had common sense come crashing in?

"The political side, the Port Huron side of me, saved me," he says. "It seemed very plausible to me that my life might end in some sorry prison cell. But as I look back on it, psychologically I also needed to believe on some level that the system worked. During the trial I became obsessive about preparing defense witnesses. I had a note pad, I could work out some logical detail every day. The judge, and Nixon, were so extreme that somehow the public, the press, other institutions would respond and see us as valid protesters, however they might disagree with our tactics and style. Maybe I was in touch with reality. But I don't say that with any pride. It could have gone the other way."[132]

Perhaps Hayden's hesitation finally came down to his own visceral recoil from the Weathermen's relentless, remorseless, absolutely resolute cultivation of hatred. "They were cold," he says looking back. "They were at best—what's that Brecht poem? 'Judge us not too harshly. . . .' "[133]

The poem is "To Those Born Later." "Hatred, even of meanness/Contorts the features," wrote Brecht in 1938. "Anger, even against injustice/Makes the voice hoarse. Oh, we/Who wanted to prepare the ground for friendliness/Could not ourselves be friendly./But you, when the time comes at last/And man is a helper to man/Think of us/With forbearance."[134]

Hayden knew Brecht's poem well. It had been posted in the offices of the Newark Community Union. He had quoted some of its lines in the course of one of his own defenses of guerrilla warfare.[135]

"The Weathermen took that poem literally," says Hayden softly. "There's a lot of truth to it. But once you take it completely"—he pauses, momentarily lost in the thought—"it justifies anything. You have no flaws. They're all written off to historical necessity."[136] Perhaps the lapsed Catholic moralist—the existentialist with a cause—was finally a stronger part of Tom Hayden's soul than the revolutionary nihilist.

As the Weathermen huddled against the cold that October night in Lincoln Park, warming themselves before a bonfire built out of park benches, Hayden, wearing tennis shoes, with his shirt tails out, as always, picked up the bullhorn. He had come, he said, to tell them that he and his colleagues who were standing trial for conspiracy supported them. He welcomed, he said, their effort to "intensify the struggle and end the war."[137]

As he spoke, the throng readied itself for its rampage through the streets of Chicago. The architect of *The Port Huron Statement* realized that his words were irrelevant. Putting down the bullhorn, he stole back into the night. He had nothing more to say.

CONCLUSION

WHOLE CRISIS OF CHRISTIANITY IN AMERICA THAT
THE MILITARY HEROES WERE ON ONE SIDE, AND THE
UNNAMED SAINTS ON THE OTHER! LET THE BUGLE
BLOW. THE DEATH OF AMERICA RIDES IN ON THE
SMOG. AMERICA—THE LAND WHERE A NEW KIND OF
MAN WAS BORN FROM THE IDEA THAT GOD WAS
PRESENT IN EVERY MAN NOT ONLY AS COMPASSION
BUT AS POWER, AND SO THE COUNTRY BELONGED TO
THE PEOPLE; FOR THE WILL OF THE PEOPLE—IF THE
LOCKS OF THEIR LIFE COULD BE GIVEN THE ART TO
TURN—WAS THEN THE WILL OF GOD. GREAT AND
DANGEROUS IDEA! IF THE LOCKS DID NOT TURN,
THEN THE WILL OF THE PEOPLE WAS THE WILL OF THE
DEVIL. WHO BY NOW COULD KNOW WHERE WAS
WHAT? LIARS CONTROLLED THE LOCKS. BROOD ON
THAT COUNTRY THAT EXPRESSES OUR WILL. . . .
RUSH TO THE LOCKS. GOD WRITHES IN HIS BONDS.
RUSH TO THE LOCKS. DELIVER US FROM OUR CURSE.
FOR WE MUST END ON THE ROAD TO THAT MYSTERY
WHERE COURAGE, DEATH, AND THE DREAM OF LOVE
GIVE PROMISE OF SLEEP.

—Norman Mailer
Armies of the Night (1968)

IT WAS LIKE A FLYING SAUCER LANDED. . . . THAT'S
WHAT THE SIXTIES WERE LIKE. EVERYBODY HEARD
ABOUT IT, BUT ONLY A FEW REALLY SAW IT.

—Bob Dylan
Biograph (1985)

CONCLUSION

A COLLECTIVE DREAM

BY THE TIME the decade reached its end with episodes like the
Weatherman rampage in Chicago, "The Sixties" represented not just
a span of time but an impetuous, extreme spirit—youthful and reckless, searching and headstrong, foolhardy, romantic, willing to try
almost anything. It was a spirit that *The Port Huron Statement* had
helped to define. By exploring its vision of participatory democracy,
a generation discovered (and eventually became addicted to) what
one young radical called "breakaway experiences"—political and
cultural moments when boundaries melted away and it seemed as if
anything could happen. Such moments did in fact occur. They arose
in the thick of passionate debate, during sit-ins, in marches, at violent confrontations—at times when people, discovering discontents
and ideas and desires in common, sensed, often for the first time and
sometimes in the teeth of danger, that together they could change
the world. But the moments quickly passed. In the mounting enthusiasm for "breakaway experiences," the original vision of democracy
was all but forgotten. The spirit of ecstatic freedom proved impossible to sustain. The Movement collapsed, leaving behind a congeries
of smaller single-issue movements, demanding peace in Vietnam,
dignity for blacks, liberation for women, respect for homosexuality,
reverence for the balance of nature. Frustrated revolutionists built
bombs, turning reveries of freedom into cruel, ineffectual outbursts
of terrorism. And one by one, the political pilgrims who had created
"the Sixties" fell back to earth.[1]

For Tom Hayden, the end came in the early Seventies, through a
dizzying series of events that left his sense of identity profoundly

317

shaken. Called on the carpet in 1971 by his comrades in "The Red Family," the Berkeley commune he had joined, he was accused of manipulation, power-mongering and "male chauvinism." Humiliated, he packed his few belongings into an old Volkswagen and headed south. He moved into an apartment in Venice, by the Pacific, and changed his name to Emmett Garity, combining his middle name and his mother's maiden name. "I wanted to know what it was like not to be Tom Hayden," he says. Becoming preoccupied with his Irish roots, he flew to Dublin—only to be turned away at the airport as an undesirable alien. "I began to feel that I'd been stripped of my identity by the American assimilation process," he says. "My government wanted to put me in jail; there was a five-year sentence hanging over me. My father hadn't talked to me in ten years. And now the Irish didn't recognize that I was their son. I felt like I had nothing." He returned to California. In an effort to clarify America's national identity, he worked in solitude on a book, *The Love of Possession Is a Disease with Them*, a bitter critique of genocide in American history, from Wounded Knee to My Lai. Several months after he finished it, Rennie Davis, one of his oldest and steadiest friends, appeared on his doorstep. "Rennie told me the most fantastic story I'd ever heard," recalls Hayden. "Some woman had given him a ticket to go to India, to go meet the guru Maharaj-Ji," the adolescent "perfect master." Davis, who badly needed a vacation, had gone "thinking that this was just a great trip, that he was going to relax, and that he wasn't going to buy into this. Then, one day he was washing his clothes in a river. A giant black bird descended on him. He had a religious experience. He became convinced that the guru Maharaj-Ji was the son of God. He sat on my lawn telling me this. I thought I was in the presence of a character from *Invasion of the Body Snatchers*. It was one of the most shattering experiences of my life."[2]

Slowly, Hayden backed away from fantasies of apocalypse. Recovering his political nerve, he returned to public life. He helped start the Indochina Peace Campaign, an effort to lobby Congress and keep pressure on the Nixon administration to cut off American aid to the South Vietnamese. "In a strange way, I had to learn it from Vietnamese propaganda," he says, "but the American people were fundamentally good. They had a good Declaration of Independence, a bill of rights, they weren't evil—and I was one of them. I had to throw off all the ideology and guilt and self-hate and hostility that was burdening me and get back to my roots in the simplest sense." "The hope," he wrote in March, 1972, "should be that each act, . . .

each organized protest, will have the effect of water dropping on stone, inevitably wearing the stone away. . . . No single drop will smash that stone. But in time, the weak become strong and the strong weak; the water continues and the stone is no more." In the fall of 1972, a federal appeals court, commenting that "the demeanor of the judge and prosecutors would require reversal if other errors did not," overturned Hayden's conviction in the Chicago conspiracy trial. By then, there was no Movement left to lead.[3]

For Paul Booth, the decade had reached its symbolic end earlier, at the last SDS convention in Chicago in 1969. "Despite everything," he says, "SDS was still the main institution of the New Left." He attended one of the convention sessions, and watched silently as different factions spouted crude Marxist slogans from the podium, in an unwitting parody of a Communist Party plenum. It had been only three years since he had given up on his efforts to convince SDS of the need for structure and discipline.[4]

After leaving Cleveland in 1967, Sharon Jeffrey had slowly drifted away from radical politics—she was alienated by the growing violence of the Movement. But her odyssey reached its true end only in 1973, when a two-week vacation in California turned into a three-month stay at the Esalen Institute in Big Sur. "It *uprooted* me entirely," she says. "It was the first time in my life that I had been in a situation where I had nothing to say." Her parents, who had supported her political activism, were distressed; old friends from Ann Arbor were bemused. "When I visited Dick and Mickey Flacks," recalls Jeffrey, "they said, 'Esalen? We know somebody who died there: committed suicide.'" Jeffrey, however, was undeterred. Studying different techniques of "self-actualization," she became convinced that authenticity was not simply a matter of creating the right kind of social structure.[5]

For Dick Flacks, by contrast, the Sixties have in a way never really ended. In his intellectual work, he remains preoccupied with understanding an era that nearly cost him his life: in 1969, shortly after the *Chicago Tribune* had named him as a radical troublemaker, an unknown assailant burst into his office at the University of Chicago, beat him up and left him for dead. Fortunate to have survived, Flacks suffered a partially severed hand and multiple skull fractures. He had just finished serving as a staff consultant for the "Skolnik Report" to the President's Commission on the Causes and Prevention of Violence.

For what purpose, finally, had so many people made such sacrifices? What, in the end, had their search for a "democracy of individual participation" produced? These are hard questions to answer, in part because the sense of what democracy ideally meant underwent such a dizzying series of metamorphoses in the minds of young radicals during the Sixties, connoting at different times everything from registering black voters in the South, to rule-by-consensus in small communes, to street fighting in chaotic demonstrations. Convincing answers would require a more detailed study of the New Left as a whole, and of parallel trends in American society in the Sixties. But this much seems clear: the Movement that the young radicals had worked so hard to build fell apart in the wake of the killings at Kent State University in the spring of 1970. The war that they had tried to stop went on for several more years, although the United States withdrew its troops from Vietman in 1973, in part in an effort to restore domestic tranquillity. Preoccupied with protesting the war and fatally handicapped by their inability to agree on what institutions (if any) were appropriate in a participatory democracy, they obviously did not succeed in reinventing "the neighborly community."

For all its failings, the New Left briefly affected the whole tone of political life in America, raising fundamental questions about the nature and limits of democracy in a modern industrial society. As the political scientist Samuel Huntington has pointed out in one of the most sharply critical evaluations of the era, "the 1960s witnessed a dramatic renewal of the democratic spirit in America"—a renewal that, in its sweep and intensity, Huntington ranks beside several other watershed periods in the development of American democracy: the revolution of 1776; the presidency of Andrew Jackson; the era of Progressive reforms. "The essence of the democratic surge of the 1960s," writes Huntington, "was a general challenge to existing systems of authority, public and private. In one form or another, this challenge manifested itself in the family, the university, business, public and private associations, politics, the governmental bureaucracy, and the military services. People no longer felt the same compulsion to obey those whom they had previously considered superior to themselves in age, rank, status, expertise, character, or talents. Within most organizations, discipline eased and differences in status became blurred."[6]

Writing in 1975, Huntington deplored these developments. American society, he felt, had come to suffer from "an excess of democracy." "The Welfare Shift" caused by the "internal democratic surge" on the part of "marginal social groups" in the Sixties had, he argued, badly strained the fiscal resources of the state, weakened its

military power and created popular skepticism about such legitimate aspects of government as "hierarchy, coercion, discipline, secrecy, and deception." Huntington recommended a more balanced
and tough-minded approach to government and a renewed respect
for traditional institutions. Five years later, under the presidency of
Ronald Reagan, such views became a commonplace of intellectual
discourse and public policy. It is as if the strategy of the young
radicals, as they had explained it in *America and the New Era*, had
in some measure succeeded, only to create new—and unintended—
opportunities for a kind of counterrevolution. Under the administration of President Reagan, it was neoconservatives who reaped the
benefits of what the New Left, before its sudden collapse, had helped
to sow—the delegitimation of liberal corporatism and the ideal of
the welfare state.[7]

Tom Hayden, speaking at the outset of Reagan's second term,
doubted the long-term effectiveness of this counterrevolution. "Reagan," he said, "has tried through administrative methods to disman-
tle as much as possible of what the Sixties created. But he's accepted
more of it than he recognizes, just as Eisenhower accepted more of
the New Deal than was recognized at the time. I think democracy is
the genie that's out of the bottle."[8]

The spirit of Port Huron certainly left a lasting mark on those who
experienced it firsthand. Al Haber, for one, remains an ardent activist. A cabinetmaker who lives in Berkeley, California, Haber in 1986
was involved with other Bay Area radicals in organizing everything
from antiapartheid rallies to peace protests. He also has stayed in
touch with most of his old friends from SDS. One of them is Bob
Ross, an associate professor at Clark University in Worcester, Massachusetts. Ross in 1986 had recently finished a book, written in
collaboration with Kent Trachte, presenting a new model of international capitalism. In addition, Ross was working as a policy ana-
lyst for Democrat Gerard D'Amico, an outspoken liberal—or "urban
populist," in Ross's words—who was a Massachusetts state senator
before becoming a candidate for lieutenant governor in 1986. Steve
Max too maintains an active interest in stimulating what he calls a
"resurgent populism." A full-time organizer who still lives in New
York City, Max for years has been the curriculum director for the
Midwest Academy, the training arm of Citizen Action, a national
federation of grass-roots citizen organizations. As Max proudly
points out, both Citizen Action and the Midwest Academy maintain
cordial relations with the Democratic Socialists of America, which
in 1986 was led by Michael Harrington—Max's old nemesis, now a

firm friend and political ally. "Few things in my life have given me
as much satisfaction as winning back the friendship of a good number of those whom I so wrongly attacked in 1962," says Harrington,
who has played a major role in regrouping the socialist movement
during the lean years of the late Seventies and Eighties. "I think I
have proved that you can go home again."[9]

"In the beginning, we were about discovering self-worth," says
Sharon Jeffrey. "We were about breaking out of traditions, about
breaking out of structures. I get angry with my friends who say that
we accomplished very little. It's as if they won't take responsibility
for what we did do—and for what we failed to do." Although she
maintains an active interest in the psychological and spiritual traditions she discovered at Esalen, Jeffrey, like Max, remains an organizer. "My understanding of what's entailed in participation," she
says, "is so much greater now than it was then." In 1986, she was
working in the San Francisco Bay Area as a free-lance consultant to
small businesses and public agencies, as well as offering seminars
on becoming a "visionary leader"—"somebody who creates desirable pictures of the future, inspires others to participate, mobilizes
resources and designs organizational structures to produce the intended result." In her effort to fuse democratic ideals with therapeu-
tic techniques of self-actualization—and in her continuing interest
in the culture of modern feminism—Jeffrey embodies two important
strands in the legacy of the New Left.

Paul Booth too has remained committed after his own lights to
the project of democratic renewal defined at Port Huron. After
nearly two decades of experience as a union organizer, he looks back
on the politics of his youth with wry skepticism. "The direct-action
model for political influence was about speaking truth to power," he
says. "It was a theory that you could be influential because your
thoughts were good and right, and you made the necessary sacrifices
to get a podium to speak. We didn't start out with very good ideas
about strategy, in part because the pacificist–direct-action people
who influenced us weren't into strategy, they were into *witness*.
And then there were the academic influences, and they weren't into
strategy because they weren't into activity. Unfortunately, the Old
Left *didn't* influence us: we viewed them as intellectually bankrupt.
But they were the only people in the society who knew what mass
action was, who knew what a mass organization was or how you
worked in one." Still, as Booth hastens to add, "the willingness of
Americans to take an activist approach to their society, which
spread so dramatically in the Sixties, hasn't subsided very much; it

is a major difference between our world in 1986 and the world we criticized in 1962."[10] In 1986, Booth was working for AFSCME, the American Federation of State, County and Municipal Employees, one of the most combative trade unions within the AFL-CIO.

Dick Flacks at the same time was putting the finishing touches on his second book, *Making History vs. Making Life*, a study of the tension between the vision of the left and mainstream American political beliefs. (His first book, *Youth and Social Change*, published in 1971, was a study of the student rebellions of the Sixties.) A professor of sociology at the University of California at Santa Barbara, Flacks, like Bob Ross and a host of other radicals from the Sixties, has found a home of sorts in the academy. "The New Left," he says, "helped open the political arena so that alternatives to capitalism can now be imagined, sought, debated and organized." One alternative—participatory democracy—still strikes Flacks as key. "I think we were on to something," he says. "I think people do have a basic impulse to have a voice in decisions about them. There certainly has been a tendency in this country for people to try to exercise that voice in more and more different areas. I mean, what is the environmental movement? It's an attempt to participate in decisions about land use and technology." The New Left fell apart at the end of the Sixties, he thinks, for a number of reasons: its inability to extend its middle-class base, its delusions of "revolutionary apocalypse," its failure to develop a durable organizational structure. "SDS," he says, "was trying to be too many things at once: a student group, an anti-war organization, and the party of the New Left. There's no way it could be all those things."[11]

Like most of his old friends, Flacks has remained active in politics —he drafted the substance of "Make the Future Ours," the campaign platform that Tom Hayden used in his unsuccessful effort to defeat incumbent U.S. Senator John Tunney in the California Democratic primary election of 1976. But Flacks has grown increasingly skeptical about left-wing efforts to win power. "Basically," he says, "I think that the left in America is a cultural rather than a political force, defining 'political' as power-oriented. The claim that you are power-oriented is typically a sign that you are turning into a sect or that you are betraying the values that you once held. If that's true, the question for the left is what forms of organization are appropriate to being an intellectual, educative, moral force."[12]

Although Tom Hayden was defeated in his bid to become the Democratic candidate for the Senate in 1976, he drew different lessons than Flacks did from his defeat. Shortly afterward, Hayden established the Campaign for Economic Democracy—in 1986, renamed Campaign California—a network of grass-roots citizen-action groups that has given him an independent base of power in California politics. Though the Campaign has concentrated on mobilizing voters and organizing "citizen lobbyists" to pepper elected officials with letters and phone calls, it also evokes the democratic ideals of the Sixties. "The process of trying to find a consensus rather than going ahead with a slim majority still strikes me as key," says Hayden of the Campaign's professed commitment to participatory democracy. "Simply counting votes doesn't encourage two people to find the best in each other and look for a deeper truth." However, he readily concedes that consensus has its limits. "Our meetings often drive people out because of their length," he says. "And if you want to participate on more than the most immediate, local level, for whatever reasons, something more than grass-roots organizing and neighborhood democracy is needed."[13]

Although its effort to stimulate "participatory democracy" has had rather modest results so far, the Campaign has been successful in fielding candidates for more than fifty local and state offices in California. In the late Seventies, it developed an alliance with Governor Jerry Brown, which led to rent control and new energy-conservation measures, among other reforms that had been sought by its predominantly middle-class membership. At the same time, traditionally socialist goals that were part of the Campaign's original agenda—above all, the redistribution of wealth—have been sharply downplayed, in an apparent effort to broaden the group's appeal. In 1982, Hayden himself returned to the electoral arena. With support from CED members and financial help from the actress Jane Fonda, whom he married in 1973, he was able to win election to the California State Assembly, in a race that cost a staggering $1.7 million. Since then, Hayden has weathered several attempts by conservative opponents to impugn his loyalty and to have him thrown out of office. He has nevertheless succeeded in building a modest reputation as a tactician and iconoclast on the progressive wing of the Democratic Party, where his views—in 1986, he said that he still favored "economic democracy," but also described himself as an "armed dove"—linked him to such pioneering "new look" liberals as California Governor Jerry Brown and Colorado Senator Gary Hart. "I believe that the analysis of *America and the New Era* is still relevant," says Hayden. "Politicians of our generation, starting with Jerry Brown, are trying to understand the new era, which is one of limits—on our economic reach, on our military reach." At the same time, Hayden stresses the need to shore up "a very feeble center" within the Democratic Party—which may be one reason the political views he expresses often seem so ambiguous. "Is it co-optation to work with the corporate liberals?" he asked rhetorically shortly after being reelected to his State Assembly seat in 1984. "Or do you have virtually to define and defend what the corporate liberal agenda is? I think that it's important to defend a centrist position that would allow a more progressive future to evolve."[14]

Looking back on the Sixties, Hayden admits to "mistakes," but is reluctant to dwell on them. "You don't get to live your life over," he says. In a widely publicized speech delivered at Hofstra University in 1986, however, Hayden did express a number of "regrets"—that he was not more critical "of the cynical motives of the Soviet Union"; that he was "infected with a hostility" that alienated him from his own country; that "I compounded the pain of many Americans who lost sons and loved ones in Vietnam." It is also clear that Hayden has modified some of his basic convictions. "I used to reject Reinhold Niebuhr's philosophy that there was a flaw in the human condition, that perfectibility was unattainable," he says. "I now think that there's quite a bit of truth to that, for individuals, for revolutions, for nations." As a result, his old enthusiasm for a politics of "vision" has waned. "Ideology is an intellectual weapon you create to get your own way," he said in one of his more cynical moments.[15]

But at other times, Hayden implies that he would do it all over again: "I don't think there's anything more satisfying politically than to be young in spirit, and to believe that the world is yours to change. And there's nothing better than to set a living example, if you can, by associating yourself with the victims of social injustice." Looking back, he also takes pride in many of the changes that the New Left triggered. "I don't know whether we caused the changes," he says, "or whether the changes were in the making and we just saw them coming. But obviously the system of segregation, which until 1960 was considered impregnable, collapsed. Students, who had never been considered a social force, became a political factor. The Vietnam War was brought to an end, partly because of the role of students. More than one President was thrown into crisis or out of office. And the Movement created an agenda. At the time, it was seen as anathema, as terrible—very unruly. But people have absorbed more of the agenda than they realize."[16]

In the early Seventies, in the immediate aftermath of the collapse of the Movement, Hayden, like other young radicals, would have been incapable of delivering this sanguine verdict with such equanimity. Always more than an effort to win piecemeal reforms, the New Left—in this respect, as American as apple pie—had hoped for a new beginning, a new, more democratic order for the ages. Those who had committed their lives to the Movement experienced its violent, vertiginous crack-up as a personal calamity.

Although with more capable leaders, a more sharply defined theory of democracy, a sturdier sense of humility and skepticism, and a shrewder grasp of political reality, the Movement might have averted its disastrous collapse, the realization of its larger objectives —particularly in the chaotic circumstances of the late Sixties—was bound to be difficult, if not impossible. To search for a "democracy of individual participation," particularly if the goal is to restore the give-and-take of face-to-face relations in the "neighborly community," is to swim against the tide of history. The main drift in modern industrial life has been toward expanding scale and complexity, the centralization of power and the growth of heirarchical bureaucracies. Popular revolts against these overwhelming realities have been only sporadically successful, in part because the demand for individual autonomy and active participation in public life must sooner or later run up against the desire for stability, privacy and the material comforts promised by the modern industrial nation-state. Like virtually every other American mass movement for democratic renewal since the Civil War—socialist or populist, progressive or right-wing, plebeian or middle-class—the New Left flourished in situations of relative moral simplicity and floundered when faced with the almost hopeless difficulties and immense strategic quandaries posed by the economic, social and political forces it wished to counteract. Its experiments in democracy perhaps most usefully demonstrated the incompatibility of rule-by-consensus with accountable, responsible government in a large organization—or even in a small group of people with divergent interests and a limited patience for endless meetings.[17] But even this modest lesson proved difficult for many activists to assimilate. At the height of its influence in the late Sixties, the New Left had some of the virtues of a utopian and romantic revolt—passion, moral intensity, a shared joy in the sheer process of change—but also some of its most glaring vices: intransigence, impatience, an irrational and ultimately self-destructive sense of self-righteousness.[18]

Nearly two decades later, the promise of democratic renewal leads a chastened existence in the thinking of intellectuals, the stubborn efforts of organizers and the disillusioned compromises of a handful of politicians. As the careers of Al Haber, Bob Ross, Steve Max, Sharon Jeffrey, Paul Booth, Richard Flacks and Tom Hayden all illustrate, many veterans of the Movement have continued to apply the precepts of Port Huron in the light of their mature experience, evincing modesty in their immediate goals, pragmatism in their tactics and a hard-earned realism in their evaluation of the prospects for social change. Numerous books, most of them aimed at an academic audience, have appeared in the wake of the New Left on the theory and practical problems of "economic democracy," "unitary democracy," "strong democracy," "empowered democracy." Left-wing legislators with power, cornered into fighting for the preservation of social reforms initiated in the Sixties, have desperately struggled to restore some luster to the liberal ideals of fairness, social justice and the welfare state. Some radical economists, no longer assuming America to be a society of potentially boundless prosperity, have argued that industrial productivity could be increased by the introduction of new forms of worker participation. At the same time, citizen-action groups and organizations like the Midwest Academy and Hayden's Campaign California have quietly continued to refine tactics honed in the Sixties, teaching techniques of grass-roots insurgency and small-scale self-government to disgruntled tenants, peace activists, environmentalists, feminists, small businessmen, labor unionists. In bits and pieces and fragments that do not always fit together, the political vision of the New Left, and some of its original spirit, has survived, helping to keep open the possibilities for change.[19]

"The American left is now powerless, distracted, and confused," wrote C. Wright Mills in 1948, in a passage that rings true for the plight of American radicals throughout most of this century: "The program of the right can be presented as an implementation of what is now happening in and to the world, but no left program can honestly be asserted in such a compelling way. What is happening is destructive of the values which the left would implant into modern society." That is why Mills, while clinging to the possibilities for democratic renewal, conceded that "the ideas available on the left today are less a program than a collective dream."[20]

But for a time in the Sixties, for a generation that first found its political voice in The Port Huron Statement, the ideas of the left did not seem like a dream at all. In city streets and on college campuses, in thousands of small experiments in participatory democracy, my generation tested for itself the limits of political freedom. Those limits proved sobering. In retrospect, our experience feels, almost literally, fantastic. Yet the spirit of Port Huron was real. A mass Movement to change America briefly flourished, touching countless lives and institutions. And for anyone who joined in the search for a democracy of individual participation—and certainly for anyone who remembers the happiness and holds to the hopes that the quest itself aroused—the sense of what politics can mean will never be quite the same again.

THE PORT HURON STATEMENT

INTRODUCTORY NOTE: This document represents the results of several months of writing and discussion among the membership, a draft paper, and revision by the Students for a Democratic Society national convention meeting in Port Huron, Michigan, June 11–15, 1962. It is presented as a document with which SDS officially identifies, but also as a living document open to change with our times and experiences. It is a beginning: in our own debate and education, in our dialogue with society.

INTRODUCTION: AGENDA FOR A GENERATION

We are people of this generation, bred in at least modest comfort, housed now in universities, looking uncomfortably to the world we inherit.

When we were kids the United States was the wealthiest and strongest country in the world; the only one with the atom bomb, the least scarred by modern war, an initiator of the United Nations that we thought would distribute Western influence throughout the world. Freedom and equality for each individual, government of, by, and for the people—these American values we found good, principles by which we could live as men. Many of us began maturing in complacency.

As we grew, however, our comfort was penetrated by events too troubling to dismiss. First, the permeating and victimizing fact of human degradation, symbolized by the Southern struggle against racial bigotry, compelled most of us from silence to activism. Second, the enclosing fact of the Cold War, symbolized by the presence of the Bomb, brought awareness that we ourselves, and our friends, and millions of abstract "others" we knew more directly because of our common peril, might die at any time. We might deliberately ignore, or avoid, or fail to feel all other human problems, but not these two, for these were too immediate and crushing in their impact, too challenging in the demand that we as individuals take the responsibility for encounter and resolution.

While these and other problems either directly oppressed us or rankled our consciences and became our own subjective concerns, we began to see complicated and disturbing paradoxes in our surrounding America. The declaration "all men are created equal . . ." rang hollow before the facts of Negro life in the South and the big cities of the North. The proclaimed peaceful intentions of the United States contradicted its economic and military investments in the Cold War status quo.

We witnessed, and continue to witness, other paradoxes. With nuclear energy whole cities can easily be powered, yet the dominant nation-states seem more likely to unleash destruction greater than that incurred in all wars of human history. Although our own technology is destroying old and creating new forms of social organization, men still tolerate meaningless work and idleness. While two-thirds of mankind suffers undernourishment, our own upper classes revel amidst superfluous abundance. Although world population is expected to double in forty years, the nations still tolerate anarchy as a major principle of international conduct and uncontrolled exploitation governs the sapping of the earth's physical resources. Although mankind desperately needs revolutionary leadership, America rests in national stalemate, its goals ambiguous and tradition-bound instead of informed and clear, its democratic system apathetic and manipulated rather than "of, by, and for the people."

Not only did tarnish appear on our image of American virtue, not only did disillusion occur when the hypocrisy of American ideals was discovered, but we began to sense that what we had originally seen as the American Golden Age was actually the decline of an era. The worldwide outbreak of revolution against colonialism and imperialism, the entrenchment of totalitarian states, the menace of war, overpopulation, international disorder, supertechnology—these trends were testing the tenacity of our own commitment to democracy and freedom and our abilities to visualize their application to a world in upheaval.

Our work is guided by the sense that we may be the last generation in the experiment with living. But we are a minority—the vast majority of our people regard the temporary equilibriums of our society and world as eternally functional parts. In this is perhaps the outstanding paradox: we ourselves are imbued with urgency, yet the message of our society is that there is no viable alternative to the present. Beneath the reassuring tones of the politicians, beneath the common opinion that America will "muddle through," beneath the stagnation of those who have closed their minds to the future, is the pervading feeling that there simply are no alternatives, that our times have witnessed the exhaustion not only of Utopias, but of any new departures as well. Feeling the press of complexity upon the emptiness of life, people are fearful of the thought that at any moment things might be thrust out of control. They fear change itself, since change might smash whatever invisible framework seems to hold back chaos for them now. For most Americans, all crusades are suspect, threatening. The fact that each individual sees apathy in his fellows perpetuates the common reluctance to organize for change. The dominant institutions are complex enough to blunt the minds of their potential critics, and entrenched enough to swiftly dissipate or entirely repel the energies of protest and reform, thus limiting human expectancies. Then, too, we are a materially improved society, and by our own improvements we seem to have weakened the case for further change.

Some would have us believe that Americans feel contentment amidst prosperity—but might it not better be called a glaze above deeply felt anxieties about their role in the new world? And if these anxieties produce a developed indifference to human affairs, do they not as well produce a yearning to believe there *is* an alternative to the present, that something *can* be done to change circumstances in the school, the workplaces, the bureaucracies, the government? It is to this latter yearning, at once the spark and engine of change, that we direct our present appeal. The search for truly democratic alternatives to the present, and a commitment to social experimentation with them, is a worthy and fulfilling human enterprise, one which moves us and, we hope, others today. On such a basis do we offer this document of our convictions and analysis: as an effort in understanding and changing the conditions of humanity in the late twentieth century, an effort rooted in the ancient, still unfulfilled conception of man attaining determining influence over his circumstances of life.

VALUES

Making values explicit—an initial task in establishing alternatives—is an activity that has been devalued and corrupted. The conventional moral terms of the age, the politician moralities—"free world," "people's democracies"—reflect realities poorly, if at all, and seem to function more as ruling myths than as descriptive principles. But neither has our experience in the universities brought us moral enlightenment. Our professors and administrators sacrifice controversy to public relations; their curriculums change more slowly than the living events of the world; their skills and silence are purchased by investors in the arms race; passion is called unscholastic. The questions we might want raised—what is really important? can we live in a different and better way? if we wanted to change society, how would we do it?—are not thought to be questions of a "fruitful, empirical nature," and thus are brushed aside.

Unlike youth in other countries we are used to moral leadership being exercised and moral dimensions being clarified by our elders. But today, for us, not even the liberal and socialist preachments of the past seem adequate to the forms of the present. Consider the old slogans: Capitalism Cannot Reform Itself, United Front Against Fascism, General Strike, All Out on May Day. Or, more recently, No Cooperation with Commies and Fellow Travellers, Ideologies Are Exhausted, Bipartisanship, No Utopias. These are incomplete, and there are few new prophets. It has been said that our liberal and socialist predecessors were plagued by vision without program, while our own generation is plagued by program without vision. All around us there is astute grasp of method, technique—the committee, the ad hoc group, the lobbyist, the hard and soft sell, the make, the projected image—but, if pressed critically, such expertise is incompetent to explain its implicit ideals. It is highly fashionable to identify oneself by old categories, or by naming a respected political figure, or by explaining "how we would vote" on various issues.

Theoretic chaos has replaced the idealistic thinking of old—and, unable to reconstitute theoretic order, men have condemned idealism itself. Doubt has replaced hopefulness—and men act out a defeatism that is labelled realistic. The decline of utopia and hope is in fact one of the defining features of social life today. The reasons are various: the dreams of the older left were perverted by Stalinism and never re-created; the congressional stalemate makes men narrow their view of the possible; the specialization of human activity leaves little room for sweeping thought; the horrors of the twentieth century, symbolized in the gas ovens and concentration camps and atom bombs, have blasted hopefulness. To be idealistic is to be considered apocalyptic, deluded. To have no serious aspirations, on the contrary, is to be "tough-minded."

In suggesting social goals and values, therefore, we are aware of entering a sphere of some disrepute. Perhaps matured by the past, we have no sure formulas, no closed theories—but that does not mean values are beyond discussion and tentative determination. A first task of any social movement is to convince people that the search for orienting theories and the creation of human values is complex but worthwhile. We are aware that to avoid platitudes we must analyze the concrete conditions of social order. But to direct such an analysis we must use the guideposts of basic principles. Our own social values involve conceptions of human beings, human relationships, and social systems.

We regard *men* as infinitely precious and possessed of unfulfilled capacities for reason, freedom, and love. In affirming these principles we are aware of countering perhaps the dominant conceptions of man in the twentieth century: that he is a thing to be manipulated, and that he is inherently incapable of directing his own affairs. We oppose the depersonalization that reduces human beings to the status of things—if anything, the brutalities of the twentieth century teach that means and ends are intimately related, that vague appeals to "posterity" cannot justify the mutilations of the present. We oppose, too, the doctrine of human incompetence because it rests essentially on the modern fact that men have been "competently" manipulated into incompetence—we see little reason why men cannot meet with increasing skill the complexities and responsibilities of their situation, if society is organized not for minority, but for majority, participation in decision-making.

Men have unrealized potential for self-cultivation, self-direction, self-understanding, and creativity. It is this potential that we regard as crucial and to which we appeal, not to the human potentiality for violence, unreason, and submission to authority. The goal of man and society should be human independence: a concern not with image of popularity but with finding a meaning in life that is personally authentic; a quality of mind not compulsively driven by a sense of powerlessness, nor one which unthinkingly adopts status values, nor one which represses all threats to its habits, but one which has full, spontaneous access to present and past experiences, one which easily unites the fragmented parts of personal history, one which openly faces problems which are troubling and unresolved; one with an intuitive awareness of possibilities, an active sense of curiosity, an ability and willingness to learn.

This kind of independence does not mean egotistic individualism—the object is not to have one's way so much as it is to have a way that is one's own. Nor do we deify man—we merely have faith in his potential.

Human relationships should involve fraternity and honesty. Human interdependence is contemporary fact; human brotherhood must be willed, however, as a condition of future survival and as the most appropriate form of social relations. Personal links between man and man are needed, especially to go beyond the partial and fragmentary bonds of function that bind men only as worker to worker, employer to employee, teacher to student, American to Russian.

Loneliness, estrangement, isolation describe the vast distance between man and man today. These dominant tendencies cannot be overcome by better personnel management, nor by improved gadgets, but only when a love of man overcomes the idolatrous worship of things by man. As the individualism we affirm is not egoism, the selflessness we affirm is not self-elimination. On the contrary, we believe in generosity of a kind that imprints one's unique individual qualities in the relation to other men, and to all human activity. Further, to dislike isolation is not to favor the abolition of privacy; the latter differs from isolation in that it occurs or is abolished according to individual will.

We would replace power rooted in possession, privilege, or circumstance by power and uniqueness rooted in love, reflectiveness, reason, and creativity. As a *social system* we seek the establishment of a democracy of individual participation, governed by two central aims: that the individual share in those social decisions determining the quality and direction of his life; that society be organized to encourage independence in men and provide the media for their common participation.

In a participatory democracy, the political life would be based in several root principles:

> that decision-making of basic social consequence be carried on by public groupings;
>
> that politics be seen positively, as the art of collectively creating an acceptable pattern of social relations;
>
> that politics has the function of bringing people out of isolation and into community, thus being a necessary, though not sufficient, means of finding meaning in personal life;
>
> that the political order should serve to clarify problems in a way instrumental to their solution; it should provide outlets for the expression of personal grievance and aspiration; opposing views should be organized so as to illuminate choices and facilitate the attainment of goals; channels should be commonly available to relate men to knowledge and to power so that private problems—from bad recreation facilites to personal alienation —are formulated as general issues.

The economic sphere would have as its basis the principles:

> that work should involve incentives worthier than money or survival. It should be educative, not stultifying; creative, not mechanical; self-directed, not manipulated, encouraging independence, a respect for others, a sense of dignity, and a willingness to accept social responsibility, since it is this experience that has crucial influence on habits, perceptions, and individual ethics;
>
> that the economic experience is so personally decisive that the individual must share in its full determination;
>
> that the economy itself is of such social importance that its major resources and means of production should be open to democratic participation and subject to democratic social regulation.

Like the political and economic ones, major social institutions—cultural, educational, rehabilitative, and others—should be generally organized with the well-being and dignity of man as the essential measure of success.

In social change or interchange, we find violence to be abhorrent because it requires generally the transformation of the target, be it a human being or a community of people, into a depersonalized object of hate. It is imperative that the means of violence be abolished and the institutions—local, national, international—that encourage non-violence as a condition of conflict be developed.

These are our central values, in skeletal form. It remains vital to understand their denial or attainment in the context of the modern world.

THE STUDENTS

In the last few years, thousands of American students demonstrated that they at least felt the urgency of the times. They moved actively and directly against racial injustices, the threat of war, violations of individual rights of conscience,

and, less frequently, against economic manipulation. They succeeded in restoring a small measure of controversy to the campuses after the stillness of the
McCarthy period. They succeeded, too, in gaining some concessions from
the people and institutions they opposed, especially in the fight against racial
bigotry.

The significance of these scattered movements lies not in their success or
failure in gaining objectives—at least, not yet. Nor does the significance lie in
the intellectual "competence" or "maturity" of the students involved—as some
pedantic elders allege. The significance is in the fact that students are breaking
the crust of apathy and overcoming the inner alienation that remain the defining characteristics of American college life.

If student movements for change are still rarities on the campus scene, what
is commonplace there? The real campus, the familiar campus, is a place of
private people, engaged in their notorious "inner emigration." It is a place
of commitment to business-as-usual, getting ahead, playing it cool. It is a place
of mass affirmation of the Twist, but mass reluctance toward the controversial public stance. Rules are accepted as "inevitable," bureaucracy as "just circumstances," irrelevance as "scholarship," selflessness as "martyrdom,"
politics as "just another way to make people, and an unprofitable one, too."

Almost no students value activity as citizens. Passive in public, they are
hardly more idealistic in arranging their private lives: Gallup concludes they
will settle for "low success, and won't risk high failure." There is not much
willingness to take risks (not even in business), no setting of dangerous goals,
no real conception of personal identity except one manufactured in the image
of others, no real urge for personal fulfillment except to be almost as successful
as the very successful people. Attention is being paid to social status (the quality
of shirt collars, meeting people, getting wives or husbands, making solid contacts for later on); much, too, is paid to academic status (grades, honors, the
med school rat race). But neglected generally is real intellectual status, the
personal cultivation of the mind.

"Students don't even give a damn about the apathy," one has said. Apathy
toward apathy begets a privately constructed universe, a place of systematic
study schedules, two nights each week for beer, a girl or two, and early marriage;
a framework infused with personality, warmth, and under control, no matter
how unsatisfying otherwise.

Under these conditions university life loses all relevance to some. Four
hundred thousand of our classmates leave college every year.

But apathy is not simply an attitude; it is a product of social institutions, and
of the structure and organization of higher education itself. The extracurricular
life is ordered according to in loco parentis theory, which ratifies the Administration as the moral guardian of the young.

The accompanying "let's pretend" theory of student extracurricular affairs
validates student government as a training center for those who want to spend
their lives in political pretense, and discourages initiative from the more articulate, honest, and sensitive students. The bounds and style of controversy are
delimited before controversy begins. The university "prepares" the student for
"citizenship" through perpetual rehearsals and, usually, through emasculation
of what creative spirit there is in the individual.

The academic life contains reinforcing counterparts to the way in which
extracurricular life is organized. The academic world is founded on a teacher-
student relation analogous to the parent-child relation which characterizes in
loco parentis. Further, academia includes a radical separation of the student

from the material of study. That which is studied, the social reality, is "objectified" to sterility, dividing the student from life—just as he is restrained in active involvement by the deans controlling student government. The specialization of function and knowledge, admittedly necessary to our complex technological and social structure, has produced an exaggerated compartmentalization of study and understanding. This has contributed to an overly parochial view, by faculty, of the role of its research and scholarship; to a discontinuous and truncated understanding, by students, of the surrounding social order; and to a loss of personal attachment, by nearly all, to the worth of study as a humanistic enterprise.

There is, finally, the cumbersome academic bureaucracy extending throughout the academic as well as the extracurricular structures, contributing to the sense of outer complexity and inner powerlessness that transforms the honest searching of many students to a ratification of convention and, worse, to a numbness to present and future catastrophes. The size and financing systems of the university enhance the permanent trusteeship of the administrative bureaucracy, their power leading to a shift within the university toward the value standards of business and the administrative mentality. Huge foundations and other private financial interests shape the under-financed colleges and universities, making them not only more commercial, but less disposed to diagnose society critically, less open to dissent. Many social and physical scientists, neglecting the liberating heritage of higher learning, develop "human relations" or "morale-producing" techniques for the corporate economy, while others exercise their intellectual skills to accelerate the arms race.

Tragically, the university could serve as a significant source of social criticism and an initiator of new modes and molders of attitudes. But the actual intellectual effect of the college experience is hardly distinguishable from that of any other communications channel—say, a television set—passing on the stock truths of the day. Students leave college somewhat more "tolerant" than when they arrived, but basically unchallenged in their values and political orientations. With administrators ordering the institution, and faculty the curriculum, the student learns by his isolation to accept elite rule within the university, which prepares him to accept later forms of minority control. The real function of the educational system—as opposed to its more rhetorical function of "searching for truth"—is to impart the key information and styles that will help the student get by, modestly but comfortably, in the big society beyond.

THE SOCIETY BEYOND

Look beyond the campus, to America itself. That student life is more intellectual, and perhaps more comfortable, does not obscure the fact that the fundamental qualities of life on the campus reflect the habits of society at large. The fraternity president is seen at the junior manager levels; the sorority queen has gone to Grosse Pointe; the serious poet burns for a place, any place, to work; the once-serious and never-serious poets work at the advertising agencies. The desperation of people threatened by forces about which they know little and of which they can say less; the cheerful emptiness of people "giving up" all hope of changing things; the faceless ones polled by Gallup who listed "international affairs" fourteenth on their list of "problems" but who also expected thermonuclear war in the next few years; in these and other forms, Americans are in withdrawal from public life, from any collective effort at directing their own affairs.

Some regard these national doldrums as a sign of healthy approval of the established order—but is it approval by consent or manipulated acquiescence? Others declare that the people are withdrawn because compelling issues are fast disappearing—perhaps there are fewer breadlines in America, but is Jim Crow gone, is there enough work and work more fulfilling, is world war a diminishing threat, and what of the revolutionary new peoples? Still others think the national quietude is a necessary consequence of the need for elites to resolve complex and specialized problems of modern industrial society—but, then, why should *business* elites help decide foreign policy, and who controls the elites anyway, and are they solving mankind's problems? Others, finally, shrug knowingly and announce that full democracy never worked anywhere in the past— but why lump qualitatively different civilizations together, and how can a social order work well if its best thinkers are skeptics, and is man really doomed forever to the domination of today?

There are no convincing apologies for the contemporary malaise. While the world tumbles toward the final war, while men in other nations are trying desperately to alter events, while the very future qua future is uncertain— America is without community impulse, without the inner momentum necessary for an age when societies cannot successfully perpetuate themselves by their military weapons, when democracy must be viable because of its quality of life, not its quantity of rockets.

The apathy here is, first, *subjective*—the felt powerlessness of ordinary people, the resignation before the enormity of events. But subjective apathy is encouraged by the *objective* American situation—the actual structural separation of people from power, from relevant knowledge, from pinnacles of decision-making. Just as the university influences the student way of life, so do major social institutions create the circumstances in which the isolated citizen will try hopelessly to understand his world and himself.

The very isolation of the individual—from power and community and ability to aspire—means the rise of a democracy without publics. With the great mass of people structurally remote and psychologically hesitant with respect to democratic institutions, those institutions themselves attenuate and become, in the fashion of the vicious circle, progressively less accessible to those few who aspire to serious participation in social affairs. The vital democratic connection between community and leadership, between the mass and the several elites, has been so wrenched and perverted that disastrous policies go unchallenged time and again.

POLITICS WITHOUT PUBLICS

The American political system is not the democratic model of which its glorifiers speak. In actuality it frustrates democracy by confusing the individual citizen, paralyzing policy discussion, and consolidating the irresponsible power of military and business interests.

A crucial feature of the political apparatus in America is that greater differences are harbored within each major party than the differences existing between them. Instead of two parties presenting distinctive and significant differences of approach, what dominates the system is a natural interlocking of Democrats from Southern states with the more conservative elements of the Republican Party. This arrangement of forces is blessed by the seniority system of Congress which guarantees congressional committee domination by conservatives—ten of 17 committees in the Senate and 13 of 21 in the House of Representatives are chaired currently by Dixiecrats.

The party overlap, however, is not the only structural antagonist of democracy in politics. First, the localized nature of the party system does not encourage discussion of national and international issues: thus problems are not raised by and for people, and political representatives usually are unfettered from any responsibilities to the general public except those regarding parochial matters. Second, whole constituencies are divested of the full political power they might have: many Negroes in the South are prevented from voting, migrant workers are disenfranchised by various residence requirements, some urban and suburban dwellers are victimized by gerrymandering, and poor people are too often without the power to obtain political representation. Third, the focus of political attention is significantly distorted by the enormous lobby force, composed predominantly of business interests, spending hundreds of millions each year in an attempt to conform facts about productivity, agriculture, defense, and social services, to the wants of private economic groupings.

What emerges from the party contradiction and insulation of privately held power is the organized political stalemate: calcification dominates flexibility as the principle of parliamentary organization, frustration is the expectancy of legislators intending liberal reform, and Congress becomes less and less central to national decision-making, especially in the area of foreign policy. In this context, confusion and blurring is built into the formulation of issues, long-range priorities are not discussed in the rational manner needed for policy-making, the politics of personality and "image" become a more important mechanism than the construction of issues in a way that affords each voter a challenging and real option. The American voter is buffeted from all directions by pseudo-problems, by the structurally initiated sense that nothing political is subject to human mastery. Worried by his mundane problems which never get solved, but constrained by the common belief that politics is an agonizingly slow accommodation of views, he quits all pretense of bothering.

A most alarming fact is that few, if any, politicians are calling for changes in these conditions. Only a handful even are calling on the President to "live up to" platform pledges; no one is demanding structural changes, such as the shuttling of Southern Democrats out of the Democratic Party. Rather than protesting the state of politics, most politicians are reinforcing and aggravating that state. While in practice they rig public opinion to suit their own interests, in word and ritual they enshrine "the sovereign public" and call for more and more letters. Their speeches and campaign actions are banal, based on a degrading conception of what people want to hear. They respond not to dialogue, but to pressure: and knowing this, the ordinary citizen sees even greater inclination to shun the political sphere. The politician is usually a trumpeter to "citizenship" and "service to the nation," but since he is unwilling to seriously rearrange power relationships, his trumpetings only increase apathy by creating no outlets. Much of the time the call to "service" is justified not in idealistic terms, but in the crasser terms of "defending the free world from communism"—thus making future idealistic impulses harder to justify in anything but Cold War terms.

In such a setting of status quo politics, where most if not all government activity is rationalized in Cold War anti-communist terms, it is somewhat natural that discontented, super-patriotic groups would emerge through political channels and explain their ultra-conservatism as the best means of Victory over Communism. They have become a politically influential force within the Republican Party, at a national level through Senator Goldwater, and at a local level through their important social and economic roles. Their political views are defined generally as the opposite of the supposed views of communists: complete individual freedom in the economic sphere, non-participation by the government in the machinery of production. But actually "anti-communism" becomes an umbrella by which to protest liberalism, internationalism, welfarism, the active civil rights and labor movements. It is to the disgrace of the United States that such a movement should become a prominent kind of public participation in the modern world—but, ironically, it is somewhat to the interests of the United States that such a movement should be a public constituency pointed toward realignment of the political parties, demanding a conservative Republican Party in the South and an exclusion of the "leftist" elements of the national GOP.

THE ECONOMY

American capitalism today advertises itself as the Welfare State. Many of us comfortably expect pensions, medical care, unemployment compensation, and other social services in our lifetimes. Even with one-fourth of our productive capacity unused, the majority of Americans are living in relative comfort—although their nagging incentive to "keep up" makes them continually dissatisfied with their possessions. In many places, unrestrained bosses, uncontrolled machines, and sweatshop conditions have been reformed or abolished and suffering tremendously relieved. But in spite of the benign yet obscuring effects of the New Deal reforms and the reassuring phrases of government economists and politicians, the paradoxes and myths of the economy are sufficient to irritate our complacency and reveal to us some essential causes of the American malaise.

We live amidst a national celebration of economic prosperity while poverty and deprivation remain an unbreakable way of life for millions in the "affluent society," including many of our own generation. We hear glib references to the "welfare state," "free enterprise," and "share-holder's democracy" while military defense is the main item of "public" spending and obvious oligopoly and other forms of minority rule defy real individual initiative or popular control. Work, too, is often unfulfilling and victimizing, accepted as a channel to status or plenty, if not a way to pay the bills, rarely as a means of understanding and controlling self and events. In work and leisure the individual is regulated as part of the system, a consuming unit, bombarded by hard-sell, soft-sell, lies and semi-true appeals to his basest drives. He is always told that he is a "free" man because of "free enterprise."

The Remote Control Economy. We are subject to a remote control economy, which excludes the mass of individual "units"—the people—from basic decisions affecting the nature and organization of work, rewards, and opportunities. The modern concentration of wealth is fantastic. The wealthiest 1 percent of Americans own more than 80 percent of all personal shares of stock.[1] From

1. Statistics on wealth reveal the "have" and "have not" gap at home. Only 5 percent of all those in the $5,000 or less bracket own any stock at all. In 1953, personally owned wealth in the U.S. stood at $1 trillion. Of this sum, $309.2 billion (30.2 percent) was owned by 1,659,000 top wealth-holders (with incomes of $60,000 or more). This elite comprised 1.04 percent of the population. Their average gross estate estimate was $182,000, as against the national average of $10,000. They held 80 percent of all corporation stock, virtually all state and local bonds, and between 10 and 33 percent of other types of property: bonds, real estate, mortgages, life insurance, unincorporated businesses, and cash. They received 40 percent of property income, rent,

World War II until the mid-Fifties, the 50 biggest corporations increased their manufacturing production from 17 to 23 percent of the national total, and the share of the largest 200 companies rose from 30 to 37 percent. To regard the various decisions of these elites as purely economic is short-sighted: their decisions affect in a momentous way the entire fabric of social life in America. Foreign investments influence political policies in underdeveloped areas—and our efforts to build a "profitable" capitalist world blind our foreign policy to mankind's needs and destiny. The drive for sales spurs phenomenal advertising efforts; the ethical drug industry, for instance, spent more than $750 million on promotions in 1960, nearly four times the amount available to all American medical schools for their educational programs. The arts, too, are organized substantially according to their commercial appeal; aesthetic values are subordinated to exchange values, and writers swiftly learn to consider the commercial market as much as the humanistic marketplace of ideas. The tendency to over-production, to gluts of surplus commodities, encourages "market research" techniques to deliberately create pseudo-needs in consumers—we learn to buy "smart" things, regardless of their utility—and introduces wasteful "planned obsolescence" as a permanent feature of business strategy. While real social needs accumulate as rapidly as profits, it becomes evident that Money, instead of dignity of character, remains a pivotal American value and Profitability, instead of social use, a pivotal standard in determining priorities of resource allocation.

Within existing arrangements, the American business community cannot be said to encourage a democratic process nationally. Economic minorities not responsible to a public in any democratic fashion make decisions of a more profound importance than even those made by Congress. Such a claim is usually dismissed by respectful and knowing citations of the ways in which government asserts itself as keeper of the public interest at times of business irresponsibility. But the real, as opposed to the mythical, range of government "control" of the economy includes only:

1 some limited "regulatory" powers—which usually just ratify industry policies or serve as palliatives at the margins of significant business activity;

2 a fiscal policy built upon defense expenditures as pump-priming "public works"—without a significant emphasis on peaceful "public works" to meet social priorities and alleviate personal hardships;

3 limited fiscal and monetary weapons which are rigid and have only minor effects, and are greatly limited by corporate veto: tax cuts and reforms; interest rate control (used generally to tug on investment but hurting the little investor most); tariffs which protect non-competitive industries with political power and which keep less-favored nations out of the large trade mainstream, as the removal of barriers reciprocally with the Common Market may do disastrously to emerging countries outside of Europe; wage arbitration, the use of government coercion in the name of "public interest" to hide the tensions between workers and business production controllers; price controls, which further maintain the status quo of big ownership and flush out little investors for the sake of "stability";

---

interest, dividends. The size of this elite's wealth has been relatively constant: 31.6 percent (1922), 30.6 percent (1939), 29.8 percent (1949), 30.2 percent (1958).

4 very limited "poverty-solving" which is designed for the organized working class but not the shut-out, poverty-stricken migrants, farm workers,
   the indigent unaware of medical care or the lower-middle-class person
   riddled with medical bills, the "unhirables" of minority groups or workers over 45 years of age, etc.
5 regional development programs—such as the Area Redevelopment Act
   —which have been only "trickle down" welfare programs without broad
   authority for regional planning and development and public works
   spending. The federal highway program has been more significant than
   the "depressed areas" program in meeting the needs of people, but it is
   generally too remote and does not reach the vicious circle of poverty
   itself.

In short, the theory of government's "countervailing" business neglects the
extent to which government influence is marginal to the basic production decisions, the basic decision-making environment of society, the basic structure
of distribution and allocation which is still determined by major corporations
with power and wealth concentrated among the few. A conscious conspiracy—
as in the case of price-rigging in the electrical industry—is by no means generally or continuously operative but power undeniably does rest in comparative
insulation from the public and its political representatives.

The Military-Industrial Complex. The most spectacular and important creation
of the authoritarian and oligopolistic structure of economic decision-making in
America is the institution called "the military-industrial complex" by former
President Eisenhower—the powerful congruence of interest and structure
among military and business elites which affects so much of our development
and destiny. Not only is ours the first generation to live with the possibility of
world-wide cataclysm—it is the first to experience the actual social preparation
for cataclysm, the general militarization of American society. In 1948 Congress
established Universal Military Training, the first peacetime conscription. The
military became a permanent institution. Four years earlier, General Motors'
Charles E. Wilson had heralded the creation of what he called the "permanent
war economy," the continuous use of military spending as a solution to
economic problems unsolved before the post-war boom, most notably the
problem of the seventeen million jobless after eight years of the New Deal.
This has left a "hidden crisis" in the allocation of resources by the American
economy.

Since our childhood these two trends—the rise of the military and the installation of a defense-based economy—have grown fantastically. The Department
of Defense, ironically the world's largest single organization, is worth $160
billion, owns 32 million acres of America and employs half the 7.5 million
persons directly dependent on the military for subsistence, has an $11 billion
payroll which is larger than the net annual income of all American corporations.
Defense spending in the Eisenhower era totaled $350 billion and President Ken-
nedy entered office pledged to go even beyond the present defense allocation of
60 cents from every public dollar spent. Except for a war-induced boom immediately after "our side" bombed Hiroshima, American economic prosperity has
coincided with a growing dependence on military outlay—from 1941 to 1959
America's Gross National Product of $5.25 trillion included $700 billion in
goods and services purchased for the defense effort, about one-seventh of the
accumulated GNP. This pattern has included the steady concentration of military spending among a few corporations. In 1961, 86 percent of Defense Depart-

ment contracts were awarded without competition. The ordnance industry of 100,000 people is completely engaged in military work; in the aircraft industry, 94 percent of 750,000 workers are linked to the war economy; shipbuilding, radio, and communications equipment industries commit 40 percent of their work to defense; iron and steel, petroleum, metal-stamping and machine shop products, motors and generators, tools and hardware, copper, aluminum and machine tools industries all devote at least 10 percent of their work to the same cause.

The intermingling of Big Military and Big Industry is evidenced in the 1,400 former officers working for the 100 corporations who received nearly all the $21 billion spent in procurement by the Defense Department in 1961. The overlap is most poignantly clear in the case of General Dynamics, the company which received the best 1961 contracts, employed the most retired officers (187), and is directed by a former Secretary of the Army. A *Fortune* magazine profile of General Dynamics said: "The unique group of men who run Dynamics are only incidentally in rivalry with other U.S. manufacturers, with many of whom they actually act in concert. Their chief competitor is the USSR. The core of General Dynamics' corporate philosophy is the conviction that national defense is a more or less permanent business." Little has changed since Wilson's proud declaration of the Permanent War Economy back in the 1944 days when the top 200 corporations possessed 80 percent of all active prime war-supply contracts.

Military-Industrial Politics. The military and its supporting business foundation have found numerous forms of political expression, and we have heard their din endlessly. There has not been a major Congressional split on the issue of continued defense spending spirals in our lifetime. The triangular relations of the business, military, and political arenas cannot be better expressed than in Dixiecrat Carl Vinson's remarks as his House Armed Services Committee reported [on] a military construction bill of $808 million throughout the 50 states, for 1960–61: "There is something in this bill for everyone," he announced. President Kennedy had earlier acknowledged the valuable anti-recession features of the bill.

Imagine, on the other hand, $808 million suggested as an anti-recession measure, but being poured into programs of social welfare: the impossibility of receiving support for such a measure identifies a crucial feature of defense spending—it is beneficial to private enterprise, while welfare spending is not. Defense spending does not "compete" with the private sector; it contains a natural obsolescence; its "confidential" nature permits easier boondoggling; the tax burdens to which it leads can be shunted from corporation to consumer as a "cost of production." Welfare spending, however, involves the government in competition with private corporations and contractors; it conflicts with immediate interests of private pressure groups; it leads to taxes on business. Think of the opposition of private power companies to current proposals for river and valley development, or the hostility of the real estate lobby to urban renewal; or the attitude of the American Medical Association to a paltry medical care bill; or of all business lobbyists to foreign aid; these are the pressures leading to the schizophrenic public-military, private-civilian economy of our epoch. The politicians, of course, take the line of least resistance and thickest support: warfare, instead of welfare, is easiest to stand up for: after all, the Free World is at stake (and our constituency's investments, too).

Automation, Abundance, and Challenge. But while the economy remains relatively static in its setting of priorities and allocation of resources, new conditions are emerging with enormous implications: the revolution of automation, and the replacement of scarcity by the potential of material abundance.

Automation, the process of machines replacing men in performing sensory, motoric, and complex logical tasks, is transforming society in ways that are scarcely comprehensible. By 1959, industrial production regained its 1957 "pre-recession" level—but with 750,000 fewer workers required. In the Fifties as a whole, national production enlarged by 43 percent but the number of factory employees remained stationary, seven-tenths of 1 percent higher than in 1947.[2] Automation is destroying whole categories of work—impersonal thinkers have efficiently labeled this "structural unemployment"—in blue-collar, service, and even middle management occupations. In addition it is eliminating employment opportunities for a youth force that numbers one million more than it did in 1950, and rendering work far more difficult both to find and to do for people in their forties and up. The consequences of this economic drama, strengthened by the force of post-war recessions, are momentous: five million becomes an acceptable unemployment tabulation, and misery, uprootedness, and anxiety become the lot of increasing numbers of Americans.

But while automation is creating social dislocation of a stunning kind, it paradoxically is imparting the opportunity for men the world around to rise in dignity from their knees. The dominant optimistic economic fact of this epoch is that fewer hands are needed now in actual production, although more goods and services are a real potentiality. The world could be fed, poverty abolished, the great public needs could be met, the brutish world of Darwinian scarcity could be brushed away, all men could have more time to pursue their leisure, drudgery in work could be cut to a minimum, education could become more of a continuing process for all people, both public and personal needs could be met rationally. But only in a system with selfish production motives and elitist control, a system which is less welfare- than war-based, undemocratic rather than "stock-holder participative" as "sold to us," does the potentiality for abundance become a curse and a cruel irony:

1 Automation brings unemployment instead of more leisure for all and greater achievement of needs for all people in the world—a crisis instead of economic utopia. Instead of being introduced into a social system in a planned and equitable way, automation is initiated according to its profitability. American Telephone and Telegraph holds back modern telephone equipment, invented with public research funds, until present equipment is *financially* unprofitable. Colleges develop teaching machines, mass-class techniques, and TV education to replace teachers: not to proliferate knowledge or to assist the qualified professors now, but to "*cut costs in education* and make the academic community more *efficient* and less *wasteful.*" Technology, which could be a blessing to society, becomes more and more a sinister threat to humanistic and rational enterprise.

2. The electronics industry lost 200,000 of 900,000 workers in the years 1953–57. In the steel industry, productive capacity has increased 20 percent since 1955, while the number of workers has fallen 17,000. Employment in the auto industry decreased in the same period from 746,000 to 614,000. The chemical industry has enlarged its productive powers 27 percent although its work force has dropped by 3 percent. A farmer in 1962 can grow enough to feed 24 people, where one generation ago only 12 could be nourished. The United States Bureau of the Census used 50 statisticians in 1960 to perform the service that required 4,100 in 1950.

2 Hard-core poverty exists just beyond the neon lights of affluence, and the "have-nots" may be driven still further from opportunity as the high-technology society demands better education to get into the production mainstream and more capital investment to get into "business." Poverty is shameful in that it herds people by race, region, and previous condition of misfortune into "uneconomic classes" in the so-called free society—the marginal worker is made more insecure by automation, high education requirements, heavier competition for jobs, the maintenance of low wages, and a high level of unemployment. People in the rut of poverty are strikingly unable to overcome the collection of forces working against them: poor health, bad neighborhoods, miserable schools, inadequate "welfare" services, unemployment and underemployment, weak political and union organization.

3 Surplus and potential plenty are wasted domestically and producers suffer impoverishment because the real needs of the world and of our society are not reflected in the market. Our huge bins of decomposing grain are classic American examples, as is the steel industry, which, in the summer of 1962, is producing at 53 percent of capacity.

The Stance of Labor. Amidst all this, what of organized labor, the historic institutional representative of the exploited, the presumed "countervailing power" against the excesses of Big Business? The contemporary social assault on the labor movement is of crisis proportions. To the average American, "big labor" is a growing cancer equal in impact to Big Business—nothing could be more distorted, even granting a sizable union bureaucracy. But in addition to public exaggerations, the labor crisis can be measured in several ways. First, the high expectations of the newborn AFL-CIO of 30 million members by 1965 are suffering a reverse unimaginable five years ago. The demise of the dream of "organizing the unorganized" is dramatically reflected in the AFL-CIO decision, just two years after its creation, to slash its organizing staff in half. From 15 million members when the AFL and CIO merged, the total has slipped to 13.5 million. During the post-war generation, union membership nationally has increased by 4 million—but the total number of workers has jumped by 13 million. Today only 40 percent of all non-agricultural workers are protected by any form of organization. Second, organizing conditions are going to worsen. Where labor now is strongest—in industries—automation is leading to an attrition of available work. As the number of jobs dwindles, so does labor's power of bargaining, since management can handle a strike in an automated plant more easily than in the older mass-operated ones.

More important, perhaps, the American economy has changed radically in the last decade, as suddenly the number of workers producing goods became fewer than the number in "nonproductive" areas—government, trade, finance, services, utilities, transportation. Since World War II "white collar" and "service" jobs have grown twice as fast as have "blue collar" production jobs. Labor has almost no organization in the expanding occupational areas of the new economy, but almost all of its entrenched strength in contracting areas. As big government hires more, as business seeks more office workers and skilled technicians, and as growing commercial America demands new hotels, service stations, and the like, the conditions will become graver still. Further, there is continuing hostility to labor by the Southern states and their industrial interests —meaning "runaway" plants, cheap labor threatening the organized trade union movement, and opposition from Dixicrats to favorable labor legislation in Congress. Finally, there is indication that Big Business, for the sake of public relations if nothing more, has acknowledged labor's "right" to exist, but has deliberately tried to contain labor at its present strength, preventing strong unions from helping weaker ones or from spreading to unorganized sectors of the economy. Business is aided in its efforts by proliferation of "right-to-work" laws at state levels (especially in areas where labor is without organizing strength to begin with), and anti-labor legislation in Congress.

In the midst of these besetting crises, labor itself faces its own problems of vision and program. Historically, there can be no doubt as to its worth in American politics—what progress there has been in meeting human needs in this century rests greatly with the labor movement. And to a considerable extent the social democracy for which labor has fought externally is reflected in its own essentially democratic character: representing millions of people, not millions of dollars; demanding their welfare, not eternal profit.

Today labor remains the most liberal "mainstream" institution—but often its liberalism represents vestigial commitments, self-interestedness, unradicalism. In some measure labor has succumbed to institutionalization, its social idealism waning under the tendencies of bureaucracy, materialism, business ethics. The successes of the last generation perhaps have braked, rather than accelerated, labor's zeal for change. Even the House of Labor has bay windows: not only is this true of the labor elites, but as well of some of the rank-and-file. Many of the latter are indifferent unionists, uninterested in meetings, alienated from the complexities of the labor-management negotiating apparatus, lulled to comfort by the accessibility of luxury and the opportunity of long-term contracts. "Union democracy" is inhibited not simply by labor-leader elitism, but by the related problem of rank-and-file apathy to the tradition of unionism. The crisis of labor is reflected in the co-existence within the unions of militant Negro discontents and discriminatory locals, sweeping critics of the obscuring "public interest" marginal tinkering of government and willing handmaidens of conservative political leadership, austere sacrificers and businesslike operators, visionaries and anachronisms—tensions between extremes that keep alive the possibilities for a more militant unionism. Too, there are seeds of rebirth in the "organizational crisis" itself: the technologically unemployed, the unorganized white-collar men and women, the migrants and farm workers, the unprotected Negroes, the poor, all of whom are isolated now from the power structure of the economy, but who are the potential base for a broader and more forceful unionism.

Horizon. In summary: a more reformed, more human capitalism, functioning at three-fourths capacity while one-third of America and two-thirds of the world goes needy, domination of politics and the economy by fantastically rich elites, accommodation and limited effectiveness by the labor movement, hard-core poverty and unemployment, automation confirming the dark ascension of machine over man instead of shared abundance, technological change being introduced into the economy by the criteria of profitability—this has been our inheritance. However inadequate, it has instilled quiescence in liberal hearts—partly reflecting the extent to which misery has been overcome, but also the eclipse of social ideals. Though many of us are "affluent," poverty, waste, elitism, manipulation are too manifest to go unnoticed, too clearly unnecessary to go accepted. To change the Cold War status quo and other social evils, concern with the challenges to the American economic machine must expand. Now, as a truly better social state becomes visible, a new poverty impends: a poverty of vision, and a poverty of political action to make that vision reality. Without new vision, the failure to achieve our potentialities will spell the inability of our society to endure in a world of obvious, crying needs and rapid change.

THE INDIVIDUAL IN THE WARFARE STATE

Business and politics, when significantly militarized, affect the whole living condition of each American citizen. Worker and family depend on the Cold War for life. Half of all research and development is concentrated on military ends. The press mimics conventional Cold War opinion in its editorials. In less than a full generation, most Americans accept the military-industrial structure as "the way things are." War is still pictured as one kind of diplomacy, perhaps a gloriously satisfying kind. Our saturation and atomic bombings of Germany and Japan are little more than memories of past "policy necessities" that preceded the wonderful economic boom of 1946. The facts that our once-revolutionary 20,000-ton Hiroshima Bomb is now paled by 50-megaton weapons, that our lifetime has included the creation of intercontinental ballistic missiles, that "greater" weapons are to follow, that weapons refinement is more rapid than the development of weapons of defense, that soon a dozen or more nations will have the Bomb, that one simple miscalculation could incinerate mankind: these orienting facts are but remotely felt. A shell of moral callus separates the citizen from sensitivity to the common peril: this is the result of a lifetime saturation with horror. After all, some ask, where could we begin, even if we wanted to? After all, others declare, we can only assume things are in the best of hands. A coed at the University of Kentucky says, "we regard peace and war as fairy tales." And a child has asked in helplessness, perhaps for us all, "Daddy, why is there a cold war?"

Past senselessness permits present brutality; present brutality is prelude to future deeds of still greater inhumanity; that is the moral history of the twentieth century, from the First World War to the present. A half-century of accelerating destruction has flattened out the individual's ability to make moral distinctions; it has made people understandably give up; it has forced private worry and public silence.

To a decisive extent, the means of defense, the military technology itself, determines the political and social character of the state being defended—that is, defense mechanisms themselves in the nuclear age alter the character of the system that creates them for protection. So it has been with America, as her democratic institutions and habits have shriveled in almost direct proportion to the growth of her armaments. Decisions about military strategy, including the monstrous decision to go to war, are more and more the property of the military and industrial arms race machine, with the politicians assuming a ratifying role instead of a determining one. This is increasingly a fact not just because of the installation of the permanent military, but because of constant revolutions in military technology. The new technologies allegedly require military expertise, scientific comprehension, and the mantle of secrecy. As Congress relies more and more on the Joint Chiefs of Staff, the existing chasm between people and decision-makers becomes irreconcilably wide, and more alienating in its effects.

A necessary part of the military effort is propaganda: to "sell" the need for Congressional appropriations, to conceal various business scandals, and to convince the American people that the arms race is important enough to sacrifice civil liberties and social welfare. So confusion prevails about the national needs, while the three major services and the industrial allies jockey for power—the

Air Force tending to support bombers and missilery; the Navy, Polaris and carriers; the Army, conventional ground forces and invulnerable nuclear arsenals; and all three feigning unity by support of the policy of weapons and agglomeration called the "mix." Strategies are advocated on the basis of power and profit, usually more so than on the basis of national military needs. In the meantime, Congressional investigating committees—most notably the House Un-American Activities Committee and the Senate Judiciary Committee—attempt to curb the little dissent that finds its way into off-beat magazines. A huge militant anti-communist brigade throws in its support, patriotically willing to do *anything* to achieve "total victory" in the Cold War; the government advocates peaceful confrontation with international Communism, then utterly pillories and outlaws the tiny American Communist Party. University professors withdraw prudently from public issues; the very style of social science writing becomes more qualified. Needs in housing, education, minority rights, health care, land redevelopment, hourly wages all are subordinated—though a political tear is shed gratuitously—to the primary objective of the "military and economic strength of the Free World."

What are the governing policies which supposedly justify all this human sacrifice and waste? With few exceptions they have reflected the quandaries and confusion, stagnation and anxiety of a stalemated nation in a turbulent world. They have shown a slowness, sometimes a sheer inability to react to a sequence of new problems.

Of these problems, two of the newest are foremost: the existence of poised nuclear weapons and the revolutions against the former colonial powers. In both areas, the Soviet Union and the various national communist movements have aggravated international relations in inhuman and undesirable ways, but hardly so much as to blame only communism for the present menacing situation.

DETERRENCE POLICY

The accumulation of nuclear arsenals, the threat of accidental war, the possibility of limited war becoming illimitable holocaust, the impossibility of achieving final arms superiority or invulnerability, the approaching nativity of a cluster of infant atomic powers: all of these events are tending to undermine traditional concepts of power relations among nations. War can no longer be considered as an effective instrument of foreign policy, a means of strengthening alliances, adjusting the balance of power, maintaining national sovereignty, or preserving human values. War is no longer simply a forceful extension of foreign policy; it can obtain no constructive ends in the modern world. Soviet or American "megatonnage" is sufficient to destroy all existing social structures as well as value systems. Missiles have (figuratively) thumbed their nose cones at national boundaries. But America, like other countries, still operates by means of national defense and deterrence systems. These are seen to be useful so long as they are never fully used: unless we as a national entity can convince Russia that we are willing to commit the most heinous action in human history, we will be forced to commit it.

Deterrence advocates, all of them prepared at least to threaten mass extermination, advance arguments of several kinds. At one pole are the minority of open partisans of preventive war—who falsely assume the inevitability of violent conflict and assert the lunatic efficacy of striking the first blow, assuming that it will be easier to "recover" after thermonuclear war than to recover now from the grip of the Cold War. Somewhat more reluctant to advocate initiating a war, but perhaps more disturbing for their numbers within the Kennedy administration, are the many advocates of the "counter-force" theory of aiming strategic nuclear weapons at military installations—though this might "save" more lives than a preventive war, it would require drastic, provocative, and perhaps impossible social change to separate many cities from weapon sites, it would be impossible to insure the immunity of cities after one or two counter-force nuclear "exchanges," it would generate a perpetual arms race for less vulnerability and greater weapons power and mobility, it would make outer space a region subject to militarization, and it would accelerate the suspicions and arms build-ups which are incentives to precipitate nuclear action.

Others would support fighting "limited wars" which use conventional (all but atomic) weapons, backed by deterrents so mighty that both sides would fear to use them—although underestimating the implications of numerous new atomic powers on the world stage, the extreme difficulty of anchoring international order with weapons of only transient invulnerability, the potential tendency for a "losing side" to push limited protracted fighting on the soil of underdeveloped countries. Still other deterrence artists propose limited, clearly defensive and retaliatory, nuclear capacity, always potent enough to deter an opponent's aggressive designs—the best of deterrence strategies, but inadequate when it rests on the equation of an arms "stalemate" with international stability.

All the deterrence theories suffer in several common ways. They allow insufficient attention to preserving, extending, and enriching democratic values, such matters being subordinate rather than governing in the process of conducting foreign policy. Second, they inadequately realize the inherent instabilities of the continuing arms race and balance of fear. Third, they operationally tend to eclipse interest and action towards disarmament by solidifying economic, political, and even moral investments in continuation of tensions. Fourth, they offer a disinterested and even patriotic rationale for the boondoggling, belligerence, and privilege of military and economic elites. Finally, deterrence strategies invariably understate or dismiss the relatedness of various dangers; they inevitably lend tolerability to the idea of war by neglecting the dynamic interaction of problems—such as the menace of accidental war, the probable future tensions surrounding the emergence of ex-colonial nations, the imminence of several new nations joining the "Nuclear Club," the destabilizing potential of technological breakthrough by either arms race contestant, the threat of Chinese atomic might, the fact that "recovery" after World War III would involve not only human survivors but, as well, a huge and fragile social structure and culture which would be decimated perhaps irreparably by total war.

Such a harsh critique of what we are doing as a nation by no means implies that sole blame for the Cold War rests on the United States. Both sides have behaved irresponsibly—the Russians by an exaggerated lack of trust, and by much dependence on aggressive military strategists rather than on proponents of nonviolent conflict and coexistence. But we do contend, as Americans concerned with the conduct of our representative institutions, that our government has blamed the Cold War stalemate on nearly everything but its own hesitations, its own anachronistic dependence on weapons. To be sure, there is more to disarmament than wishing for it. There are inadequacies in international rule-making institutions—which could be corrected. There are faulty inspection mechanisms—which could be perfected by disinterested scientists. There are Russian intransigency and evasiveness—which do not erase the face that the Soviet Union, because of a strained economy, an expectant population, fears of Chinese potential, and interest in the colonial revolution, is increasingly disposed to real disarmament with real controls. But there is, too, our own reluctance to face the uncertain world beyond the Cold War, our own shocking assumption that the risks of the present are fewer than the risks of a policy re-orientation to disarmament, our own unwillingness to face the implementation of our rhetorical commitments to peace and freedom.

Today the world alternatively drifts and plunges towards a terrible war—when vision and change are required, our government pursues a policy of ma-cabre dead-end dimensions—conditioned, but not justified, by actions of the Soviet bloc. Ironically, the war which seems so close will not be fought between the United States and Russia, not externally between two national entities, but as an international civil war throughout the unrespected and unprotected *civitas* which spans the world.

THE COLONIAL REVOLUTION

While weapons have accelerated man's opportunity for self-destruction, the counter-impulse to life and creation is superbly manifest in the revolutionary feelings of many Asian, African, and Latin American peoples. Against the indi-vidual initiative and aspiration, and social sense of organicism, characteristic of these upsurges, the American apathy and stalemate stand in embarrassing con-trast.

It is difficult today to give human meaning to the welter of facts that sur-rounds us. That is why it is especially hard to understand the facts of "under-development": in India, man and beast together produced 65 percent of the nation's economic energy in a recent year, and of the remaining 35 percent of inanimately produced power almost three-fourths was obtained by burning dung. But in the United States, human and animal power together account for only 1 percent of the national economic energy—that is what stands humanly behind the vague term "industrialization." Even to maintain the misery of Asia today at a constant level will require a rate of growth tripling the national income and the aggregate production in Asian countries by the end of the cen-tury. For Asians to have the (unacceptable) 1950 standard of Europeans, less than $2,000 per year for a family, national production must increase 21-fold by the end of the century, and that monstrous feat only to reach a level that Europeans find intolerable.

What has America done? During the years 1955–57 our total expenditures in economic aid were equal to one-tenth of 1 percent of our total Gross National Product. Prior to that time it was less; since then it has been a fraction higher. Immediate social and economic development is needed—we have helped little, seeming to prefer to create a growing gap between 'have" and "have not" rather than to usher in social revolutions which would threaten our investors and our military alliances. The new nations want to avoid power entanglements that will open their countries to foreign domination—and we have often demanded loyalty oaths. They do not see the relevance of uncontrolled free enterprise in societies without accumulated capital and a significant middle class—and we have looked calumniously on those who would not try "our way." They seek empathy—and we have sided with the old colonialists, who now are trying to take credit for "giving" all the freedom that has been wrested from them, or we "empathize" when pressure absolutely demands it.

With rare variation, American foreign policy in the Fifties was guided by a concern for foreign investment and a negative anti-communist political stance linked to a series of military alliances, both undergirded by military threat. We participated unilaterally—usually through the Central Intelligence Agency—in revolutions against governments in Laos, Guatemala, Cuba, Egypt, Iran. We permitted economic investment to decisively affect our foreign policy: sugar in Cuba, oil in the Middle East, diamonds and gold in South Africa (with whom we trade more than with any other African nation). More exactly: America's "foreign market" in the late Fifties, including exports of goods and services plus overseas sales by American firms, averaged about $60 billion annually. This represented twice the investment of 1950, and it is predicted that the same rates of increase will continue. The reason is obvious; *Fortune* said in 1958, "foreign earnings will more than double in ten years, more than twice the probable gain in domestic profits." These investments are concentrated primarily in the Middle East and Latin America, neither region being an impressive candidate for the long-run stability, political caution, and lower-class tolerance that American investors typically demand.

Our pugnacious anti-communism and protection of interests has led us to an alliance inappropriately called the "Free World." It includes four major parliamentary democracies: ourselves, Canada, Great Britain, and India. It also has included through the years Batista, Franco, Verwoerd, Salazar, De Gaulle, Boun Oum, Ngo Dinh Diem, Chiang Kai-shek, Trujillo, the Somosas, Saud, Ydigoras —all of these non-democrats separating us deeply from the colonial revolutions.

Since the Kennedy administration began, the American government seems to have initiated policy changes in the colonial and underdeveloped areas. It accepted "neutralism" as a tolerable principle; it sided more than once with the Angolans in the United Nations; it invited Souvanna Phouma to return to Laos after having overthrown his neutralist government there; it implemented the Alliance for Progress that President Eisenhower proposed when Latin America appeared on the verge of socialist revolution; it made derogatory statements about the Trujillos; it cautiously suggested that a democratic socialist government in British Guiana might be necessary to support; in inaugural oratory, it suggested that a moral imperative was involved in sharing the world's resources with those who have been previously dominated. These were hardly sufficient to heal the scars of past activity and present associations, but nevertheless they were motions away from the Fifties. But quite unexpectedly, the President ordered the Cuban invasion, and while the American press railed about how we had been "shamed" and defied by that "monster Castro," the colonial peoples of the world wondered whether our foreign policy had really changed from its old imperialist ways (we had never supported Castro, even on the eve of his taking power, and had announced early that "the conduct of the Castro government toward foreign private enterprise in Cuba" would be a main State Department concern). Any heralded changes in our foreign policy are now further suspect in the wake of the Punta del Este foreign ministers' conference where the five countries representing most of Latin America refused to cooperate in our plans to further "isolate" the Castro government.

Ever since the colonial revolution began, American policy-makers have reacted to new problems with old "gunboat" remedies, often thinly disguised. The feeble but desirable efforts of the Kennedy administration to be more flexible are coming perhaps too late, and are of too little significance to really change the historical thrust of our policies. The hunger problem is increasing rapidly mostly as a result of the worldwide population explosion that cancels out the meager triumphs gained so far over starvation. The threat of population to economic growth is simply documented: in 1960–70 population in Africa south of the Sahara will increase 14 percent; in South Asia and the Far East by 22 percent; in North Africa 26 percent; in the Middle East by 27 percent; in

Latin America 29 percent. Population explosion, no matter how devastating, is neutral. But how long will it take to create a relation of trust between America and the newly developing societies? How long to change our policies? And what length of time do we have?

The world is in transformation. But America is not. It can race to industrialize the world, tolerating occasional authoritarianisms, socialisms, neutralisms along the way—or it can slow the pace of the inevitable and default to the eager and self-interested Soviets and, much more importantly, to mankind itself. Only mystics would guess we have opted thoroughly for the first. Consider what our people think of this, the most urgent issue on the human agenda. Fed by a bellicose press, manipulated by economic and political opponents of change, drifting in their own history, they grumble about "the foreign aid waste," or about "that beatnik down in Cuba," or how "things will get us by" ... thinking confidently, albeit in the usual bewilderment, that Americans can go right on as always, 5 percent of mankind producing 40 percent of its goods.

ANTI-COMMUNISM

An unreasoning anti-communism has become a major social problem for those who want to construct a more democratic America. McCarthyism and other forms of exaggerated and conservative anti-communism seriously weaken democratic institutions and spawn movements contrary to the interests of basic freedoms and peace. In such an atmosphere even the most intelligent of Americans fear to join political organizations, sign petitions, speak out on serious issues. Militaristic policies are easily "sold" to a public fearful of a demonic enemy. Political debate is restricted, thought standardized, action inhibited by the demands of "unity" and "oneness" in the face of the declared danger. Even many liberals and socialists share static and repetitious participation in the anti-communist crusade and often discourage tentative, inquiring discussion about "the Russian question" within their ranks—often by employing "stalinist," "stalinoid," "trotskyite," and other epithets in an oversimplifying way to discredit opposition.

Thus much of the American anti-communism takes on the characteristic of paranoia. Not only does it lead to the perversion of democracy and to the political stagnation of a warfare society, but it also has the unintended consequence of preventing an honest and effective approach to the issues. Such an approach would require public analysis and debate of world politics. But almost nowhere in politics is such a rational analysis possible to make.

It would seem reasonable to expect that in America the basic issues of the Cold War should be rationally and fully debated, between persons of every opinion—on television, on platforms, and through other media. It would seem, too, that there should be a way for a person or an organization to oppose communism *without* contributing to the common fear of associations and public actions. But these things do not happen; instead, there is finger-pointing and comical debate about the most serious of issues. This trend of events on the domestic scene, towards greater irrationality on major questions, moves us to greater concern than does the "internal threat" of domestic communism. Democracy, we are convinced, requires every effort to set in peaceful opposition the basic viewpoints of the day; only by conscious, determined, though difficult, efforts in this direction will the issue of communism be met appropriately.

COMMUNISM AND FOREIGN POLICY

As democrats we are in basic opposition to the communist system. The Soviet Union, as a system, rests on the total suppression of organized opposition, as well as a vision of the future in the name of which much human life has been sacrificed, and numerous small and large denials of human dignity rationalized. The Communist Party has equated falsely the "triumph of true socialism" with centralized bureaucracy. The Soviet state lacks independent labor organizations and other liberties we consider basic. And despite certain reforms, the system remains almost totally divorced from the image officially promulgated by the Party. Communist parties thoughout the rest of the world are generally undemocratic in internal structure and mode of action. Moreover, in most cases they have subordinated radical programs to requirements of Soviet foreign policy. The communist movement has failed, in every sense, to achieve its stated intention of leading a worldwide movement for human emancipation.

But present trends in American anti-communism are not sufficient for the creation of appropriate policies with which to relate to and counter communist movements in the world. In no instance is this better illustrated than in our basic national policy-making assumption that the Soviet Union is inherently expansionist and aggressive, prepared to dominate the rest of the world by military means. On this assumption rests the monstrous American structure of military "preparedness"; because of it we sacrifice values and social programs to the alleged needs of military power.

But the assumption itself is certainly open to question and debate. To be sure, the Soviet state has used force and the threat of force to promote or defend its perceived national interests. But the typical American response has been to equate the use of force—which in many cases might be dispassionately interpreted as a conservative, albeit brutal, action—with the initiation of a worldwide military onslaught. In addition, the Russian-Chinese conflicts and the emergence of rifts throughout the communist movement call for a re-evaluation of any monolithic interpretations. And the apparent Soviet lack of interest in building a first-strike arsenal of weapons challenges the weight given to protection against surprise attack in formulations of American policy toward the Soviets.

Almost without regard to one's conception of the dynamics of Soviet society and foreign policy, it is evident that the American military response has been more effective in deterring the growth of democracy than communism. Moreover, our prevailing policies make difficult the encouragement of skepticism, [or] anti-war or pro-democratic attitudes in the communist systems. America has done a great deal to foment the easier, opposite tendency in Russia: suspicion, suppression, and stiff military resistance. We have established a system of military alliances which are even of dubious deterrence value. It is reasonable to suggest that "Berlin" and "Laos" have become earth-shaking situations partly because rival systems of deterrence make impossible the withdrawal of threats. The "status quo" is not cemented by mutual threat but by mutual fear of receding from pugnacity—since the latter course would undermine the "credibility" of our deterring system. Simultaneously, while billions in military aid were propping up right-wing Laotian, Formosan, Iranian, and other regimes, American leadership never developed a purely political policy for offering concrete alternatives to either communism or the status quo for colonial revolutions. The results have been: fulfillment of the communist belief that capitalism is stagnant, its only defense being dangerous military adventurism; destabilizing incidents in numerous developing countries; an image of America allied with corrupt oligarchies counterposed to the Russian-Chinese image of rapid, though brutal, economic development. Again and again, America mistakes the static area of defense, rather than the dynamic area of development, as the master need of two-thirds of mankind.

Our paranoia about the Soviet Union has made us incapable of achieving agreements absolutely necessary for disarmament and the preservation of peace. We are hardly able to see the possibility that the Soviet Union, though not "peace-loving," may be seriously interested in disarmament.

Infinite possibilities for both tragedy and progress lie before us. On the one hand, we can continue to be afraid, and out of fear commit suicide. On the other hand, we can develop a fresh and creative approach to world problems which will help to create democracy at home and establish conditions for its growth elsewhere in the world.

DISCRIMINATION

Our America is still white.

Consider the plight, statistically, of its greatest nonconformists, the "nonwhite" (a Census Bureau designation).

LITERACY: One out of every four "nonwhites" is functionally illiterate; half do not complete elementary school; one in five finishes high school or better. But one in twenty whites is functionally illiterate; four of five finish elementary school; half go through high school or better.

SALARY: In 1959 a "nonwhite" worker could expect to average $2,844 annually; a "nonwhite" family, including a college-educated father, could expect to make $5,654 collectively. But a white worker could expect to make $4,487 if he worked alone; with a college degree and a family of helpers he could expect $7,373. The approximate Negro-white wage ratio has remained nearly level for generations, with the exception of the World War II employment "boom" which opened many better jobs to exploited groups.

WORK: More than half of all "nonwhites" work at laboring or service jobs, including one-fourth of those with college degrees; one in 20 works in a professional or managerial capacity. Fewer than one in five of all whites are laboring or service workers, including one in every 100 of the college-educated; one in four is in professional or managerial work.

UNEMPLOYMENT: Within the 1960 labor force of approximately 72 million, one of every ten "nonwhites" was unemployed. Only one of every twenty whites suffered that condition.

HOUSING: The census classifies 57 percent of all "nonwhite" houses substandard, but only 27 percent of white-owned units so exist.

EDUCATION: More than 50 percent of America's "nonwhite" high school students never graduate. The vocational and professional spread of curriculum categories offered "nonwhites" is 16 as opposed to the 41 occupations offered to the white student. Furthermore, in spite of the 1954 Supreme Court decision, of all "nonwhites" educated, 80 percent are educated actually, or virtually, under segregated conditions. And only one of twenty "nonwhite" students goes to college as opposed to the 1:10 ratio for white students.

VOTING: While the white community is registered above two-thirds of its potential, the "nonwhite" population is registered below one-third of its capacity (with even greater distortion in areas of the Deep South).

Even against this background some will say that progress is being made. The facts belie it, however, unless it is assumed that America has another century to deal with its racial inequalities. Others, more pompous, will blame the situation on "those people's inability to pick themselves up," not understanding the automatic way in which such a system can frustrate reform efforts and diminish the aspirations of the oppressed. The one-party system in the South,

APPENDIX   353

attached to the Dixiecrat-Republican complex nationally, cuts off the Negro's
independent powers as a citizen. Discrimination in employment, along with
labor's accommodation to the "lily-white" hiring practices, guarantees the low-
est slot in the economic order to the "nonwhite." North or South, these oppressed are conditioned by their inheritance and their surroundings to expect
more of the same: in housing, schools, recreation, travel, all their potential is
circumscribed, thwarted, and often extinguished. Automation grinds up job
opportunities, and ineffective or nonexistent retraining programs make the al-
ready-handicapped "nonwhite" even less equipped to participate in "technological progress."

Horatio Alger Americans typically believe that the "nonwhites" are being
"accepted" and "rising" gradually. They see more Negroes on television and so
assume that Negroes are "better off." They hear the President talking about
Negroes and so assume they are politically represented. They are aware of black
peoples in the United Nations and so assume that the world is generally moving
towards integration. They don't drive through the South, or through the slum
areas of the big cities, so they assume that squalor and naked exploitation are
disappearing. They express generalities about "time and gradualism" to hide
the fact that they don't know what is happening.

The advancement of the Negro and other "nonwhites" in America has not
been altogether by means of the crusades of liberalism, but rather through
unavoidable changes in social structure. The economic pressures of World War
II opened new jobs, new mobility, new insights to Southern Negroes, who then
began great migrations from the South to the bigger urban areas of the North
where their *absolute* wage was greater, though unchanged in relation to the
white man of the same stratum. More important than the World War II openings
was the colonial revolution. The world-wide upsurge of dark peoples against
white colonial domination stirred the aspiration and created an urgency among
American Negroes, while simultaneously it threatened the power structure of
the United States enough to produce concessions to the Negro. Produced by
outer pressure from the newly moving peoples rather than by the internal conscience of the Federal government, the gains were keyed to improving the
American "image" more than to reconstructing the society that prospered on
top of its minorities. Thus the historic Supreme Court decision of 1954, theoretically desegregating Southern schools, was more a proclamation than a har-
binger of social change—and is reflected as such in the fraction of Southern
school districts which have desegregated, with Federal officials doing little to
spur the process.

It has been said that the Kennedy administration did more in two years than
the Eisenhower administration did in eight. Of this there can be no doubt. But
it is analogous to comparing whispers to silence when positively stentorian
tones are demanded. President Kennedy leaped ahead of the Eisenhower record
when he made his second reference to the racial problem; Eisenhower did not
utter a meaningful public statement until his last month in office when he
mentioned the "blemish" of bigotry.

To avoid conflict with the Dixiecrat-Republican alliance, President Kennedy
has developed a civil rights philosophy of "enforcement, not enactment," implying that existing statutory tools are sufficient to change the lot of the Negro.
So far he has employed executive power usefully to appoint Negroes to various
offices, and seems interested in seeing the Southern Negro registered to vote.
On the other hand, he has appointed at least four segregationist judges in areas
where voter registration is a desperate need. Only two civil rights bills, one to

abolish the poll tax in five states and another to prevent unfair use of literacy tests in registration, have been proposed—the President giving active support to neither. But even this legislation, lethargically supported, then defeated, was intended to extend only to Federal elections. More important, the Kennedy interest in voter registration has not been supplemented with interest in giving the Southern Negro the economic protection that only trade unions can provide.

It seems evident that the President is attempting to win the Negro permanently to the Democratic Party without basically disturbing the reactionary one-party oligarchy in the South. Moreover, the administration is decidedly "cool" (a phrase of Robert Kennedy) toward mass nonviolent movements in the South, though by the support of racist Dixiecrats, the administration makes impossible gradual action through conventional channels. The Federal Bureau of Investigation in the South is composed of Southerners and their intervention in situations of racial tension is always after the incident, not before. Kennedy has refused to "enforce" the legal prerogative to keep Federal marshals active in Southern areas before, during, and after any "situations" (this would invite Negroes to exercise their rights and it would infuriate the Southerners in Congress because of its "insulting" features).

While corrupt politicians, together with business interests happy with the absence of organized labor in Southern states and with the profits that result from paying the Negro half a "white wage," stymie and slow fundamental progress, it remains to be appreciated that the ultimate wages of discrimination are paid by individuals and not by the state. Indeed the other sides of the economic, political, and sociological coins of racism represent their more profound implications in the private lives, liberties, and pursuits of happiness of the citizen. While hungry nonwhites the world around assume rightful dominance, the majority of Americans fight to keep integrated housing out of the suburbs. While a fully interracial world becomes a biological probability, most Americans persist in opposing marriage between the races.

While cultures generally interpenetrate, white America is ignorant still of nonwhite America—and perhaps glad of it. The white lives almost completely within his immediate, close-up world where things are tolerable, where there are no Negroes except on the bus corner going to and from work, and where it is important that daughter marry right. White, like might, makes right in America today. Not knowing the "nonwhite," however, the white knows something less of himself. Not comfortable around "different people," he reclines in whiteness instead of preparing for diversity. Refusing to yield objective social freedoms to the "nonwhite," the white loses his personal subjective freedom by turning away "from all these damn causes."

White American ethnocentrism at home and abroad reflects most sharply the self-deprivation suffered by the majority of our country, which effectively makes it an isolated minority in the world community of culture and fellowship. The awe inspired by the pervasiveness of racism in American life is matched only by the marvel of its historical span in American traditions. The national heritage of racial discrimination via slavery has been a part of America since Christopher Columbus' advent on the new continent. As such, racism antedates not only the Republic and the thirteen Colonies, but even the use of the English language in this hemisphere. And it is well that we keep this as a background when trying to understand why racism stands as such a steadfast pillar in the culture and custom of the country. Racial xenophobia is reflected in the admission of various racial stocks to the country. From the nineteenth century Oriental Exclusion Acts to the most recent up-dating of the Walter-

McCarran Immigration Acts, the nation has shown a continuous contemptuous regard for "nonwhite." More recently, the tragedies of Hiroshima and Korematsu, and our cooperation with Western Europe in the United Nations, add treatment to the thoroughness of racist overtones in national life.

But the right to refuse service to anyone is no longer reserved to the Americans. The minority groups, internationally, are changing places.

WHAT IS NEEDED?

How to end the Cold War? How to increase democracy in America? These are the decisive issues confronting liberal and socialist forces today. To us, the issues are intimately related, the struggle for one inevitably being a struggle for the other. What policy and structural alternatives are needed to obtain these ends?

1. Universal controlled disarmament must replace deterrence and arms control as the national defense goal.

The strategy of mutual threat can only temporarily prevent thermonuclear war, and it cannot but erode democratic institutions here while consolidating oppressive institutions in the Soviet Union. Yet American leadership, while giving rhetorical due to the ideal of disarmament, persists in accepting mixed deterrence as its policy formula: under Kennedy we have seen first-strike and second-strike weapons, counter-military and counter-population inventions, tactical atomic weapons and guerrilla warriors, etc. The convenient rationalization that our weapons *potpourri* will confuse the enemy into fear of misbehaving is absurd and threatening. Our own intentions, once clearly retaliatory, are now ambiguous since the President has indicated we might in certain circumstances be the first to use nuclear weapons. We can expect that Russia will become more anxious herself, and perhaps even prepare to "pre-empt" us, and we (expecting the worst from the Russians) will nervously consider "pre-emption" ourselves. The symmetry of threat and counter-threat leads not to stability but to the edge of hell.

It is necessary that America make disarmament, not nuclear deterrence, "credible" to the Soviets and to the world. That is, disarmament should be continually avowed as a national goal; concrete plans should be presented at conference tables; real machinery for a disarming and disarmed world—national and international—should be created while the disarming process itself goes on. The long-standing idea of unilateral initiative should be implemented as a basic feature of American disarmament strategy: initiatives that are graduated in their risk potential, accompanied by invitations to reciprocation, done regardless of reciprocation, openly planned for a significant period of future time. Their functions should not be to strip America of weapons, but to induce a climate in which disarmament can be discussed with less mutual hostility and threat. They might include: a unilateral nuclear test moratorium; withdrawal of several bases near the Soviet Union; proposals to experiment in disarmament by stabilization of zone of controversy; cessation of all apparent first-strike preparations, such as the development of 41 Polaris submarines by 1963 while naval theorists state that about 45 constitute a provocative force; inviting a special United Nations agency to observe and inspect the launchings of all American flights into outer space; and numerous others.

There is no simple formula for the content of an actual disarmament treaty. It should be phased: perhaps on a region-by-region basis, the conventional weapons first. It should be conclusive, not open-ended, in its projection. It should be controlled: national inspection systems are adequate at first, but should be soon replaced by international devices and teams. It should be more than denuding: world or at least regional enforcement agencies, an international civil service and inspection service, and other supranational groups must come in to reality under the United Nations.

2. Disarmament should be seen as a political issue, not a technical problem.

Should this year's Geneva negotiations have resulted (by magic) in a disarmament agreement, the United States Senate would have refused to ratify it, a domestic depression would have begun instantly, and every fiber of American life would be wrenched drastically: these are indications not only of our unpreparedness for disarmament, but also that disarmament is not "just another policy shift." Disarmament means a deliberate shift in most of our domestic and foreign policy.

A. It will involve major changes in economic direction. Government intervention in new areas, government regulation of certain industrial price and investment practices to prevent inflation, full use of national productive capacities, and employment for every person in a dramatically expanding economy all are to be expected as the "price" of peace.
B. It will involve the simultaneous creation of international rule-making and enforcement machinery beginning under the United Nations, and the gradual transfer of sovereignties—such as national armies and national determination of "international" law—to such machinery.
C. It will involve the initiation of an explicitly political—as opposed to military—foreign policy on the part of the two major superstates. Neither has formulated the political terms in which they would conduct their behavior in a disarming or disarmed world. Neither dares to disarm until such an understanding is reached.

3. A crucial feature of this political understanding must be the acceptance of status quo possessions.

According to the universality principle all present national entities—including the Vietnams, the Koreas, the Chinas, and the Germanys—should be members of the United Nations as sovereign, no matter how desirable, states.

Russia cannot be expected to negotiate disarmament treaties for the Chinese. We should not feed Chinese fanaticism with our encirclement but Chinese stomachs with the aim of making war contrary to Chinese policy interests. Every day that we support anti-communist tyrants but refuse to even allow the Chinese Communists representation in the United Nations marks a greater separation of our ideals and our actions, and it makes more likely bitter future relations with the Chinese.

Second, we should recognize that an authoritarian Germany's insistence on reunification, while knowing the impossibility of achieving it with peaceful means, could only generate increasing frustrations among the population and nationalist sentiments which frighten its Eastern neighbors who have historical reasons to suspect Germanic intentions. President Kennedy himself told the editor of *Izvestia* that he fears an independent Germany with nuclear arms, but American policies have not demonstrated cognizance of the fact that Chancellor Adenauer too is interested in continued East-West tensions over the Germany and Berlin problems and nuclear arms precisely because this is the rationale for extending his domestic power and his influence upon the NATO–Common Market alliance.

A world war over Berlin would be absurd. Anyone concurring with such a proposition should demand that the West cease its contradictory advocacy of "reunification of Germany through free elections" and "a rearmed Germany in NATO." It is a dangerous illusion to assume that Russia will hand over East Germany to a rearmed reunited Germany which will enter the Western camp, although this Germany might have a Social Democratic majority which could prevent a reassertion of German nationalism. We have to recognize that the Cold War and the incorporation of Germany into the two power blocs was a decision of both Moscow and Washington, of both Adenauer and Ulbricht. The immediate responsibility for the Berlin Wall is Ulbricht's. But it had to be expected that a regime which was bad enough to make people flee is also bad enough to prevent them from fleeing. The inhumanity of the Berlin Wall is an ironic symbol of the irrationality of the Cold War, which keeps Adenauer and Ulbricht in power. A reduction of the tension over Berlin, if by internationalization or by a recognition of the status quo and reducing provocations, is a necessary but equally temporary measure which could not ultimately reduce the basic Cold War tension to which Berlin owes its precarious situation. The Berlin problem cannot be solved without reducing tensions in Europe, possibly by a bilateral military disengagement and creating a neutralized buffer zone. Even if Washington and Moscow were in favor of disengagement, both Adenauer and Ulbricht would never agree to it because Cold War keeps their parties in power.

Until their regimes' departure from the scene of history, the Berlin status quo will have to be maintained while minimizing the tensions necessarily arising from it. Russia cannot expect the United States to tolerate its capture by the Ulbricht regime, but neither can America expect to be in a position to indefinitely use Berlin as a fortress within the communist world. As a fair and bilateral disengagement in Central Europe seems to be impossible for the time being, a mutual recognition of the Berlin status quo, that is, of West Berlin's and East Germany's security, is needed. And it seems to be possible, although the totalitarian regime of East Germany and the authoritarian leadership of West Germany have until now succeeded in frustrating all attempts to minimize the dangerous tensions of Cold War.

The strategy of securing the status quo of the two power blocs until it is possible to depolarize the world by creating neutralist regions in all trouble zones seems to be the only way to guarantee peace at this time.

    4. Experiments in disengagement and demilitarization must be conducted as part of the total disarming process.

These "disarmament experiments" can be of several kinds, so long as they are consistent with the principles of containing the arms race and isolating specific sectors of the world from the Cold War powerplay. First, it is imperative that no more nations be supplied with, or locally produce, nuclear weapons. A 1959 report of the National Academy of Sciences predicted that 19 nations would be so armed in the near future. Should this prediction be fulfilled, the prospects of war would be unimaginably expanded. For ths reason, the United States, Great Britain, and the Soviet Union should band against France (which wants its own independent deterrent) and seek, through United Nations and other machinery, the effective prevention of the spread of atomic weapons. This not only would involve declarations of "denuclearization" in whole areas of

Latin America, Africa, Asia, and Europe, but would attempt to create inspection machinery to guarantee the peaceful use of atomic energy.

Second, the United States should reconsider its increasingly outmoded European defense framework, the North Atlantic Treaty Organization. Since its creation in 1949, NATO has assumed increased strength in overall determination of Western military policy, but has become less and less relevant to its original purpose, which was the defense of Central Europe. To be sure, after the Czech coup in 1948, it might have appeared that the Soviet Union was on the verge of a full-scale assault on Europe. But that onslaught has not materialized, not so much because of NATO's existence but because of the general unimportance of much of Central Europe to the Soviets. Today, when even American-based ICBM's could smash Russia minutes after an invasion of Europe, when the Soviets have no reason to embark on such an invasion, and when "thaw sectors" are desperately needed to brake the arms race, one of the least threatening but most promising courses for America would be toward the gradual diminishment of the NATO force, coupled with the negotiated "disengagement" of parts of Central Europe.

It is especially crucial that this be done while America is entering into favorable trade relations with the European Economic Community: such a gesture, combining economic ambition with less dependence on the military, would demonstrate the kind of competitive "coexistence" America intends to conduct with the communist-bloc nations. If the disengaged states were the two Germanys, Poland, and Czechoslovakia, several other benefits would accrue. First, the United States would be breaking with the lip-service commitment of "liberation" of Eastern Europe which has contributed so much to Russian fears and intransigence, while doing too little about actual liberation. But the end of "liberation" as a proposed policy would *not* signal the end of American concern for the oppressed in East Europe. On the contrary, disengagement would be a real, rather than a rhetorical, effort to ease military tensions, thus undermining the Russian argument for tighter controls in East Europe based on the "menace of capitalist encirclement." This policy, geared to the needs of democratic elements in the satellites, would develop a real bridge between East and West across the two most pro-Western Russian satellites. The Russians in the past have indicated some interest in such a plan, including the demilitarization of the Warsaw Pact countries. Their interest should be publicly tested. If disengagement could be achieved, a major zone could be removed from the Cold War, the German problem would be materially diminished, and the need for NATO would diminish, and attitudes favorable to disarming would be generated.

Needless to say, these proposals are much different than what is currently being practiced and praised. American military strategists are slowly acceding to the NATO demand for an independent deterrent, based on the fear that America might not defend Europe from military attack. These tendencies strike just the opposite chords in Russia than those which would be struck by disengagement themes: the chords of military alertness, based on the fact that NATO (bulwarked by the German Wehrmacht) is preparing to attack Eastern Europe or the Soviet Union. Thus the alarm which underlies the NATO proposal for an independent deterrent is likely itself to bring into existence the very Russian posture that was the original cause of fear. Armaments spiral and belligerence will carry the day, not disengagement and negotiation.

THE INDUSTRIALIZATION OF THE WORLD

Many Americans are prone to think of the industrialization of the newly developed countries as a modern form of American *noblesse*, undertaken sacrificially for the benefit of others. On the contrary, the task of world industrialization, of eliminating the disparity between have and have-not nations, is as important as any issue facing America. The colonial revolution signals the end of an era for the old Western powers and a time of new beginnings for most of the people of the earth. In the course of these upheavals, many problems will emerge; American policies must be revised or accelerated in several ways.

1. The United States' principal goal should be creating a world where hunger, poverty, disease, ignorance, violence, and exploitation are replaced as central features by abundance, reason, love, and international cooperation.

To many this will seem the product of juvenile hallucination: but we insist it is a more realistic goal than is a world of nuclear stalemate. Some will say this is a hope beyond all bounds: but it is far better to us to have a positive vision than a "hard-headed" resignation. Some will sympathize, but claim it is impossible: if so, then, we, not Fate, are the responsible ones, for we have the means at our disposal. *We should not give up the attempt for fear of failure.*

2. We should undertake here and now a fifty-year effort to prepare for all nations the conditions of industrialization.

Even with far more capital and skill than we now import to emerging areas, serious prophets expect that two generations will pass before accelerating industrialism is a world-wide act. The needs are numerous: every nation must build an adequate infrastructure (transportation, communication, land resources, waterways) for future industrial growth; there must be industries suited to the rapid development of differing raw materials and other resources; education must begin on a continuing basis for everyone in the society, especially including engineering and technical training; technical assistance from outside sources must be adequate to meet present and long-term needs; atomic power plants must spring up to make electrical energy available. With America's idle productive capacity, it is possible to begin this process immediately without changing our military allocations. This might catalyze a "peace race" since it would demand a response of such magnitude from the Soviet Union that arms spending and "coexistence" spending would become strenuous, perhaps impossible, for the Soviets to carry on simultaneously.

3. We should not depend significantly on private enterprise to do the job.

Many important projects will not be profitable enough to entice the investment of private capital. The total amount required is far beyond the resources of corporate and philanthropic concerns. The new nations are suspicious, legitimately, of foreign enterprises dominating their national life. World industrialization is too huge an undertaking to be formulated or carried out by private interests. Foreign economic assistance is a national problem, requiring long-range planning, integration with other domestic and foreign policies, and considerable public debate and analysis. Therefore the Federal government should have primary responsibility in this area.

4. We should not lock the development process into the Cold War: we should view it as a way of ending that conflict.

When President Kennedy declared that we must aid those who need aid because it is right, he was unimpeachably correct—now principle must become practice. We should reverse the trend of aiding corrupt anti-communist regimes. To support dictators like Diem while trying to destroy ones like Castro will only enforce international cynicism about American "principle," and is bound to lead to even more authoritarian revolutions, especially in Latin America where we did not even consider foreign aid until Castro had challenged the status quo. We should end the distinction between communist hunger and anti-communist hunger. To feed only anti-communists is to directly fatten men like Boun Oum, to incur the wrath of real democrats, and to distort our own sense of human values. We must cease seeing development in terms of communism and capitalism. To fight communism by capitalism in the newly developing areas is to fundamentally misunderstand the international hatred of imperialism and colonialism and to confuse the needs of 19th century industrial America with those of contemporary nations.

Quite fortunately, we are edging away from the Dullesian "either-or" foreign policy ultimatum towards an uneasy acceptance of neutralism and nonalignment. If we really desire the end of the Cold War, we should now welcome nonalignment—that is, the creation of whole blocs of nations concerned with growth and with independently trying to break out of the Cold War apparatus.

Finally, while seeking disarmament as the genuine deterrent, we should shift from financial support of military regimes to support of national development. Real security cannot be gained by propping up military defenses, but only through the hastening of political stability, economic growth, greater social welfare, improved education. Military aid is temporary in nature, a "shoring up" measure that only postpones crisis. In addition, it tends to divert the allocations of the nation being defended to supplementary military spending (Pakistan's budget is 70 percent oriented to defense measures). Sometimes it actually creates crisis situations, as in Latin America where we have contributed to the growth of national armies which are opposed generally to sweeping democratization. Finally, if we are really generous, it is harder for corrupt governments to exploit unfairly economic aid—especially if it is so plentiful that rulers cannot blame the absence of real reforms on anything but their own power lusts.

5. America should show its commitment to democratic institutions not by withdrawing support from undemocratic regimes, but by making domestic democracy exemplary.

Worldwide amusement, cynicism, and hatred towards the United States as a democracy is not simply a communist propaganda trick, but an objectively justifiable phenomenon. If respect for democracy is to be international, then the significance of democracy must emanate from American shores, not from the "soft sell" of the United States Information Agency.

6. America should agree that public utilities, railroads, mines, plantations, and other basic economic institutions should be in the control of national, not foreign, agencies.

The destiny of any country should be determined by its nationals, not by outsiders with economic interests within. We should encourage our investors to turn over their foreign holdings (or at least 50 percent of the stock) to the national governments of the countries involved.

7. Foreign aid should be given through international agencies, primarily the United Nations.

The need is to eliminate political overtones, to the extent possible, from economic development. The use of international agencies, with interests transcending those of American or Russian self-interest, is the feasible means of working on sound development. Second, internationalization will allow more long-range planning, integrate development plans adjacent countries and regions may have, and eliminate the duplication built into national systems of foreign aid. Third, it would justify more strictness of supervision than is now the case with American foreign aid efforts, but with far less chance of suspicion on the part of the developing countries. Fourth, the humiliating "handout" effect would be replaced by the joint participation of all nations in the general development of the earth's resources and industrial capacities. Fifth, it would eliminate national tensions, e.g. between Japan and some southeast Asian areas, which now impair aid programs by "disguising" nationalities in the common pooling of funds. Sixth, it would make easier the task of stabilizing the world market prices of basic commodities, alleviating the enormous threat that decline in prices of commodity exports might cancel out the gains from foreign aid in the new nations. Seventh, it would improve the possibilities of non-exploitative development, especially in creating "soft-credit" rotating-fund agencies which would not require immediate progress or financial return. Finally, it would enhance the importance of the United Nations itself, as the disarming process would enhance the UN as a rule-enforcement agency.

8. Democratic theory must confront the problems inherent in social revolutions.

For Americans concerned with the development of democratic societies, the anti-colonial movements and revolutions in the emerging nations pose serious problems. We need to face the problems with humility: after 180 years of constitutional government we are still striving for democracy in our own society. We must acknowledge that democracy and freedom do not magically occcur, but have roots in historical experience; they cannot always be demanded for any society at any time, but must be nurtured and facilitated. We must avoid the arbitrary projection of Anglo-Saxon democratic forms onto different cultures. Instead of democratic capitalisms we should anticipate more or less authoritarian variants of socialism and collectivism in many emergent societies.

But we do not abandon our critical faculties. Insofar as these regimes represent a genuine realization of national independence, and are engaged in constructing social systems which allow for personal meaning and purpose where once exploitation was, economic systems which work for the people where once they oppressed them, and political systems which allow for the organization and expression of minority opinion and dissent, we recognize their revolutionary and positive character. Americans can contribute to the growth of democracy in such societies not by moralizing, nor by indiscriminate prejudgment, but by retaining a critical identification with these nations, and by helping them to avoid external threats to their independence. Together with students and radicals in these nations we need to develop a reasonable theory of democracy which is concretely applicable to the cultures and conditions of hungry people.

TOWARDS AMERICAN DEMOCRACY

Every effort to end the Cold War and expand the process of world industrialization is an effort hostile to people and institutions whose interests lie in perpetuation of the East-West military threat and the postponement of change in the "have not" nations of the world. Every such effort, too, is bound to establish greater democracy in America. The major goals of a domestic effort would be:

1. America must abolish its political party stalemate.

Two genuine parties, centered around issues and essential values, demanding allegiance to party principles shall supplant the current system of organized stalemate which is seriously inadequate to a world in flux. It has long been argued that the very overlapping of American parties guarantees that issues will be considered responsibly, that progress will be gradual instead of intemperate, and that therefore America will remain stable instead of torn by class strife. On the contrary: the enormous party overlap itself confuses issues and makes responsible presentation of choice to the electorate impossible, guarantees Congressional listlessness and the drift of power to military and economic bureaucracies, directs attention away from the more fundamental causes of social stability, such as huge middle class, Keynesian economic techniques, and Madison Avenue advertising. The ideals of political democracy, then, the imperative need for flexible decision-making apparatus make a real two-party system an immediate social necessity. What is desirable is sufficient party disagreement to dramatize major issues, yet sufficient party overlap to guarantee stable transitions from administration to administration.

Every time the President criticizes a recalcitrant Congress, we must ask that he no longer tolerate the Southern conservatives in the Democratic Party. Every time a liberal representative complains that "we can't expect everything at once" we must ask if we received much of anything from Congress in the last generation. Every time he refers to "circumstances beyond control" we must ask why he fraternizes with racist scoundrels. Every time he speaks of the "unpleasantness of personal and party fighting" we should insist that pleasantry with Dixiecrats is inexcusable when the dark peoples of the world call for American support.

2. Mechanisms of voluntary association must be created through which political information can be imparted and political participation encouraged.

Political parties, even if realigned, would not provide adequate outlets for popular involvement. Institutions should be created that engage people with issues and express political preference, not as now with huge business lobbies which exercise undemocratic *power*, but which carry political *influence* (appropriate to private, rather than public, groupings) in national decision-making enterprise. Private in nature, these should be organized around single issues (medical care, transportation systems reform, etc.), concrete interest (labor and minority group organizations), multiple issues, or general issues. These do not exist in America in quantity today. If they did exist, they would be a significant politicizing and educative force bringing people in touch with public life and affording them means of expression and action. Today, giant lobby representatives of business interests are dominant, but not educative. The Federal government itself should counter the latter forces whose intent is often public deceit for private gain, by subsidizing the preparation and decentralized distribution of objective materials on all public issues facing government.

3. Institutions and practices which stifle dissent should be abolished, and the promotion of peaceful dissent should be actively promoted.

The First Amendment freedoms of speech, assembly, thought, religion and press should be seen as guarantees, not threats, to national security. While society has the right to prevent active subversion of its laws and institutions, it has the duty as well to promote open discussion of all issues—otherwise it will be in fact promoting real subversion as the only means of implementing ideas. To eliminate the fears and apathy from national life it is necessary that the institutions bred by fear and apathy be rooted out: the House Un-American Activities Committee, the Senate Internal Security Committee, the loyalty oaths on Federal loans, the Attorney General's list of subversive organizations, the Smith and McCarran Acts. The process of eliminating the blighting institutions is the process of restoring democratic participation. Their existence is a sign of the decomposition and atrophy of participation.

4. Corporations must be made publicly responsible.

It is not possible to believe that true democracy can exist where a minority utterly controls enormous wealth and power. The influence of corporate elites on foreign policy is neither reliable nor democratic; a way must be found to subordinate private American foreign investment to a democratically constructed foreign policy. The influence of the same giants on domestic life is intolerable as well; a way must be found to direct our economic resources to genuine human needs, not the private needs of corporations nor the rigged needs of maneuvered citizenry.

We can no longer rely on competition of the many to insure that business enterprise is responsive to social needs. The many have become the few. Nor can we trust the corporate bureaucracy to be socially responsible or to develop a "corporate conscience" that is democratic. The community of interest of corporations, the anarchic actions of industrial leaders should become structurally responsible to the people—and truly to the people rather than to an ill-defined and questionable "national interest." Labor and government as presently constituted are not sufficient to "regulate" corporations. A new re-ordering, a new calling of responsibility is necessary: more than changing "work rules" we must consider changes in the rules of society by challenging the unchallenged politics of American corporations. Before the government can really begin to control business in a "public interest," the public must gain more substantial control of government: this demands a movement for political as well as economic realignments. We are aware that simple government "regulation," if achieved, would be inadequate without increased worker participation in management decision-making, strengthened and independent regulatory power, balances of partial and/or complete public ownership, various means of humanizing the conditions and types of work itself, sweeping welfare programs, and regional *public* development authorities. These are examples of measures to re-balance the economy toward public—and individual—control.

5. The allocation of resources must be based on social needs. A truly "public sector" must be established, and its nature debated and planned.

At present the majority of America's "public sector," the largest part of our public spending, is for the military. When great social needs are so pressing, our concept of "government spending" is wrapped up in the "permanent war economy."

In fact, if war is to be avoided, the "permanent war economy" must be seen as an "*interim* war economy." At some point, America must return to other mechanisms of economic growth besides public military spending. We must plan economically in peace. The most likely, and least desirable, return would be in the form of private enterprise. The undesirability lies in the fact of inherent capitalist instability, noticeable even with the bolstering effects of government intervention. In the most recent post-war recessions, for example, private expenditures for plant and equipment dropped from $16 billion to $11.5 billion, while unemployment surged to nearly 6 million. By good fortune, investments in construction industries remained level, else an economic depression would have occurred. This will recur, and our growth in national per capita living standards will remain unsensational, while the economy stagnates.

The main *private* forces of economic expansion cannot guarantee a steady rate of growth, nor acceptable recovery from recession—especially in a demilitarizing world. Government participation will inevitably expand enormously, because the stable growth of the economy demands increasing "public" investments yearly. Our present outpour of more than $500 billion might double in a generation, irreversibly involving government solutions. And in future recessions, the compensatory fiscal action by the government will be the only means of avoiding the twin disasters of greater unemployment and a slackening rate of growth. Furthermore, a close relationship with the European Common Market will involve competition with numerous planned economies and may aggravate American unemployment unless the economy here is expanding swiftly enough to create new jobs.

All these tendencies suggest that not only solutions to our present social needs but our future expansion rests upon our willingness to enlarge the "public sector" greatly. Unless we choose war as an economic solvent, future public spending will be of a non-military nature—a major intervention into civilian production by the government. The issues posed by this development are enormous:

A. How should public vs. private domain be determined? We suggest these criteria: 1) when a resource has been discovered or developed with public tax revenues, such as a space communications system, it should remain a public resource, not be given away to private enterprise; 2) when monopolization seems inevitable, the public should maintain control of an industry; 3) when national objectives conflict seriously with business objectives as to the use of the resource, the public need should prevail.

B. How should technological advances be introduced into a society? By a public process, based on publicly determined needs. Technological innovations should not be postponed from social use by private corporations in order to protect investment in older equipment.

C. How shall the "public sector" be made public, and not the arena of a ruling bureaucracy of "public servants"? By steadfast opposition to bureaucratic coagulation, and to definitions of human needs according to problems easiest for computers to solve. Second, the bureaucratic pile-ups must be at least minimized by local, regional, and national economic *planning*—responding to the interconnection of public problems by comprehensive programs. Third, and most important, by experiments in *decentralization*, based on the vision of man as master of his machines and his society. The personal capacity to cope with life has been reduced everywhere by the introduction of technology that only minorities of men (barely) understand. How the process can be reversed—and we believe it can be—is one of the greatest sociological and economic tasks before human people today. Polytechnical schooling, with the individual adjusting to several work and life experiences, is one method. The transfer of certain mechanized tasks back into manual forms, allowing men to make whole, not partial, products, is not unimaginable. Our monster cities, based historically on the need for mass labor, might now be humanized, broken into smaller communities, powered by nuclear energy, arranged according to community decision. These are but a fraction of the opportunities of the new era: serious study and deliberate experimentation, rooted in a desire for human fraternity, may now result in blueprints of civic paradise.

6. America should concentrate on its genuine social priorities: abolish squalor, terminate neglect, and establish an environment for people to live in with dignity and creativeness.

A. A program against *poverty* must be just as sweeping as the nature of poverty itself. It must not be just palliative, but directed to the abolition of the structural circumstances of poverty. At a bare minimum it should include a *housing* act far larger than the one supported by the Kennedy administration, but one that is geared more to low- and middle-income needs than to the windfall aspirations of small and large private entrepreneurs, one that is more sympathetic to the quality of communal life than to the efficiency of city-split highways. Second, *medical care* must become recognized as a lifetime human right just as vital as food, shelter, and clothing—the Federal government should guarantee health insurance as a basic social service, turning medical treatment into a social habit, not just an occasion of crisis, fighting sickness among the aged, not just by making medical care financially feasible, but by reducing sickness among children and younger people. Third, existing institutions should be expanded so the welfare state cares for *everyone's* welfare according to need. *Social Security* payments should be extended to everyone and should be proportionately greater for the poorest. A *minimum wage* of at least $1.50 should be extended to all workers (including the 16 million currently not covered at all). Programs for equal *educational opportunity* are as important a part of the battle against poverty.
B. A full-scale public initiative for civil rights should be undertaken despite the clamor among conservatives (and liberals) about gradualism, property rights, and law and order. The executive and legislative branches of the Federal government should work by enforcement *and* enactment against any form of exploitation of minority groups. No Federal cooperation with racism is tolerable—from financing of schools, to the development of Federally supported industry, to the social gatherings of the President. Laws hastening school desegregation, voting rights, and economic protection for Negroes are needed right now. The moral force of the Executive Office should be exerted against the Dixiecrats specifically, and the national complacency about the race question generally. Especially in the North, where one-half of the country's Negro people now live, civil rights is not a problem to be solved in isolation from other problems. The fight against poverty, against slums, against the stalemated Congress, against McCarthyism are all fights against the discrimination that is nearly endemic to all areas of American life.
C. The promise and problems of long-range *Federal economic development* should be studied more constructively. It is an embarrassing paradox that the Tennessee Valley Authority is a wonder to most foreign visitors but a "radical" and barely influential project to most Americans. The Kennedy decision to permit private facilities to transmit power from the

$1 billion Colorado River Storage Project is a disastrous one, interposing privately owned transmitters between publicly owned generators and their publicly (and cooperatively) owned distributors. The contrary trend, to public ownership of power, should be generated in an experimental way.

The Area Redevelopment Act of 1961 is a first step in recognizing the underdeveloped areas of the United States. It is only a drop in the bucket financially and is not keyed to public planning and public works on a broad scale. It consists only of a few loan programs to lure industries and some grants to improve public facilities to lure these industries. The current public works bill in Congress is needed—and a more sweeping, higher-priced program of regional development with a proliferation of "TVA's" in such areas as the Appalachian region are needed desperately. However, it has been rejected already by Mississippi because of the improvement it bodes for the unskilled Negro worker. This program should be enlarged, given teeth, and pursued rigorously by Federal authorities.

D. We must meet the growing complex of "city" problems; over 90 percent of Americans will live in urban areas within two decades. Juvenile delinquency, untended mental illness, crime increase, slums, urban tenantry and non-rent-controlled housing, the isolation of the individual in the city—all are problems of the city and are major symptoms of the present system of economic priorities and lack of public planning. Private property control (the real estate lobby and a few selfish landowners and businesses) is as devastating in the cities as corporations are on the national level. But there is no comprehensive way to deal with these problems now amidst competing units of government, dwindling tax resources, suburban escapism (saprophitic to the sick central cities), high infrastructure costs and no one to pay them.

The only solutions are national and regional. "Federalism" has thus far failed here because states are rural-dominated; the Federal government has had to operate by bootlegging and trickle-down measures dominated by private interests, with their appendages through annexation or federation. A new external challenge is needed, not just a Department of Urban Affairs but a thorough national *program* to help the cities. The *model* city must be projected—more community decision-making and participation, true integration of classes, races, vocations—provision for beauty, access to nature and the benefits of the central city as well, privacy without privatism, decentralized "units" spread horizontally with central, regional democratic control—provision for the basic facility needs, for everyone, with units of planned *regions* and thus public, democratic control over the growth of the civic community and the allocation of resources.

E. *Mental health* institutions are in dire need; there were fewer mental hospital *beds* in relation to the numbers of mentally ill in 1959 than there were in 1948. Public hospitals, too, are seriously wanting; existing structures alone need an estimated $1 billion for rehabilitation. Tremendous staff and faculty needs exist as well, and there are not enough medical students enrolled today to meet the anticipated needs of the future.

F. Our *prisons* are too often the enforcers of misery. They must either be re-oriented to rehabilitative work through public supervision or be abolished for their dehumanizing social effects. Funds are needed, too, to make possible a decent prison environment.

G. *Education* is too vital a public problem to be completely entrusted to the province of the various states and local units. In fact, there is no good reason why America should not progress now toward internationalizing, rather than localizing, its education system—children and young adults studying everywhere in the world, through a United Nations program, would go far to create mutual understanding. In the meantime, the need for teachers and classrooms in America is fantastic. This is an area where "minimal" requirements should hardly be considered as a goal—there always are improvements to be made in the education system, e.g., smaller classes and many more teachers for them, programs to subsidize the education for the poor but bright, etc.

H. America should eliminate *agricultural policies* based on scarcity and pent-up surplus. In America and foreign countries there exist tremendous needs for more food and balanced diets. The Federal government should finance small farmers' cooperatives, strengthen programs of rural electrification, and expand policies for the distribution of agricultural surpluses throughout the world (by Food for Peace and related UN programming). Marginal farmers must either be helped to become productive enough to survive "industrialized agriculture" or given help in making the transition out of agriculture—the current Rural Area Development program must be better coordinated with a massive national "area redevelopment" program.

I. *Science* should be employed to constructively transform the conditions of life throughout the United States and the world. Yet at the present time the Department of Health, Education, and Welfare and the National Science Foundation together spend only $300 million annually for scientific purposes, in contrast to the $6 billion spent by the Defense Department and the Atomic Energy Commission. One half of all research and development in America is directly devoted to military purposes. Two imbalances must be corrected—that of military over nonmilitary investigation, and that of biological-natural-physical science over the sciences of human behavior. Our political system must then include planning for the human use of science: by anticipating the political consequences of scientific innovation, by directing the discovery and exploration of space; by adapting science to improved production of food, to international communications systems, to technical problems of disarmament, and so on. For the newly developing nations, American science should focus on the study of cheap sources of power, housing and building materials, mass educational techniques, etc. Further, science and scholarship should be seen less as an apparatus of conflicting power blocs, but as a bridge toward supra-national community: the International Geophysical Year is a model for continuous further cooperation between the science communities of all nations.

ALTERNATIVES TO HELPLESSNESS

The goals we have set are not realizable next month, or even next election—but that fact justifies neither giving up altogether nor a determination to work only on immediate, direct, tangible problems. Both responses are a sign of helplessness, fearfulness of vision, refusal to hope, and tend to bring on the very conditions to be avoided. Fearing vision, we justify rhetoric or myopia. Fearing hope, we reinforce despair.

The first effort, then, should be to state a vision: what is the perimeter of human possibility in this epoch? This we have tried to do. The second effort, if we are to be politically responsible, is to evaluate the prospects for obtaining at least a substantial part of that vision in our epoch: what are the social forces that exist, or that must exist, if we are to be at all successful? And what role have we ourselves to play as a social force?

1. In exploring the existing social forces, note must be taken of the Southern civil rights movement as the most heartening because of the justice it insists upon, exemplary because it indicates that there can be a passage out of apathy.

This movement, pushed into a brilliant new phase by the Montgomery bus boycott and the subsequent nonviolent action of the sit-ins and Freedom Rides, has had three major results: first a sense of self-determination has been instilled in millions of oppressed Negroes; second, the movement has challenged a few thousand liberals to new social idealism; third, a series of important concessions have been obtained, such as token school desegregation, increased Administration help, new laws, desegregation of some public facilities.

But fundamental social change—that would break the props from under Jim Crow—has not come. Negro employment opportunity, wage levels, housing conditions, educational privileges—these remain deplorable and relatively constant, each deprivation reinforcing the impact of the others. The Southern states, in the meantime, are strengthening the fortresses of the status quo, and are beginning to camouflage the fortresses by guile where open bigotry announced its defiance before. The white-controlled one-party system remains intact; and even where the Republicans are beginning, under the pressures of industrialization in the towns and suburbs, to show initiative in fostering a two-party system, all Southern state Republican committees (save Georgia) have adopted militant segregationist platforms to attract Dixiecrats.

Rural dominance remains a fact in nearly all the Southern states, although the reapportionment decision of the Supreme Court portends future power shifts to the cities. Southern politicians maintain a continuing aversion to the welfare legislation that would aid their people. The reins of the Southern economy are held by conservative businessmen who view human rights as secondary to property rights. A violent anti-communism is rooting itself in the South, and threatening even moderate voices. Add the militaristic tradition of the South, and its irrational regional mystique, and one must conclude that authoritarian and reactionary tendencies are a rising obstacle to the small, voiceless, poor, and isolated democratic movements.

The civil rights struggle thus has come to an impasse. To this impasse, the movement responded this year by entering the sphere of politics, insisting on citizenship rights, specifically the right to vote. The new voter-registration stage of protest represents perhaps the first major attempt to exercise the conventional instruments of political democracy in the struggle for racial justice. The vote, if used strategically by the great mass of now-unregistered Negroes, theoretically eligible to vote, will be a decisive factor in changing the quality of Southern leadership from low demagoguery to decent statesmanship.

More important, the new emphasis on the vote heralds the use of *political* means to solve the problems of equality in America, and it signals the decline of the shortsighted view that "discrimination" can be isolated from related social problems. Since the moral clarity of the civil rights movement has not always been accompanied by precise political vision, and sometimes not even by a real political consciousness, the new phase is revolutionary in its implications. The intermediate goal of the program is to secure and insure a healthy respect and realization of Constitutional liberties. This is important not only to terminate the civil and private abuses which currently characterize the region, but also to prevent the pendulum of oppression from simply swinging to an alternate extreme with a new unsophisticated electorate, after the unhappy example of the last Reconstruction. It is the *ultimate* objectives of the strategy which promise profound change in the politics of the nation. An increased Negro voting rate in and of itself is not going to dislodge racist controls of the Southern power structure; but an accelerating movement through the courts, the ballot boxes, and especially the jails is the most likely means of shattering the crust of political intransigency and creating a semblance of democratic order on local and state levels.

Linked with pressure from Northern liberals to expunge the Dixiecrats from the ranks of the Democratic party, massive Negro voting in the South could destroy the vise-like grip reactionary Southerners have on the Congressional legislative process.

2. The broadest movement for *peace* in several years emerged in 1961–62. In its political orientation and goals it is much less identifiable than the movement for civil rights: it includes socialists, pacifists, liberals, scholars, militant activists, middle-class women, some professionals, many students, a few unionists. Some have been emotionally single-issue: Ban the Bomb. Some have been academically obscurantist. Some have rejected the System (sometimes both systems). Some have attempted, also, to "work within" the system. Amidst these conflicting streams of emphasis, however, certain basic qualities appear. The most important is that the "peace movement" has operated almost exclusively through peripheral institutions—almost never through mainstream institutions. Similarly, individuals interested in peace have nonpolitical social roles that cannot be turned to the support of peace activity. Concretely, liberal religious societies, anti-war groups, voluntary associations, and ad hoc committees have been the political units of the peace movement; and its human movers have been students, teachers, housewives, secretaries, lawyers, doctors, clergy. The units have not been located in spots of major social influence; the people have not been able to turn their resources fully to the issues that concern them. The results are political ineffectiveness and personal alienation.

The organizing ability of the peace movement thus is limited to the ability to state and polarize issues. It does not have an institution or a forum in which the conflicting interests can be debated. The debate goes on in corners; it has little connection with the continuing process of determining allocations of resources. This process is not necessarily centralized, however much of the peace movement is estranged from it. National policy, though dominated to a large degree by the "power elites" of the corporations and the military, is still partially founded in consensus. It can be altered when there actually begins a shift in the allocation of resources and the listing of priorities by the people in the institutions which have social influence, e.g., the labor unions and the schools. As long as the debates of the peace movement form only a protest, rather than an opposition viewpoint within the centers of serious decision-making, then it is neither a movement of democratic relevance, nor is it likely to have any effectiveness except in educating more outsiders to the issue. It is vital, to be sure, that this educating go on (a heartening sign is the recent proliferation of books and journals dealing with peace and war from newly developing countries); the possibilities for making politicians responsible to "peace constituencies" become greater.

But in the long interim before the national political climate is more open to deliberate, goal-directed debate about peace issues, the dedicated peace "movement" might well prepare a *local base*, especially by establishing civic commit-

tees on the techniques of converting from military to peacetime production. To
make war and peace *relevant* to the problems of everyday life, by relating it to
the backyard (shelters), the baby (fallout), the job (military contracts)—and making a turn toward peace seem desirable on these same terms—is a task the peace
movement is just beginning and can profitably continue.

3. Central to any analysis of the potential for change must be an appraisal of
organized labor. It would be ahistorical to disregard the immense influence of
labor in making modern America a decent place in which to live. It would be
confused to fail to note labor's presence today as the most liberal of mainstream
institutions. But it would be irresponsible not to criticize labor for losing much
of the idealism that once made it a driving movement. Those who expected a
labor upsurge after the 1955 AFL-CIO merger can only be dismayed that one
year later, in the Stevenson-Eisenhower campaign, the AFL-CIO Committee on
Political Education was able to obtain solicited $1.00 contributions from only
one of every 24 unionists, and prompt only 40 percent of the rank-and-file to
vote.

As a political force, labor generally has been unsuccessful in the post-war
period of prosperity. It has seen the passage of the Taft-Hartley and Landrum-
Griffin laws, and while beginning to receive slightly favorable National Labor
Relations Board rulings, it has made little progress against right-to-work laws.
Furthermore, it has seen less than adequate action on domestic problems, especially unemployment.

This labor "recession" has been only partly due to anti-labor politicians and
corporations. Blame should be laid, too, to labor itself for not mounting an
adequate movement. Labor has too often seen itself as elitist, rather than mass-
oriented, and as a pressure group rather than as an 18-million-member body
making political demands for all America. In the first instance, the labor bureaucracy tends to be cynical towards, or afraid of, rank-and-file involvement in
the work of the union. Resolutions passed at conventions are implemented only
by high-level machinations, not by mass mobilization of the unionists. Without
a significant base, labor's pressure function is materially reduced since it becomes difficult to hold political figures accountable to a movement that cannot
muster a vote from a majority of its members.

There are some indications, however, that labor might regain its missing
idealism. First, there are signs within the movement: of workers' discontent
with their economic progress, of collective bargaining, of occasional splits
among union leaders on questions such as nuclear testing or other Cold War
issues. Second, and more important, are the social forces which prompt these
feelings of unrest. Foremost is the permanence of unemployment, and the threat
of automation. But important, too, is the growth of unorganized ranks in white-
collar fields. Third, there is the tremendous challenge of the Negro movement
for support from organized labor: the alienation from and disgust with labor
hypocrisy among Negroes ranging from the NAACP to the Black Muslims (crystallized in the formation of the Negro American Labor Council) indicates that
labor must move more seriously in its attempts to organize on an interracial
basis in the South and in large urban centers. When this task was broached
several years ago, "jurisdictional" disputes prevented action. Today, many of
these disputes have been settled—and the question of a massive organizing
campaign is on the labor agenda again.

These threats and opportunities point to a profound crisis: either labor will
continue to decline as a social force, or it must constitute itself as a mass
political force demanding not only that society recognize its rights to organize

but also a program going beyond desired labor legislation and welfare improvements. Necessarily this latter role will require rank-and-file involvement. It might include greater autonomy and power for political coalitions of the various trade unions in local areas, rather than the more stultifying dominance of the international unions now. It might include reductions in leaders' salaries, or rotation from executive office to shop obligations, as a means of breaking down the hierarchical tendencies which have detached elite from base and made the highest echelons of labor more like businessmen than workers. It would certainly mean an announced independence of the center and Dixiecrat wings of the Democratic Party, and a massive organizing drive, especially in the South to complement the growing Negro political drive there.

A new politics must include a revitalized labor movement: a movement which sees itself, and is regarded by others, as a major leader of the breakthrough to a politics of hope and vision. Labor's role is no less unique or important to the needs of the future than it was in the past; its numbers and potential political strength, its natural interest in the abolition of exploitation, its reach to the grass roots of American society combine to make it the best candidate for the synthesis of the civil rights, peace, and economic reform movements.

The creation of bridges is made more difficult by the problems left over from the generation of "silence." Middle-class students, still the main actors in the embryonic upsurge, have yet to overcome their ignorance, and even vague hostility, for what they see as "middle class labor" bureaucrats. Students must open the campus to labor through publications, action programs, curricula, while labor opens its house to students through internships, requests for aid (on the picket line, with handbills, in the public dialogue), and politics. And the organization of the campus can be a beginning—teachers' unions can be advocated as both socially progressive and educationally beneficial; university employees can be organized—and thereby an important element in the education of the student radical.

But the new politics is still contained; it struggles below the surface of apathy, awaiting liberation. Few anticipate the breakthrough and fewer still exhort labor to begin. Labor continues to be the most liberal—and most frustrated—institution in mainstream America.

4. Since the Democratic Party sweep in 1958, there have been exaggerated but real efforts to establish a liberal force in Congress, not to balance but to at least voice criticism of the conservative mood. The most notable of these efforts was the Liberal Project begun early in 1959 by Representative Kastenmeier of Wisconsin. The Project was neither disciplined nor very influential, but it was concerned at least with confronting basic domestic and foreign problems, in concert with several liberal intellectuals.

In 1960 five members of the Project were defeated at the polls (for reasons other than their membership in the Project). Then followed a "post mortem" publication of *The Liberal Papers*, materials discussed by the Project when it was in existence. Republican leaders called the book "further out than Communism." The New Frontier administration repudiated any connection with the statements. Some former members of the Project even disclaimed their past roles.

A hopeful beginning came to a shameful end. But during the demise of the Project, a new spirit of Democratic Party reform was occurring: in New York City, Ithaca, Massachusetts, Connecticut, Texas, California, and even in Mississippi and Alabama, where Negro candidates for Congress challenged racist political power. Some were for peace, some for the liberal side of the New

Frontier, some for realignment of the parties—and in most cases they were supported by students.

Here and there were stirrings of organized discontent with the political stalemate. Americans for Democratic Action and the *New Republic*, pillars of the liberal community, took stands against the president on nuclear testing. A split, extremely slight thus far, developed in organized labor on the same issue. The Rev. Martin Luther King, Jr., preached against the Dixiecrat-Republican coalition across the nation.

5. From 1960 to 1962, the campuses experienced a revival of idealism among an active few. Triggered by the impact of the sit-ins, students began to struggle for integration, civil liberties, student rights, peace, and against the fast-rising right-wing "revolt" as well. The liberal students, too, have felt their urgency thwarted by conventional channels: from student governments to Congressional committees. Out of this alienation from existing channels has come the creation of new ones; the most characteristic forms of liberal-radical student organizations are the dozens of campus political parties, political journals, and peace marches and demonstrations. In only a few cases have students built bridges to power: an occasional election campaign; the sit-ins, Freedom Rides, and voter-registration activities; some relatively large Northern demonstrations for peace and civil rights; and infrequently, through the United States National Student Association, whose notable work has not been focused on political change.

These contemporary social movements—for peace, civil rights, civil liberties, labor—have in common certain values and goals. The fight for peace is one for a stable and racially integrated world; for an end to the inherently volatile exploitation of most of mankind by irresponsible elites; and for freedom of economic, political, and cultural organization. The fight for civil rights is also one for social welfare for all Americans; for free speech and the right to protest; for the shield of economic independence and bargaining power; for the reduction of the arms race, which takes national attention and resources away from the problems of domestic injustices. Labor's fight for jobs and wages is also one against exploitation of the Negro as a source of cheap labor; for the right of petition and strike; for world industrialization; for the stability of a peacetime economy instead of the instability of a wartime economy; for expansion of the welfare state. The fight for a liberal Congress is a fight for a platform from which these concerns can issue. And the fight for students, for internal democracy in the university, is a fight to gain a forum for the issues.

But these scattered movements have more in common: a need for their concerns to be expressed by a political party responsible to their interests. That they have no political expression, no political channels, can be traced in large measure to the existence of a Democratic Party which tolerates the perverse unity of liberalism and racism, prevents the social change wanted by Negroes, peace protesters, labor unions, students, reform Democrats, and other liberals. Worse, the party stalemate prevents even the raising of controversy—a full Congressional assault on racial discrimination, disengagement in Central Europe, sweeping urban reform, disarmament and inspection, public regulation of major industries; these and other issues are never heard in the body that is supposed to represent the best thoughts and interests of all Americans.

An imperative task for these publicly disinherited groups, then, is to demand a Democratic Party responsible to their interests. They must support Southern voter registration and Negro political candidates and demand that Democratic Party liberals do the same (in the last Congress, Dixiecrats split with Northern

Democrats on 119 of 300 roll calls, mostly on civil rights, area redevelopment, and foreign-aid bills; the breach was much larger than in the previous several sessions). Labor (either independent or Democratic) should be formed to run against big-city regimes on such issues as peace, civil rights, and urban needs. Demonstrations should be held at every Congressional or convention seating of Dixiecrats. A massive publicity and research campaign should be initiated, showing to every housewife, doctor, professor, and worker the damage done to their interests every day a racist occupies a place in the Democratic Party. Where possible, the peace movement should challenge the "peace credentials" of the otherwise-liberals by threatening or actually running candidates against them.

The University and Social Change

There is perhaps little reason to be optimistic about the above analysis. True, the Dixiecrat-GOP coalition is the weakest point in the dominating complex of corporate, military, and political power. But the civil rights, peace, and student movements are too poor and socially slighted, and the labor movement too quiescent, to be counted with enthusiasm. From where else can power and vision be summoned? We believe that the universities are an overlooked seat of influence.

First, the university is located in a permanent position of social influence. Its educational function makes it indispensable and automatically makes it a crucial institution in the formation of social attitudes. Second, in an unbelievably complicated world, it is the central institution for organizing, evaluating, and transmitting knowledge. Third, the extent to which academic resources presently are used to buttress immoral social practice is revealed, first, by the extent to which defense contracts make the universities engineers of the arms race. Too, the use of modern social science as a manipulative tool reveals itself in the "human relations" consultants to the modern corporations, who introduce trivial sops to give laborers feelings of "participation" or "belonging," while actually deluding them in order to further exploit their labor. And, of course, the use of motivational research is already infamous as a manipulative aspect of American politics. But these social uses of the universities' resources also demonstrate the unchangeable reliance by men of power on the men and storehouses of knowledge: this makes the university functionally tied to society in new ways, revealing new potentialities, new levers for change. Fourth, the university is the only mainstream institution that is open to participation by individuals of nearly any viewpoint.

These, at least, are facts, no matter how dull the teaching, how paternalistic the rules, how irrelevant the research that goes on. Social relevance, the accessibility to knowledge, and internal openness—these together make the university a potential base and agency in a movement of social change.

1. Any new left in America must be, in large measure, a left with real intellectual skills, committed to deliberativeness, honesy, reflection as working tools. The university permits the political life to be an adjunct to the academic one, and action to be informed by reason.

2. A new left must be distributed in significant social roles throughout the country. The universities are distributed in such a manner.

3. A new left must consist of younger people who matured in the post-war world, and partially be directed to the recruitment of younger people. The university is an obvious beginning point.

4. A new left must include liberals and socialists, the former for their rele-

vance, the latter for their sense of thoroughgoing reforms in the system. The university is a more sensible place than a political party for these two traditions to begin to discuss their differences and look for political synthesis.

5. A new left must start controversy across the land, if national policies and national apathy are to be reversed. The ideal university is a community of controversy, within itself and in its effects on communities beyond.

6. A new left must transform modern complexity into issues that can be understood and felt close up by every human being. It must give form to the feelings of helplessness and indifference, so that people may see the political, social, and economic sources of their private troubles and organize to change society. In a time of supposed prosperity, moral complacency, and political manipulation, a new left cannot rely on only aching stomachs to be the engine force of social reform. The case for change, for alternatives that will involve uncomfortable personal efforts, must be argued as never before. The university is a relevant place for all of these activities.

But we need not indulge in illusions: the university system cannot complete a movement of ordinary people making demands for a better life. From its schools and colleges across the nation, a militant left might awaken its allies, and by beginning the process towards peace, civil rights, and labor struggles, reinsert theory and idealism where too often reign confusion and political barter. The power of students and faculty united is not only potential; it has shown its actuality in the South, and in the reform movements of the North.

The bridge to political power, though, will be built through genuine cooperation, locally, nationally, and internationally, between a new left of young people and an awakening community of allies. In each community we must look within the university and act with confidence that we can be powerful, but we must look outwards to the less exotic but more lasting struggles for justice.

To turn these possibilities into realities will involve national efforts at university reform by an alliance of students and faculty. They must wrest control of the educational process from the administrative bureaucracy. They must make fraternal and functional contact with allies in labor, civil rights, and other liberal forces outside the campus. They must import major public issues into the curriculum—research and teaching on problems of war and peace is an outstanding example. They must make debate and controversy, not dull pedantic cant, the common style for educational life. They must consciously build a base for their assault upon the loci of power.

As students for a democratic society, we are committed to stimulating this kind of social movement, this kind of vision and program in campus and community across the country. If we appear to seek the unattainable, as it has been said, then let it be known that we do so to avoid the unimaginable.

A NOTE ON SOURCES

The most important collection of SDS documents, held by the Wisconsin State Historical Society in Madison, is available on microfilm. In quoting from documents included in this microfilm collection, I have cited the relevant series and document section numbers. The other major source of SDS documents, particularly for the period prior to 1965, is the Tamiment Library of Labor History at New York University. In several cases, I have also had access to papers held privately by the individuals I was interviewing, which I have noted accordingly. One caveat: if a footnote cites a document from a private collection of papers, that does not necessarily mean that the document is unavailable in the Wisconsin State Historical Society collection; whenever possible, I cite the microfilm location of a document, but under the pressure of my publishing deadline, I have been unable to cross-check the public availability of every reference.

An invaluable source for the New Left in Ann Arbor is the oral-history project on this topic supervised by Bret Eynon in the late Seventies; the vivid and intimate sense of a small circle of friends conveyed through Eynon's interviews helped me enormously in focusing my own biographical approach. Since Eynon is planning his own book based on this material, it cannot be quoted directly; but scholars may consult his interview transcripts in the "Contemporary History Project" in the Michigan Historical Collections, Bentley Historical Library, University of Michigan. Another important source, Tom Hayden's articles and editorials for *The Michigan Daily*, can be consulted on microfilm in the University of Michigan's main library.

My own interviews were conducted between 1984 and 1986. Anticipating a need to refresh memories, I generally brought along to each interview some of the primary source material. In some cases, this precaution proved unnecessary; in other cases, the prompting was essential. For example, when I showed Tom Hayden some of his draft notes from 1962 on the idea of democracy, he gazed at the page with faint recognition. "I haven't seen these in twenty-five years," he said after a long pause; "I obviously pulled together an enormous amount of stuff." The limits of oral testimony in such cases are obvious. Still, I was often surprised by the sharpness of recollections, particularly when measured against contemporary documents, which of course remained my primary source whenever they were available. In a further effort to achieve accuracy, I sent a draft of my manuscript to everyone I interviewed, soliciting corrections and second thoughts, which I have incorporated into the final text where relevant. The forthrightness of my subjects will, I think, speak for itself.

Tom Hayden presents a special case. I interviewed him on five separate occasions, including two sessions held, at his request, after he had read a draft of the finished manuscript. On all these occasions, he spoke as an elected official as well as a figure in the history I was trying to reconstruct. Under the circumstances, his comments on some sensitive issues were understandably circumspect. However, of all my subjects, Hayden has written the most and said the most, in interviews that he has granted with some frequency since 1967. And of all my subjects, Hayden went out of his way to help me the most. In addition to arranging two extra interview sessions (one of them with Richard and Mickey Flacks present), he sent me detailed remarks on my manuscript, returning his copy with a number of marginal comments. I have gratefully incorporated new material from all these sources into my narrative where it seemed appropriate; quotations from notes that Hayden wrote on the margin of my manuscript are identified as "Hayden's marginal comments." Some of this material posed a dilemma, however. Hayden's comments in a few instances, particularly in matters relating to the demonstrations in Chicago in August, 1968, called into question the accuracy of contemporary newspaper reports. As I know from firsthand experience, journalists working without a tape recorder can easily misquote somebody. But as a historian, I am generally inclined to place more stock in contemporary reports; in several cases, I have decided to stick with the primary sources, while registering Hayden's objections in my end notes. Hayden also wished on a few occasions to modify the description of events that he had given in earlier interviews. In some cases, his current version simply added some nuance or texture; in other cases, his differences in perception may reflect a genuine ambivalence that he felt at the time. But I have sometimes been inclined to rely on interviews conducted closer to the events recalled. And at several points, I have decided to offer Hayden's current recollection in my end notes. In this regard, one particular Hayden interview, published in 1972 by *Rolling Stone* magazine, merits special attention. At the time, Hayden was in transition, having lost his faith in the imminence of revolution, without having yet become a professional politician. I have quoted extensively from this particular interview, believing it to be one of the most revealing glimpses of Hayden's experience that we shall have—at least until Hayden himself chooses to publish his memoirs, a draft of which he completed during the Seventies.

The secondary literature on the New Left, though plentiful, is not, on the whole, distinguished. Many of the scholarly studies written in the late Sixties and early Seventies—Kenneth Kenniston's *Young Radicals* is a good example —have not worn well. Much of this early literature is marred by *parti pris* and unexamined assumptions, sometimes liberal, sometimes radical, sometimes conservative. Apart from anthologies, I found a handful of historical accounts to be essential: Kirkpatrick Sale, *SDS* (New York, 1972); Jack Newfield, *A Pro-*

phetic Minority (New York, 1966); Sara Evans, *Personal Politics* (New York, 1979); James Forman, *The Making of Black Revolutionaries* (Washington, D.C., 1985); Clayborne Carson, *In Struggle: SNCC and the Black Awakening of the 1960s* (Cambridge, Mass., 1981); and Nancy Zaroulis and Gerald Sullivan, *Who Spoke Up?: American Protest Against the War in Vietnam, 1963–1975* (New York, 1984). The scholarly interpretations that I found most thought-provoking were Todd Gitlin, *The Whole World Is Watching* (Berkeley, 1981), an exploration of the impact of the mass media on the New Left, filled with shrewd comments and interesting digressions; Wini Breines, *Community and Organization in the New Left, 1962–1968* (New York, 1982), a perceptive and sympathetic account of the New Left's utopian impulse that faithfully transcribes its inner tensions; and Nigel Young, *An Infantile Disorder? The Crisis and Decline of the New Left* (London, 1977), a thoroughly researched study of how the erosion of the New Left's commitment to pacifism helped lead to its self-destruction. In a class by itself is Jane J. Mansbridge, *Beyond Adversary Democracy* (New York, 1980), a book avowedly defending "unitary democracy" that in fact rigorously documents and analyzes some of its most critical flaws.

NOTES

Introduction

1. See, e.g., Allen J. Matusow, *The Unraveling of America: A History of Liberalism in the 1960s* (New York, 1984), pp. 309–13. Matusow's book is a good barometer, for it is an excellent general history, distinguished by solid scholarship and thoughtful analysis. The source for many of the misconceptions about the early New Left seems to be Kirkpatrick Sale, whose *SDS* (New York, 1973) is justifiably regarded as the standard history of the organization. Meticulous in his marshaling of facts—anyone who has had to sift through the SDS archives knows the extent of his accomplishment— Sale was less rigorous in his approach to the theoretical debates through which the New Left understood itself. His interpretation of the early New Left is also marred by a subtle anachronism caused, in part, by Sales's enthusiasm for the rhetoric of revolution, which was still fashionable when he completed his book. Even more misleading is Irwin Unger's widely cited *The Movement: A History of the American New Left, 1959–1972* (New York, 1974); see esp. pp. 54–55, where, without blinking, he declares that *The Port Huron Statement* "echoed . . . old-fashioned libertarians and adherents of the Anarchist Black International" and that the same statement nevertheless "took the student dissenters only a short step beyond the New Deal–Fair Deal–New Frontier tradition." On the left at the time, similar misunderstandings were propagated by neo-Marxists like James Weinstein, who mistook the lack of a Marxist ideology and strategy for the lack of an ideology and strategy *tout court*; see, e.g., Weinstein, *The Decline of Socialism in America, 1912–1925* (New York, 1967), p. vii.
2. Daniel Bell, "Columbia and the New Left," *The Public Interest*, Fall, 1968, pp. 61–101. Tom Hayden, quoted in *Time*, August 15, 1977, p. 67.
3. Sale, *SDS*, p. 69.

Chapter One

1. See Tom Hayden, *Rebellion and Repression* (New York, 1969), pp. 186, 78n. Cf. Milton Viorst, *Fire in the Streets* (New York, 1979), p. 459.

2. Tim Findley, "Tom Hayden: Rolling Stone Interview, Part 2," *Rolling Stone*, November 9, 1972, p. 28.

3. Hayden, *Rebellion and Repression*, p. 34.

4. See Al Haber, "From Protest to Radicalism: An Appraisal of the Student Movement 1960" (originally published in *Venture*, September, 1960), in Mitchell Cohen and Dennis Hale, *The New Student Left* (Boston, 1967), pp. 34–42.

5. Haber interview, 2–28–85; unless otherwise indicated, all subsequent Haber quotations in this chapter come from this interview.

6. Ruth Bordin, *The University of Michigan: A Pictorial History* (Ann Arbor, 1967), pp. 129, 135. *The President's Report for 1958–59* (Ann Arbor, 1959), p. 7.

7. Bordin, *Michigan: A Pictorial History*, pp. 128–29. Allen Matusow, *The Unraveling of America*, p. xiii.

8. Angus T. Campbell, Philip E. Converse, Warren E. Miller and Donald E. Stokes, *The American Voter* (New York, 1960), p. 543.

9. For Boulding, see Morton A. Kaplan, "Systems Analysis: International Systems," in David L. Sills, ed., *International Encyclopedia of the Social Sciences* (New York, 1968), Vol. 15, p. 483.

10. [Harlan Hatcher], "Conclusion of an Unhappy Episode," *The Michigan Alumnus*, Vol. 61, No. 7 (November 13, 1954), p. 78. See also *The Michigan Alumnus*, Vol. 61, No. 3 (October 16, 1954), pp. 17, 25–28. For an extended account of the Davis case—he eventually served six months in prison—see Ellen W. Schrecker, *No Ivory Tower: McCarthyism and the Universities* (New York, 1986), pp. 3–4, 219–34.

11. See Yamada's correspondence with the Student League for Industrial Democracy, esp. letter of 11–29–56; Tamiment.

12. For the history of SLID, see the appendix to Sale, *SDS*, pp. 673–93. For Debs and the republican tradition, see Nick Salvatore, *Eugene V. Debs: Citizen and Socialist* (Urbana, Ill., 1982), esp. pp. 148–55; Debs's allegiance to republican principles was so profound that he hesitated to embrace "socialism" as a word and as a movement.

13. See Harvey Klehr, *The Heyday of American Communism* (New York, 1984), pp. 312–19.

14. Robert T. Yamada to Susan, 12–29–57; Tamiment.

15. Sale, *SDS*, p. 692.

16. Alan Haber to Charles Van Tassel, 7–31–58; Tamiment.

17. Jeffrey interview, 2–26–85; unless otherwise indicated, all subsequent Jeffrey quotations in this chapter come from this interview.

18. "SDS Conference: Human Rights in the North," *Venture*, Vol. 1, No. 4 (Spring, 1960), pp. 10–11. "Act Now . . . To Combat Discrimination in the North," flyer for SDS 1960 Conference for Human Rights in the North, April 28–May 1, 1960; Tamiment.

19. Jeffrey interview, 2–26–85; and see also Bret Eynon's interview with Jeffrey, 10–78, pp. 3, 5, in the "Contemporary History Project"; Michigan Historical Collections, Bentley Historical Library, University of Michigan.

20. Clayborne Carson, *In Struggle: SNCC and the Black Awakening of the 1960s* (Cambridge, Mass., 1981), pp. 9–11, 15. Howell Raines, *My Soul Is*

NOTES FOR PAGES 35–45

Rested: The Story of the Civil Rights Movement in the Deep South (New York, 1983), pp. 75–82. Aldon D. Morris, *The Origins of the Civil Rights Movement* (New York, 1984), pp. 197–99.

21. Thomas Hayden, "This Land Is Your Land ... ," *The Michigan Daily*, March 12, 1960.
22. Hayden interview, 3–6–85. Hayden's marginal comment: "I wanted to become a national or foreign correspondent. I was not ready to make a primary commitment to action."
23. Ross interview, 1–23–85; unless otherwise indicated, all subsequent Ross quotations in this chapter come from this interview.
24. James Farmer, *Lay Bare the Heart* (New York, 1985), pp. 70, 72, 75, 93, 100–102, 117, 119, 175–78, 188, 193–95.
25. Michael Harrington, *Fragments of the Century* (New York, 1973), pp. 1, 8, 18, 20, 36–38, 92–93.
26. Cf. Jack Newfield, *A Prophetic Minority* (London, 1967), p. 130.
27. "Student Radicalism—1960," *SDS Voice*, July, 1960, pp. 1–5.
28. Sale, *SDS*, p. 663.
29. Haber, "From Protest to Radicalism," in Cohen and Hale, *The New Student Left*, pp. 34–42.

Chapter Two
1. Hayden quoted in Steven V. Roberts, "Will Tom Hayden Overcome?," *Esquire*, December, 1968, p. 179. Tim Findley, "Tom Hayden: Rolling Stone Interview, Part 1," *Rolling Stone*, October 26, 1972, p. 38.
2. Gary Wills, review of Tom Hayden's book, *Trial*, in *The New York Times Book Review*, November 8, 1970, p. 8.
3. Hayden interview, 3–6–85.
4. "Tom Hayden's Remarks, June 8, 1982" (on his father's death); Hayden papers. Hayden marginal comments. Also see Roberts, "Will Tom Hayden Overcome?," p. 178. And Joel Kotkin, "Tom Hayden's Manifest Destiny," *Esquire*, May, 1980, p. 40. For Father Coughlin and Royal Oak, see Alan Brinkley, *Voices of Protest* (New York, 1982), esp. pp. 89, 268. *Current Biography*, April, 1976, erroneously gives Hayden's birth date as December 12, 1940.
5. Steve Max interview, 5–7–85.
6. Kotkin, "Hayden's Manifest Destiny," p. 40. The information on his mother's attitude toward Coughlin comes from Hayden's unpublished memoir; Hayden papers.
7. Roberts, "Will Tom Hayden Overcome?," p. 178.
8. Kotkin, "Hayden's Manifest Destiny," p. 40. Roberts, "Will Tom Hayden Overcome?," p. 178.
9. Ibid., p. 178, plus details from Hayden's marginal comments.
10. Hayden interview, 3–6–85. Roberts, "Will Tom Hayden Overcome?," p. 178. Hayden's marginal comment: "My roommate's brother was already planning a political career, but it didn't attract me. He became the governor of Colorado, Dick Lamm."
11. Roberts, "Will Tom Hayden Overcome?," p. 178.
12. Viorst, *Fire in the Streets*, p. 167.

13. Hayden interview, 3–6–85.
14. David Horowitz, *Student* (New York, 1962), p. 39. Horowitz' is the most comprehensive account of the Berkeley student movement in this period.
15. Ibid., pp. 36–37, 41–45.
16. Ibid., pp. 67–81.
17. Findley, "Hayden: Rolling Stone Interview, Part 1," p. 38.
18. Thomas Hayden, "A Niche for Stevenson," *The Michigan Daily*, July 12, 1960. Thomas Hayden, "Youth, Ambivalence Mark Candidate Kennedy," *The Michigan Daily*, July 15, 1960. Thomas Hayden, "Student Movements: Common Goal," *The Michigan Daily*, July 9, 1960. For the civil rights demonstration, see Thomas Hayden, "To Back Stiff Rights Plank," *The Michigan Daily*, July 12, 1960.
19. Hayden interview, 3–6–85.
20. Thomas Hayden, "American Student Requires Value Stimulation," *The Michigan Daily*, August 6, 1960.
21. Findley, "Hayden: Rolling Stone Interview, Part 1," p. 40.
22. Tom Hayden, "NSA Congress—A Post Mortem," *Common Sense*, Vol. 4, No. 1 (October 13, 1962), p. 14; Max papers. The NSA–CIA connection was first revealed by *Ramparts* magazine in its February, 1967 issue.
23. "SNCC Founding Statement," in Massimo Teodori, ed., *The New Left: A Documentary History* (Indianapolis, 1969), pp. 99–100. For Sandra Cason's background, see Sara Evans, *Personal Politics* (New York, 1979), esp. pp. 33–34.
24. See Bret Eynon's interview with Hayden, 9–29–78, in the "Contemporary History Project"; Michigan Historical Collections, Bentley Historical Library, University of Michigan.
25. Viorst, *Fire in the Streets*, p. 172.
26. Thomas Hayden, "Why This Erupting Generation?," *The Michigan Daily*, September 22, 1960.
27. Thomas Hayden, "New Student Action in a World of Crisis," *The Michigan Daily*, September 16, 1960. Hayden, "Why This Erupting Generation?"
28. Hayden, "New Student Action in a World of Crisis." Albert Camus, *The Rebel*, trans. Anthony Bower (New York, 1956), p. 285. Cf. Albert Camus, *The Myth of Sisyphus*, trans. Justin O'Brien (New York, 1955), p. 12.
29. Thomas Hayden, "Continuing Sit-In Struggle Demands Respect, Introspection," *The Michigan Daily*, September 25, 1960. Thomas Hayden, "The American Student—1960," *The Michigan Daily*, September 21, 1960. Hayden, "Why This Erupting Generation?" See also Camus, *The Myth of Sisyphus*, p. v.
30. Hayden, "American Student—1960."
31. Ross interview, 1–23–85. Richard Flacks interview, 3–4–85.
32. Thomas Hayden, "Myopic Realism No Answer to Needs," *The Michigan Daily*. Hayden, "Sit-In Struggle Demands Respect."
33. Jeffrey interview, 2–26–85; all subsequent Jeffrey quotations in this chapter come from this interview. For more on this scandal, see comments by Hayden, Ross and Jeffrey in their interviews with Bret Eynon in the "Contemporary History Project"; Michigan Historical Collections, Bentley Historical Library, University of Michigan.

34. Thomas Hayden and Philip Power, "Conference on the University," *The Michigan Daily*, March 8, 1961.
35. Hayden interview, 11–27–84.
36. Harrington interview, 11–27–84.
37. Thomas Hayden, "Who Are the Student Boat-Rockers?," *Mademoiselle*, August, 1961, distributed as an SDS pamphlet; SDS Microfilm, Series 1, No. 11.
38. Hayden marginal comments. Herbert Parmet, *JFK: The Presidency of John F. Kennedy* (New York, 1983), pp. 3–5. Alan Guskin, one of Hayden's Ann Arbor friends, played a key role in persuading Kennedy and his aides to take seriously the idea of a Peace Corps.
39. Ibid., pp. 252–56. Matusow, *The Unraveling of America*, pp. 71–74.
40. Ibid., p. 75. See also "L.I.D. Executive Committee Meeting," September 21, 1961; SDS Microfilm, Series 1, No. 7. 37.
41. Hayden interview, 3–6–85.
42. Roberts, "Will Tom Hayden Overcome?," p. 179. For SNCC's political differences with King, see James Forman, *The Making of Black Revolutionaries* (Washington, D.C., 1985), pp. 217–18.
43. Thomas Hayden, "Story of Fayette and Haywood: Bitter Revolution," *The Michigan Daily*, February 15, 1961. See also Forman, *The Making of Black Revolutionaries*, pp. 116–45.
44. Hayden interview, 3–6–85. Roberts, "Will Tom Hayden Overcome?," p. 179.
45. Thomas Hayden, "Report on McComb, Mississippi," p. 1; SDS Microfilm, Series 1, No. 11.
46. See Forman, *The Making of Black Revolutionaries*, pp. 224–24, 233; Newfield, *A Prophetic Minority*, pp. 72–75; and Robert Parris Moses, "Mississippi: 1961–1962," in John S. Friedman, ed., *First Harvest: The Institute for Policy Studies, 1963–1983* (New York, 1983), pp. 185–200.
47. See Carson, *In Struggle*, pp. 45–50; Forman, *The Making of Black Revolutionaries*, pp. 223–33; and Newfield, *A Prophetic Minority*, pp. 69–83.
48. Findley, "Hayden: Rolling Stone Interview, Part 1," p. 42.
49. Hayden interview, 3–6–85.
50. Hayden, "Report on McComb," p. 15. Tom Hayden, "Revolution in Mississippi" (pamphlet first printed by SDS in January, 1962), p. 5; SDS Microfilm, Series 4B, No. 159.
51. Carson, *In Struggle*, p. 54. Hayden to [Al] Haber, "Re: SNCC meeting, Jackson, Mississippi, September 14–17, 1961," p. 4; Hayden papers. Hayden to SDS Friends, "Re: December meeting," from Albany City Jail, Albany, Georgia, December 11, 1961; SDS Microfilm, Series 1, No. 3.
52. Betty Garman, quoted in Sale, *SDS*, p. 36. Caroline Dow, "Hayden Symbolizes Conflict," *The Michigan Daily*, October 13, 1961. In his interview of 5–16–86, Hayden described how he and Potter, after being beaten in McComb, "went to Atlanta, talking to the FBI along the way, and then straight to Washington, to Robert Kennedy's Justice Department, where we met with Burke Marshall. And we presented to him the entire episode as one example of what could happen, even to whites from the North. That's because we still believed that he could do something. On the other hand,

what he said to us had a decisive impact on me. It was a one-hour discussion, but I only remember one sentence: he asked us to help get Bob Moses and the SNCC workers to leave Mississippi, because he thought they could not be protected and would all be killed."

53. Hayden, "Revolution in Mississippi," p. 28; SDS Microfilm, Series 4B, No. 159. Cf. Ignazio Silone, *Bread and Wine*, trans. Harvey Fergusson (New York, 1963), p. 43.

54. Ibid., p. 30.

Chapter Three

1. LID Executive Committee Meeting, September 21, 1961; SDS Microfilm, Series 1, No. 7.

2. Haber's memory of meeting the old guard of the LID in 1960 parallels to an uncanny degree Irving Howe's description of the "old guard" of the Socialist Party in the 1930s; see Irving Howe, *Socialism and America* (San Diego, 1985), pp. 54–55.

3. Minutes, [LID] Student Activities Committee, December 12, 1960; Tamiment. Robert A. Haber, "Where Can the Students Go From Here," *LID News Bulletin*, Vol. 1, No. 2 (Fall, 1960), p. 1; SDS Microfilm, Series 1, No. 7.

4. Haber interview, 2–28–85; unless otherwise indicated, all subsequent Haber quotations in this chapter come from this interview.

5. Al Haber to Frank Trager, March 11, 1961; Tamiment. William Haber to Frank Trager, May 4, 1961; SDS microfilm, Series 1, No. 10.

6. Al Haber, "Memorandum on the Students for a Democratic Society," May 20, 1961, pp. 1–2; Tamiment.

7. Ibid., p. 4.

8. Ibid., pp. 4, 6.

9. [Al Haber,] "Campus Report," [Summer, 1961], p. 2; Tamiment. Haber, "Memorandum," May 20, 1961, p. 7; Tamiment. "Conference on the New Left: The Ideology, Politics and Controversies of the Student Movement," September 8–10, 1961, Conference Schedule, p. 1; Tamiment.

10. "Campus Report," p. 4 (emphasis added).

11. Haber, "Memorandum," May 20, 1961, pp. 18–19. R. A. Haber, "Memorandum on Conference of the Student Democratic Left: Democracy and the Student Movement," June 6, 1961; Tamiment.

12. Al Haber, Sandra Cason, "Memo Re: Proposed student project in voter registration," August 3, 1961; Tamiment.

13. Ross interview, 1–23–85.

14. Booth interview, 9–23–84. Plus details from Hayden's marginal comment.

15. Davis quoted in Viorst, *Fire in the Streets*, p. 178.

16. Philip Sutin, "Hayden Hits Student Failure," *Michigan Daily*, November 22, 1961. The quote from the Talmud should run: "If I am not for myself, who am I? If I am only for myself, what am I? And if not now, when?"

17. Max interview, 5–7–85; all subsequent Max quotations in this chapter come from this interview.

18. See Harrington, *Fragments of the Century*, pp. 71–77. Murray Kempton, "Three Who Didn't Make a Revolution," *The New York Review of Books*, January 7, 1971, p. 39.

19. Hayden to: SDS Friends, Re: December meeting, December 11, 1961; SDS Microfilm, Series 1, No. 3. The Albany movement had been initiated by SNCC; see Forman, *The Making of Black Revolutionaries*, pp. 247–62.
20. Hayden to SDS, December 5, 1961; SDS Microfilm, Series 1, No. 3. Haber, P.S. to Hayden to SDS, December 11, 1961.
21. "Proposed Agenda, Students for a Democratic Society Organizational Discussion, December 29–31, 1961;" SDS Microfilm, Series 1, No. 3. Jeffrey interview, 2–26–85.
22. Al Haber, "SDS Convention," *Common Sense*, Vol. III, No. 4 (January 20, 1962); Max papers. SDS "Memo" [no date; first line: "The National convention of the Students for a Democratic Society has been set for 14 to 17 June 1962"]; Flacks papers.
23. Tom Hayden, "Proposed Book of Essays;" SDS Microfilm, Series 1, No. 11.

Chapter Four
1. Hayden to: SDS executive committee, Re: manifesto [c. April, 1962; hereafter "Issues"], pp. 1, 2–3; SDS Microfilm, Series 1, No. 6.
2. "References of Interest" for "Conference on the New Left," September 8–10, 1961; Tamiment. Hayden marginal comment.
3. Tom Hayden, "Manifesto Notes: A Beginning Draft," Convention Document #1, March 19, 1962 [hereafter "Beginning Draft"], pp. 1, 2; SDS Microfilm, Series 1, No. 6.
4. Hayden, "Who Are the Student Boat-Rockers?"; SDS Microfilm, Series 1, No. 11. (In this article, Hayden mentioned two other adults of relevance to the student left, but they were both activists: Norman Thomas and Michael Harrington.) Proposed Agenda, December 29–31, 1961; SDS Microfilm, Series 1, No. 3. Max interview, 5–7–85.
5. See Hayden and Power, "Conference on the University," *The Michigan Daily*, March 8, 1961; [Haber,] "Campus Report" [Summer, 1961], p. 4; Hayden, "Proposed Book of Essays," p. 3; SDS Microfilm, Series 1, No. 11.
6. Hayden interview, 3–6–85.
7. C. Wright Mills, "The Structure of Power in American Society" (1958), in Irving Louis Horowitz, ed., *Power, Politics and People* (New York, 1963), p. 24. The most famous example of Mills's sloganeering is *The Causes of World War Three* (New York, 1958); see, e.g., pp. 31–35 (on democracy as a "fairy tale").
8. C. Wright Mills, "On Knowledge and Power" (1955), in *Power, Politics and People*, p. 613. One contemporary who appreciated Mills's obsession with powerlessness was Ralph Miliband: see his essay, "Mills and Politics," in Irving Louis Horowitz, ed., *The New Sociology* (New York, 1964), esp. p. 81.
9. Hans Gerth, "C. Wright Mills, 1916–1962," *Studies on the Left*, Vol. 2, No. 3 (1962), p. 10. Biographical details are drawn from this essay and from Irving Louis Horowitz, *C. Wright Mills: An American Utopian* (New York, 1983), pp. 6, 14. See also C. Wright Mills, "The Powerless People: The Role of the Intellectual in Society" (1944), in *Power, Politics and People*, p. 148; *White Collar* (New York, 1952), p. 292; and "Pragmatism, Politics and Religion" (1942), in *Power, Politics and People*, p. 168.

10. Mills to Kurt H. Wolff, 4–15–53, quoted in Irving Louis Horowitz, *C. Wright Mills*, p. 84. Mills's outburst as a clerk is cited in Richard Gillam, "White Collar from Start to Finish," *Theory and Society*, Vol. 10, No. 1 (January, 1981), p. 18. See also Dan Wakefield, "Taking It Big: A Memoir of C. Wright Mills," *The Atlantic Monthly*, September, 1971, pp. 65, 71.

11. The quotes from Charles Frankel come from an interview conducted in preparation for a piece on Mills that appeared in *Newsweek*, May 11, 1964, and appear here by permission of the editors of *Newsweek* magazine. Wakefield, "Taking It Big," p. 71.

12. Mills, "The Powerless People," in *Power, Politics and People*, pp. 292–304.

13. Mills, *White Collar* (New York, 1952), p. 161. Mills, *The Power Elite* (New York, 1956), p. 225. On "sociological poetry," see Mills's review of James Agee and Walker Evans, *Let Us Now Praise Famous Men*, in *Politics*, Vol. 5, No. 2 (Spring, 1948), pp. 125–26.

14. C. Wright Mills, "The Political Gargoyles" (1943), in *Power, Politics and People*, pp. 75–76. C. Wright Mills, "Letter to the New Left" (1960), ibid., p. 256. C. Wright Mills, *The New Men of Power*, p. 252.

15. On ideal-types, see Hans Gerth and C. Wright Mills, *From Max Weber* (New York, 1946), pp. 59–60. For the centrality of "mass" vs. "public" in Mills's work, see especially *The Power Elite*, pp. 298–324, and *The Causes of World War Three*, pp. 31–35; see also *The Sociological Imagination* (New York, 1959), pp. 187–190. The notion of mass society is crucial in *White Collar*—see pp. 332–340—and the idea of the public is pivotal in *The New Men of Power*—see pp. 13–30.

16. C. Wright Mills, "Mass Media and Public Opinion" (1950), in *Power, Politics and People*, pp. 577–98.

17. Mills, *The Power Elite*, pp. 300, 310, 320, 322–23.

18. Mills, *The Sociological Imagination*, p. 213. Mills, *The New Men of Power*, p. 273. Cf. Hans Gerth and C. Wright Mills, *Character and Social Structure* (New York, 1953), pp. 288, 298. The clearest contemporary appreciation of Mills as a moral visionary is Harvey Swados, "C. Wright Mills: A Personal Memoir," *Dissent*, Vol. 10, No. 1. (Winter, 1963), esp. p. 40.

19. Mills, *The Causes of World War Three*, p. 141. On Ian Ballantine, see Kenneth C. Davis, *Two-Bit Culture: The Paperbacking of America* (New York, 1984), pp. 330–33, 372. Wakefield, "Taking It Big," p. 70.

20. Mills, "Letter to the New Left," in *Power, Politics and People*, pp. 259, 254, 257.

21. Hayden interview, 3–6–85.

22. Booth interview, 9–23–84. Ross interview, 1–21–85.

23. Proposed Agenda, December 29–31, 1961; SDS Microfilm, Series 1, No. 3. See Tom Hayden, "Student Social Action" (a speech delivered in March, 1962, at the University of Michigan), pp. 4–5; SDS Microfilm, Series 4B, No. 160; and for the impact on feminism, see Sara Evans, *Personal Politics*, esp. pp. 104–5.

24. Robert A. Dahl, *After the Revolution* (New Haven, 1970), p. 4.

25. Mills, *White Collar*, p. 345. For references to G. D. H. Cole, see Mills, *The New Men of Power*, pp. 253, 258. For Cole's Rousseauistic premises, see his *Social Theory* (London, 1920). For Hofstadter on the agrarian myth, see

Richard Hofstadter, *The Age of Reform* (New York, 1955), pp. 23–59; Mills's involvement in the book is credited on p. 330.

26. Mills, *The Causes of World War Three*, p. 37. Mills, *The Power Elite*, pp. 236, 301. Mills, "The Structure of Power in American Society," in *Power, Politics and People*, pp. 37–38.

27. Wakefield, "Taking It Big," p. 66. Gerth, "C. Wright Mills, 1916–1962," pp. 9, 11.

28. George Orwell, "Inside the Whale" (1940), in *An Age Like This*, ed., Sonia Orwell and Ian Angus (New York, 1968), pp. 525–26.

29. Thomas Hayden, "A Letter to the New (Young) Left" (originally published in *The Activist*, Winter, 1961), in Cohen and Hale, *The New Student Left*, p. 3. For Mills on fraternity, see Irving Howe, *A Margin of Hope* (New York, 1982), p. 244. For Hayden's view of Mills in his finished thesis, see Thomas Hayden, *Radical Nomad: Essays on C. Wright Mills and His Times*, esp. pp. 8–9, 195–96; distributed as a mimeographed "preprint" in July, 1964, by the Center for Research on Conflict Resolution in Ann Arbor; Flacks papers.

30. Hayden to: SDS executive committee, re: manifesto, p. 5; SDS Microfilm, Series 1, No. 6.

31. Mills, *The New Men of Power*, pp. 250, 260, 261, 265. Cf. Mills, "Letter to the New Left," in *Power, Politics and People*.

Chapter Five

1. Hayden, *Radical Nomad*, pp. 8–9. Hayden interview, 3–6–85.

2. Hayden, "Beginning Draft"; SDS Microfilm, Series 1, No. 6. The quotes come from Iris Murdoch, "A House of Theory," in McKenzie, ed., *Conviction* (London, 1958). Like E. P. Thompson at roughly the same time, Murdoch implies a new respect for the romantic socialism of William Morris and explicitly commends the Guild Socialists.

3. Tom Hayden, "Manifesto Notes: Problems of Democracy," Convention Document #2, March 19, 1962 [hereafter "Democracy"], p. 7; SDS Microfilm, Series 1, No. 6. See also Erich Fromm, *The Sane Society* (New York, 1967) [first published in 1955], pp. 297–98; Sheldon S. Wolin, *Politics and Vision* (Boston, 1960), pp. 20–21.

4. A similar phrase—"participative democracy"—was used in 1949 by Sidney Lens, who distinguished it from "manipulative democracy." But Hayden says—and there is no evidence to the contrary—that he had not read Lens's book. See Sidney Lens, "The New Left and the Establishment," *Liberation*, September, 1965, p. 9. Lens first used the phrase in his book *Left, Right and Center*.

5. Arnold Kaufman, "Human Nature and Participatory Democracy," in Carl J. Friedrich, ed., *Nomos III: Responsibility* (New York, 1960), pp. 279, 272, 274.

6. Hayden, "Democracy," p. 1; SDS Microfilm, Series 1, No. 6.

7. Ibid., p. 2. Cf. Wolin, *Politics and Vision*, pp. 388–93, a critique of constitutionalism as a species of organization theory: "The question, in other words, was to constitutionalize a Hobbesian society. . . . We look in vain for any theory of political education, of political leadership, or, until re-

cently, of social consensus." See also "Draft Paper for S.D.S. Manifesto, for consideration in convention 11–15 June, F.D.R. Labor Center, Port Huron, Michigan," pp. 7 (a paraphrase of Wolin), 44 (where the phrase "inactive democracy" appears); Tamiment.

8. Hayden, "Democracy," p. 3; SDS Microfilm, Series 1, No. 6.
9. Ibid., p. 4.
10. Ibid., pp. 4–5.
11. Ibid., p. 5.
12. Ibid., p. 5.
13. Ibid., p. 6.
14. Hayden, "Issues," esp. pp. 7–8; SDS Microfilm, Series 1, No. 6.
15. Tom Hayden, "Freedom of the Student Press" [a 1961 speech delivered to the Student Editors of America Conference], p. 5; Tamiment.
16. [Tom Hayden,] "Politics, the Intellectual and SDS"; SDS Microfilm, Series 1, No. 6.
17. Hayden interview, 3–10–85; Ross interview, 2–18–85.
18. Tom Hayden, "Politics, the Intellectual and SDS"; SDS Microfilm, Series 1, No. 6. Hayden, "Issues," pp. 1, 8; SDS Microfilm, Series 1, No. 6. Cf. Camus, *The Myth of Sisyphus*, p. 4: "Solely the balance between evidence and lyricism can allow us to achieve simultaneously emotion and lucidity."
19. See "Minutes, Meeting of the SDS National Executive Committee, Chapel Hill, May 6–7," p. 3; SDS Microfilm, Series 1, No. 5.
20. Tom Hayden, "Student Social Action"; SDS Microfilm, Series 4B, No. 160.
21. Flacks interview, 3–4–85.
22. "To: SDS From: Hayden Re: 'Race and Politics' Conference, Chapel Hill, N.C., May 4–6"; SDS Microfilm, Series 1, No. 4. Hayden interview, 3–6–85. Hayden felt these views important enough to reiterate them in *The Port Huron Statement:* see p. 55. For developments in SNCC in this period, see Forman, *The Making of Black Revolutionaries*, pp. 262–69.
23. Hayden, "Issues," p. 8; SDS Microfilm, Series 1, No. 6.
24. Max interview, 5–7–85.
25. "Minutes, Meeting of the SDS National Executive Committee, Chapel Hill, May 6–7," pp. 2, 3; SDS Microfilm, Series 1, No. 5.
26. Al Haber, "Aims and Purposes of SDS: Some Comments," p. 3; SDS Microfilm, Series 1, No. 6.
27. Robb Burlage to Al Haber and Tom Hayden, 5–26–62. Jeffrey interview, 2–28–85.
28. See Tom Hayden, "Writing the Port Huron Statement," in Linda Obst, *The Sixties* (New York, 1977), p. 70.

Chapter Six
1. Ross interview, 2–18–85. Unless otherwise indicated, all subsequent Ross quotations in this chapter come from this interview.
2. Jeffrey interview, 2–28–85. All subsequent Jeffrey quotations in this chapter come from this interview.
3. See "Registration List—SDS Convention, Port Huron, Mich., June 11–15, 1962"; SDS Microfilm, Series 1, No. 6. Cf. "Appeal, 7–12–62," p. 5.
4. Flacks interview, 3–4–85. All subsequent Flacks quotations in this chapter come from this interview.

5. Max interview, 5–7–85. All subsequent Max quotations in this chapter come from this interview.

6. Booth interview, 9–23–84. Unless otherwise indicated, all subsequent Booth quotations in this chapter come from this interview.

7. "Draft Paper for S.D.S. Manifesto, for consideration in convention 11–15 June, F.D.R. Labor Center, Port Huron, Michigan" [hereafter "Working draft"], pp. 10, 20, 23; Tamiment (and for pp. 31–32, which the Tamiment copy is missing, Flacks papers).

8. Hayden interview, 3–10–85; unless otherwise identified, all the following Hayden quotations come from this interview. Cf. "To: LID Executive Committee From: SDS National Executive Committee Re: Relationship Between SDS and LID, Thursday, July 12, 1962" [hereafter, "Appeal, 7–12–62"], p. 5; Tamiment.

9. See the agenda, "S.D.S. National Convention, 14–17 June, 1962, Place to be announced"; SDS Microfilm, Series 1, No. 6. Cf. the changes agreed to in "Minutes, Meeting of the SDS National Executive Committee, Chapel Hill, May 6–7," pp. 1–2; SDS Microfilm, Series 1, No. 5.

10. Haber interview, 2–28–85. All subsequent Haber quotations in this chapter come from this interview. "Report on SDS convention, 6/29/62," p. 1; SDS Microfilm, Series 1, No. 6. This skeletal four-page report, together with Haber's five-paragraph press release, reprinted in *New America* and reproduced in SDS Microfilm, Series 1, No. 6, represent the basic contemporary documentation of the Port Huron convention. In what follows, I have tried to reconstruct the week's happenings by welding together the recollections of all the participants I interviewed, sifting out inconsistencies and giving greater weight to the reports that seemed most detailed and most consistent with the contemporary documentation. Of all the participants, it was Richard Flacks who had the clearest memory of events, perhaps because he was older than most of the others, perhaps because he had come at first as a reporter (for the *National Guardian*) and therefore took notes, perhaps because he has maintained a scholarly interest in the New Left. In any event, the reader should be aware of this primary source, and also of the numerous ambiguities that an 'oral history' simply cannot resolve.

11. "The Young Radicals, A Symposium," *Dissent*, Vol. 9, No. 2 (Spring, 1962), p. 132.

12. Harrington interview, 11–27–84. All subsequent Harrington quotations in this chapter come from this interview. For the original soviet form of democracy, see Oskar Anweiler, *The Soviets*, trans. Ruth Hein (New York, 1974); and for their impact on left-wing Marxism, see Richard Gombin, *Les origines du gauchisme* (Paris, 1971), esp. pp. 101–51.

13. Working draft, pp. 10, 11, 48, 22, 20–21.

14. "Appeal, 7–12–62," p. 5; Harrington's letter has apparently been lost.

15. See "Memo to: LID Executive Board, From: Vera Rony, Re: Decision of LID Executive Committee to Suspend SDS and Resultant Action by SDS, EMERGENCY BOARD MEETING, Thursday, July 12th," Tamiment; and "Appeal, 7–12–62," p. 5.

16. "Appeal, 7–12–62," p. 5. Steve Max, who knew Hawley, recalls that Hawley really wasn't that interested in SDS, and felt awkward being at the center of a squabble.

17. Mickey Flacks interview, 3–4–85.
18. Cf. *The Port Huron Statement* (New York, 1964), pp. 58, 62, and first draft, pp. 45–46, 48–49. (All references to *The Port Huron Statement* come from the second edition of 1964, the only complete edition set in type rather than mimeographed.)
19. Cf. *The Port Huron Statement*, p. 31, and first draft, p. 21.
20. Hayden, "Writing the Port Huron Statement," in Obst, ed., *The Sixties*, p. 70.
21. Cf. *The Port Huron Statement*, p. 6, and working draft, p. 29.
22. Working draft, pp. 16, 38.
23. Ibid., p. 31.
24. Ibid., p. 7. This is a paraphrase of Sheldon Wolin, *Politics and Vision*, pp. 388–93.
25. *The Port Huron Statement*, p. 3 (from the new "introduction" Hayden had completed before the end of the convention). Working draft, pp. 5–6, 49, 29, 30—in some cases, the final printed version reflects slight differences in the cited wording.
26. Booth, quoted in Sale, *SDS*, p. 58.
27. Ross, quoted in Newfield, *A Prophetic Minority*, p. 131.

Chapter Seven
1. See "Report on SDS Convention, 6–29–62," p. 1; SDS Microfilm, Series 1, No. 6. This report stresses that "the draft is no longer to be considered an SDS document and should not be distributed further."
2. Harrington interview, 11–27–84; unless otherwise indicated, all subsequent Harrington quotations in this chapter come from this interview.
3. Horowitz phone interview, 4–30–86.
4. Harrington, *Fragments of the Century*, p. 148.
5. "Memo to: Members of LID Executive Committee, From: Vera Rony, *Urgent* Outline Report of SDS Policy Statement, July 2, 1962"; Tamiment. Hayden's recollection of what he said about the Soviets and disarmament is one of his marginal comments. He also comments: "This is someone writing the *gist* of whatever I said. This is not me [directly talking]."
6. Max interview, 5–7–85; Flacks interview, 3–4–85; unless otherwise indicated, all subsequent Max and Flacks quotations in this chapter come from these interviews. "Appeal, 7–12–62," p. 7; Tamiment.
7. LID memo of 7–3–62, quoted in "Appeal, 7–12–62," p. 7; Tamiment.
8. "To: National Executive Committee, From: Thomas Hayden, SDS President, Re: immediate organizational problem, July 4th, 1962"; Tamiment.
9. "To: The Officers of the L.I.D., From: Al Haber and Tom Hayden, July 4, 1962"; Tamiment.
10. Quotations from "extensive handwritten notes taken by an SDSer," quoted by Sale, *SDS*, pp. 61–64; the hearing was tape-recorded by SDS (see "Appeal, 7–12–62," p. 7; Tamiment), so it is likely that these notes are a transcription (although I could not locate this transcript in the SDS microfilm). See also Newfield, *A Prophetic Minority*, p. 134.
11. "Appeal, 7–12–62," pp. 8, 13; Tamiment.
12. Ross quoted in Newfield, *A Prophetic Minority*, p. 134. Booth interview, 9–23–84.

13. Hayden to Vera Rony, 7–24–62, p. 3; Tamiment.
14. "Memo to: LID Executive Board, From: Vera Rony, Re: Decision of LID Executive Committee to Suspend SDS and Resultant Action by SDS, EMERGENCY BOARD MEETING, Thursday, July 12"; Tamiment.
15. "Appeal, 7–12–62," p. 2; Tamiment.
16. Ibid., pp. 2, 17.
17. Ibid., pp. 22, 23, 18–19. There was some anti-Communist language in Hayden's original draft: see working draft, p. 21.
18. Ibid., pp. 25, 26.
19. Harold Taylor, *Students Without Teachers* (New York, 1969), p. 40.
20. Norman Thomas, "Preface" to "Proposed LID–SDS Agreement," in "Memo from Vera Rony To Al Haber" [July, 1962], p. 2; Tamiment.
21. *The Port Huron Statement*, pp. 32–33.
22. Mickey Flacks interview, 3–4–85; Bob Ross interview, 1–23–85; unless otherwise indicated, all subsequent Mickey Flacks and Ross quotations in this chapter come from these interviews. For the "Americanization" of the Party, see Klehr, *The Heyday of American Communism*, esp. pp. 210–22; and Howe, *Socialism and America*, pp. 96–97. For the impact of the Nazi–Soviet pact on Party policy, see Klehr, op. cit., pp. 386–409.
23. Haber interview, 2–28–85.
24. Hayden to Vera Rony, 7–24–85, p. 3 et passim; Tamiment.
25. For the "armistice" agreement, see "League for Industrial Democracy Statement of Principles, with Emphasis on the Relationship between the LID and the SDS"; Tamiment.
26. "To: National Executive Committee [SDS], From: Jim Monsonis, Office Report, CONFIDENTIAL, 10–30–62," p. 2; Flacks papers. Harrington, *Fragments of the Century*, p. 148.
27. Hayden, quoted in Newfield, *A Prophetic Minority*, p. 134.
28. Hayden, "Writing the Port Huron Statement," in Obst, ed., *The Sixties*, p. 71.

Chapter Eight
1. Hayden interview, 3–10–85; unless otherwise indicated, all subsequent Hayden quotations in this chapter come from this interview.
2. Hayden, quoted in Viorst, *Fire in the Streets*, p. 195. Ross interview, 2–18–85; all subsequent Ross quotes in this chapter come from this interview. Vivian Franklin to Robb Burlage, August, 1962, quoted in Sale, *SDS*, p. 69.
3. *The Port Huron Statement*, p. 7 (emphasis added).
4. Flacks interview, 3–4–85; all subsequent Flacks quotations in this chapter come from this interview.
5. Harrington, *Fragments of the Century*, p. 147. Booth interview, 9–23–84; all subsequent Booth quotations in this chapter come from this interview.
6. *The Port Huron Statement*, pp. 11, 7. "Aims and Purposes of SDS: Some Comments," p. 3; SDS Microfilm, Series 1, No. 6.
7. Haber interview, 2–28–85.
8. Jeffrey interview, 2–28–85.
9. Max interview, 5–7–85.
10. A. D. Lindsay, *The Modern Democratic State* (London, 1943), p. 77. For Mills, see Ch. 4 above, esp. pp. 11–12. In *Fire in the Streets*, Milton Viorst

credits James Lawson's "group-centered" decision-making as the source for participatory democracy. This is false. But Lawson, who had worked with the Quaker Fellowship of Reconciliation (like James Farmer before him) and who profoundly influenced SNCC's original philosophy (he drafted its first statement of purpose), *was* pivotal in introducing rule-by-consensus into the civil rights movement. See Viorst, *Fire in the Streets*, pp. 105–6; Carson, *In Struggle*, pp. 23–25; and Morris, *The Origins of the Civil Rights Movement*, pp. 124, 162–67. The information about Quaker influences on SDS members comes, in part, from interviews with Jeffrey, Haber and Bob Ross, who recalls how Hayden one dreary, damp day in Ann Arbor, pointed out Boulding, who was holding a solitary vigil for peace, and declared, "He lives as a man ought." Left-wing ideas about workers' control and socialism from the bottom up were expressed in the Twenties and Thirties by writers like Karl Korsch, Antonio Gramsci and Anton Pannekoek, maverick Marxists who would be rediscovered by the New Left later in the decade. See, e.g., Dick Howard and Karl E. Klare, eds., *The Unknown Dimension: European Marxism since Lenin* (New York, 1972), an anthology of essays largely written by young scholars who had been partisans of the New Left.

11. Hayden, quoted in Viorst, *Fire in the Streets*, p. 192. Marshall Berman, *All That Is Solid Melts into Air* (New York, 1982), p. 121. Perhaps the most sophisticated theoretical expression of the modernist impulse behind the radical democratic politics of the Sixties is to be found in Guy Debord, *La Société du spectacle* (Paris, 1971), e.g., nos. 205 and 221. The impact of modernism on the American New Left was eventually noted by New York intellectuals like Lionel Trilling, who, after witnessing the Columbia student uprising of 1968, decried "modernism in the streets." See Mark Krupnick, *Lionel Trilling and the Fate of Cultural Criticism* (Evanston, Ill., 1986), pp. 143–47. A similar idea has been carried forward into the Eighties by neoconservatives: see, e.g., Norman Podhoretz, "The Adversary Culture and the New Class," in *The Bloody Crossroads* (New York, 1986), esp. pp. 121–26.

12. Camus, *The Myth of Sisyphus*, p. 40.

13. Hayden to: SDS executive committee, Re: manifesto, p. 5; SDS Microfilm, Series 1, No. 6.

14. Walter Lippmann, *Public Opinion* (New York, 1922), p. 94. Walter Lippmann, *The Phantom Public* (New York, 1925), p. 155.

15. John Dewey, *The Public and its Problems* (Chicago, 1927), pp. 157, 158, 213, 218; Dewey records his debt to Lippmann on p. 116n; his critique of Progressive thought is developed on pp. 96–109; see esp. p. 101.

16. *The Port Huron Statement*, p. 52(on decentralization), 56 (on "serious decision-making"), and 46–53 passim. For C. Wright Mills on Lippmann, see Mills, *White Collar*, p. 325: "The difficulties of liberalism's assumption of the alert citizen were well stated by Walter Lippmann in the early 'twenties. . . . No one of liberal persuasion has refuted Lippmann's analysis."

17. The SNCC slogan is quoted in Tom Hayden (with Herb Mills), "SDS Southern Report #4," 29 November 1961, p. 3; SDS Microfilm, Series 1, No. 10. For McComb, see Carson, *In Struggle*, pp. 13–14, 38–39, 48–49. Hayden, phone interview, 7–5–86. Cf. Viorst, *Fire in the Streets*, p. 183.

18. Hayden to: SDS executive committee, Re: manifesto, p. 5; SDS Microfilm, Series 1, No. 6.
19. See Gordon S. Wood, *The Creation of the American Republic, 1776–1789* (New York, 1969), esp. p. 374 (where Rush is quoted). Alexander Hamilton, James Madison, John Jay, *The Federalist Papers,* nos. 63 ("exclusion of the people") and 10. Cf. James Madison, *The Forging of American Federalism,* ed. Padover (New York, 1953), p. 40. Beard's classic work of muckracking scholarship is *An Economic Interpretation of the Constitution of the United States.*
20. First draft, p. 7. Hayden, "Student Social Action" (emphasis added); SDS Microfilm, Series 4B, No. 160.
21. Hayden marginal comment.
22. The size of the printings for *The Port Huron Statement* is indicated on the inside front cover of the third printing: see SDS Microfilm, Series 4B, No. 328. This third printing used the same excerpts selected by Cohen and Hale, *The New Student Left*: see pp. 9–16, 215–18, 292–307. Paul Jacobs and Saul Landau, *The New Radicals* (New York, 1966), reprints only the introductory sections: see pp. 150–62.
23. "A Letter to a Young Democrat"; SDS Microfilm, Series 4B, No. 276. "Why SDS?"; SDS Microfilm, Series 3, No. 3.
24. *The Port Huron Statement,* pp. 5, 8, 63.

Chapter Nine
1. Richard Flacks, Review of Todd Gitlin's *The Whole World Is Watching* [hereafter "Gitlin Review"], *Theory and Society,* Vol. 10, No. 4 (July, 1981), p. 579. Richard Flacks, "Making History vs. Making Life," *Working Papers for a New Society,* Vol. 2, No. 2 (Summer, 1974), p. 64.
2. Ross quoted in Roberts, "Will Tom Hayden Overcome?," p. 179. See also Eynon Flacks interview, p. 13.
3. Richard Flacks, "Student Power and the New Left: The Role of SDS," in Howard Gadlin and Bertram E. Garskof, *The Uptight Society* (Belmont, Calif., 1970), p. 202.
4. Flacks, "Gitlin Review," p. 579.
5. Ibid.
6. Flacks interview, 3–4–85; unless otherwise indicated, all subsequent Flacks quotations in this chapter come from this interview.
7. See Bret Eynon's interview with Flacks, 9–25–78 [hereafter referred to as "Eynon Flacks interview"], pp. 2–3, in the "Contemporary History Project"; Michigan Historical Collections, Bentley Historical Library, University of Michigan. Also see Lloyd Barenblatt, "Theodore M. Newcombe," in Sills, ed., *International Encyclopedia of the Social Sciences* (New York, 1968), Vol. 18, pp. 584–86.
8. His collaboration with Newcombe resulted in two published studies: *Deviant Subcultures on a College Campus* (1964) and *Persistence and Change: Bennington College and its Students after 25 Years* (with Koenig, Newcombe and Warwick, 1967).
9. Mills, *The Sociological Imagination,* pp. 20, 176.
10. Flacks interview, 3–4–85. And Richard Flacks, ed., *Conformity, Resis-*

tance, and Self-Determination: The Individual and Authority (Boston, 1973), p. 15.

11. See Eynon Flacks interview, p. 9.

12. See Dick Flacks to Leo Huberman, 9–21–62; Flacks papers.

13. See Eynon Flacks interview, pp. 12, 15.

14. For this and other details about the Missile Crisis, see Herbert S. Parmet, *JFK: The Presidency of John F. Kennedy* (New York, 1983), pp. 277–300. No evidence has ever been presented to prove that the Cuban missiles had in fact been armed with nuclear warheads.

15. See "Widespread Student Opposition to Blockade," *Common Sense*, Vol. 4, No. 2 (December, 1962), pp. 1, 4–5; Max papers.

16. Findley, "Hayden: Rolling Stone Interview, Part 1," p. 42 (includes Flacks quote).

17. Ibid., p. 42.

18. Tom Hayden and Dick Flacks, "Cuba and USA," *Common Sense*, Vol. 4, No. 2 (December, 1962), pp. 11–12.

19. See Eynon Flacks interview, p. 13.

20. Al Haber and Barbara Jacobs to Friends, 12–15–62, p. 8; SDS Microfilm, Series 2A, No. 1.

21. Robb Burlage to the SDS National Executive Committee, 12–25–62, p. 4; SDS Microfilm, Series 2A, No. 1. Minutes, National Council Meeting, Ann Arbor, December 26 through 31, rough draft, p. 7; SDS Microfilm, Series 2A, No. 1.

22. Ibid., pp. 2–4.

23. Haber and Jacobs to Friends, 12–15–62, p. 8.

24. "National Council 1962: Report of the National Secretary," pp. 6–7; SDS Microfilm, Series 2A, No. 1.

25. Minutes, National Council Meeting, Ann Arbor, December 26th through 31st, rough draft, pp. 5–7.

26. Proposal on spring organizing strategy; SDS Microfilm, Series 2A, No. 1.

27. David Riesman and Michael Macoby, "The American Crisis," in James Roosevelt, ed., *The Liberal Papers* (Garden City, N.Y., 1962), pp. 31, 32, 45.

28. See John S. Friedman, ed., *First Harvest: The Institute for Policy Studies, 1963–83* (New York, 1983), p. xi.

29. C. Wright Mills, "Liberal Values in the Modern World" (1952), in Horowitz, ed., *Power, Politics and People*, p. 191. Mills, *The New Men of Power*, pp. 160, 229, 230, 233.

30. "The Ultra-Right and Cold War Liberalism," *Studies on the Left*, Vol. 3, No. 1 (1962), p. 6.

31. [Stanley Aronowitz, Ray Brown, Terence Cannon, Bob Heifitz, Beth Roy,] "Working Papers for Nyack Conference on Unemployment and Social Change" (June, 1963), p. 6; Flacks papers. See also Ray Brown, "Our Crisis Economy: The End of the Boom" (a paper delivered at the Nyack Conference in June, 1963); Flacks papers. And see Stanley Aronowitz, "When the New Left Was New," in Sohnya Sayres, Anders Stephanson, Stanley Aronowitz and Fredric Jameson, *The 60s Without Apology* (Minneapolis, 1984), pp. 20–21.

32. William Appleman Williams, *The Contours of American History* (Cleveland, Ohio, 1961), pp. 477, 351, 428.

33. Ibid., pp. 257, 376–77.
34. Ibid., pp. 481, 483, 487.
35. Dick Flacks, "Some Thoughts on the Current Scene," *Peace Research and Education Newsletter*, No. 1 (May, 1963), pp. 9–10. William Appleman Williams believed that revolutions like Castro's in Cuba "could shock Americans into recognition of the failure of the frontier-expansionist outlook." See *The Contours of American History*, p. 477. Cf. Thomas Hayden and Richard Flacks, "The New Possibilities for Peace," a mimeographed essay published by the Peace Research and Education Project, Ann Arbor, Michigan, August, 1963; Booth papers.
36. Tom Hayden, "Outline of Draft of the SDS Convention Document"; SDS Microfilm, Series 2A, No. 2.
37. Jeffrey interview, 2–28–85.
38. Richard Flacks, "American Scene Document (Draft) 6–7–63," pp. I-1, I-2, I-6, I-8, I-3–5; SDS Microfilm, Series 2A, No. 3.
39. Ibid., p. I-2.
40. Ibid., p. I-1.
41. Ibid., pp. II-1, II-2, II-3.
42. Ibid., pp. II-1, II-3. Richard Flacks, "The New Left and American Politics After Ten Years," *Journal of Social Issues*, Vol. 27, No. 1 (1971), p. 27.
43. See "Roster for the 1963 SDS Convention" and "SDS National Convention, 1963/Schedule"; both in SDS Microfilm, Series 2A, No. 2.
44. See Todd Gitlin, "SDS Convention Stresses Integrality of Movement," *Common Sense*, Vol. 4, No. 5 (Summer 1963), pp. 1, 5–6; Flacks papers. See also [Lee Webb,] "Convention Report"; SDS Microfilm, Series 2A, No. 2.
45. Paul Potter, "The Intellectual as an Agent of Social Change," pp. 3, 5, 6; SDS Microfilm, Series 4B, No. 275.
46. Sale, *SDS*, p. 92.
47. Richard Flacks, "Student Activists: Result, Not Revolt," *Psychology Today*, Vol. 1, No. 6 (October, 1967), p. 18.
48. See [Jim Monsonis,] "1963 National Convention—National Secretary's Report," p. 6; and [Lee Webb,] "Convention Report."
49. On the teach-ins, see Eynon Flacks interview, p. 13; and Nancy Zaroulis and Gerald Sullivan, *Who Spoke Up?: American Protest Against the War in Vietnam, 1963–1975* (Garden City, N.Y., 1984), p. 37.
50. See Richard Flacks, "Chicago: Organizing the Unemployed"; SDS Microfilm, Series 4B, No. 91.
51. Richard Flacks, *Youth and Social Change* (Chicago, 1971), p. 101.
52. Hayden and Flacks, "The New Possibilities for Peace," p. ii. The top-ten version was by Peter, Paul and Mary, not Dylan himself.

Chapter Ten
1. Jeffrey interview, 2–28–85; unless otherwise indicated, all subsequent Jeffrey quotations in this chapter come from this interview.
2. Richard Flacks, "The Liberated Generation: An Exploration of the Roots of Student Protest," reprinted in Flacks, ed., *Conformity, Resistance, and Self-Determination: The Individual and Authority*, pp. 109–11. For a critique of the research of Flacks, see Stanley Rothman and S. Robert Lichter, *Roots of Radicalism* (New York, 1982), esp. pp. 62–65.

3. Sharon Jeffrey to Dickie [Magidoff], July 3, 1962, carbon to Dick Flacks; Flacks papers.
4. Northern Student Movement, "Building a New Reality" [pamphlet, 1963]. For the history of NSM, see James Brook, "Ghetto Students," *Common Sense*, February, 1962, pp. 8–10; Max papers.
5. Sharon Jeffrey to Dick and Mickey [Flacks], [n.d.; c. August, 1963]; Flacks papers.
6. Sharon Jeffrey to all [SDS group in Ann Arbor], February 23, 1963; Flacks papers.
7. Tom Hayden, [untitled comment], *S.D.S. Bulletin*, No. 4 (March–April, 1963), p. 16; Tamiment.
8. I. Frederick Shotkin to Don McKelvey, June 17, 1963; SDS Microfilm, Series 2A, No. 3.
9. Tom Hayden to Walter Reuther, March 29, 1963; SDS Microfilm, Series 2A, No. 25. Tom Hayden to Todd Gitlin, August 2, 1963; SDS Microfilm, Series 2A, No. 25.
10. See Richard Rothstein, "A Short History of ERAP" [3/66]; SDS Microfilm, Series 2B, No. 21. And Richard Rothstein, "Evolution of the ERAP Organizers," in Priscilla Long, ed., *The New Left: A Collection of Essays* (Boston, 1969), pp. 272–88.
11. Sharon Jeffrey to Tom-Al, Monday, September [1963]; Flacks papers.
12. See Richard Flacks, "Chicago: Organizing the Unemployed," SDS Microfilm, Series 4B, No. 91; and Carl Wittman, "Students and Economic Action," in Teodori, *The New Left: A Documentary History*, p. 130.
13. See Wittman, "Students and Economic Action," p. 131.
14. Ibid., p. 132.
15. Tom Hayden, "Liberal Analysis and Federal Power," pp. 1, 3, 6; Booth papers.
16. Carl Wittman and Thomas Hayden, "An Interracial Movement of the Poor?," in Cohen and Hale, *The New Student Left*, pp. 206, 208, 196, 203.
17. Paul Potter, *A Name for Ourselves* (Boston, 1971), pp. 142, 149.
18. Al Haber, "The National Council: A Reply to the President's Report," *SDS Bulletin*, Vol. 2, No. 6 (March, 1964), pp. 23–25.
19. Sale, *SDS*, p. 106.
20. Matusow, *The Unraveling of America*, pp. 123–24, 245.
21. Dick Flacks to the National Office, February 16, 1964.
22. The Ad Hoc Committee on the Triple Revolution, "The Triple Revolution: An Appraisal of the Major U.S. Crises and Proposals for Action," pp. 13, 12; Flacks papers.
23. Herman D. Stein, ed., *The Crisis in Welfare in Cleveland: Report of the Mayor's Commission* (Cleveland, 1969), p. 113. Andrew Kopkind, "Introduction: The Young Radicals," in Kopkind, ed., *Thoughts of the Young Radicals* (New Jersey, 1966), p. 3.
24. Sharon Jeffrey to Steve [Max], 5/4/64; SDS Microfilm, Series 2B, No. 89.
25. "To: ERAP community staff, From: Rennie Davis, Re: ERAP Summer Institute"; SDS Microfilm, Series 2B, No. 17.
26. Flacks interview, 3–4–85.
27. "A Statement by Paul Potter . . . submitted for the consideration of the SDS 1964 National Convention in Pine Hill," pp. 1, 2; Flacks papers.

28. Dick Flacks, "SDS 1964 Convention, Draft Statement #2," p. 25; Flacks papers. Swarthmore College Chapter of SDS, "SDS 1964 Convention, Draft Statement #1," p. 3; Flacks papers. See also C. Clark Kissinger, "1964 Convention Summary," [SDS] *Bulletin*, Vol. 2, No. 10 (July, 1964), pp. 1, 30–33.

29. "Confidential for Staff Use ERAP Project Report: Report from Cleveland Community Project, June 20–28," p. 1 [hereafter "Cleveland Report, 6–28–64"]; SDS Microfilm, Series 2B, No. 2.

30. See untitled fragments on "Cleveland 6/64," source unclear, in SDS Microfilm, Series 2B, No. 95. Kathy Boudin—later a Weatherman and fugitive, arrested in 1981 after a Brink's car robbery and a shoot-out that left two dead—was briefly a member of the Cleveland project in 1964, and rejoined Jeffery and McEldowney in 1965. See John Castellucci, *The Big Dance* (New York, 1986), pp. 96–100.

31. See "Cleveland Report, 6–28–64," pp. 1, 6.

32. Ibid., p. 6.

33. Ibid., pp. 1–2.

34. Ibid., p. 2. For the Mississippi Summer Project, see Forman, *The Making of Black Revolutionaries*, pp. 371–86,

35. "Cleveland Report, 6–28–64," pp. 7–8.

36. "Cleveland Report, July 23 [1964]," p. 4; SDS Microfilm, Series 2B, No. 2.

37. Potter, *A Name for Ourselves*, p.145.

38. "Cleveland Report, July 23 [1964], pp. 2–3, 5–6, 8.

39. Potter, *A Name for Ourselves*, pp. 145–46.

40. "Cleveland [Report], July 27," p. 1; SDS Microfilm, Series 2B, No. 2. "Cleveland [Report], August 9," p. 4; SDS Microfilm, Series 2B, No. 2. "Cleveland [Report; n.d.—probably August 10–17, 1964, n.p.]"; SDS Microfilm, Series 2B, No. 2.

41. "Cleveland Report," July 23 [1964], pp. 4, 6.

42. Ibid., p. 8.

43. "Cleveland [Report], August 9 [1964]," pp. 1–2; SDS Microfilm, Series 2B, No. 2.

44. Potter, *A Name for Ourselves*, p. 149.

45. Hayden, "Student Social Action," p. 7. Flacks, "Student Activists: Result, Not Revolt," *Pyschology Today*, October, 1967, p. 22.

46. For Mills, see above, Ch. 4.

47. For SNCC's informal structures of decision-making at the time, see Forman, *The Making of Black Revolutionaries*, pp. 235, 418–19.

48. Paul Jacobs and Saul Landau, *The New Radicals*, pp. 30–31. For more on Quaker concepts of democracy, see Margaret Hope Bacon, *The Quiet Rebels* (Philadelphia, 1985), pp. 171–75.

49. Jean-Jacques Rousseau, *The Social Contract*, Bk. III, Ch. 15.

50. Potter, *A Name for Ourselves*, pp. 182–83.

51. "Cleveland Report" [September 10–20, 1964], p. 3; SDS Microfilm, Series 2B, No. 101.

52. Ibid., p. 2. "Cleveland Report" [October 4–11, 1964]; SDS Microfilm, Series 2B, No. 101. Sharon Jeffrey to ———, October 4, 1964; SDS Microfilm, Series 2B, No. 91.

53. "Students for a Democratic Society respectfully requests $13,450 to support

a political education program for three indigenous community organiza-
tions in a low-income white neighborhood of Cleveland, Ohio" [hereafter
"Cleveland Grant Request"], pp. 1, 2; SDS Microfilm, Series 2B, No. 97.
This request was made to cover operating expenses for the year 1965.

54. Ibid., p. 3.
55. Ibid., pp. 7–9.
56. Ibid., pp. 10–15.
57. Quoted in Connie Brown, "Cleveland: Conference of the Poor," *Studies on
the Left*, Vol. 5, No. 2 (Spring, 1965), p. 73.
58. "Reports on Cleveland's Rat March," *ERAP Newsletter*, August 27, 1965;
SDS Microfilm, Series 2B, No. 24. See also Rothstein, "A Short History of
ERAP," p. 4; SDS Microfilm, Series 2B, No. 21.
59. Ibid., p. 4. Sale *SDS*, p. 146–47. For the National Welfare Rights Organization, see Frances Fox Piven and Richard A. Cloward, *Poor People's Movements: Why They Succeed, How They Fail* (New York, 1977), esp. pp.
290–92. For the SDS influence on SNCC, see Forman, *The Making of Black
Revolutionaries*, p. 419. Forman became a Marxist convinced of the need
for disciplined organization; he considers the SDS influence on SNCC
"middle class" and pernicious. See ibid., p. 413: "An organization that is
seeking revolution, and willing to use violence, cannot afford the fear of
power." Forman regards Bob Moses as the SNCC leader most crippled by
this "liberal" attitude. See also Staughton Lynd, "The New Radicals and
Participatory Democracy," *Dissent*, Vol. 12, No. 3 (Summer, 1965), pp.
324–26. And see the chronology in Newfield, *A Prophetic Minority*, pp.
100–101. Cf. Carson, *In Struggle*, pp. 176–77. Carson assumes, erroneously,
that "participatory democracy" inhered in "moribund American traditions" that SNCC reactivated, thus inspiring the SDS use of the phrase (see
ibid., p. 141). It is hard to tell precisely, but the currency of the actual phrase
"participatory democracy" in SNCC seems to coincide roughly with the
Waveland retreat of November, 1964—long after SDS had made the phrase
into a guiding slogan. Hayden volunteered the information about the Peace
Corps job offer in his marginal comments, adding details in his interview
of 5–16–86: "It was a grandiose offer: 'Will I take the Andes?' They were
exploring whether I would be interested in working with the Peace Corps
in Latin America, primarily as a trainer. They thought that I would be a
good organizer of organizers, staying within the bounds of realism, but
organizing insurgents. I was so remote from official life that I didn't take it
[the offer] seriously."
60. "Cleveland ERAP Report for Sept. 28–Oct. 4" [1964]; SDS Microfilm, Series
2B, No. 101. For talk of "counter-institutions," see Carol McEldowney's
letter of May 19, 1965, on the ERAP summer institute, esp. p. 7; SDS
Microfilm, Series 2B, No. 18.
61. "Cleveland Community Project Summer 1966 An Introduction"; Flacks
papers.
62. Rothstein, "A Short History of ERAP," p. 2.
63. Paul Potter, "Research and Education in Community Action Projects," p.
1; SDS Microfilm, Series 4B, No.278. "To: ERAP staff and friends From:
Cleveland project Re: Summer institute," May 5, 1965, p. 4; SDS Micro-

film, Series 2B, No. 18. On the ERAP decision to decentralize, see Rothstein, "Evolution of the ERAP Organizers," pp. 283–84. Hayden's marginal comment: "It was the reverse of the usual organizational dynamic of centralism, bureaucracy, stagnation, etc."

64. Sharon Jeffrey, "Vietnam in Poor Black and White Communities," from *National Vietnam Newsletter*, No. 3 (August 26, 1965); SDS Microfilm, Series 2B, No. 65.

65. See "A Movement of Many Voices," the recruiting pamphlet that ERAP published in the spring of 1965: "Talk helps people consider the possibilities open for social change. . . . Movements begin when people get together to think out loud about the kind of city they might help to create. One person said, 'Freedom is an endless meeting.' " "1965 SDS National Convention Working Paper, from Ken McEldowney (Cleveland Project)"; Flacks papers. In her valuable study of the utopian strand in the New Left, Wini Breines asserts that participatory democracy "worked well in small groups." She also suggests that of all the reasons for the ultimate failure of the ERAP projects, "the democratic nature of ERAP community organizations was probably the least important." See Breines, *Community and Organization in the New Left, 1962–1968*, pp. 63, 145. There is some truth in these observations: as we have just seen, the Cleveland ERAP project managed to operate smoothly through consensus for a number of months. But the eventual fate of the Cleveland project suggests that Breines underestimates the enormous difficulties that the group's commitment to a radical form of direct democracy created—the amount of time and level of self-sacrifice that were required were simply too great, even for committed young radicals with no other responsibilities.

66. Potter, *A Name for Ourselves*, p. 152.

67. For a detailed and fascinating account of one such democratic commune, full of shrewd observations, see Jane J. Mansbridge, *Beyond Adversary Democracy* (New York, 1980), pp. 129–230.

Chapter Eleven

1. Booth interview, 12–28–85; unless otherwise indicated, all subsequent Booth quotations in this chapter come from this interview.

2. For the Gulf of Tonkin incident and the Vietnam War generally, see Stanley Karnow, *Vietnam: A History* (New York, 1983), pp. 360–76; and Gabriel Kolko, *Anatomy of a War: Vietnam, the United States and the Modern Historical Experience* (New York, 1986), pp. 122–25.

3. Paul Booth, "National Secretary's Report 12–65," p. 1; Flacks papers.

4. Booth interview, 9–23–84.

5. See, e.g., Paul Booth, "Peace Politics" [February, 1964]; SDS Microfilm, Series 4B, No. 24. See also: Paul Booth, "Peace Politics—1962," from a speech delivered in March, 1963; SDS Microfilm, Series 2A, No. 19. And Paul Booth, "Converting America" [1964]; SDS Microfilm, Series 4B, No. 22.

6. Dick Flacks, "To: SDS Work List and others; Re: NEW CRISIS IN VIETNAM"; SDS Microfilm, Series 2A, No. 55.

7. Karnow, *Vietnam*, pp. 360–76.

8. I. F. Stone, "What Few Knew About the Tonkin Bay Incidents" [August 24, 1964], reprinted in Stone, *In a Time of Torment* (New York, 1968), p. 195. Stone's conclusions have since been borne out by extensive contemporary documentation. See, e.g., George McT. Kahin, *Intervention* (New York, 1986), pp. 219–25.

9. "Toward an Effective Program on Campus," PREP, Fall, 1964, pp. 2–3; Flacks papers. Wayne Morse to Douglas Ireland, September 4, 1964; SDS Microfilm, Series 2A, No. 55.

10. For a brief overview of the organized peace movement in 1963–64, see Nancy Zaroulis and Gerald Sullivan, *Who Spoke Up?* (Garden City, N.Y., 1984), pp. 7–16.

11. Ibid., p. 10.

12. "Working Papers—NC PREP Committee"; SDS Microfilm, Series 2A, No. 12. Paul Booth, Todd Gitlin, "Draft Resolution on Vietnam"; SDS Microfilm, Series 2A, No. 12.

13. The best source for the Berkeley uprising is Seymour Martin Lipset and Sheldon S. Wolin, eds., *The Berkeley Student Revolt* (Garden City, N.Y., 1965). For the SDS response, see Robert J. Ross, "Primary Groups in Social Movements: A Memoir and Interpretation," *Journal of Voluntary Action Research*, Vol. 6, Nos. 3–4 (July–October, 1977), p. 143. Also see Richard Flacks, "Student Power and the New Left: The Role of SDS," in Howard Gadlin and Bertram E. Garskof, eds., *The Uptight Society* (Belmont, Calif., 1970), p. 202.

14. See Todd Gitlin to Robb and Dorothy Burlage, 9–12–64; quoted in Todd Gitlin, *The Whole World Is Watching* (Berkeley, 1980), p. 134.

15. "Report of the Committee on the Establishment of the Political Education Project" [Fall, 1964].

16. Eugene Feingold and Tom Hayden, "Politics 1965—Corporatism and Crisis," pp. 11–12; SDS Microfilm, Series 4B, No. 157 [also published as "What happened to democracy?" in *New University Thought*, Vol. 4, No. 1 (Summer, 1964), pp. 39–48]. Tom Hayden, "SNCC: The Qualities of Protest," *Studies on the Left*, Vol. 5, No. 1 (Winter, 1965), p. 120.

17. See "Intro." [to "letter by Dick Flacks. . . . written just after the Christmas 1964 National Council meeting"], in "December Conference" packet of papers, p. 5; Flacks papers. See also Sale, *SDS*, pp. 156–57.

18. See Milton Mankoff and Richard Flacks, "The Changing Social Base of the American Student Movement," in Philip G. Altbach and Robert S. Laufer, eds., *The New Pilgrims: Youth Protest in Transition* (Boston, 1972), pp. 46–62.

19. Sale, *SDS*, pp. 206, 209. Fred Powledge, "The New Student Left: Movement Represents Serious Activists in Drive for Changes," *The New York Times*, Monday, March 15, 1965.

20. Jeffrey Shero, "SDS, Organization and the South"; SDS Microfilm, Series 2A, No. 130.

21. The first two Hayden quotes come from Sale, *SDS*, pp. 158–59; the second two from Hayden, "SNCC: The Qualities of Protest," p. 118. See also Steven V. Roberts, "Will Tom Hayden Overcome?," *Esquire*, Vol. 70, No. 6 (December, 1968), p. 179.

22. "Minutes of SDS NC Plenary Session—Wednesday, 30. 12. 64"; SDS Microfilm, Series 2A, No. 12. Further details about the parliamentary maneuvering and Hayden's speech were communicated in a phone interview with Bob Ross, 4–15–86. Cf. Sale, *SDS*, pp. 170–72; and "Report from the Editors: The SDS March on Washington" [hereafter "SDS March"], *Studies on the Left*, Vol. 5, No. 2 (Spring, 1965), p. 62.

23. Booth letter, 1–18–65, quoted in Sale, *SDS*, p. 172.

24. See Todd [Gitlin] to Izzy [Stone], 1–15–65; SDS Microfilm, Series 2A, No. 59. C. Clark Kissinger to "Dear Friend," 1–3–65; SDS Microfilm, Series 2A, No. 60. And "SDS March," *Studies on the Left*, p. 63.

25. "2/11/65 FOR IMMEDIATE RELEASE: STUDENTS OPPOSE VIETNAM POLICY" [SDS press release]; SDS microfilm, Series 2A, No. 60. Zaroulis and Sullivan, *Who Spoke Up?*, p. 37.

26. Paul Booth to Mike James, 3–5–65; SDS Microfilm, Series 2A, No. 19.

27. The details of the wrangling over the April SDS march are recounted in "SDS March," *Studies on the Left*, pp. 64–65.

28. On the teach-ins, see Zaroulis and Sullivan, *Who Spoke Up?*, pp. 37–38 and Sale, *SDS*, p. 183.

29. For the poster and songs, see "SDS March," *Studies on the Left*, pp. 66–67.

30. On the background to Johnson's speech, see Karnow, *Vietnam*, p. 418.

31. Ibid., pp. 418–19.

32. ". . . THAT BRIGHT AND NECESSARY DAY OF PEACE . . . ," April 8, 1965; SDS Microfilm, Series 2A, No. 61. Cf. the behind-the-scenes account of Johnson's thinking in Kahin, *Intervention*, pp. 324–25.

33. The statement is included in the SDS Microfilm, Series 2A, No. 60. See also the *New York Post*, April 17, 1965; SDS Microfilm, Series 2A, No. 60. And see "SDS March," *Studies on the Left*, pp. 67–68.

34. Details on the march and the speeches come from: Paul Booth, "March on Washington," *Students for a Democratic Society Bulletin*, Vol. 3, No. 7 (May, 1965), pp. 1, 9–10; Flacks papers. Dave Dellinger, "The March on Washington and Its Critics," *Liberation*, Vol. 10, No. 3 (May, 1965). "15,000 White House Pickets Denounce Vietnam War," *The New York Times*, April 18, 1965. Zaroulis and Sullivan, *Who Spoke Up?*, pp. 40–42. Newfield, *A Prophetic Minority*, pp. 190–91. On Bob Moses' name change, see Forman, *The Making of Black Revolutionaries*, p. 439.

35. From the text of Potter's speech reprinted by SDS as a pamphlet; Flacks papers. See also Andrew Kopkind, "Of, By and For the Poor," *The New Republic*, Vol. 152, No. 25 (June 19, 1965), p. 19.

36. Potter, *A Name for Ourselves*, p. 101.

37. "Petition to Congress"; SDS Microfilm, Series 2A, No. 60.

38. Staughton Lynd, "Coalition Politics or Nonviolent Revolution?," *Liberation*, June–July, 1965; reprinted in Jacobs and Landau, *The New Radicals*, pp. 318–19.

39. Tom Hayden, "The Politics of 'The Movement,'" in Irving Howe, ed., *The Radical Papers* (Garden City, N.Y., 1966), pp. 376–77. See also Paul Cowan, "An Open Letter to Tom Hayden" [a working paper for the 1965 SDS national convention], p. 1; SDS Microfilm, Series 2A, No. 16.

40. See Paul Booth, "Working Papers; Summer Projects," p. 1; SDS Microfilm,

Series 2A, No. 16; and Sale, *SDS*, p. 194. For the break with LID, see ibid., pp. 237–40.

41. Booth, "March on Washington," *Students for a Democratic Society Bulletin*, Vol. 3, No. 7 (May, 1965), p. 10.

42. Fred Powledge, "The New Student Left: Movement Represents Serious Activists in Drive for Changes," *The New York Times*, March 15, 1965.

43. "15,000 White House Pickets Denounce Vietnam War," *The New York Times*, April 18, 1965, p. 3.

44. "The Peace Opposition," *The Nation*, Vol. 200, No. 18 (May 3, 1965), p. 462. "Rebels with Cause," *The New Republic*, May 1, 1965, Vol. 152, No. 18, pp. 5–6.

45. Jack Newfield, "The Student Left: Revolt Without Dogma," *The Nation*, Vol. 200, No. 19 (May 10, 1965), pp. 491–95. Andrew Kopkind, "Of, By and For the Poor: The New Generation of Student Organizers," *The New Republic*, Vol. 152, No. 25 (June 19, 1965), p. 15. Jack Newfield, "Idealism and Action: The Student Left," *The Nation*, Vol. 201, No. 15 (November 8, 1965), p. 330. Andrew Kopkind, "Looking Backward: The Sixties and the Movement," *Ramparts*, Vol. 11, No. 8 (February, 1973), p. 29. In his invaluable study of how media coverage affected the growth of the New Left, Todd Gitlin does not even mention the articles by Newfield and Kopkind. Yet on the basis of personal experience, it was *these* accounts (both subsequently reprinted in books) that attracted the attention of scores of liberal-minded students in 1965 and 1966—not the articles in *The New York Times*, which in those days was not widely available in most of the country. See Gitlin, *The Whole World Is Watching*, esp. pp. 32–133. Kopkind's article was also reprinted as the introduction to *Thoughts of the Young Radicals* (1966), a collection of essays by Hayden, Flacks and others that originally appeared in *The New Republic*.

46. Jacobs and Landau, *The New Radicals*, pp. 27–28.

47. Ibid., pp. 28, 35. The Dylan line alluded to is from "Subterranean Homesick Blues." See Bob Dylan, *Lyrics: 1962–1985* (New York, 1985), p. 164. Hayden's marginal comment: "Very important . . . Dylan more important than Mills et al. in some ways. . . . More important than Kerouac."

48. Jacobs and Landau, *The New Radicals*, p. 29. Steve [Max] to Paul [Booth]; SDS Microfilm, Series 3, No. 2.

49. "Workshops for the 1965 SDS National Convention;" SDS Microfilm, Series 2A, No. 14.

50. Booth, "Working Papers: Summer Projects," p. 7; SDS Microfilm, Series 2A, No. 16.

51. Paul Potter, "SDS and Foreign Policy," p. 1. Paul Cowan, "An Open Letter to Tom Hayden," pp. 3, 4. Ken McEldowney, "Dear National Office," p. 2. Dick Flacks, "Some Problems, Issues, Proposals," p. 1. All 1965 SDS National Convention working papers: see SDS Microfilm, Series 2A, No. 16.

52. Jacobs and Landau, *The New Radicals*, p. 31.

53. "Workshops for the 1965 SDS National Convention"; SDS Microfilm, Series 2A, No. 16. See also "Notes for the December National Council"; SDS Microfilm, Series 2A, No. 12.

54. Shero quoted in Sale, *SDS*, p. 209n. Shero's argument is taken from his

working paper for the 1965 convention, "M.D.S.—Movement for a Democratic Society," p. 2; SDS Microfilm, Series 2A, No. 16.

55. Ibid., p. 2.

56. Steve Max, "The 1965 SDS Convention: From Port Huron to Maplehurst," p. 2, in "December Conference" packet of papers; Flacks papers. See also Booth, "National Secretary's Report 12–65," p. 4, in "December Conference" packet of papers; Flacks papers.

57. Max, "From Port Huron to Maplehurst," p. 2.

58. Paul Booth to Todd Gitlin, 5–29–65; quoted in Gitlin, *The Whole World Is Watching*, p. 83.

59. Oglesby quoted in Zaroulis and Sullivan, *Who Spoke Up?*, p. 50.

60. "Interviews with SDS Staffers," in Jacobs and Landau, *The New Radicals*, pp. 176, 177. Booth is unnamed, but unmistakably the person quoted, as he himself has confirmed.

61. "From: Paul Booth, Oakland Community Project," *National Vietnam Newsletter*, #3, August 26, 1965; SDS Microfilm, Series 2A, No. 65. Paul Booth, "Strategy for the Peace Movement," *Liberation*, Vol. 11, No. 5 (August, 1966), p. 50.

62. Jeffrey Shero, "The S.D.S. National Office: Bureaucracy, Democracy and Decentralization," p. 3 [a paper for the 1965 December Conference]; Flacks papers. Sale, *SDS*, pp. 216–17.

63. See Magidoff letter in "December Conference" packet of papers, pp. 4–5; Flacks papers.

64. "SDS NC—or "How to build a movement; Sept. 7" [minutes for National Council meeting, September, 1965], pp. 10, 13; SDS Microfilm; Series 3, No. 6.

65. See ibid., p. 8: "Does participatory democ[racy] work in office—tied to decision making and delegation of respons[ibility]—difficult to collectivize these with people in N[ational] O[ffice] who don't completely understand SDS—staff is transient and is expanding to people who are not capable of making polit[ical] decisions—lack of inter[nal] dem[ocracy]—whole ques[tion] of partici[patory] democ[racy]—need to refine 'partic. democ.'— this theoretical aspect has been lacking—problem of commitment, developing this and understanding of this."

66. See Shero, "The S.D.S. National Office: Bureaucracy, Democracy and Decentralization," p. 4; and Booth, "National Secretary's Report 12–65," p. 3.

67. *The New York Times*, quoted in Gitlin, p. 102. See also Newfield, *A Prophetic Minority*, p. 117.

68. See Booth, "National Secretary's Report 12–65," pp. 7, 10.

69. Shero, "The S.D.S. National Office: Bureaucracy, Democracy and Decentralization," p. 4. Booth, quoted in Newfield, *A Prophetic Minority*, p. 124.

70. Booth, quoted in Thomas R. Brooks, "Voice of the New Campus Underclass," *The New York Times Magazine*, November 7, 1965, p. 135. Booth, "National Secretary's Report 12–65," p. 7.

71. Shero, "The S.D.S. National Office: Bureaucracy, Democracy and Decentralization," p. 3.

72. Jeff Shero to Dick Howard, 12–15–65; SDS Microfilm, Series 3, No. 1. Sale, *SDS*, p. 224.

73. Paul Booth to David Hunter, Stern Family Fund, 9–28–65; SDS Microfilm, Series 3, No. 1.
74. Gitlin, *The Whole World Is Watching*, pp. 88–89, 90. In what follows, I make extensive use of Gitlin's detailed reconstruction of these events. Stephen D. Lerner, "Paul Booth," *The Harvard Crimson*, November 2, 1965.
75. See [SDS] *Worklist*, #23, October 22, 1965; SDS Microfilm, Series 3, No. 126.
76. Gitlin, *The Whole World Is Watching*, pp. 89, 93, 94.
77. Chicago *Sun-Times*, October 16, 1965, pp. 1, 6. See also Richard Rothstein, "Make Love Not War: The Campaign Against the Draft," *Liberation*, December, 1965, p. 24.
78. Gitlin, *The Whole World Is Watching*, pp. 95–98.
79. [SDS] *Worklist*, #23, October 22, 1965. Gitlin, *The Whole World Is Watching*, p. 102.
80. Booth, "National Secretary's Report 12–65," p. 4.
81. "Students for a Democratic Society: 'Build, Not Burn' "; SDS Microfilm, Series 3, No. 1.
82. Paul Booth to Richard Reiss, Americans for Reappraisal of Far Eastern Policy, 10–21–65; SDS Microfilm, Series 3, No. 1.
83. [SDS] *Worklist*, #23, October 11, 1965. *The New Republic*, October 30, 1965, quoted in Sale, *SDS*, p. 237. Booth, "National Secretary's Report 12–65," p. 5.
84. Ken McEldowney to Paul Booth, 11–21–65; SDS Microfilm, Series 3, No. 1. Shero, "The S.D.S. National Office: Bureaucracy, Democracy and Decentralization," p. 8.
85. Judy Pardun to N.[ational] O.[ffice] People, 11–1–65; SDS Microfilm, Series 3, No. 1.
86. Paul Booth to Erwin Rosen, 11–19–65; SDS Microfilm, Series 3, No. 1.
87. [SDS] *Worklist*, No. 27, November 17, 1965; SDS Microfilm, Series 3, No. 126.
88. Mansbridge, *Beyond Adversary Democracy*, p. 211.
89. Paul Booth to Mike Davis [Nov–Dec?, 1965]; SDS Microfilm, Series 3, No. 1.
90. Booth, quoted in Newfield, "The Student Left: Idealism and Action," *The Nation*, Vol. 201, No. 15 (November 8, 1965), p. 333. Todd Gitlin, "Movement," *The Nation*, November 8, 1965, p. 331. The membership estimate comes from Sale, *SDS*, p. 664.
91. Andrew Kopkind, "Radicals on the March," *The New Republic*, Vol. 153, No. 24 (December 11, 1965), pp. 15–19.
92. Carl Oglesby, "Let Us Shape the Future," reprinted in *Liberation*, Vol. 10, No. 10 (January, 1966), p. 14.
93. A number of papers were circulated before the December conference in a stapled packet; others were circulated separately at the conference. The papers (and passages) alluded to in this paragraph are, in order: C. George Benello, "Some Key Issues in Participative Democracy," p. 2; Dick Howard, "SDS: Present and Future," p. 12; Michael Zweig, "Some Reflections on a Radical Movement," p. 12; Robert Pardun, "Organizational Democracy," pp. 3–4; C. Clark Kissinger, "There's a Change Gotta Come!," p. 3; Paul Booth, "National Secretary's Report 12–65," p. 9; Jeffrey Shero, "The S.D.S.

National Office: Bureaucracy, Democracy and Decentralization," p. 13. See SDS Microfilm, Series 3, No. 3; and Series 3, No. 130.

94. Lee Webb and Paul Booth, "The Anti-War Movement: From Protest to Radical Politics," pp. 1, 11, in December conference packet; Flacks papers. Shero, "The S.D.S. National Office: Bureaucracy, Democracy and Decentralization," p. 13. The metaphor comes from Louis Hartz, *The Liberal Tradition in America* (New York, 1955), p. 90.

95. Ross, "Primary Groups in Social Movements: A Memoir and Interpretation," *Journal of Voluntary Action Research*, p. 144.

96. Jeffrey interview 2–28–85. For the roots of modern feminism in the New Left, see Evans, *Personal Politics*, esp. pp. 156–69. Evans includes extensive quotes from Sharon Jeffrey and Carol McEldowney. "Notes" from the small-group discussion on women and women's roles at the December conference; these notes are in the private possession of Vivian Rothstein.

97. Gitlin, *The Whole World Is Watching*, p. 31.

98. See Paul Booth, "Student and Workers," *Ramparts*, Vol. 8, No. 3 (September, 1969), pp. 19–20.

Chapter Twelve

1. Staughton Lynd and Thomas Hayden, *The Other Side* (New York, 1966), pp. 57, 9. Tom Hayden, "A Visit to Hanoi," *Liberation*, Vol. 11, No. 3 (May–June, 1966), pp. 23, 25.

2. Roberts, "Will Tom Hayden Overcome?," p. 209. Andrew Kopkind, "Looking Backward," *Ramparts*, February, 1973, p. 29.

3. Hayden, *Radical Nomad*, pp. 195–96.

4. "Summer Report: Newark Community Union" [1964], p. 4; SDS Microfilm, Series 4B, No. 154. See also Stanley Aronowitz, "When the New Left was New," *The 60's Without Apology*, p. 23.

5. Tom Hayden, "The Politics of 'The Movement,' " in Howe, ed., *The Radical Papers* (Garden City, N.Y., 1966), p. 375. Tom Hayden, "The Ability to Face Whatever Comes," in Kopkind, ed., *Thoughts of the Young Radicals* (New York, 1966), pp. 40–41. Tom Hayden, "SNCC: The Qualities of Protest," *Studies on the Left*, Vol. 5, No. 1 (Winter, 1965), pp. 118, 119, 120. "Summer Report: Newark Community Union," p. 6.

6. See Tom Hayden, Norm Fruchter, Alan Cheuse, "Up from Irrelevance," *Studies on the Left*, Vol. 5, No. 2 (Spring, 1965), p. 5 (where Bayard Rustin's quip about Rousseau is recorded). Also see the "Reply" in the same issue of *Studies* signed by James Weinstein, Stanley Aronowitz, Lee Baxandall, Eugene D. Genovese and Helen Kramer, esp. pp. 8–9.

7. Hayden, Fruchter, Cheuse, "Up From Irrelevance," pp. 6, 7. Hayden interview, 1–25–86.

8. Findley, "Hayden: Rolling Stone Interview, Part 1," p. 46.

9. Ibid., p. 46. Lynd and Hayden, *The Other Side*, p. 5.

10. Findley, "Hayden: Rolling Stone Interview, Part 1," p. 46. See Lynd and Hayden, *The Other Side*, p. 22.

11. Findley, "Hayden: Rolling Stone Interview, Part 1," p. 46, with bracketed correction of the printed transcript by Hayden, from phone interview, 7–5–86.

12. Lynd and Hayden, *The Other Side*, p. 22.

13. Findley, "Hayden: Rolling Stone Interview, Part 1," pp. 46–48. Roberts, "Will Tom Hayden Overcome?," p. 208.
14. Findley, "Hayden: Rolling Stone Interview, Part 1," p. 48.
15. Staughton Lynd, "Socialism, the Forbidden Word," *Studies on the Left*, Vol. 3, No. 3 (Summer, 1963), pp. 19, 18. For Lynd's career, see Newfield, *A Prophetic Minority*, pp. 195–96.
16. Lynd and Hayden, *The Other Side*, pp. 80, 69, 65.
17. Ibid., pp. 146–47, 92, 200.
18. Douglas Pike, *PAVN: People's Army of Vietnam* (Novato, Calif., 1986), p. 238. Kolko, *Anatomy of a War*, p. 270.
19. Cf. Hayden interview, 3–10–85: "Parliamentary leaders are prosaic. Visionary leaders are poetic. The prosaic leader elicits participation primarily on the level of an occasional vote. The poetic leader elicits curiously greater participation from people who are in fact not just an anonymous mass of followers. At the same time that they're followers in one sense, they are doing more than voting. They are involved in neighborhood or union or political associations, they're reading, they're studying, they're arguing, they're *developing*—even though they seem to have been triggered by an authoritarian or dominating kind of leader."
20. Rosa Luxemburg, *"The Russian Revolution" and "Leninism or Marxism?"* (Ann Arbor, Mich., 1961), p. 77. Cf. Christopher Lasch, "Journey to Hanoi," *The New York Times Book Review*, April 23, 1967: Lasch immediately recognized *The Other Side* as a minor classic of revolutionary romance.
21. Hayden interview, 1–25–86.
22. Findley, "Hayden: Rolling Stone Interview, Part 1," p. 46.
23. Barbara and Alan Haber, "Getting By with a Little Help from Our Friends," in Priscilla Long, ed., *The New Left: A Collection of Essays* (Boston, 1969), p. 292.
24. Hayden interview, 3–10–85.
25. "Newark report and reprints from NCUP paper," *ERAP Newsletter*, July 23, 1965; SDS Microfilm, Series 2B, No. 24.
26. Findley, "Hayden: Rolling Stone Interview, Part 1," p. 44.
27. Tom Hayden, *Trial* (New York, 1970), p. 109.
28. Jeffrey interview, 2–28–85. Flacks interview, 5–16–86. Irving Howe, *A Margin of Hope* (New York, 1982), p. 293.
29. Hayden interview, 5–16–86.
30. See Tom Hayden, *Rebellion in Newark* (New York, 1977), and Matusow, *The Unraveling of America*, pp. 362–63.
31. Ibid., pp. 362, 353–55. See also Carson, *In Struggle*, pp. 190–211.
32. Hayden in the *National Guardian*, quoted in Hayden, *Rebellion and Repression*, p. 74. Hayden, *Rebellion in Newark*, pp. 26, 5–7. See also Roberts, "Will Tom Hayden Overcome?," p. 208. Plus details from Hayden's marginal comment.
33. Findley, "Hayden: Rolling Stone Interview, Part 1," pp. 44–46. "Improbable Radical: Thomas Emmett Hayden," Man in the News profile, *The New York Times*, November 13, 1967.
34. Findley, "Hayden: Rolling Stone Interview, Part 1," p. 46. Hayden marginal comment.

35. Findley, "Hayden: Rolling Stone Interview, Part 1," p. 46. In "Growing Up with America: The Life Story of Tom Hayden," a campaign biography distributed in 1982, the text asserts that "Hughes followed Hayden's advice and the riots ended"—an assertion that Hayden himself, in his interview of 1–25–86, told me he has no way of verifying: "I really don't know what role in that history I played. I think he [Hughes] would have made the same decision whether or not I'd been there."

36. Hayden, *Rebellion in Newark*, pp. 4, 69.

37. Ibid., pp. 68, 69, 32, 71, 72.

38. Kopkind interview, 1–7–86. Andrew Kopkind's piece was "Soul Power," *The New York Review of Books*, Vol. 9 (August 24, 1967).

39. Hayden interview, 5–16–86.

40. Matusow, *The Unraveling of America*, p. 327. See also Carson, *In Struggle*, pp. 274–75.

41. Karnow, *Vietnam*, pp. 457–59.

42. Langdon Winner, quoted in Greil Marcus, "The Beatles," in Jim Miller, ed., *The Rolling Stone Illustrated History of Rock and Roll* (New York, 1980), p. 183. See also Timothy Leary, *Flashbacks* (Los Angeles, 1983), esp. pp. 43–44, for the debate with Huxley. For drugs and the New Left generally, see Martin A. Lee and Bruce Shlain, *Acid Dreams* (New York, 1985), esp. pp. 126–38.

43. Hayden marginal comment. Kopkind, "Looking Backward," p. 32. For the Bratislava conference generally, see: "Promise vs. Performance," *Newsweek*, September 25, 1985. Findley, "Hayden: Rolling Stone Interview, Part 1," p. 46. Roberts, "Will Tom Hayden Overcome?," p. 208. Zaroulis and Sullivan, *Who Spoke Up?*, pp. 130–32.

44. Hayden interview, 5–16–86. Hayden phone interview, 4–30–86.

45. Roberts, "Will Tom Hayden Overcome?," p. 208. Kopkind, "Looking Backward," p. 32. Kopkind, phone interview, 5–5–86. Flacks interview, 5–16–86.

46. Hayden marginal comment.

47. Cf. "Promise vs. Performance," *Newsweek*, September 25, 1985. Hayden insists that the *Newsweek* version, widely quoted since—"We are all Viet Cong *now*"—is a misquote.

48. Hayden interview, 5–16–86.

49. Ibid.

50. Ibid.

51. Ibid.

52. See Dave Dellinger, *More Power than We Know* (New York, 1975), p. 53; Dellinger, in *Liberation*, November, 1967, and Zaroulis and Sullivan, *Who Spoke Up?*, pp. 135–36.

53. Norman Mailer, *Armies of the Night* (New York, 1968), p. 285.

54. Zaroulis and Sullivan, *Who Spoke Up?*, pp. 137–41.

55. Hayden interview, 5–16–86.

56. Ibid. Cf. Rennie Davis, who implicitly confirms Hayden's account, in his interview with Zaroulis and Sullivan, *Who Spoke Up?*, pp. 131–32.

57. See Dellinger, *More Power Than We Know*, pp. 131–32.

58. Findley, "Hayden: Rolling Stone Interview, Part 2," p. 28. Tom Hayden,

"Post-Chicago Interview" [from *The Movement*], in Walter Schneir, ed., *Telling It like It Was: The Chicago Riots* (New York, 1969), p. 127.

59. Rennie Davis and Tom Hayden, "Movement Campaign 1968: An Election Year Offensive," pp. 1, 2–3, 4, 16; Flacks papers. Dellinger, *More Power Than We Know*, p. 127.

60. Greg Calvert and Carol Neiman, *A Disrupted History: The New Left and the New Capitalism* (New York, 1971), p. 140. Greg Calvert, "Participatory Democracy, Collective Leadership and Political Responsibility," *New Left Notes*, December 18, 1967, pp. 1, 7. Calvert changed his views on participatory democracy after witnessing the triumph of the Progressive Labor Party and the madness of the Weathermen.

61. Mike Spiegel and Jeff Jones, "Don't Take Your Guns to Town," *New Left Notes*, March 4, 1968. See also Zaroulis and Sullivan, *Who Spoke Up?*, pp. 206–7.

62. Abbie Hoffman, "Why We're Going to Chicago" [from *The Realist*], in Schneir, ed., *Telling It like It Was*, pp. 11–12. Daniel Walker, *Rights in Conflict* (New York, 1968), pp. 44–45. Viorst, *Fire in the Streets*, pp. 446–47. See also Abe Peck, *Uncovering the Sixties* (New York, 1985), p. 103.

63. On the Yippie agenda, see ibid., pp. 118–19.

64. Roberts, "Will Tom Hayden Overcome?," p. 208. Hayden, "Rolling Stone Interview, Part 2," p. 30.

65. "Improbable Radical: Thomas Emmett Hayden," Man in the News profile, *The New York Times*, November 13, 1967.

66. See "Growing Up with America," p. 11. Tom Hayden, "The Impasse in Paris," *Ramparts*, Vol. 7, No. 3 (August 24, 1968), pp. 18–19.

67. Newfield phone interview, 5–13–86. Arthur M. Schlesinger, Jr., *Robert Kennedy and His Times* (New York, 1978), p. 829. Findley, "Hayden: Rolling Stone Interview, Part 1," p. 50. Hayden marginal comments. By 1968, Hayden was calling for "immediate withdrawal"; see Tom Hayden, "Talk, Talk; Fight, Fight," *Ramparts*, Vol. 6, No. 12 (June 29, 1968), p. 6.

68. Hayden interview, 1–25–86.

69. See Findley, "Hayden: Rolling Stone Interview, Part 1," p. 50. Hayden recalled his hopes for an American Mendès-France in his marginal comments and in his interview on 5–16–86.

70. See Kolko, *Anatomy of a War*, pp. 303–11. Cf. Col. Harry G. Summers, *On Strategy* (Novato, Calif., 1982), p. 112: "During Tet 1968 both the North Vietnamese and the Viet Cong suffered heavy losses but, while it may have been a tactical failure, it was a strategic success since, by eroding our will, they were able eventually to capture the political initiative." See also Pike, *PAVN: People's Army of Vietnam*, pp. 226–27.

71. See Viorst, *Fire in the Streets*, pp. 418–20.

72. Findley, "Hayden: Rolling Stone Interview, Part 1," p. 48. Cf. Hayden, "The Impasse in Paris," pp. 18–19; in his Rolling Stone interview, Hayden conflates Harriman's birthday party and the riots.

73. Hayden's marginal comment: "Did I seem so difficult to understand? I thought everything should be tried to head off chaos, but chaos too had to be expected as a possibility."

74. Hayden's marginal comment. Roberts, "Will Tom Hayden Overcome?," p. 176. See Jerry L. Avorn et al., *Up Against the Ivy Wall* (New York, 1968), pp. 37–59.

75. Ibid., pp. 52–53, 29–30, 294.

76. Hayden interview, 5–17–86. Avorn et al., *Up Against the Ivy Wall*, pp. 111–12.

77. Ibid., pp. 117–18, 129. Findley, "Hayden: Rolling Stone Interview, Part 2," p. 28. Dotson Rader, "More About Columbia," in Terrence E. Cook and Patrick M. Morgan, eds., *Participatory Democracy* (San Francisco, 1971), p. 336. Stephen Spender, *The Year of the Young Rebels* (New York, 1969), p. 6.

78. Roberts, "Will Tom Hayden Overcome?," p. 176.

79. Tom Hayden, "Two, Three, Many Columbias," in Teodori, *The New Left*, pp. 346–47.

80. Hayden interview, 5–16–86. Cf. Findley, "Hayden: Rolling Stone Interview, Part 1," p. 50.

81. Ibid., p. 50. Cf. Schlesinger, *Robert Kennedy and His Times*, p. 983.

82. Findley, "Hayden: Rolling Stone Interview, Part 1," p. 50.

83. Ibid.

84. Hayden interview, 5–16–86 (reading a passage from his unpublished memoirs).

85. Ibid.

86. Hayden marginal comment. Findley, "Hayden: Rolling Stone Interview, Part 1," p. 50.

87. Ross interview, 1–23–85.

88. Findley, "Hayden: Rolling Stone Interview, Part 1," p. 50.

89. See Tom Hayden, "Democracy Is . . . in the Streets," *Rat*, Vol. 1, No. 14 ["Convention Special"], p. 5. Hayden [from a letter from the National Mobilization in *Liberation*, July–August, 1968], quoted in Walker, *Rights in Conflict*, p. 90. Rennie Davis, quoted in Zaroulis and Sullivan, *Who Spoke Up?*, p. 179.

90. Ibid., pp. 182–83. Walker, *Rights in Conflict*, pp. 3, 14, 57–95 (on permit negotiations), 95–128 (on the city's security preparations). See Viorst, *Fire in the Streets*, pp. 450–51.

91. Dellinger, *More Power Than We Know*, pp. 121, 126.

92. Hayden interview, 1–25–86. For his trip to Paris, see Hayden, "The Impasse in Paris," pp. 18–21.

93. Peck, *Uncovering the Sixties*, p. 110. I called Peck on 5–6–86 to confirm this story, and he told me that he had checked it with Paul Krassner, who was present. Hayden's marginal comment: "I think I said 'CIA or LSD'— meaning Peck was not in control of himself. This makes me sound as though [I thought] Peck was literally an agent." This remains Peck's (and Krassner's) impression.

94. David Wise, *The American Police State* (New York, 1976), p. 318. Gitlin, *The Whole World Is Watching*, pp. 188–89. Zaroulis and Sullivan, *Who Spoke Up?*, p. 182. Tom Hayden, "Me and My Shadows: From Chicago to Watergate," *New Times*, November 2, 1973, pp. 27–29. Hayden interview, 1–25–86.

95. [Tom] Hayden, "The Machine Can Be Stopped," *The Ramparts Wall Poster*, No. 2 (August 25, 1968).

96. Hayden, "Democracy Is . . . in the Streets," p. 14. Tom Hayden, "The Reason Why," *The Ramparts Wall Poster*, No. 1 (August 24, 1968). Hayden's marginal comment on the Chairman Mao quotation: "I don't quite remember, but I think this was the line of SDS National Office, which had [belatedly] endorsed the action. Rennie and I were now speaking for a many-sided coalition of factions." In my interview with Hayden on 5–16–86, I asked him how conscious of his rhetoric he was in 1968. "Not very," he said after thinking it over. "I think that I was carried away. But it is true that when you're leading a coalition, or to some extent speaking for a coalition, you develop what I call 'coalition thought,' which starts with your ideas, and then becomes your personal merging of all the ideas of all the various elements in the coalition. So there was a little Yippie/counterculture language, some 'Up Against the Wall' street language, some pious reform language." What's hard to find in this document, however, is the "pious reform language."

97. This paragraph is a paraphrase of the thoughtful summary of the unique circumstances of Chicago in Dellinger, *More Power Than We Know*, pp. 99–103. For Hayden's remarks in the Mobilization meeting, see Todd Gitlin, "MOB Debates Street Plans," *The Ramparts Wall Poster*, No. 3 (August 26, 1968).

98. Ibid. Hayden's marginal comments on his remarks as quoted by Gitlin: "This may be someone's notes, but it's clearly not me in reality. It's not the way I talked."

99. Gitlin, "MOB Debates," op. cit. Hayden interview, 5–16–86. The police informer was Irwin Bock, who testified for the prosecution at the conspiracy trial: see Judy Clair and John Spitzer, *The Conspiracy Trial* (Indianapolis, 1970).

100. Walker, *Rights in Conflict*, pp. 154–55. Potter, *A Name for Ourselves*, p. 33.

101. "Editorial" and "Crazed Cops to Hayden: 'We'll Kill You,' " *The Ramparts Wall Poster*, [No. 4], August 27, 1968. Jack Newfield and Paul Cowan, "Outside the Arena: Prelims Are Bloody," in Newfield, *Bread and Roses, Too* (New York, 1971), pp. 106–9. The police testimony in these cases is summarized in Arthur Kinoy, Helene E. Schwartz, Doris Peterson, *Conspiracy on Appeal* (New York, 1971), pp. 254–56n.

102. "Editorial," in *The Ramparts Wall Poster*, August 27, 1968. "Loop the Loop," *Handwriting on the Wall*, No. 3 [SDS Wall Poster]. Walker, *Rights in Conflict*, pp. 187, 204.

103. Ibid., pp. 211–12, 214. Hayden's marginal comment: "This is wacko—again, not my words, but someone's notes. I don't even know the point here."

104. Hayden interview, 1–25–86. Hayden marginal comment. Cf. Fred Gardner, "See Tom and Jane Run," *City* [San Francisco], Vol. 9, No. 5 (August 3, 1975), p. 32. Gardner's piece is a diatribe and not always accurate, but helpful on events in Chicago, which he witnessed firsthand; he recalls Hayden's taped message as "This is Tom Hayden. I've made it inside the Hilton. It is your revolutionary responsibility to get into the Hilton by

any means necessary!" Hayden calls Gardner's version "not true." Other Hayden marginal comments: "There was no way to 'storm' [the hotel]. . . . This was an idea that went nowhere, yet other 'strange' things *really* happened." I have confirmed the gist of this incident with two of the people who actually smuggled Hayden's tape into the Hilton, but both prefer to remain anonymous.

105. For the events of Wednesday, August 28, in Grant Park and in front of the Conrad Hilton, see: Walker, *Rights in Conflict*, pp. 215–85. Kinoy, Schwartz, Peterson, *Conspiracy on Appeal*, pp. 264–66. Zaroulis and Sullivan, *Who Spoke Up?*, pp. 190–91. Viorst, *Fire in the Streets*, pp. 456–57. Dellinger, *More Power Than We Know*, pp. 123, 142–43. Clair and Spitzer, *The Conspiracy Trial*, p. 211. Gardner, "See Tom and Jane Run," p. 32. I have also drawn from my interviews with Hayden on 1–25–86 and 5–16–86, as well as my experience as a participant at the rally and in the crowd in front of the Conrad Hilton. Hayden's speech was *so* garbled that it is not even mentioned in the Walker report!

106. Donald Jansen, "Hayden, in Disguise, Fools Policemen and Friends," *The New York Times*, August 30, 1968.

107. Walker, *Rights in Conflict*, p. 337. Hayden's marginal comment: "Again, someone formulating my speech."

108. Hayden, "Post-Chicago Interview," in *Telling It Like It Was*, pp. 119, 123. Hayden in *The New York Times*, August 31, 1968.

109. For a detailed philosophical defense of this assertion about the injustice of the war in Vietnam, see Michael Walzer, *Just and Unjust Wars* (New York, 1977), pp. 97–101, 186–96, 299–303.

110. Hayden, *Rebellion and Repression*, pp. 175, 179.

111. Hayden, "Democracy Is . . . in the Streets," p. 5. Hayden in *The New York Times*, August 31, 1968. Alexander Cockburn and James Ridgeway, "Hayden: From Chicago Back to the Mainstream," *The Village Voice*, June 23, 1981. I have been influenced here by the astute comments of Christopher Lasch in *The Agony of the American Left* (New York, 1969), pp. 211–12.

112. Hayden's marginal comment: "This is a little like a British journalist writing about bloody riots in Boston in the 1700s."

113. Findley, "Hayden: Rolling Stone Interview, Part 2," p. 28. Hayden, *Trial*, p. 159.

114. Ibid., pp. 158–65. (First published in *Ramparts*, Vol. 9, No. 1 [July, 1970].)

115. Hayden, *Rebellion and Repression*, p. 16. Hayden's marginal comment. See also Dellinger, *More Power Than We Know*, p. 130.

116. Hayden, *Trial*, pp. 44, 151.

117. Hayden, "Post-Chicago Interview," in *Telling It Like It Was*, p. 133. Hayden, *Trial*, p. 11.

118. For Nixon's attacks on the anti-war movement, see Jonathan Schell, *The Time of Illusion* (New York, 1976), pp. 35–37.

119. Findley, "Hayden: Rolling Stone Interview, Part 2," p. 30.

120. Jason Epstein, *The Great Conspiracy Trial: An Essay in Law, Liberty and the Constitution* (New York, 1970), pp. 24, 116, 306. Cf. Kinoy, Schwartz, Peterson, *Conspiracy on Appeal*. For a condensed version of the trial transcript, see Clair and Spitzer, *The Conspiracy Trial*.

121. Hayden interview, 5–16–86.,

122. Hayden, *Trial,* pp. 30, 108. Alexander Cockburn and James Ridgeway, "Tom Hayden: From Innocence to Chicago," *The Village Voice,* June 16, 1981.

123. Hayden, *Trial,* p. 107. Murray Kempton, "Three Who Didn't Make a Revolution," *The New York Review of Books,* January 7, 1971, p. 37. Jack Newfield, in his phone interview of 5–13–86, suggested that he was one (radical) liberal ally who felt grave reservations about Hayden's turn to revolutionary rhetoric. Many of these reservations Newfield expressed at the time, without mentioning his friend by name: see, e.g., "SDS: From Port Huron to La Chinoise," in *Bread and Roses, Too,* pp. 119–29.

124. Up Against the Wall Motherfuckers, "Respect for Lawlessness," *New Left Notes,* September 16, 1968, p. 4. Tom Hayden, "The Battle for Survival" [adapted from a speech at UCLA, May, 1969], in Peter and Deborah Babcox and Bob Abel, eds., *The Conspiracy* (New York, 1969), pp. 171, 172. Findley, "Hayden: Rolling Stone Interview, Part 2," p. 30. See also Richard Flacks and Milton Mankoff, "Why They Burned the Bank," *The Nation,* March 23, 1970, pp. 337–40.

125. Hayden phone interview, 4–30–86. Hayden's marginal comments. Schell, *Time of Illusion,* pp. 90–91. Zaroulis and Sullivan, *Who Spoke Up?,* pp. 308–09. Unger, *The Movement,* p. 185.

126. Zaroulis and Sullivan, *Who Spoke Up?,* pp. 319–20.

127. Kathy Boudin, Bernadine Dohrn and Terry Robbins, "Bringing the War Home: Less Talk, More National Action," *New Left Notes,* Vol. 4, No. 28 (August 28, 1969), p. 6. Also see Sale, *SDS,* pp. 557–79.

128. See Hayden, *Trial,* pp. 92–93, and Sale, *SDS,* p. 603. In a phone interview on 7–5–86, Hayden stressed (as he had in *Trial*) that the extent of the violence that followed his speech on the night of October 8 came as a shock to him. The Weathermen had told him, he says, that they were planning a "demonstration"—and he expected another militant confrontation between protesters and police, like that in Chicago during the 1968 convention. It is true that the Weathermen did not publicly spell out their full intentions beforehand; it is also true that paramilitary posturing was by now such a common feature of New Left rhetoric that it was easy not to take it too seriously. Still, several days before Hayden made his address, the Weathermen had led protesters into the streets of Chicago, where "storefronts and pig wagons were stoned," as the group happily reported in its newspaper. (See "Take the Blues to Chicago," *New Left Notes,* Vol. 4, No. 31 [October 2, 1969], p. 1.) And by the evening of October 8, it was clear that the Weathermen, with their military gear, were girding for some kind of pitched battle. Perhaps that is one of the reasons why John Froines and Abbie Hoffman, who accompanied Hayden to address the crowd that night, "thought better of it and disappeared," as Hayden later wrote. (See *Trial,* p. 92.)

129. Hayden interview, 5–16–86.

130. Ibid. Findley, "Hayden: Rolling Stone Interview, Part 2," p. 29. Cockburn and Ridgeway, "Tom Hayden: From Innocence to Chicago, *The Village Voice,* June 16, 1981.

131. Hayden interview, 5–16–86.

132. Ibid.

133. Hayden interview, 3–10–85.

134. Bertolt Brecht, *Poems, 1913–1956*, ed. John Willett and Ralph Manheim (New York, 1976), p. 320.

135. See: Sale, *SDS*, p. 150. Lynd and Hayden, *The Other Side*, p. 204.

136. Hayden interview, 3–10–85.

137. Epstein, *The Great Conspiracy Trial*, p. 17. Sale, *SDS*, p. 605. Hayden, *Trial*, pp. 92–94.

Conclusion

1. On the idea of "breakaway" experience and its limits, see Paul Potter, *A Name for Ourselves*, pp. 44–45.

2. Hayden interview, 5–16–86. Hayden marginal comments. See also Kotkin, "Tom Hayden's Manifest Destiny," p. 44.

3. Hayden interview, 5–16–85. Tom Hayden, *The Love of Possession Is a Disease With Them* (New York, 1972), pp. 98, 103, 127. *United States* v. *Dellinger*, 472 F.2d 340, p. 391 (7th Cir. 1972). On the Indochina Peace Campaign, see Zaroulis and Sullivan, *Who Spoke Up?*, pp. 393–94.

4. Booth interview, 12–28–85.

5. Jeffrey interview, 2–28–85; all subsequent Jeffrey quotations come from this interview.

6. Samuel P. Huntington on "The United States," in Michael J. Crozier, Samuel P. Huntington, Joji Watanuki, *The Crisis of Democracy* (New York, 1975), pp. 59, 74–75. Cf. Huntington, *American Politics: The Promise of Disharmony* (Cambridge, Mass., 1981), pp. 1–5. Consider, too, the rhetoric in President Nixon's "State of the Union" speech in 1971: "To all Americans let us say: We hear you and we will give you a chance. We are going to give you a new chance to have more to say about the decisions that affect your future—to participate in government." (Quoted in Cook and Morgan, eds., *Participatory Democracy*, p. ix.)

7. Ibid., pp. 113, 65, 114, 93.

8. Hayden interview, 3–11–85.

9. Haber phone interview, 5–15–86. Ross phone interview, 5–4–86. Max phone interview, 5–10–86.

10. Booth interview, 9–23–84. Booth phone interview, 5–21–86.

11. Richard Flacks, "The Importance of the Romantic Myth for the Left," *Theory and Society*, Vol. 2, No. 3 (Fall, 1975), pp. 410–11. Flacks interviews, 5–16–86 and 3–4–85.

12. Flacks interview, 3–4–85.

13. Hayden interview, 1–25–86. See also "Building the Future," a CED pamphlet being distributed in 1986. In practice, the Campaign's commitment to "participation" seems to have been progressively compromised by the exigencies of practical politics: see Mark E. Kann, *Middle Class Radicalism in Santa Monica* (Philadelphia, 1986), pp. 100–103, 145–68, 215–19.

14. Hayden interviews, 5–16–86 and 3–11–85.

15. Hayden interviews, 1–25–86 and 5–16–86; "Transcript of Remarks by Tom Hayden, Symposium on LBJ and Vietnam, Hofstra University, April 11, 1986," pp. 4–5.

16. Hayden interviews, 5–17–86 and 3–11–85.

17. The classic discussion of this lesson—although the author herself is reluctant to take the full measure of her findings—is Jane Mansbridge's *Beyond Adversary Democracy*. See also Michael Walzer, "A Day in the Life of a Socialist Citizen," in Walzer, *Radical Principles* (New York, 1980), pp. 128–38.

18. See, e.g., Brinkley, *Voices of Protest*, for the fate of right-wing populism during the New Deal; Richard Hofstadter, *The Age of Reform* (New York, 1955), for the fate of the Progressive movement; Lawrence Goodwyn, *Democratic Promise* (New York, 1979), for a more sympathetic account of agrarian populism; James Weinstein, *The Decline of Socialism in America, 1912–1925* (New York, 1967); and Gabriel Kolko, "The Decline of American Radicalism in the Twentieth Century," *Studies on the Left*, Vol. 6, No. 5 (September–October, 1966), pp. 9–26.

19. Recent work on the political theory of democracy includes Benjamin Barber, *Strong Democracy: Participatory Politics for a New Age* (Berkeley, 1984); Robert Dahl, *A Preface to Economic Democracy* (Berkeley, 1985); Mansbridge, *Beyond Adversary Democracy*; Martin Carnoy and Derek Shearer, *Economic Democracy* (White Plains, N.Y., 1980); and Roberto Mangabeira Unger, *The Critical Legal Studies Movement* (Cambridge, 1986). See also Sheldon Wolin's editorials and essays in his short-lived journal *Democracy*. My book *Rousseau: Dreamer of Democracy* (New Haven, 1984) was conceived in a similar spirit of intellectual and historical reappraisal. This strand in academic political theory dates back to the Sixties: see especially Peter Bachrach, *The Theory of Democratic Elitism* (Boston, 1967), and Carole Pateman, *Participation and Democratic Theory* (Cambridge, 1970). Relevant works by economists include Gar Alperovitz and Jeff Faux, *Rebuilding America* (New York, 1984), and Samuel Bowles, David M. Gordon and Thomas E. Weisskopf, *Beyond the Waste Land: A Democratic Alternative to Economic Decline* (Garden City, N.Y., 1983); and, in a more philosophical vein, Samuel Bowles and Herbert Gintis, *Democracy and Capitalism* (New York, 1986). Although unconnected with the New Left (and properly critical of some of its adherents), perhaps the most important recent study on the prospects for democracy in a socialist economy is Alec Nove, *The Economics of Feasible Socialism* (London, 1983). For community organizing in the aftermath of the New Left, see Harry Boyte, *The Backyard Revolution: Understanding the New Citizen Movement* (Philadelphia, 1980); David Morris and Karl Hess, *Neighborhood Power: The New Localism* (Boston, 1975); Michael Walzer, "The Pastoral Retreat of the New Left," in Walzer, *Radical Principles*, pp. 175–85; Gary Delgado, *Organizing the Movement: The Roots and Growth of ACORN* (Philadelphia, 1986); and—for a detailed and critical study of the "revolution" in Hayden's own "backyard"—Kann, *Middle Class Radicalism in Santa Monica*.

20. Mills, *The New Men of Power*, p. 250.

ACKNOWLEDGMENTS

Raphael Sagalyn, my literary agent, first suggested my doing a book on *The Port Huron Statement;* Bob Asahina, my editor at Simon and Schuster, saw it through, offering timely comments and suggestions. Annalyn Swan and the editors of *Newsweek* kindly permitted me to go on a half-time schedule there, allowing me fourteen months to research and write the book; without their flexibility, I could never have completed the task.

The staff librarians at *The Michigan Daily,* particularly Shawn Howard, went out of their way to help me by tracking down and copying Tom Hayden's articles and editorials for the *Daily.* The staff of the Bentley Historical Library at the University of Michigan offered similar assistance on several occasions. And Rebecca Cox, 1987 editor-in-chief of *The Michiganensian,* the university's yearbook, kindly helped me out with photographs, as did John Demeter of *Radical America,* Bruce Kluckhorn of *The Harvard Crimson,* Barbara Blake of Tom Hayden's office and Yaroslava Mills, C. Wright Mills's widow.

While I was working on the manuscript, I had the benefit of two special experiences. At a conference on intellectuals at Skidmore College organized by Bob Boyers and sponsored by *Salmagundi* magazine, I was able to air some of my ideas about C. Wright Mills before an audience that included Christopher Lasch and Norman Birnbaum, whose comments and encouragement helped me to persevere. And at the Rockefeller Foundation's Study and Conference Center in Bellagio, Italy, I had the good fortune to complete the manuscript in an idyllic setting; to David and Mary Wightman, who both read part of the manuscript there, and to Judith Shklar, who cheerfully argued with me about politics, go my special thanks.

While I was on the road conducting interviews, I was lucky to have as hosts my friends Darrell Hawthorne, David Turner, Lee and Claire McDonald, and Craig Unger. In checking some of the legal details of the text, I had invaluable help from my friend Mike Boudin.

Various drafts of the whole text were read by Ande Zellman, Greil Marcus, Joe Boskin, Langdon Winner and Sarah Minden, my wife. Jean Strouse, Andrew

Kopkind, Bruce Miroff, James Schmidt, Stan Draenos and James E. Miller, Jr., my father, all read parts of the manuscript too. The comments of these readers on matters of substance and style helped me immeasurably.

My friends Wini and Paul Breines contributed more than helpful comments. From the inception of the project, Wini, who is one of the few serious scholars of the New Left, and Paul, who is an unrepentant but skeptical veteran of the Movement, offered expert advice, moral support and a sense of intellectual community.

I also received unusual assistance from George Abbott White. In 1968, he contracted to write a history, with Paul Garber as his coauthor, of SDS. Though Kirkpatrick Sale beat them to it, White has kept an extensive collection of SDS documents, photographs and interview transcripts, including many things unavailable elsewhere. I first met him when my own manuscript was virtually finished; but he set aside time to offer comments, and with Garber's approval generously helped me out by supplying many extremely rare photographs.

Finally, to the central subjects of this book I owe a special debt. Bob Ross, Paul Booth, Michael Harrington, Sharon Jeffrey, Alan Haber, Richard Flacks, Tom Hayden and Steve Max all gave generously of their time and patience. It was not always easy for them to rehearse for me the joys and follies of youth, or to explain the intricacies of dimly remembered disputes. Still, the New Left had been their precocious attempt to "make history." And it is only thanks to their cooperation that I have been able, two decades later, to write history.

J.M.
West Roxbury, Massachusetts
June, 1986

INDEX

417

Students for a Democratic Society (SDS)
  (cont.)
  leadership and, 225–26, 239–40, 242,
    270, 285
  LID break with, 235
  LID criticism of, 126–35, 139–40, 231
  LID support of, 66–70
  male dominance in, 257, 272
  march on Washington sponsored by,
    226–29, 231–34
  membership of, 65, 158, 177
  Mills's influence on, 79, 84, 86–87, 90
  "new insurgency" of, 176–77, 181–83,
    187, 188
  news coverage of, 236–37, 248–52
  organizational structure of, 165, 240–
    242, 244–46, 253–56
  origins of, 23, 38
  Pine Hill conventions of, 174, 177–79,
    194–97
  Progressive Labor Party infiltration of,
    139, 284–85, 311
  recommended reading list of, 78
  recruitment for, 40, 41–42, 49, 54–55,
    70–75, 186
  Tom Hayden and, 54, 61, 225–26, 239–
    240, 241
  Young People's Socialist League and, 74–
    76, 127
  see also Port Huron convention
"Student Social Action" (Hayden), 100–
  102, 151, 205
Studies on the Left, 169, 170
Supreme Court, U.S., segregation
  decisions by, 34
Survey Research Center, 25–26, 159
Swarthmore College, SDS chapter at, 166,
  188, 196, 219, 254

tax-exempt status, activism and, 67, 132,
  187, 235
Taylor, Harold, 111, 134
Taylor, Maxwell, 200
teach-in movement, 180, 229
tenants'-council project, 201–3
Tet Offensive, 289
Theobald, Robert, 192, 204
"Theses on Feuerbach" (Marx), 11
Third World:
  American interest in, 25, 181
  peace movement and, 173
  revolutionary insurgencies in, 230
  Sharon Jeffrey and, 186
Thomas, Norman:
  Intercollegiate Socialist Society and,
    28
  LID-SDS mediation by, 134–35, 140
  SDS march and, 229, 230

William Haber and, 23
young left and, 30, 38, 114
troop-train blockades, 243–44, 282
Tropic of Cancer (Miller), 11
Trotsky, Leon, 74, 112, 135
Tunney, John, 323
Turner, Felton, 35
Turner, Frederick Jackson, 171

unemployment, ERAP projects on, 201,
  202
United Auto Workers (UAW):
  ERAP funded by, 182, 186, 188
  Reuther and, 29, 32, 173
  Sharon Jeffrey and, 31, 32, 105
united frontism, 131, 231
United States:
  Gross National Product of, 25, 340
  military foreign policy of, 127–28
  unprecedented affluence in, 25
  William A. Williams's history of, 170–
    172

Varela, Mary, 107, 118, 122
Veblen, Thorstein, 79
Vester, Michael, 107, 123
Viet Cong, 228, 239, 280
Vietnam:
  bomb damage in, 277
  Communism in, 267–68, 269
  establishment liberals, 182
  France and, 288
  Gulf of Tonkin incidents in, 218–21
  POWs released from, 280–81, 287
  Tet Offensive in, 289
  U.S. ambassadors to, 200
  war escalation in, 182, 259
  see also anti-war movement; Hanoi;
    National Liberation Front; North
    Vietnamese; specific protests
Vinson, Carl, 341
VOICE, 53, 186
voter registration:
  Cleveland ERAP project and, 198
  SNCC projects on, 56, 57–58, 70, 102,
    149–50

Wakefield, Dan, 81
Waskow, Arthur, 169, 177, 219, 222
Watts riot, 273, 277
Weathermen, 311–13, 317
Webb, Beatrice, 27
Webb, Sidney, 27
Weber, Max, 84
Weinstein, James, 177
Weisman, Gary, 72
welfare recipients, community organizing
  and, 201, 203–4, 232

A NOTE ABOUT THE AUTHOR

JAMES MILLER, a native of Chicago, studied politics, philosophy and intellectual history at Pomona College and Brandeis University, where he received his Ph.D. in 1975. Before becoming a book and music critic for *Newsweek* magazine in 1981, he taught in the government department at the University of Texas at Austin. His scholarly work has appeared in *History and Theory, Salmagundi, Telos* and the anthology *Hannah Arendt: The Recovery of the Public World.* Twice a winner of the ASCAP–Deems Taylor award for excellence in writing about music, he has contributed essays on popular music to *The New Republic, Rolling Stone, New Times* and the anthology *Stranded: Rock and Roll for a Desert Island.* He is the author of two previous books, *Rousseau: Dreamer of Democracy* (1984), a study of the origins of modern democracy in the thinking of Jean-Jacques Rousseau and the French Revolution, and *History and Human Existence—From Marx to Merleau-Ponty* (1979), an analysis of Marx and the French existentialists. In addition, he is the editor of *The Rolling Stone Illustrated History of Rock and Roll* (1976). He lives with his wife and two sons in West Roxbury, Massachusetts.